THE LISBON TREATY AND SOCIAL EUROPE

On 1 December 2009 the Treaty of Lisbon entered into force. Although often described as primarily technical it significantly amended the Treaty on the European Union (TEU) and the old EC Treaty (now the Treaty on the Functioning of the European Union, TFEU). The authors' aim in this book is to explore what the Treaty means for social law and social policy at the European level. The first part of the book on the general framework looks—at a time of financial crisis—for new foundations for Europe's Social market economy, questions the balance between fundamental social rights and economic freedoms, analyses the role of the now binding Charter of Fundamental Rights of the European Union, maps the potential impact of the horizontal clauses on social policy, and addresses the possibilities for social partners to enlarge their role in labour law and industrial relations.

The importance of fundamental rights is not only highlighted by the legally binding Charter of Fundamental Rights. The Lisbon Treaty has also tightened the relationship to the European Convention on Human Rights. Aware of this fact and of the new case-law of the European Court of Human Rights in respect of in particular collective social rights several authors are working on a publication which will deal with these problems and opportunities.

The second part, on the social framework of the Treaty, focuses on the development of the Union's competences. In it the authors evaluate the consequences of the new general framework on social competences, analyse the evolution of the principle of subsidiarity and its impact in the new Treaty, look at the coordination of economic policies in the light of fundamental rights, and analyse the adoption in the Treaty of a new architecture for services of general interest.

The manuscript was completed in the summer of 2011 and therefore does not cover the most recent developments in respect of the impact of the economic and financial crisis on the EU Treaties and European social law. However, the authors are currently working on a new publication dealing with the consequences of the economic and financial crisis on European social policy fields.

The Lisbon Treaty and Social Europe

Edited by
Niklas Bruun
Klaus Lörcher
and
Isabelle Schömann

etui.

• HART •
PUBLISHING
OXFORD AND PORTLAND, OREGON
2012

Published in the United Kingdom by Hart Publishing Ltd
16C Worcester Place, Oxford, OX1 2JW
Telephone: +44 (0)1865 517530
Fax: +44 (0)1865 510710
E-mail: mail@hartpub.co.uk
Website: http://www.hartpub.co.uk

Published in North America (US and Canada) by
Hart Publishing
c/o International Specialized Book Services
920 NE 58th Avenue, Suite 300
Portland, OR 97213-3786
USA
Tel: +1 503 287 3093 or toll-free: (1) 800 944 6190
Fax: +1 503 280 8832
E-mail: orders@isbs.com
Website: http://www.isbs.com

British Library Cataloguing in Publication Data
Data Available

ISBN: 978-1-84946-253-2

Typeset by Compuscript Ltd, Shannon
Printed and bound in Great Britain by
CPI Group (UK) Ltd, Croydon CR0 4YY

Foreword

The Treaty of Lisbon, which came into force on 1 December 2009, takes its inspiration from the so-called European Convention held from 2001 to 2003 and originally intended to give birth to a European Constitution. While the Lisbon Treaty fails to live up to such a far-reaching expectation, it does, nonetheless, significantly amend the Treaty on the European Union (TEU) as well as the former EC Treaty, now renamed Treaty on the Functioning of the European Union (TFEU). Though the European Union was originally launched as primarily an economic project—in the form of the European Economic Community—its social competences and regulations have developed over the years, enriched by references to fundamental rights which are now legally binding and thus serve to underpin legislation and case law relating to European social law and European social policy.

In view of a widespread tendency to regard these new social elements in the Treaty as little more than programmatic declarations of scant legal significance—especially during situations such as the present economic and financial crisis—there is a need for an in-depth analysis of the new implications as they stem from the new legal framework enshrined in the Lisbon Treaty. This book, conceived from a primarily labour law perspective, represents an attempt to fill this gap.

The authors' aim is to enquire what the new Treaty means for social law and social policy, at both the European and the national level. In a first part on the general framework of the social dimension of the European Union, the authors seek to explore, during a period marked by financial crisis, some of the possible new foundations for Europe's Social market economy. They explore, to this end, whether the distinction, as well as the relationship, between *values* and *objectives* might provoke a shift in the 'balance' between fundamental (social) rights and fundamental economic freedoms; they question the role of the Charter of Fundamental Rights; they analyse the potential impact of the horizontal clauses on social policy on the basis of the experience of gender mainstreaming; and they address the possibility given to social partners to enlarge their role in labour law and industrial relations at all EU institutional levels.

In a second part devoted more specifically to the social framework of the Lisbon Treaty itself, the authors focus on the developments of the Union's competences by evaluating the consequences of the new general framework on (social) competences. Here they analyse the evolution of the principle of subsidiarity and its impact in the new frame of the Treaty; examine the coordination of economic policies, as a reading of the Treaty which takes its policy goals seriously by stipulating that EU economic governance must incorporate social policy and fundamental rights assessments of all proposed policy measures; and finally analyse the services of general interest, as the Treaty marks an important stage in the adoption of a new architecture to govern and underpin Services of General Interest.

The Transnational trade union rights experts' network of the European Trade Union Institute (ETUI), comprising labour law academics from different EU member states—Niklas Bruun (Finland) and Klaus Lörcher (Germany), the two coordinators of this volume, Thomas Blanke (Germany), Simon Deakin (Great Britain), Filip Dorssemont (Belgium), Antoine Jacobs (Netherlands), Csilla Kollonay-Lehoczky (Hungary), Bruno Veneziani (Italy), and Isabelle Schömann (ETUI)—undertook the task of analysing the impact of the Lisbon Treaty on social Europe out of a belief that such an analysis could provide, particularly during the current period of economic crisis, a new understanding of the Lisbon Treaty's potential to influence social Europe. The critical commentary of the social dimension of the new Treaty presented in this book is an attempt to contribute to public debate as well as to the academic arena of the future framing of social Europe. The intention is to stimulate research and deepen reflection upon the process of European integration as well as to develop arguments that may be used in legal proceedings, including before the Court of Justice of the European Union. The project was started under the leadership of the late Brian Bercusson. The authors could have paid no better tribute to Brian's memory than to complete this book in the spirit of promotion of a social Europe.

The ETUI wishes to thank the authors for their in-depth analysis which shows how a comprehensive interpretation of the Lisbon Treaty could contribute to the achievement of a better and more social Europe.

Maria Jepsen

ETUI
Director of the Research Department

Contents

List of Contributors

Thomas Blanke is former Professor of Labour Law at the Carl-von-Ossietzky-University, Oldenburg, Germany.

Niklas Bruun is Professor of Private Law at the University of Helsinki, Finland. He is leader of the research programme ReMarkLab, Stockholm University, and member of the research team of the Centre of Excellence in the Foundations of European Law and Polity, University of Helsinki.

Simon Deakin is Professor of Law at the University of Cambridge, UK.

Filip Dorssemont is Professor of Law at the Catholic University of Louvain, Belgium.

Antoine Jacobs is former Professor of Law at the University of Tilburg, The Netherlands.

Csilla Kollonay-Lehoczky is Professor of Law, Eötvös Lóránd University, Faculty of Law and Central European University, Legal Studies Department, Budapest, Hungary.

Klaus Lörcher is former Legal adviser to the European Trade Union Confederation (ETUC) and former Legal secretary to the Civil Service Tribunal of the European Union.

Isabelle Schömann is senior researcher at the European Trade Union Institute (ETUI).

Bruno Veneziani is former Professor of Labour Law and Comparative Trade Union Law, University of Bari, Italy.

Pascale Vielle is Professor of Law at the University of Louvain, Belgium.

Introduction

ON 1 DECEMBER 2009, the Treaty of Lisbon entered into force. Its content was developed around 2001–03 by the so-called European Convention, convened especially to give birth to a European Constitution. However, after the negative results of the referendums in France and the Netherlands it was decided to strip this document of the controversial epithet 'European Constitution', but to insert its text, slightly modified, into the existing European Treaties. That has been done through the Treaty of Lisbon. Under this treaty, the Treaty on the European Union (TEU) has changed significantly. The same applies to the old EC Treaty, which in future will be known as the Treaty on the Functioning of the European Union (TFEU).[1]

The EEC was launched in 1957 primarily as an economic project. The social component was largely neglected. The founding fathers had confidence in the ability of the common market to prompt social progress so that only some coordinating incentives would be needed. Consequently, the EEC Treaty did not contain many specific competences enabling the EC institutions to issue social regulations.[2]

It was only at the summit in Paris, April 1972, that it was formally recognised that the social objectives of the EEC are as important as its economic objectives. Since that time, the EEC rules in this area have increased. Even so, the harvest initially was small, because in those days European social legislation could be created only by a unanimous vote in the EC Council of Ministers, and that was seldom achievable.

However, since 1986, in successive Treaty amendments, on a steadily growing number of social issues the unanimity rule in the Council of Ministers has been converted into qualified majority voting. This has made decision making on social matters slightly—although not much—easier. Since 1992, certain provisions have also been included in the European Treaties which open up the possibility of creating, alongside heteronomous law (law created by public authorities), autonomous European social law (law created by trade unions and employers). Finally, since 1997 the EU Treaties have been enriched by references to fundamental rights, which

[1] See the consolidated versions of the Treaties in OJ C 30.3.2010.

[2] The Treaty provisions which expressed this (Articles 117 and 118 of the Treaty of Rome, 1957) have been retained almost unchanged and are now in Articles 151 and 156 TFEU.

may support legislation and case law relating to European social law and European social policy. Now there is the Treaty of Lisbon.

What do the new texts mean for social law and social policy, both at the European level and at the national level?[3] That is the theme of this book. We will deal with the economic versus the social constitution; the values and objectives; the European Court of Justice (ECJ) in conjunction with the European Convention on Human Rights (ECHR); the role of the social partners in Europe; the social competences and the law making process in social matters; the principle of solidarity; the coordination of social and economic policies; services of general interest; EU governance; and references to the EU Charter.

I. THE ECONOMIC VERSUS THE SOCIAL CONSTITUTION

In recent years it has become increasingly clear that the EU is not necessarily a boon for social justice and social policy, but entails great risks as the EU embraces the 'laws of the market' and 'free competition'.[4] The oldest text of the Treaty, which offered a very liberal market model, inspired the European authorities—notably the European Commission and the European Court of Justice—to take strong action against so-called distortions of competition and against state aid by Member States in favour of their own industries.

Over the years, however, anxiety has increased among citizens in many countries that the freedoms of the European market have led to much collateral destruction of acquired rights. European policy on the 'distortion of free competition' and state aid are understandable in relation to the major economic players. However, they have also led to highly questionable interference on the part of 'Europe' in the maintenance of employment in regional context; decent working conditions and social security; public services; and aspects of the socio-cultural policies of the Member States, for example in the areas of support for social housing, sport, public broadcasting and even zoos.

Under pressure from a restive public, politicians are more and more reluctant to apply the 'laws of the market' consistently. For instance, fear

[3] See also C Barnard, 'Social policy revisited in the light of the constitutional debate' in C Barnard (ed), *The Fundamentals of EU Law Revisited* (Oxford, 2007) ch 5; E Sabatakis, 'A propos du Traité de Lisbonne et de l'Europe sociale' (2008) *Revue du Marché commun et de l'Union européenne* 432–41; P Syrpis, 'The Treaty of Lisbon: Much Ado … But About What?' (2008) 37 *Industrial Law Journal* 219–35; B Bercusson, 'The Lisbon Treaty and Social Europe' (2009) 10 *ERA-Forum* 87–105.

[4] ATJM Jacobs, 'The social Janus head of the European Union: social market economy versus ultraliberal policies' in J Wouters et al (eds), *European Constitutionalism beyond Lisbon* (Antwerp, 2009) 111–28.

of the replacement of their own workers by cheaper foreign workers (the 'Polish plumber') has led to a substantial dilution of the Services Directive.[5] Some Member States, such as France and Spain, continue to protect their key industries and in 2006 took emergency measures to prevent the acquisition of their energy giants by Italian and German rivals, respectively. Also, state aid to national industries still frequently rears its head (see the proposed German aid to Opel, 2009). And the European Commission immediately rallied to support some Member States when their main banks got into trouble in 2008.

At present, it is notably the EU Court of Justice which in various judgments is showing its attachment to market liberalism by giving it priority over other values. In the cases *Viking*[6] and *Laval*[7] the right to take collective action was held to be inferior to the economic freedoms in an open European market. In *Rüffert*,[8] based on the grounds of the same philosophy, a German regional government was prohibited from imposing social conditions on public procurement, a tried and tested device for achieving social progress, recommended by the ILO.[9] In *Commission v Luxembourg*,[10] a Member State was prohibited from requiring higher labour standards for the employment of foreigners than prescribed in the EU Posted Workers Directive.

These judgments have brought to light two fundamental problems of social law and social policy:

— Which rules apply if the social rights come into conflict with the 'laws of the market'?[11]
— Do Member States still have the freedom to enact or maintain their labour and social security law as long as it is more favourable to the workers?

It is interesting to consider the extent to which the entry into force of the Treaty of Lisbon has changed the answers to those questions. This is the theme of the chapter by Simon Deakin.

[5] Directive 2006/123/EC.

[6] Case C-438/05, 2007 ECR I- 10779 (*Viking*).

[7] Case C-341/05, 2007 ECR I-11767 (*Laval*); see R Blanpain (ed), 'The Laval and Viking Cases' (2009) 69 *Bulletin of Comparative Labour Relations*.

[8] Case C-346/06 CoJ EC 3.4.2008 (*Rüffert*).

[9] N Bruun, A Jacobs and M Schmidt, 'ILO Convention No 94 in the aftermath of the *Rüffert* case' (2010) 16(4) *Transfer* 473–89.

[10] Case C-319/06 CoJ EC 19.6.2008 (*Commission v Luxembourg*).

[11] A Vimercati, *Il Conflitto Sbilanciato* (Bari, 2009); U Carabelli, *Europa dei mercati e conflitto sociale* (Bari, 2009).

II. VALUES AND OBJECTIVES

Regarding the first question, it should be noted that at the European Convention 2002–03 there was little discussion of whether the character of Europe as a social market economy was to be confirmed in the proposed European Constitution. There were various proposals to reinforce the social face of the EU by inserting principles such as human dignity, equality, social justice, solidarity,[12] sustainable development, social progress, full employment and the battle against social exclusion. All these concepts have finally entered the European Treaties by way of the Treaty of Lisbon and found a place in Articles 2 and 3 TEU and Article 67 TFEU.[13] Moreover, during the Intergovernmental Conference (IGC) of 2003–04 a so-called horizontal social clause was developed, which states that in defining and implementing its policies and actions, the Union shall take into account requirements linked to the promotion of a high level of employment, the guarantee of adequate social protection, the fight against social exclusion and a high level of education, training and protection of human health (Article 9 TFEU). This provision is seen as an expression of the desire to mainstream social policies in all areas of policy.

However, references to social values are counterbalanced by that other great EU objective, namely to maintain an 'internal market' (Article 3 TEU), characterised by an open market economy with free competition, with stable prices, sound public finances and monetary conditions and a sustainable balance of payments, among other things. In the reformed European Treaties all this has found a place in Articles 119 and 120 TFEU and is further developed in numerous Articles on the free market and competition. However, it is significant that, at the insistence of France, at the European Council in June 2007 it was decided[14] not to retain in the Lisbon Treaty the passage in the text of the draft European Constitution in the Article on the aims of the Union (Article I-3(2)) which stated that 'the Union ... will offer its citizens an internal market where competition is free and undistorted'. Apparently, the politicians found it a bit over the top to give the open market economy with free competition equal rank with the

[12] European Commission, 'Renewed social agenda: opportunities, access and solidarity in 21st century Europe' COM 2008 (412); T Hieronymi, *Solidarität als Rechtsprinzip in der Europäischen Union* (Frankfurt am Main, 2003); S Stjerno, *Solidarity in Europe: The History of an Idea* (Cambridge, 2005); L Wilde, 'The concept of solidarity: emerging from the theoretical shadows?' (2007) *British Journal of Politics and International Relations* 171; W Rehg, 'Solidarity and the Common Good. An analytical framework' (2007) *Journal of Social Philosophy* 7; N Karagiannis (ed), *European Solidarity* (Liverpool, 2007); M Ross, *Solidarity in EU Law* (Oxford, 2009).

[13] See K Lenaerts and M Desomer, 'Bricks for a Constitutional Treaty of the European Union: values, objectives and means' (2002) *ELRev* 377–407; T Koopmans, 'De Europese Conventie—een tussenstand' (2003) *SEW* 195.

[14] Document, European Council 11177/07, p 24.

other aims, including the social objectives of the EU. Free competition is now relegated to Protocol No 27 to the reformed European Treaties, which states that 'the European Union includes a system ensuring that competition is not distorted' and that 'the Union shall, if necessary, take action'.[15]

Finally, we may recall the elaborate 'Solemn declaration on the rights of workers, social policy and other issues' which the European Council adopted on 18/19 June 2009 as part of the overall package of facilities to ease the concerns of the Irish people regarding the Treaty of Lisbon.[16] While this statement contains nothing new—the content can also result from the various provisions of the reformed Treaties—it still signals that the politicians want to give the social rights extra emphasis. As such, it was endorsed in June 2009 by a petition signed by about 100 labour lawyers from many EU Member States. In all this sufficient arguments were discernible to suggest that in a future conflict between social rights and the laws of the market priority would be given to social rights. And 'priority' is stronger than the solution formula of 'proportionality' which permits limitations on social rights with regard to the laws of the free market, as the EU Court of Justice in its earlier cited decisions has used it.

Turning to the relationship between the EU and the ECHR, the Treaty of Lisbon says that the EU shall accede to the European Convention for the Protection of Human Rights and Fundamental Freedoms (Article 6(2) TEU), a provision which provides the necessary legal basis for such membership at any time in the future.[17] However, the realisation of this intention requires a Treaty which must be voted in the Council of Ministers with unanimity and endorsed by all EU Member States in conformity with their national procedures (Article 218(8) TFEU) and by all 45 Member States of the Council of Europe. Moreover, it is added that accession shall not affect the Union's competences as defined in the Treaties (Article 6(2), last sentence TEU) and that statement is repeated again in Protocol No 8 to the reformed Treaties (Article 2, first sentence), which ensures that accession shall not affect the competences of the Union and of its institutions nor the situation of Member States in relation to the ECHR.[18] This Protocol No 8 and Declaration No 2 in the Final Act of the IGC 2007 underline that the

15 See Protocol No 27 on the internal market and competition, added to TEU and TFEU; Document, European Council 11177/07, p 24, note 16.

16 Document, European Council 11225/09, pp 20–21.

17 Such a legal basis was considered indispensable by the EC Court of Justice in its Opinion 2/94.

18 Protocol No 8 specifies as such the special Protocols to the ECHR, measures taken by Member States derogating from the ECHR in accordance with Article 15 thereof and reservations to the ECHR made by Member States in accordance with Article 57 thereof. This is a current issue, for instance in view of a decision of the German Bundesverfassungsgericht of October 2004, in which it was stated that the ECHR is not the highest legal authority in Germany.

accession of the EU to the ECHR will be arranged in such a way that the specific characteristics of the EU and of EU law will be left untouched.

Serious problems may lie ahead when national courts are faced with a dual system of monitoring compliance with fundamental rights: the Court of Justice of the EU in Luxembourg and the European Court of Human Rights in Strasbourg.[19] This situation brings the potential risk that the number of legal disputes will double, as claimants may try to obtain adjustments of national law along two lines—in Luxembourg and in Strasbourg—and that these two courts have to rule on similar but not entirely congruent sets of rights. For labour and social security law one may think, by way of example, of the trade union rights, as mentioned in Article 11 ECHR[20] and in Articles 12 and 28 in the EU Charter of Fundamental Rights. Filip Dorssemont reflects on this in his chapter.

III. REFERENCE TO THE EU CHARTER OF FUNDAMENTAL RIGHTS

In recent decades, within the EU, increasing attention has been paid to fundamental rights. In the first place the Treaties of Maastricht and Amsterdam inserted amendments on the applicability of fundamental rights in the European Treaties. In particular, the Treaty of Amsterdam brought in a basic standard by which the ECHR and the fundamental rights enshrined in the constitutional traditions common to the Member States were recognised as general principles of Community law.[21] Moreover, the Treaty of Amsterdam inserted a few specific fundamental rights in the European Treaties.[22] Secondly, it was considered whether the EU as such could join the European Convention on Human Rights. Thirdly, the EU itself engaged in the preparation of a Charter of Fundamental Rights. This latter process was taken up in 2000 by a convention that drafted the so-called Charter of Fundamental Rights of the European Union.[23] This Charter was adopted in December 2000 by the European Council of Nice, but at that time it did not receive a legally binding character.

The European Convention that prepared the European Constitution departed from these points. It suggested therefore, first, inserting the EU Charter of Fundamental Rights in full into the European Constitution, thus making it

[19] LA Geelhoed, 'Een Europawijde Europese Unie: een grondwet zonder staat' (2003) *SEW* 299.

[20] J van Drongelen and ATJM Jacobs, 'Nieuwe vleugels voor de vakverenigingsvrijheid van art 11 ECHR' (2009) *NJB* 1781.

[21] Article 6(2) TEU as it stood until 1 December 2009.

[22] J Wouters, 'Institutionele aspecten van het Verdrag van Amsterdam' in R Blanpain et al (eds), *Europa na het Verdrag van Amsterdam* (Leuven, 1998) 77–84.

[23] G de Búrca, 'The drafting of the European Union Charter of Fundamental Rights' (2001) *ELRev* 126–38; B Bercusson (ed), *European Labour Law and the EU Charter of Fundamental Rights* (Baden-Baden, 2006).

legally binding. To gain enough support for that idea the Convention designed a number of additional provisions to limit the scope of the Charter. This was necessary to overcome the opposition of a number of governments—including those of the UK and the Netherlands—which strongly opposed the possibility that the Charter could become a source of dispute that could give the citizens direct claims against governments or employers. During the 2003–04 IGC stage the resistance to the inclusion of the Charter in the Constitution continued until the last moment. To overcome that resistance a few more sentences were added to the 'general provisions' of the Charter, particularly on the status of the official Explanations of the Charter. However, since the referendums in France and the Netherlands things have gone in a different direction. The IGC of 2007 at the insistence of (again) Britain and the Netherlands agreed to keep the full text of the Charter outside the reformed European Treaties. For the Dutch Government especially this was one of the most important points in order to provide it with enough arguments to convince the Dutch people that the Lisbon Treaty was substantially different from the European Constitution and thus that there was no need to call a new referendum. Instead of a complete incorporation of the full text of the Charter in the European Treaties, there is now only one reference to the Charter in the Treaty of the European Union, in which the Union recognises the rights, freedoms and principles set out in the Charter. It is added that the Charter shall have the same legal value as the Treaties, but it is also explicitly asserted that the Charter shall not extend in any way the competences of the Union as defined in the Treaties and that the Charter shall be interpreted in accordance with the general provisions in Title VII of the Charter governing its interpretation and application and with due regard to the Explanations referred to in the Charter that set out the sources of those provisions (Article 6 TEU). The version of the Charter established by the IGC in 2003–04 was agreed by the IGC in 2007 with another small modification and then endorsed by the EU institutions in Strasbourg on 12 December 2007 and published in the EU *Official Journal*.[24]

Many people believe that the Charter will be an engine for EU activities in the social field due to the fact that many fundamental rights have a social nature. Csilla Kollonay-Lehoczky, Klaus Lörcher and Isabelle Schömann reflect on this subject in their contribution.

IV. HOW THE HORIZONTAL SOCIAL CLAUSE CAN BE MADE TO WORK: THE LESSONS OF GENDER MAINSTREAMING

The new Article 9 of the Treaty on the Functioning of the European Union (TFEU) requires the EU institutions and the Member States to assess all their

[24] OJ EC C 303/1 of 14.12.2007.

policies, laws and activities in light of their implications for the achievement of social goals. In combination with the Charter of Fundamental Rights and the future accession of the EU to the Convention for the Protection of Human Rights and Fundamental Freedoms, it may contribute to a fundamental reorientation of EU legislation and jurisprudence towards social aims. The implementation of gender mainstreaming over the last 10 years enables identification of the key factors required if horizontal European policies are to succeed. The experience of gender mainstreaming shows in particular that, in order to develop its full potential, the new Horizontal Social Clause will require firm commitment on the part of all European actors involved in the fields of employment, social protection, the fight against social exclusion, education and training and human health. Subject to impetus by a strong political will, Article 9 has the potential to prompt significant redirection of the most liberal European policies towards social ends and to contribute to the emergence of a European social model.

V. THE ROLE OF THE SOCIAL PARTNERS IN EUROPE

In the Treaty of Maastricht (1992), the so-called social dialogue was anchored in the European Treaties. This is a remarkable process by which the European social partners have been given legislative powers of a kind (Articles 138–139 TEC). Since then, the European Commission in all its social policy initiatives must consult the European social partners. If the social partners so desire, the European Commission temporarily stops its preparatory work in order to enable the European social partners to take the matter into their own hands and to conclude an agreement on that matter. Subsequently, the social partners via the European Commission may offer their agreement to the Council of Ministers of the EU, which may convert it into a Directive, which is just as binding as other EC Directives.[25] These procedures over the past 10 years have been very little used and only for a few high profile issues.[26] Nevertheless, this possibility gives the EU a distinctive neo-corporatist streak. Not remarkable for the Benelux countries, Austria and the Scandinavian countries, but for many other EU countries it is extraordinary.

At the European Convention the European social dialogue was not called into question at all. On the contrary, it was embraced as an element of

[25] Alternatively, these agreements may be implemented in accordance with the procedures and practices specific to management and labour and the Member States (see Articles 138–139 TEC).

[26] E Franssen, *Legal Aspects of the European Social Dialogue* (Antwerp, 2002); M de Vos, *A Decade beyond Maastricht: The European Social Dialogue Revisited* (The Hague, 2003); ATJM Jacobs, 'European social consultation' in *Comission Consultative Nacional de Convenios Colectivos* (*Collective Bargaining in Europe*) (Madrid, 2004) 347–93; JH Even, *Transnational Collective Bargaining in Europe* (The Hague, 2008).

participatory democracy and given an honourable mention in Article I-48 of the Constitution:

> The Union recognizes and promotes the role of social partners at its level, taking into account the diversity of national systems. It shall facilitate dialogue between the social partners, respecting their autonomy. The Tripartite Social Summit for Growth and Employment shall contribute to social dialogue.

In the Treaty of Lisbon, this text is moved to the Title on Social Policy (Article 152 TFEU) and it remains to be seen whether this recognition of social dialogue will prove fruitful. The European Trade Union Congress[27] hopes that this provision may stimulate the European Commission to provide the European social partners more often with more information[28] and consultation on a wider range of issues and may stimulate the EU Court of Justice to hear it on social matters.[29]

The provisions in the European Treaties on the European Social Dialogue have been largely consolidated by the Treaty of Lisbon (Articles 154–155 TFEU),[30] although here too a few minor adjustments have been made. It has been added that the European Parliament shall be informed about the state of affairs with the agreements of the social partners (Article 155(2) TFEU), something which is already happening in practice. The European Parliament will continue to find it unsatisfactory that it is in fact outflanked if the social partners have reached an agreement that is implemented by a Directive. If that matter had been settled under Article 153 TFEU, the European Parliament—at least in cases falling under the ordinary legislative procedure—would have had the possibility of amending the contents of the measure and even of stopping it. In Directives under Article 155 TFEU, however, this is not possible.

Employers are naturally reluctant to contribute to an increase in 'hard law' in the labour market. Only two things can persuade them to make concessions: collective action and the threat of legislation. Collective action at European level still appears hardly possible. They rarely have to fear threats of legislation ('bargaining in the shadow of the law') because of the cumbersome decision-making procedures in the Council of Ministers, which are outlined in the next chapter.[31]

[27] See the Resolution of the Executive Board of the ETUC of 1–2 December 2009, at: www.etuc.org/a/6741.

[28] For instance, it is remarkable that in the Consultative Committee on Employment the social partners have only the right to consultation, not information (Article 150 TFEU).

[29] I have elaborated this point in A Jacobs, 'The European Court of Justice, social law, and the European social partners' in R Blanpain (ed), *Labour Law, Human Rights and Social Justice* (The Hague, 2001) 139–50.

[30] No answer has been given on the question whether the social partners in their competence to conclude agreements are limited by Article 153(5) TFEU (former Article 137(5) TEC).

[31] See B Bercusson, 'The implementation and monitoring of cross-border agreements: The potential role of cross-border collective industrial action' in ETUI publication *Labour Law and Social Europe. Selected Writings of Brian Bercusson* (Brussels, 2009) 656.

Can we expect that the European Social Dialogue under the Treaty of Lisbon will produce more than was the case over the past 15 years of its existence?

This is the question that Bruno Veneziani tries to answer.

VI. THE SOCIAL POWERS AND THE LAWMAKING PROCESS IN SOCIAL MATTERS

The European Union is a supranational organisation, which may exercise only those powers expressly conferred on it (Article 5(2) TEU). In 2002–03 at the European Convention, there were significant differences on the role of the European Union in the social field. Many argued that the EU had to be rather reticent in social affairs and to leave most initiatives to the Member States. There were also opposing voices that argued in favour of a stronger European social policy. The outcome of the fight was a draw. The Lisbon Treaty has indeed brought a number of smaller changes, but on the essential points it is the same old story.

The Articles on social policy in general as they read up until 1 December 2009[32] have been barely changed in the reformed European Treaties (now Articles 151–164 TFEU). They authorise the EU to promote the coordination of the social legislation of the Member States (Article 156 TFEU) and to issue its own European rules with regard to most aspects of social policy (Articles 153–155 TFEU).

The Maastricht Treaty (1991) had already divided the social field into one domain in which decisions by the Council of Ministers have to be adopted unanimously and another domain in which decisions are taken by qualified majority. The Treaty of Nice (2000) only went a small step further. It opened up the possibility that all decisions in the social field, except those relating to social security and social protection, in future could be taken by the Council of Ministers with a qualified majority if this Council decides that unanimously (the so-called 'passarelle' clause).[33] However, such a decision was never taken. At the European Convention 2002–03 the Presidium had proposed bringing almost the entire field of social policy under the normal legislative procedure (that is, qualified majority voting in the Council of Ministers and a co-legislative role for the European Parliament).[34] This text was inexplicably deleted during one of the last sessions of the Convention[35] and the final text of the Convention's draft for a European Constitution contained exactly the same assignment of social

[32] Articles 136–148 TEC.
[33] See Article 137(2), last sentence, TEC.
[34] CONV 725/03 p 67 on Article III-99 (ex-Article 137 TEC).
[35] CONV 811/03 p 54 on Article III-99 (ex-Article 137 TEC).

issues partly to the unanimity procedure and partly to the procedure of qualified majority, as was already the case, as well as the same 'passarelle' clause as in the Treaty of Nice.[36] During the 2003–04 IGC, France tried to take that further step of the Presidium in the text of the Constitution, but that attempt was met with resistance from several countries, including the UK. Finally, also in the now reformed European Treaties, only half the social issues are assigned under the ordinary legislative procedure (qualified majority voting in the Council of Ministers) and the other half under the special legislative procedure (unanimity in the Council), exactly as it has been since the Maastricht Treaty plus the 'passarelle' from the Nice Treaty (Article 153(2), last sentence TFEU).

All this raises the question of whether one can expect a more dynamic role for EU labour law. Klaus Lörcher addresses this question.

VII. SUBSIDIARITY

A major hurdle for European social legislation may be the principle of subsidiarity. That principle requires that the Union, in areas which do not fall within its exclusive competence, shall act only if and in so far as the objectives of the proposed action cannot be sufficiently achieved by the Member States, either at central level or at regional and local level, but can rather, by reason of the scale or effects of the proposed action, be better achieved at Union level. The principle has been in the European Treaties since 1992 and was formalised in a Protocol,[37] but little has been done with it since then[38] because it has always been perceived as vague.[39] Some doubt whether it is at all able to erect a barrier against the mania for regulation in Brussels.[40]

However, especially under pressure from Germany, the importance of the subsidiarity principle has been strengthened in the reformed European Treaties.[41] It now has a prominent place in the reformed European Treaties

[36] Article III-104.3 of the Convention—Proposal.

[37] Geelhoed (n 19) p 300; see Wouters (n 22) p 70.

[38] See the first cases mentioned by Wouters (n 22) p 70; also K Boutens, 'Het subsidiariteitsbeginsel, een kwestie van toepassing' (2003) (57) 3 *Internationale Spectator*; H Ischia, *Zentralisierung und Subsidiarität* (Frankfurt am Main, 2004); A Estella, *The EU Principle of Subsidiarity and its Critique* (Oxford, 2002); CAW Timmermans, 'Is het Subsidiariteitsbeginsel vatbaar voor rechterlijke controle?' (2007) 6 *SEW* 224–30; M Schmitt, *Autonomie Collective des partenaires sociaux et principe de subsidiarité dans l'ordre juridique communautaire* (Aix-Marseille, 2009).

[39] Although it has been provided by the European Council with an Explanatory Memorandum, see the Conclusions of the Presidency of the European Council of Edinburgh, Bulletin EC 12-1992, point I.4.

[40] See L Siedentop, *Democracy in Europe* (London, 2000).

[41] See M Schröder, 'Vertikaler Kompetenzverleihung und Subsidiarität in Konventzentwurf für eine europäische Verfassung' (2004) *Juristenzeitung* 11; P de Jonge, 'Het subsidiariteitsbeginsel in de Europese Grondwet: panacee of Paard van Troje' (December 2006) *AA* 857–67.

(Article 5(3) TEU).[42] To meet the needs of regional authorities in Member States with strong 'devolution' of government (Germany, Spain, Austria, Belgium, Great Britain and so on), the regional and local dimensions are included in the definition of subsidiarity. New also is the enforcement system as set out in Protocol No 2 on Proportionality and Subsidiarity. It is a kind of 'yellow card' or 'early warning system'.[43]

National parliaments now have eight weeks to draw a 'yellow card'.[44] If a simple majority of national parliaments[45] considers that a proposal by the European Commission violates the subsidiarity principle, it should be reconsidered. Moreover, the EU Council of Ministers (with a 55 per cent majority) and the European Parliament (by a simple majority) may decide to halt further consideration of the proposal.[46] Finally, the Committee of the Regions and the national parliaments through the *locus standi* of the Member States may approach the ECJ on the applicability of this principle.[47]

Although this procedure has certainly strengthened the relevance of the subsidiarity principle compared with the situation that existed until 1 December 2009, Thomas Blanke in his chapter asks whether this new arrangement will constitute a serious hindrance to the activism of the European legislator.

VIII. THE COORDINATION OF ECONOMIC POLICIES

In the Treaty of Lisbon virtually nothing has changed in the Articles on the coordination of national employment policy as they previously existed[48] and so in this area the 'guidelines' within the framework of which policies can be made (Article 148(2) TFEU) remain as non-binding ('soft law') as before (Articles 2(3), 5(2) and 5(3) and 145–150 TFEU).

[42] R Barents, 'Het subsidiariteitsbeginsel in het Hervormingsverdrag' (2007) *NTER* 253–61.

[43] D Wyatt, 'Could a "yellow card" for national parliaments strengthen judicial as well as political policing of subsidiarity?' (2006) *Croatian Yearbook of European Law and Policy* 17; J Maaten, (November 2003) *Openbaar Bestuur* 9.

[44] This is an extension compared with the text in Protocol No 2 of the European Constitution, which mentioned a term of six weeks.

[45] This is a limitation compared with the text in Protocol No 2 of the European Constitution, which mentioned a threshold of one-third or one-quarter.

[46] See Protocol No 2 on the application of the principles of subsidiarity and proportionality.

[47] See Articles 6 and 7 of the new Protocol No 2 on subsidiarity and proportionality. See also A Dashwood and A Johnston, 'The institutions of the enlarged EU under the regime of the Constitutional Treaty' (2004) *CMLRev* 1488–89; J Peters, 'National parliaments and subsidiarity. Think twice' (2005) *ECLRev* 68.

[48] Articles 125–130 TEC.

The texts on social cohesion,[49] too, are virtually unchanged (Articles 174–178 TFEU). They have been decorated with fine words,[50] but with no extra money or power.

In the same vein, the Treaty of Lisbon has codified the views on the place of Europe in the world as they stood in 2002–03. In that period most Member States were absolutely against forceful economic governance on the part of the EU. The competences in this area are even weaker than in the social area. In the meantime, first the banks and then entire Member States have been tormented by the financial crisis. This requires more effective economic governance. In the absence of this the financial assistance to Greece, Ireland, Romania and Portugal has been made subject to strict conditions, including cuts in wages, social subsidies, pension systems and so on. Financial discipline is imposed at the expense of the wider, social objectives enshrined in the Treaties.

This makes the following question (already mentioned) a matter of urgency: do countries retain the freedom to enact or maintain labour laws which are more favourable for the workers than the rules of the European Union? Earlier it was written that the EU and the Member States have shared competence in social matters. In practice, this is so. European social law and social policy are still modest in nature, and that may be regarded as an essential part of the European Social Model. However, there is still so much room left for national social law and social policy because—as indicated above—the EU has used so little of its social competence, and where it has done so it often did it with soft law. This much room is also preserved because of the rule of thumb that, even in those areas where hard EU social law is enacted, the Member States retained leeway to enact or maintain rules that are more favourable to workers. This idea is often expressed in the Preamble and the final Articles of the social law Directives of the EU. However, the Court of Justice in the aforementioned *Laval*, *Rüffert* and *Commission v Luxembourg* cases has determined that the EU standards of the Posted Workers Directive are not only a minimum, but a maximum. This has cast doubt on whether the aforementioned rule of thumb of EU law is still functional.

This principle of the more favourable rule has been expressly stated in the Treaties for a number of years and returns unchanged in the European Treaties with the revision by the Treaty of Lisbon (Article 153(4), second indent TFEU). Some say that it applies only to the standards of the social policy of the EU and not to the standards of freedom of movement, on

[49] Articles 158–162 TEC.

[50] The European Treaties now specify that particular attention shall be paid to rural areas, areas affected by industrial transition and regions which suffer from severe and permanent natural or demographic handicaps, such as the northernmost regions with very low population density and island, cross-border and mountain regions (Article 174(3) TFEU).

which the Posted Workers Directive is founded. This interpretation would be analogous to the American doctrine of 'pre-emption'[51] which considers some standards as both minimum and maximum. However, this too narrow view is to be avoided on the basis of the Treaty of Lisbon seen in its historical context. The entire operation of the 'European Constitution' was originally set up to stop the excessive drift of the competences of the Member States to Europe. This has resulted in a reformulation of the allocation of competences,[52] a strengthening of the principle of subsidiarity and the introduction of provisions useful for the defence of social policy (see above). All this suggests that the 'principle of the more favourable rule' in the relationship between national and European social law is broadly applicable, and not only with regard to measures based on Article TFEU 153 (ex-Article 137 EC). In short, this principle of the more favourable rule is well anchored in the Lisbon Treaty. However, will this convince the Court? The first ruling by the Court in this area after the entry into force of the Treaty of Lisbon, *Commission v Germany*, is not reassuring. The priority of the rights of the market over fundamental social rights was repeated.[53] For the European Trade Union Confederation this was a reason to reiterate its call that at the next amendment of the European Treaties a 'social progress clause' or a 'social progress protocol' should be included, guaranteeing a better balance between the laws of the market and the social rights.[54]

Niklas Bruun deals in his contribution with these issues related to the economic governance of the European Union especially from the perspective of the recent economic crisis.

IX. SERVICES OF GENERAL INTEREST

The questionable character of the operation of the laws of the market and free competition has also become quite apparent in the area of services of general economic interest (postal services, public transport, waste management, energy, health care and so on). Already in the Treaty of Rome of 1957 it was determined that these services would be subject to the rules of the free market, but only 'in so far as the application of such rules does not obstruct the performance, in law or in fact, of the particular tasks assigned to them'.[55] The Treaty of Amsterdam sang the praises of 'the place occupied by services of general economic interest in the shared values of the Union' (Article 16 TEC) and the Charter of Fundamental Rights called the

[51] See ATJM Jacobs, *Sociale Rechten in Amerika* (Utrecht, 2003) 16–17.
[52] *Cf* Article 48(2) TEU, Articles 4(1) and 5(2) TFEU and Protocol No 25.
[53] Case C-271/08 CoJ EU 15.7.2010 (*Commission v Germany*).
[54] See: www.etuc.org/a/7521 and 6741.
[55] Article 82(2) TEC.

access to these services a fundamental right.[56] This generous recognition of services of general economic interest has been fully maintained in the Treaty of Lisbon (Article 14 TEU and Article 106(2) TFEU) along with the insertion of some not insignificant additions.[57]

The first addition is in the final sentence of Article 14 TEU, which at the insistence of France provides that 'the European Parliament and the Council, acting by means of regulations ... shall establish these principles and set these conditions'.[58] Apparently, this was not enough to reassure the citizens of Europe with regard to their worries about the dismantling of postal services and the breakup of railway, energy and other services. The French have always been very critical and this point was certainly one of the reasons for the French 'no' to the European Constitution. At the IGC 2007 not only France but also the Netherlands revisited this item. Together they managed to achieve that via the Lisbon Treaty Protocol No 26 has been added to the European Treaties, specifying which shared values of the Union in particular are meant in Article 14 TFEU (Article 1) and guaranteeing that the provisions of the Treaties do not affect in any way the competence of Member States to provide, commission and organise non-economic services of general interest (Article 2).

The second provision is not very helpful as, according to the case law of the EU Court of Justice, most public services are economic services and therefore remain subject to all the rules of the internal market, state aid and competition, whatever precious values they may represent. Thus, the drive of the European Commission to split up our railways, privatise our electricity and liberalise the financial markets, and so on, can just continue. Antoine Jacobs examines whether the new texts will do a better job than the previous ones in preventing these services being increasingly exposed to the trends of privatisation and free competition.

[56] Article 36 of the EU Charter on Fundamental Rights.

[57] See C Einem, 'Eine Verfassung für Europa. Anmerkungen zu ausgewählten Aspekten des Verfassungsentwurfs' (2004) *EuR* 202–06.

[58] S Rodrigues, 'Vers une loi européenne des services publics' (2003) *Revue du Marché commun et de l'Union européenne* 503–11.

Part I

The General Framework or Primacy of the Social Dimension (Principles)

1

The Lisbon Treaty, the Viking *and* Laval *Judgments and the Financial Crisis: In Search of New Foundations for Europe's 'Social Market Economy'*

SIMON DEAKIN

I. INTRODUCTION

THE AIM OF this chapter is to consider the relationship between the economic and social dimensions of European integration in the light of a number of recent legal and institutional developments, including the *Viking* and *Laval* judgments,[1] the changes to EU law made by the Lisbon Treaty and the unfolding financial crisis. *Viking* and *Laval*, and the subsequent case law clarifying and extending those rulings, radically altered the nature of the relationship between social policy and internal market law by asserting that national labour law rules were liable, in and of themselves, to distort competition within the internal market, and as such had to be justified by reference to a strict test of proportionality. Prior to *Viking* and *Laval*, strong national labour law systems, setting standards above a basic floor of rights guaranteed by a combination of Treaty provisions and Directives, had been not just accepted, but actively encouraged as providing a counterweight to the effects of market integration. With the emergence of open coordination methods, differences in levels of regulation between systems had been seen as providing a basis for experimentation in the social policy field. By associating the application of the labour laws of the Member States with the concept of distortion of competition, *Viking*

[1] Case C-438/05 *ITF v Viking Line ABP* [2007] ECR I-10779; Case C-341/05 *Laval v Svenska Byggnadsarbetareförbundet* [2007] ECR I-11767.

and *Laval* undermined these approaches to social policy and threatened to initiate a race to the bottom between national systems.[2]

The Lisbon Treaty does not amend the core social policy provisions of the EC Treaty, now contained in Title X of the TFEU, but it does make a number of changes which could have an impact on the evolution of European labour law in the aftermath of *Viking* and *Laval*. Three in particular are relevant: (i) a new reference to 'social market' goals in the objectives of the EU; (ii) a restatement of the competences of the Union and the Member States in the social policy field; and (iii) greater recognition of the legal effects of fundamental social rights within the EU legal order.[3]

These changes are already starting to have an impact on the way the Court is approaching the issue of balancing social policy and internal market freedoms post-*Viking* and *Laval*. There are some signs that economic freedoms will no longer be placed in a clearly hierarchical position with regard to social rights, and that a more flexible approach to the issue of proportionality may be possible in future.[4] How far the Court will row back from *Viking* and *Laval* is not easy to assess. The significance of the Lisbon Treaty changes will be addressed here by placing *Viking* and *Laval* in the context of the long-run evolution of EU law and in particular by considering the significance of successive Treaty amendments for the EU's 'economic constitution'.

The idea of the 'economic constitution' refers to the ways in which a given polity views the relationship between the organs of the state (including the legal system) and the market (or economic system).[5] This chapter will argue that there is no single, predominant conception of the state–market relationship in EU law and that, instead, several different versions of this idea are present in the corpus of law made up by the Treaties, secondary legislation, case law and so on. In evolutionary terms, the EU moved from an 'ordoliberal' conception of the economic constitution in the 1950s to a 'neoclassical' one in the 1990s and 2000s.[6] Ordoliberal elements remained, but, as exemplified by the case of the Treaty's freedom-of-movement

[2] S Deakin, 'Regulatory Competition after *Laval*' (2008) 10 *Cambridge Yearbook of European Legal Studies* 581.

[3] P Syrpis, 'The Treaty of Lisbon: Much Ado… But About What?' (2008) 37 *Industrial Law Journal* 219.

[4] C Barnard and S Deakin, 'European Labour Law after *Laval*' in I Ulasiuk (ed), *Before and After the Economic Crisis: What Implications for the 'European Social Model'?* (Cheltenham: Edward Elgar, 2011).

[5] C Joerges and F Rödl, 'Informal Politics, Formalized Law and "Social Deficit" of European Integration: Reflections after the Judgments of the ECJ in *Viking* and *Laval*' (2009) 15 *European Law Journal* 1.

[6] R Salais, 'Employment and the Social Dimension of Europe: What Constitutive Convention of the Market?' in R Rogowski, R Salais and N Whiteside (eds), *Transforming European Employment Policy: Labour Market Transitions and the Promotion of Capability* (Cheltenham: Edward Elgar, 2011).

provisions, were increasingly reinterpreted by reference to a neoclassical logic. The *Viking*, *Laval*, *Rüffert*[7] and *Luxembourg*[8] judgments embody this approach in context of the application of free movement rules to social policy. As such they constitute, without doubt, a marginalisation of labour law within the EU legal order. However, EU law contains a third, emergent conception of the state–market relationship, which will be referred to here as a 'human-developmental' one, from which assistance can be drawn in countering the logic of *Viking* and *Laval*. It will be argued in this chapter that advancing a developmental conception of EU social policy will prove more useful, as a strategic approach, than attempting to limit *Viking* and *Laval* by reverting to the ordoliberal logic of the Rome Treaty, particularly in the conditions created by the current financial crisis.

II. THE SHIFT FROM 'ORDOLIBERAL' TO 'NEOCLASSICAL' CONCEPTIONS OF THE MARKET IN EU LAW

A. Ordoliberal Theory, the Rome Treaty and the Original 'Social Market' Economy

An ordoliberal conception of the state–market relationship is one in which the legal system has the task of establishing the conditions for a functioning market order.[9] This process involves the active construction, through the legal order, of an economic-political environment within which market relations can develop. The legal system must do more than recognise and enforce, through private law, the property and contract rights which form the subject matter of economic exchange. Going beyond private law, the legal system must be deployed so as to ensure that competition is maintained by, for example, regulating monopolies and cartels through the mechanisms of antitrust law. At the same time, ordoliberalism does not envisage a state-directed economy. A complementary role of the legal system is to constrain the arbitrary use of governmental power. Thus ordoliberalism requires limits on state ownership of industry and constraints on direct government intervention in, or planning of, economic processes.

The ordoliberal model of the legally-constituted market order heavily influenced the approach taken in the Treaty of Rome to the process of economic integration.[10] It was given concrete expression in the Rome Treaty's

[7] Case C-346/06 *Dirk Rüffert v Land Niedersachsen* [2008] ECR I-1989.
[8] Case C-319/06 *Commission v Luxembourg* [2007] ECR I-4323.
[9] See C Joerges and F Rödl, '"Social Market Economy" as Europe's Social Model?' EUI Working Paper LAW No 2004/8 and C Joerges, 'What is left of the European Economic Constitution?' EUI Working Paper LAW No 20045/13, for accounts of ordoliberal thought and analyses of its relevance to the development of EU law.
[10] Joerges and Rödl, 'Social Market Economy' (n 9).

provisions on competition and freedom of movement. It also informed the concept of 'distortion of competition', which is referred to in the Spaak Report (1956) on which the Treaty was, in part, based.[11] The creation of a market free of 'distortions' implied a transnational trading regime in which the factors of production could move across borders in response to economic signals, to the same extent as they would do within the unitary jurisdictional space of individual Member States. It also presupposed markets which were not divided or partitioned along national lines. This could have been read as implying a need for the harmonisation of regulations (including those of labour law) affecting the factors of production, with the goal of establishing uniform costs within the common, or later, internal market. That view was rejected at the time of the Rome Treaty, in a way which expressed acceptance of an active role for the state in the social policy field, but at national level.

The acceptance of a role for social policy within the broadly ordoliberal orientation of the Rome Treaty turned on a particular analysis of the relationship between means and ends in the construction of a transnational market order. Functional convergence of regulatory norms and practice, and hence of costs, was expected to follow from the removal of the more visible obstacles to inter-state trade. This approach made formal convergence unnecessary: on the one hand, it ruled out a comprehensive European labour code or transnational floor of rights in social policy; on the other, it preserved Member State autonomy in the social policy field.

Member State autonomy over social policy was not simply the result of political obstacles to agreement between the Member States, initially or at successive stages of enlargement, on the content of a European labour code. There was indeed no political consensus but, at the same time, the decision to leave competence in social policy mostly in the hands of the Member States was presented in structural terms as a part of the integration process. The Ohlin Report (1956), commissioned from the ILO prior to the Rome Treaty, argued that strong labour law systems at national level were understood to be necessary in order to provide a counterweight against the dislocating effects of the economic growth that was expected to follow from market integration. The 'strength of the trade union movement in European countries and ... the sympathy of European governments for social aspirations' were, in this sense, necessary preconditions for the creation of a common (or internal) market.[12] While the Member States might not have agreed on the content of a common labour code, they were all in agreement—up to the mid-1970s—on the need for strong labour

[11] *Rapport des Chefs de Délégation aux Ministres des Affaires Étrangères* ('Spaak Report') (Brussels, Comité Intergouvernemental créé par la conférence de Méssine, 1956).

[12] 'Social Aspects of European Economic Cooperation' ('Ohlin Report') (1956) 74 *International Labour Review* 99, 112.

laws at national level. They also supported complementary labour market institutions in respect of social insurance, and governmental promotion of full employment through 'Keynesian' techniques of demand management, during this period. In addition, most of the Member States had made constitutional guarantees of one kind or another regarding social rights in the immediate postwar period. The commitment of the drafters of the Rome Treaty to strong labour market institutions at national level can be seen in their willingness to accept the need for social policy harmonisation in those areas where, for one reason or another, they did not expect a spontaneous process of 'levelling up' to occur.[13] This principle of selective intervention at transnational level was the origin of the Treaty of Rome's provisions on equal pay, which were to have far-reaching significance in the development of European Union labour law, as well as those relating to working time, whose influence turned out to be minimal.

The use of national labour law regimes as a counterweight to transnational economic integration gave expression to one of the elements of ordoliberal thought, namely the idea that the market was not a natural order but was constituted by, and embedded in, legal and political processes. In the 1950s and 1960s, if not all then at least some adherents of ordoliberal economic theory were able to accept the case for minimum wages, collective bargaining and social insurance as mechanisms complementing the operation of product and financial markets.[14] Wealth creation—and societal wellbeing in a wider sense—were seen as ultimately dependent on the harnessing of economic resources through private enterprise, and on a market-oriented division of labour. Social cohesion was understood, in large part, to be the consequence of economic growth, but for that growth to be sustainable, it was also accepted that elements of the social fabric had to be maintained. This was the essence of the 'social market' philosophy which influenced German economic policy debates of the 1950s and 1960s. The 'social market' idea promoted market forces and required limits to state intervention which were not compatible, for example, with macroeconomic policies aimed at achieving full employment through the management of demand which the Member States mostly followed at that time. To that extent it operated more as a model than as a representation of the practice of the Member States, Germany included.[15] Nevertheless, in so far as EU labour law could be said to have had a guiding principle during this period, the concept of the 'social market' economy provided it. The Keynesian model of redistributive and growth-oriented economic policy which held sway at Member State level was not embedded at EU level.

[13] Spaak Report (1956) p 60.
[14] Joerges and Rödl, 'Social Market Economy' (n 9) pp 14–17.
[15] Ibid pp 18–19.

B. The Impact of *Viking* and *Laval* on Member State Autonomy in Social Policy

The decisions in *Viking* and *Laval* involve a rejection of the compromise struck at the time of the Rome Treaty between economic integration at transnational level and strong labour law institutions at national level. Prior to *Viking* and *Laval*, the Court had accepted the broad terms of that compromise, and had translated them into legal principles which more or less held the deregulatory tendencies of free movement law at bay. In *Rush Portuguesa*[16] it had endorsed the principle of the territorial effect of national labour laws in the face of the Treaty-based provisions protecting the free movement rights of service providers. In *Albany*[17] it insulated national-level labour law and collective bargaining from the full application of competition policy rules. These decisions, and others like them, were seen by their critics as carving out artificial and unjustified exemptions to the operation of internal market rules, but they were arguably consistent with, and followed from, the institutional architecture of the Rome Treaty. That architecture was nevertheless coming under increasing strain as a result of the changes set in train by the Single European Act and the Maastricht and Amsterdam Treaties in the 1980s and 1990s. The 'old' ordoliberal economic constitution was never formally revoked, and its core provisions on free movement and competition remained the same. However, the assumptions on which the old constitution had been based were being eroded by the deepening of the internal market programme and by the process of economic and monetary union. *Viking* and *Laval* are part of a wider realignment of the Court's case law which took place alongside this process.

The common idea underpinning *Viking*, *Laval* and the subsequent case law in the same line is that national-level labour law rules are capable of constituting a distortion of competition within the internal market and, as such, must be justified by reference to a strict test of proportionality. Although ostensibly expressed in terms which are familiar from free movement case law, the principle put forward in *Viking* and *Laval* goes far beyond the Court's earlier decisions on the application of internal market law to social policy. Neither of the two tests conventionally relied on in free movement cases—the older and limited 'discrimination' test and the more recent, and more interventionist, 'market access' or 'restriction test'—was clearly satisfied in these cases.[18] There was no discrimination on the grounds of nationality in either case. In *Viking*, the reflagging of the vessel and not the nationality of its owner was the issue. In *Laval*, the collective agreements which the unions were seeking to enforce were intended to

[16] Case C-113/89 *Rush Portuguesa* [1990] ECR I-1417, para 18.
[17] Case C-67/96 *Albany* [1999] ECR I-5751.
[18] See Deakin, 'Regulatory Competition' (n 2).

apply to all employers engaged in construction work on Swedish territory, on an equal basis. On one view, the Lex Britannia was discriminatory in its treatment of overseas collective agreements, but even this is not clear,[19] and the Court's broad interpretation of Article 56 (ex-49) did not in any event turn on this aspect of the Lex Britannia.

In its earlier decision in the free-movement decision of *Säger*,[20] the Court had moved away from a requirement of discrimination on grounds of nationality in free-movement cases, and it relied in *Viking* and *Laval* on this wider concept of a restriction on market access to trigger the application of Article 56. It is difficult to see, however, that even the market access test was met. The issue in *Viking* was not access to Estonian markets, but—an entirely different proposition—access to Estonian jurisdiction as a low-cost alternative to the Finnish one. Similarly, the service provider in *Laval* had access to the Swedish construction market; its complaint was that it could not operate in Sweden while simultaneously taking advantage of the less stringent labour laws that would have applied had the work been done in Latvia.

In what sense can it be said, in the context of posting, that the application of the normal labour law rules of the 'host state' in these cases constitutes a 'restriction' on cross-border trade? There are two possibilities. One is that the restriction arises from differences in labour law rules and practices between the home and host states (a comparative standard); the other is that labour law rules, once they exceed a certain (unclearly defined) level of strictness, are inherently restrictive (an absolute standard). *Laval* and *Rüffert* have mostly been interpreted as turning on the application of a comparative test: from this point of view, the critical issue was that Latvian and Polish labour laws were less 'restrictive' than, respectively, Swedish and German laws. The problem with this reading of the decisions arises from the lack of any obvious connection between the establishment of a company (which determines its nationality for free-movement purposes) and the labour law rules which it observes in relations with employees and other labour market actors. A company established in a given Member State may, as a matter of law and practice, observe the labour law of that state in its relations with employees who work there, but this does not follow from the company's establishment; it results from the choice of law made by the parties to the employment contract, supplemented by the territorial effect of any mandatory labour law rules of the state concerned. If a company's establishment does not determine which labour law rules apply to it in the absence of a supposed 'restriction', the converse is also true: the applicable labour law rules do not determine the establishment. Thanks to the Court's

[19] Joerges and Rödl, 'Informal Politics' (n 5) p 16.
[20] Case C-76/90 *Säger* [1991] ECR I-4221.

Centros[21] decision and the increasing move away from the 'real seat' principle at Member State level, in favour of freedom of incorporation, a company's main seat of business or operations can, if its controllers choose, be detached from the jurisdiction in which it has its establishment.

It is also relevant to bear in mind that the parties whose free-movement rights had apparently been infringed in *Laval* and *Rüffert* were not even established in the low-cost states whose laws they were trying to access. The industrial action in *Laval* was targeted against a Swedish company which was a subsidiary of the Latvian parent which appeared as a party before the Court, while the company whose bankruptcy triggered proceedings in *Rüffert* was a German construction firm that had employed a Polish company as one of its sub-contractors.

For these various reasons, there is a case for seeing *Laval* and *Rüffert* as turning on an absolute, as opposed to a comparative, notion of what constitutes a 'restriction'. Labour law rules which impose undue regulatory costs on service providers are, in this view, seen as inherently restrictive. To trigger the free-movement principle, there must be a transnational dimension to the dispute. But this is very easily satisfied, as the facts of *Laval* and *Rüffert* make clear: a home-state parent of a host-state subsidiary (*Laval*) and a host-state client of a home-state supplier (*Rüffert*) can equally well invoke it. It is not out of the question that the principle applied in those cases will operate to disallow the application of labour law rules to service providers established in the host state and predominantly operating there, where they can show that they are competing in that state with overseas providers who can take advantage of lower cost labour law regimes to which they have some connection. The Court was invited to make just such a ruling in the *Omalet* case, which, however, it declined to take up on that occasion.[22]

Viking can also be understood as a case based on an absolute as opposed to a comparative approach to defining a 'restriction'. On one view, a restriction arose in *Viking* because of differences between Estonian and Finnish labour law and collective agreements which made the former more attractive to the employer. On another view, the Court was articulating a rule according to which strike action becomes subject to review when it weighs on any decision of the employer which has transnational elements. Relocations involving cross-border flows of assets or resources clearly enough come into this category, but once the principle is extended, as it was in *Viking*, to virtual relocations, such as the reflagging of a vessel, it becomes potentially much more open ended and its link to the original rationale of the free-movement rules becomes tenuous, because there is no sense in which there is either discrimination or a denial of market access.

[21] Case C-212/97 *Centros Ltd v Erhvervs-og Selkabsstryrelsen* [1999] ECR I-1459.
[22] Case C-245/09 *Omalet v Rijksdienst voor Sociale Zekerheid*, Judgment of 22.12.2010.

The purpose of raising these points is not simply to highlight the doctrinal murkiness of *Viking* and *Laval*, but to stress how radically they depart from the ordoliberal assumptions which informed the foundation of the EU legal order, and hence by extension, from the social market model, at least in its original ordoliberal sense. This is so whether we take a narrow view of the decisions as turning on a comparative approach to defining what a restriction is, or a broader one based on an absolute standard. If the former interpretation is correct, the decisions are incompatible with the Spaak Report's rejection of the argument that a common (or internal) market requires uniform rules in the area of labour law (or any other area of regulatory policy). If the latter interpretation is correct, they are incompatible with the idea of national-level labour law regimes as a necessary counterweight to the effects of economic integration.

The Ohlin and Spaak reports were written over 50 years ago, and there may be a case for seeing them as having diminished significance in today's environment. There is indeed a sense in which the analysis they advanced has been superseded by changing circumstances, but not in a way which is capable of justifying the Court's approach in *Viking* and *Laval*. In making the argument against a comprehensive European labour code, the Ohlin Report emphasised the inherent flexibility provided by separate national currencies and adjustable exchange rates. In the same way, the Spaak Report argued that differences in exchange rates could be expected to cancel out the potentially distorting effects of cross-national differences in nominal wage rates. Where the flexibility provided by exchange rates was thought to be absent, as in the case of the advantage enjoyed by employers in states with weak sex discrimination legislation, both Spaak and Ohlin accepted the logic of harmonisation of labour laws at transnational level, hence the incorporation of the equal pay principle into the Rome Treaty. By the same logic, the advent of the single currency, and the restrictions placed on national economic policymaking by the stability pact and associated measures, constitute a case for strengthening, not weakening, national-level labour law regimes, if necessary through further harmonisation.[23]

C. *Viking/Laval* and the Open Method of Coordination

Social policy has also moved on since the mid-1950s, but *Viking* and *Laval* are at odds with these more recent developments too. The most significant of them has been the application to social policy of the regulatory techniques associated with open coordination methods. The open method of coordination ('OMC') is premised on the value of having, within

[23] See section III.A, below.

the economic space of the internal market, a diverse range of regulatory approaches to policy issues. Within the parameters set by policy guidelines at central level, Member States have leeway over the choice of mechanisms used to arrive at common goals. The circulation of information between the Member States and the central organs, together with reflection on their different experiences, provide the basis for a learning process.[24] This model of coordination, while associated initially with 'soft law' measures in such areas as the employment strategy, has wider validity as an account of the Union's law-making method. The Spaak Report emphasised the value of regulatory diversity, and the OMC is perhaps best seen as a continuation and extension of that approach, rather than a radical departure from it.

Thus the OMC is compatible with certain 'hard law' developments in the social policy field since the 1970s. Because social policy Directives mostly use a floor of rights model, allowing Member States to set more protective standards than those set out in harmonising measures, they create a space for learning based on diversity above the floor. The development of social dialogue since the early 1990s added a further dimension to this process, making it possible for a number of additional sources of regulation—beyond those of the legal systems of the Member States—to be mobilised. There is evidence that this approach has been successful in stimulating new responses at Member State level to long-standing social policy dilemmas in such areas as worker representation and work–life balance laws, and has helped push the labour laws of the Member States in the direction of a 'race to the top' at a time when political agreement at central level was becoming more difficult to achieve.[25]

Viking and *Laval* strike at the basis of the social policy OMC by seeking to impose on national labour law systems a common set of constraints, justified by the idea of creating an 'undistorted' economic space. They do this not simply by extending the notion of 'restriction' within free movement jurisprudence, but by a highly constraining approach to issues of proportionality and justification. In the context of the Posted Workers Directive, this meant giving the Directive a 'pre-emptive' interpretation, implying that it set both a floor and a ceiling of rights. The protections set out in Article 3(1) were defined in terms of the lowest minima set by national systems, and Member States were given very little leeway to set additional mandatory rules of law governing the employment contract under Article 3(10). In these various respects, the Court marked a clear departure from the interpretive logic that had previously been applied to Directives with a social dimension. There was no recognition in these judgments that the laws and practices being challenged represented a

[24] C Sabel and J Zeitlin, 'Learning from Difference? The New Architecture of Experimentalist Governance in the EU' (2008) 14 *European Law Journal* 271.

[25] S Deakin, 'Reflexive Harmonisation and European Company Law' (2009) 15 *European Law Journal* 224.

solution to labour market coordination issues which was not only a valid response to particular national contexts, but one which should be factored into the wider learning process of the OMC as it applied to social policy.

The sector-wide labour standards which were at issue in *Laval* play a role beyond that of protecting labour interests, narrowly conceived. Within the Nordic systems they are part of a wider set of norms and institutions which operate as 'beneficial constraints',[26] requiring firms to compete on the basis, not of low pay, but by investing in productivity-enhancing techniques and organisational methods. They thereby operate in a complementary way to the active labour market policies and flexible employment protection laws which won the approval of the Commission in its Green Paper on the modernisation of labour law.[27] This is a model which EU law does not seek to impose on other Member States, but which, in the context of the OMC, provides an example of an approach to labour market regulation which has proved successful in certain national settings, and from which other Member States might have something to learn. In those settings, the various institutional mechanisms of labour market regulation are mutually supporting; to remove one puts in doubt the effectiveness of the others. *Viking* and *Laval* threaten to undermine a core component of one of the more obviously successful institutional responses to dilemmas and difficulties of labour market regulation within the EU.

D. The Neoclassical Economic Constitution

The logic of *Viking* and *Laval* runs contrary both to the ordoliberal origins of the EU and to the more recent adoption of open coordination methods as a way of encouraging regulatory learning. It is consistent, on the other hand, with what may be called a neoclassical interpretation of the EU's economic constitution.[28] Neoclassical models of the law–economy relationship see markets as essentially self-equilibrating. They share with ordoliberalism a distrust of direct state intervention in the economy, but they go further in denying that legal regulation is necessary to create the conditions for effective competition. While opposing extensive antitrust law interventions as unnecessary, neoclassical approaches nevertheless view labour law rules and collective bargaining practices as inherently inefficient. Thus, in the neoclassical approach, a principal role of the courts is to remove, through deregulation,

[26] W Streeck, 'Beneficial Constraints: On the Economic Limits of Rational Voluntarism' in R Hollingsworth and R Boyer (eds), *Contemporary Capitalism: The Embeddedness of Institutions* (Cambridge: Cambridge University Press, 1997).

[27] Green Paper, *Modernising Labour Law to Meet the Challenges of the Twenty-First Century* COM (2006)708, 22.11.2006.

[28] Salais, 'Employment and the Social Dimension' (n 6).

legislative interventions which may have arisen in the past on the basis of what are seen as misguided notions of 'social justice', and to deploy the power of the legal system to break up collusive arrangements through which private actors seek to capture the surplus ('rents') generated by the productive process. According to this logic, few protective rules are required for labour markets to operate: rules against forced labour—by ruling out the institution of slavery and requiring 'free' contracting—provide one example.

This view of labour law regulation as inherently restrictive and potentially justifiable only within a very narrow range, is what lies at the basis of the Court's analysis in *Viking* and *Laval*. The rise of the 'restriction' test in free movement law, following the *Säger* decision, represents the growing displacement of the old, ordoliberal economic constitution by the more contemporary neoclassical one. *Viking* and *Laval* extended this approach to the social policy field. Strikingly, rules against forced labour are one of the very few measures which, in *Luxembourg*, the Court said Member States could adopt as mandatory rules of law under the residual provisions of Article 3(10) of the Posted Workers Directive ('PWD').

The growing influence of neoclassical economic thought on the design of EU laws and institutions can be found at various points in the evolution of the Treaties from the Single European Act onwards. The Member States, with the UK in the lead, made the move away from Keynesian economic policies from the late 1970s onwards. The emerging neoliberal policy orthodoxy stressed the need for control of the money supply, wage restraint and fiscal stability as responses to the combination of high inflation and persistent unemployment which characterised economies at that time. The Single Act began the process of transferring these policies to EU level. They received their clearest expression in the mechanisms put in place, initially by the Maastricht Treaty, for the operation of the single currency. The convergence criteria and stability pact were intended to limit the discretion of Member States to run their own economic policies, and in particular to curb the use of fiscal deficits as a response to recessions. The ECB's Constitution formally bars it from undertaking many of the functions traditionally performed by central banks at national level in various countries, which include supporting industrial policy and promoting full employment through active monetary policy. The ECB's overarching legal obligation is to maintain price stability. The assumption underlying its institutional design is that once stable prices are ensured by control of the money supply, markets will operate in such a way as to generate full employment without the need for demand management. Any remaining unemployment in the system is the effect of 'distortions' induced, in large part, by labour laws and collective bargaining which artificially raise the price of labour and depress demand.[29]

[29] For an economic discussion and critique of the ECB's constitution, see R Schettkat, 'Will Only an Earthquake Shake Up Economics?' (2010) 149 *International Labour Review* 185.

Thus the view that labour laws are inherently restrictive of market relations is a central aspect of the ECB's policy remit and modus operandi, even if it is rarely stated as such (references instead being made to the importance of 'structural' reforms to accompany economic integration). In addition, currency union within a transnational trading area is intended to operate as a mechanism which renders national-level differences in regulatory regimes more visible, and thereby increases the pressures for deregulation. In this perspective, a 'race to the bottom' in labour law is not just an incidental feature of economic integration, but one of its intended consequences, although empirical studies suggest that labour market deregulation did not occur on any significant scale in response to the introduction of the euro.[30]

The argument here is not that the ECB constitution or the stability pact directly influenced *Viking* or *Laval*, in the sense of providing a doctrinally recognisable legal source for the reasoning in those decisions. The argument, rather, is that developments in the constitutional architecture of the EU, of which the ECB is one of the most prominent examples, have helped to legitimise a way of thinking about the relationship between the legal system and the process of economic integration which, over time, has found expression in the case law of the Court, including in *Viking* and *Laval* and the cases which succeeded them.

The ECB is, of course, only one of a number of institutions charged with the promotion of economic integration, and not all Member States are part of the currency union, or even aiming to join it. One of the arguments this chapter seeks to make is that the EU's economic constitution is multifaceted and subject to a number of distinct influences. As part of the EU's trajectory, there has been a 'layering' of ideas and institutions, with the result that as new mechanisms have emerged (such as currency union) they have been grafted on what came before, rather than completely replacing it. Thus many elements of the original ordoliberal foundation remain in place. They can be called in aid to question the legitimacy and validity, in a more technical, doctrinal sense, of the neoclassical version of the economic constitution. Critiques of *Viking* and *Laval* which invoke the cautious and nuanced approach to market integration of the Spaak Report can be seen in this light. Similarly, the reference in the Lisbon Treaty to the EU's 'social market economy' has echoes of the acceptance of a prominent role for labour-market regulation which was part of 1950s ordoliberal thought. But in the face of the institutional and economic constraints that national labour law regimes are increasingly subject to, it is unlikely to be sufficient as a bulwark against further deregulation. Alternative conceptions of the law–market relationship must be considered, together with a basis for their

[30] A Alesina, S Ardagna and V Galasso, 'The Euro and Structural Reforms' in A Alesina and F Giavazzi (eds), *Europe and the Euro* (Cambridge, MA: National Bureau of Economic Research, 2010).

operationalisation within the current framework of European labour law at both transnational and national level.

III. TOWARDS A HUMAN-DEVELOPMENTAL INTERPRETATION OF THE EU'S ECONOMIC CONSTITUTION

A. The Economic Constitution under Pressure: The Impact of the Financial Crisis

The neoclassical turn taken by the EU in the 1990s and 2000s has had far-reaching consequences not just for labour law and social policy, but for the direction of economic policy more generally. The Court's validation of the neoclassical constitution in *Viking* and *Laval* nevertheless came at a very late stage in the process of its diffusion, when its limits and contradictions were becoming clear. The judgments were handed down a few weeks after the beginning of the credit crunch of 2007, and within nine months of the onset of the global financial crisis in the autumn of 2008. Events, rather than theoretical refutations, shift paradigms and the idea of the self-equilibrating market has come under severe pressure following the near collapse of the global financial system in September 2008. A major depression was averted only by the use of traditional Keynesian measures of fiscal expansion, and by the automatic stabilisers provided by welfare states and employment protection laws.[31] Discredited ideas take time to fade away, however, and as the immediate crisis passed, much of the impetus for policy reform was lost.

For the EU, the need to consider alternative approaches to the neoclassical orthodoxy is nevertheless an urgent one. The post-Maastricht economic constitution has begun to unravel as a consequence of the financial crisis. The Member States have been locked into an economic model which stresses price stability and fiscal conservatism above all else, and which treats the welfare state as a fetter on the operation of the self-equilibrating market.[32] Under these circumstances there are very strong pressures for a race to the bottom in labour and social standards and macroeconomic policy. Notwithstanding the deepening of market integration, economic growth in the EU Member States has been at historically low levels since the 1980s, below the trend in the period of Keynesian policy dominance from the 1940s to the 1970s, and inequality has increased in more or less

[31] See IMF/ILO (2010) *The Challenges of Growth, Employment and Social Cohesion* Discussion Document, Joint ILO-IMF conference in cooperation with the office of the Prime Minister of Norway, Oslo, August 2010 (www.osloconference2010.org/discussionpaper.pdf).

[32] Schettkat, 'Will Only an Earthquake?' (n 29).

all countries along with the share of national product allocated to wages.[33] In the circumstances of the current crisis, the operation of the currency union will most likely exacerbate these trends. The Member States most severely affected by the crisis cannot restore economic growth through exchange rate adjustments as they would previously have done. They have few options for reducing fiscal deficits. One route, to which they are guided by the terms of the Maastricht criteria, is through internally-generated deflation and a further downgrading of the protections provided by the welfare state. According to neoclassical theory, and to the current orthodoxy in EU economic and monetary policy, the removal of internal barriers to growth through 'structural' reforms should facilitate a private sector revival which will permit growth to resume. This is a highly optimistic scenario. It is at least as likely that deficit-reduction policies will lower growth rates while exacerbating social inequalities. However, this is precisely the policy which the EU now seems set on enforcing through the agenda of financial stabilisation which emerged in the course of 2010–11.

The reaction to the sovereign debt crises in Greece, Ireland and Portugal has taken the form of concerted efforts on the part of the EU institutions (including the Council, the Commission and the ECB) and the Euro-area Member States to put in place mechanisms for ensuring financial stability in the Eurozone which have potentially far-reaching implications for social policy.[34] The Memorandum of Understanding agreed between the IMF, the European Commission, acting on behalf of the Eurozone states, and Greece in May 2010 included provisions under which the Greek Government agreed to introduce reforms designed to 'render labour and product markets more efficient and flexible'.[35] Changes subsequently introduced to labour legislation in Greece have, among other things, narrowed the scope of application of sector-level collective bargaining, and weakened employment protection legislation. In Ireland, the National Recovery Plan agreed in December 2011 as a condition of financial aid from the IMF and EU Member States also incorporates a social policy dimension.[36] In the course of 2010 and 2011 the Irish Government used emergency legislative powers to restrict the scope of collective bargaining and to make cuts to the minimum wage, social security benefits and the wages of public sector workers. In Portugal, financial aid provided by the Eurozone states was made conditional on an economic policy programme drawn up within the framework of the newly

[33] S Deakin and F Wilkinson, 'Marchés du travail, crise financière et nouvelle réglementation: les futures orientations du droit du travail' in *L'Homme et la société* (forthcoming).

[34] See Bruun, 'Economic Governance' (ch 8 in this volume).

[35] *Greece: Memorandum of Economic and Financial Policies*, 3 May 2010, available at: www.imf.org/external/pubs/ft/scr/2010/cr10111.pdf.

[36] Government of Ireland, *The National Recovery Plan 2011–14* (Dublin: Stationery Office, 2010).

established European Financial Stabilisation Mechanism (EFSM).[37] The March 2011 European Council meeting proposed a permanent European Stability Mechanism (ESM) which would in due course replace the EFSM. The ESM is designed to provide a basis for financial support for Eurozone states on a basis of conditionality, that is to say, the imposition strict macro-economic and fiscal policy disciplines on any Member States receiving aid. The same Council meeting proposed an amendment to Article 136 TFEU to incorporate the future ESM into the framework of EU law.[38]

Further institutional changes along these lines occurred throughout 2011. The Euro Plus Pact, which was agreed in the course of the European Council meeting of March 2011, committed the Eurozone states to a regime of economic surveillance with direct implications for labour law.[39] The Pact envisages regular monitoring of unit labour costs at national level, with the aim of ensuring that they evolve 'in line with productivity';[40] the setting of targets for long-term and youth unemployment and labour market participation rates; and the taking of steps to ensure that state expenditures in the areas of pensions, health care and social security benefits do not threaten the 'sustainability' of public finances. Since the Pact primarily addresses 'areas that fall under national competence'[41] it implies a further extension of economic and monetary policy at EU level into the area of social policy which had previously been understood to be largely the domain of the Member States. The Pact is intended to operate through a version of the OMC, with each state free to adopt specific policy measures but with a view to achieving the common goals of wage competitiveness, employment growth and financial sustainability.[42] Thus the Pact contemplates oversight of wage-setting arrangements and, while stopping short of ruling out wage indexation, requires the degree of centralisation of wage bargaining to be kept under review. Its provisions on employment growth make reference to the desirability of labour market reforms aimed at promoting 'flexicurity' and to the need for reform of employment taxation systems. In the autumn of 2011 further institutional reforms were made, in the form of the 'six pack' of measures amending and extending the budgetary and macroeconomic surveillance mechanisms originally put in place under

[37] Council Regulation (EU) No 407/2010 of 11 May 2010 establishing a European financial stabilisation mechanism, OJ L/118, 12.05.2010, pp 1–4.

[38] See Bruun, 'Economic Governance' (ch 8 in this volume).

[39] European Council, 24/25 March 2011, Conclusions, EUCO 10/1/11 REV 1, Annex I.

[40] EUCO 10/1/11 REV 1, at p 16.

[41] EUCO 10/1/11 REV 1, at p 14.

[42] 'Progress towards the common objectives … will be monitored politically by the Heads of State or Government on the basis of a series of indicators covering competitiveness, employment, fiscal sustainability and financial stability. Countries facing major challenges in any of these areas will be identified and will have to commit to addressing these challenges in a given timeframe': EUCO 10/1/11 REV 1, at p 15.

the Stability and Growth Pact in the late 1990s.[43] These measures have few direct implications for labour law and social policy, but their indirect impact in embedding a regime of monetary and fiscal discipline at the level of the Member States is likely to prove considerable in coming years. The December 2011 European Council failed to reach agreement on additional changes that would have led to a further tightening of economic surveillance mechanisms, but the 'EU-26' (that is, the Member States aside from the United Kingdom) agreed a 'fiscal compact' embodying these rules and putting in place a commitment to balanced budgets.[44]

Thus the context of the financial crisis has given the debate about the role of social policy in the EU a new and very hard edge. Social policy can no longer be seen as a marginal issue for the EU. Defenders of the current orthodoxy will press for further and more rapid deregulation of labour law at Member State level, and for a deepening of the *Viking/Laval* approach at transnational level, as means of allowing labour markets to adjust and re-equilibrate more quickly to the shock of the crisis. An emerging counter-critique, given some validation by the IMF and the ILO in their joint paper of August 2010,[45] runs as follows. The financial crisis was not an exogenous shock or freak event, but was brought about by the application of deregulatory policies to financial, product and labour markets, and triggered by the inequalities and imbalances which characterised the neoliberal growth regime of the 1990s and 2000s. Such is the severity of the crisis that, in the short run, national governments should continue to adopt policies of fiscal expansion; deficit reduction would lead only to a continuation and deepening of the recession. In the longer run, economies should be put on to a more stable growth path. In the labour market context, this implies a combination of measures aimed at restoring real wage growth, limiting income inequality and providing the basis for long-term productive investment in skills and resources. This option, while in principle capable of offering a coherent, socially progressive response to the crisis, is not currently on the policy agenda as far as the EU is concerned, because it is incompatible with the post-Maastricht economic settlement. Whether the EU's position will change in the immediate future seems doubtful, but the tensions inherent in the current policy make it likely that there will be a re-evaluation of the relationship between social and economic policy at some point. When that occurs, alternative approaches will be back on the policy agenda.

[43] For an overview of these measures, see C Barnard, 'The Financial Crisis and the Euro Plus Pact: A (Labour) Lawyer's Perspective' (2012) 41 *Industrial Law Journal*, March, forthcoming.

[44] Ibid.

[45] IMF/ILO, *The Challenges of Growth* (n 31).

B. A Human-developmental View of Labour Law Reform

One such alternative is the 'human-developmental' view of labour law. This uses the notion of human development to inform policy goals and the means of their implementation. The use of human development goals to benchmark national social and economic performance is not just relevant in the context of so-called emerging or transition systems. It cannot be assumed that 'development' is a state of affairs which mature economic systems, such as those of the Member States of the EU, have safely achieved. So-called advanced or developed systems are increasingly unable to ensure that basic developmental outcomes are being met for all their citizens. Since the rise of neoliberal policies from the early 1980s, inequality has increased in the advanced industrial economies, along with unemployment and social exclusion. The recent recession has seen a rapid rise in the poverty rate in some of the countries most severely exposed to the financial shock, including the UK and the US, which were also the systems in which neoliberal policy prescriptions had previously had their greatest impact.[46]

In the human development perspective, the role of social and economic policy is to provide a framework within which individual 'capabilities', understood as substantive economic freedoms, are advanced within the constraints set by given resources. Institutions, such as markets and other mechanisms of economic coordination on the one hand, are viewed as potential means to this end, and not as ends in themselves. The same principle applies to social rights and to the redistributive and protective mechanisms of the welfare state: they are means of enhancing the freedom of action of individuals.

This way of thinking about the goals and functions of labour law can help to clarify its relationship to issues of economic efficiency and growth. An economic efficiency-based case for labour law can be made. Certain labour law rules serve to constitute and underpin labour-market relations, and to counteract externalities which would otherwise result in the misallocation of resources.[47] At the same time, labour law systems also aim at outcomes which cannot be rationalised in purely economic terms. Economic growth can, under certain circumstances, be compatible with increased inequality of income. Such inequality is a principal cause of inferior developmental outcomes in terms of the health, wellbeing and autonomy of individuals.[48] Protective labour law rules and solidaristic forms of collective bargaining are

[46] Deakin and Wilkinson, 'Marchés du travail' (n 33).

[47] S Deakin and F Wilkinson, 'Labour Law and Economic Theory: A Reappraisal' in G De Geest, J Siegers and R van den Bergh (eds), *Law and Economics and the Labour Market* (Cheltenham: Edward Elgar, 1999).

[48] R Wilkinson and K Pickett, *The Spirit Level: Why More Equal Societies Almost Always Do Better* (London: Allen Lane, 2009).

highly effective in maintaining conditions of equality of outcome, and their weakening invariably brings about greater inequality.[49] Thus labour law rules and social policy mechanisms more generally, play a critical role in market economies of channelling economic policy in favour of a set of human-developmental objectives which go beyond a narrow focus on growth.

This tension between economic growth and human-developmental goals should not be overstated. Over the long run, growth regimes which perpetuate inequality are not sustainable. Because the market is not a 'natural' order, but is embedded in society and instituted by the legal system, a pattern of economic growth which erodes solidarity and social cohesion, and which places the impartiality of the legal system under strain, cannot be indefinitely maintained. How 'long' the long run is, however, is not certain, and the point at which a growth regime based on inequality begins to unravel cannot be precisely predicted. The experience of the economic crisis suggests that we are now living through just such a period. Had labour law systems been more effective in limiting the adverse consequences for social cohesion of the financially driven growth of the past three decades, it is unlikely that the recent shock to the system would have been so severe. This is already becoming clear from the greater capacity to absorb the social and economic effects of the crisis of those national systems which had stronger social safety nets in place.[50]

The case for labour law and social policy mechanisms more generally, then, is that they seek to reconcile economic growth and developmental goals, that is, to make them mutually complementary. If growth at the expense of human development is ultimately unsustainable, it is equally the case that the mere articulation of developmental goals, through formal social rights and labour codes, is insufficient for their achievement. Labour law involves a search for mechanisms which can render social rights compatible, as far as possible, with economic growth regimes which make the best use of society's available resources, in such a way as to ensure their mutual, long-run sustainability.

C. Human-developmental Goals and the Lisbon Treaty

To see labour law in developmental terms would by no means be an entirely novel approach in the context of EU social policy. Significant elements of

[49] R Freeman, 'Labour Market Institutions without Blinders: the Debate over Flexibility and Labour Market Performance' NBER Working Paper No 11286 (2005).

[50] ILO, 'Building an Employment-Oriented Framework for Strong, Sustainable and Balanced Growth' in *The Challenges of Growth, Employment and Social Cohesion*, Discussion Document, Joint ILO-IMF conference in cooperation with the office of the Prime Minister of Norway, Oslo, August 2010 (www.osloconference2010.org/discussionpaper.pdf).

the existing corpus of EU labour law can be understood using this model. The substantial body of equal treatment law—which originated in the equal pay provisions of the Treaty of Rome and was later broadened to include a much wider range of prohibited grounds of discrimination—provides one example.[51] It is in this context that the use of the capability approach to justify a social rights-based interpretation of discrimination law has already entered the discourse of the Court.[52] There is considerable scope for the further operationalisation of the capability approach at the level of juridical analysis.

The issue to consider here is how far this process can be advanced by the changes made by the Lisbon Treaty. As stated above, there are three changes of particular relevance to labour law: (i) the restatement of the values and objectives of the EU; (ii) the clarification of the competences of the EU and the Member States; and (iii) the recognition accorded to fundamental social rights in the form of the Charter.

Article 3 TEU states that the Union 'shall establish an internal market' and goes on to say that in addition it

> shall work for the sustainable development of Europe based on balanced economic growth and price stability, a highly competitive social market economy, aiming at full employment and social progress, and a high level of protection and improvement of the quality of the environment.

The internal market is to be 'established', while sustainable development is a goal to be 'worked for' through mechanisms which include the social market economy but also price stability and 'balanced' growth. The social market economy is, apparently, put on an equal footing with price stability as a means to an end, while the establishment of the internal market is stated to be a goal in itself. This is not at first sight an advance on the old Article 2 of the EC Treaty, under which the establishment of the common market, along with economic and monetary union and a number of other common policies, was stated to be a means of achieving various ends, namely,

> a harmonious, balanced and sustainable development of economic activities, a high level of employment and of social protection, equality between men and women, sustainable and non-inflationary growth, a high degree of competitiveness and convergence of economic performance, a high level of protection and improvement of the quality of the environment, the raising of the standard of living and quality of life, and economic and social cohesion and solidarity among Member States.

[51] S Deakin, '*Capacitas*: Contract Law, Capabilities, and the Legal Foundations of the Market' in S Deakin and A Supiot (eds), *Capacitas: Contract Law and the Institutional Foundations of a Market Economy* (Oxford: Hart Publishing, 2009).

[52] Case 478/03 *Astley v Celtec Ltd* [2007] IRLR 647, Opinion (Maduro AG).

The internal market, together with the other objectives set out in the new Article 3 TEU, can however been seen as means of achieving the values listed in Article 2 of that Treaty, namely 'human dignity, freedom, democracy, equality, the rule of law and respect for human rights, including the rights of persons belonging to minorities'. Thus the internal market remains a means to various ends, not an end in itself.

Moreover, the objectives set out in Article 3 include not just the reference to sustainable development based on (among other things) the 'social market economy', but the '[combating] of social exclusion and discrimination' and the '[promotion] of social justice and protection, equality between women and men, solidarity between generations and protection of the rights of the child'. The structure of Article 3 implies that the promotion of these social objectives is seen as a goal of the Union on a par with the establishment of the internal market, rather than being viewed as a consequence of it, as the old Article 2 TEC implied. On this interpretation, the taking of active steps to promote social goals separately from those taken to establish the internal market is now one of the Union's principal purposes.

In the context of these changes, it would be inappropriate to confine the idea of the social market economy by reference to its ordoliberal origins. The reference to the social market economy in the draft Constitutional Treaty was described as not simply conceptually flawed, but as 'empty' of meaning given that the 'the historical compromise that the concept once embodied is no longer alive'.[53] The postwar conditions in which the idea of the social market was mobilised no longer hold. Ordoliberalism, as a body of thought, has become increasingly aligned with Hayekian and neoliberal positions, thereby losing any sense that it offers a justification for social policy within a market-based economic order. Leaving aside the anachronism of the idea of the social market, the view that labour law is needed to offset some of the negative consequences of economic integration retains some validity. But this is a very limited conception of the economic role of labour law. To see labour law as intervening, ex post, to soften the worst effects of an integration process that in other respects is allowed to be carried on without restraint, would be to return social policy to the marginal and subordinate role that it occupied in the Rome Treaty.

The promotion of social justice and protection, gender equality and solidarity between generations, as set out in Article 3 TEU, imply a more ambitious role for social policy within the EU legal order, which is compatible with a human development agenda. It is nevertheless the case that the Lisbon Treaty creates no new powers at EU level for the implementation of these objectives. This brings us onto a consideration of the issue of competences.

[53] Joerges, 'What is left?'(n 9) p 34.

Under Article 2 TFEU, social policy is an area of shared competence, meaning that the Member States may exercise law-making powers to the extent that the EU has not exercised its competence. This does not in itself appear to change the asymmetry between free-movement law and national labour law-making powers under *Viking* and *Laval*: the Court can, apparently, use freedom of movement jurisprudence to create a new layer of industrial action law at EU level, while the Member States are prevented by Article 153(5) TFEU from enacting a new Directive in this field. The Court's formalist view, that its free-movement jurisdiction is in no way affected by the absence of powers to adopt harmonising legislation in the collective labour law field, is just one of the ways in which it explicitly rejected the original compromise over competences put in place by the Rome Treaty. The Court simply refused to see European labour law in the round, as consisting of complementary levels of regulation at state and transnational level.

In practice, however, the Court's intervention on this point is less powerful, and less destructive of the powers of the Member States than appears at first sight. The Court rulings in *Viking* and *Laval* have been not enough in themselves, so far, to trigger a race to the bottom. Precisely because the Member States retain the critical competences which the Lisbon Treaty confirmed, their response to *Viking* and *Laval* has makes all the difference to how those decisions impact on national labour law regimes. The response to *Laval* in the Nordic systems has taken the form of attempts to shore up the national models which that decision put in question. The Swedish legislature has gone furthest in accommodating the Court's rulings, but even then has taken steps to restore the right to strike over the application of national-level collective agreements to foreign service providers. The most significant concession to *Laval* was the restriction of strike action to the defence of the minimum forms of protection set out in collective agreements, in line with the Court's ruling in *Luxembourg*.[54] Post-*Laval* legislation in Denmark did not go this far in accommodating the Court, reaffirming the right to take strike action in support of a range of collectively-bargained terms and conditions. The Norwegian courts and the EFTA Surveillance Authority have so far upheld extension legislation in Norway which enables terms of collective agreements above the basic floor to be applied to service providers.[55] In Germany, the *Land* of Lower Saxony has responded to *Rüffert* by re-enacting its law on the application of sector-level agreements

[54] M Rönnmar, '*Laval* Returns to Sweden: the Final Judgment of the Swedish Labour Court and Swedish Legislative Reforms' (2010) 39 *Industrial Law Journal* 280.

[55] T Skjeie, 'European Economic Integration: A Threat to the Scandinavian Labour Law Systems?' (LL.M. Dissertation, Faculty of Law, University of Cambridge, 2010). See now case E-2/11, *STX Norway Offshore As V Norwegian State*, EFTA Court, Judgment, 23.12.2012.

by extending it beyond public procurement cases, in an attempt to comply with the Court's reading of Article 3(8).[56]

These legislative initiatives illustrate the continuing vitality of labour law systems at Member State level, and a determination on the part of legislatures to maintain the distinctive features of national models wherever possible. The Lisbon Treaty's reaffirmation of Member State competence in areas where the Union has not acted is a reminder that the Union's competences remain limited, even in respect of the free-movement principle, and that the Court's attempts to use internal market law to level down labour law protections at national level will generate a response in favour of preserving national models as long as local political conditions are favourable to this.

Article 152 TFEU commits the EU to recognising and promoting 'the role of the social partners at [EU] level, taking into account the diversity of national systems'. The reference to national diversity in this particular context is double-edged. While it could imply a constraint on the use of social dialogue to establish norms of general application, it can equally well be taken as an indication of the role social dialogue can play in preserving national diversity in the face of the levelling down that arises from free-movement jurisprudence. In this regard, it is relevant that among the responses to *Viking* has been an EU-wide framework agreement on the implications of the reflagging of vessels for the social protection of workers, which has been implemented in the form of a Directive. This, in turn, is intended to come into force alongside an ILO Convention on which it is modelled.[57] The conjunction of social dialogue with ILO standards in this case suggests that there are numerous options for filling gaps left by the Court's deregulatory interventions.

The legal recognition granted to the Charter of Fundamental Rights is also potentially significant. The Charter does not operate as a floor of rights, and no new legal competences are associated with the status conferred on it by the Lisbon Treaty.[58] While referring to a long (if still somewhat incomplete) list of social rights, it also incorporates entrepreneurial and economic rights which could in future be invoked in support of the Court's approach in *Viking* and *Laval*. These caveats notwithstanding, the Charter makes it more difficult to argue that economic freedoms prevail over social rights, as the Court decided in those cases. It is more plausible to argue that

[56] S Sciarra, 'Notions of Solidarity in Times of Economic Uncertainty' (2010) 39 *Industrial Law Journal* 223.

[57] Council Directive 2009/13 implementing the agreement concluded by the European Community Ship Owners' Associations and the European Transport Workers' Federation, OJ [2009] L 124/30; ILO Convention No. 186 on Maritime Labour, adopted 23.02.2006; see Sciarra, 'Notions of Solidarity' (n 50) pp 232–233.

[58] Syrpis, 'Much Ado' (n 3); see also the chapter by Filip Dorssemont (ch 2 in this volume).

the relationship between them is one of parity.[59] This view is compatible with the human-developmental conception of European labour law set out above.

IV. CONCLUSION

Viking and *Laval* were part of a wider shift from an ordoliberal conception of the EU's economic constitution to a neoclassical one, associated with the deepening of the internal market programme and the implementation of economic and monetary union. The Lisbon Treaty provides some basis for a rebalancing of economic freedoms and social rights, and points the way to what this chapter has described as a 'human-developmental' conception of labour law. The context provided by the financial crisis is highly significant in this respect. In the long run, the near collapse of the global financial system in 2008 makes the idea of the self-equilibrating market implausible. The idea will not, however, fade immediately. In the context of the EU, a continuing problem remains the embedding of the self-equilibrating market model in the constitution of the ECB and the institutional design of the currency union and, now, of mechanisms for financial stabilisation. This currently poses an even greater threat of a race to the bottom in social policy than *Viking* and *Laval*.

The first phase of the financial crisis ended with the stabilisation of the banking system in the first half of 2009, but it then gave way to a sovereign debt crisis which has had far-reaching implications for the single currency and for social policy. Throughout 2010 and 2011, Member States within and outside the Eurozone used this new phase of the crisis to initiate 'austerity' measures aimed at reducing budget deficits. Meanwhile, a new agenda of 'economic governance' was emerging alongside the financial stability mechanisms put in place in an attempt to deal with fiscal imbalances and the associated risk of sovereign debt default in certain Member States. The loans organised by the Eurozone states and IMF were made conditional on 'structural reforms' which included cuts to welfare benefits and measures of labour law deregulation in the Member States receiving financial support. These developments threaten to undermine national autonomy in social policy still further.

The practical lesson to draw from these unfolding events is that if the Union is to realise the value and objectives set out in the Lisbon Treaty, it will have to address the linking of economic and social policy in a more systematic way than in the recent past. In the short run, economic stabilisation

[59] On this, see Case C-515/08 *Santos Palhota* [2010] ECR I-000, Opinion, paras 51–53 (Cruz Villalon AG); Case 271/08 *Commission v Germany (Occupational Pensions)* [2010] ECR I-000, Opinion, paras 183–190 (Trstenjak AG).

measures which ignore the social context of the financial crisis or, worse still, use the crisis as a pretext for further weakening of the welfare state, are likely to prove counterproductive. In the longer run, institutional reforms are needed which will address the adverse social implications of fiscal and economic imbalances, and not simply their impact on the financial system.

Such reforms might look far off at present. The financial stabilisation agenda will have to run its course before they can be implemented. However, the end of orthodoxy may come sooner than we think. The contradictions inherent in a policy of enforced deflation and deregulation will inevitably come to the fore. When that happens, the next phase of the EU's institutional development can begin. This chapter has suggested a future role for social policy which would be consistent with the EU's long-term goal of promoting social progress within the framework of an open market economy.

2

Values and Objectives

FILIP DORSSEMONT

Article 2 TEU on the Union's values is not only a political and symbolic statement. It has concrete legal effects.[1]

I. INTRODUCTION

TO DATE, RELATIVELY little consideration has been given to the added value of the Treaty establishing a Constitution for Europe or the Lisbon Treaty with regard to what is generally called the 'social dimension' of the European Union.[2] 'Social policy' is covered by Part III, Chapter III, Section II of the Constitution ('Internal policies and action') and by Title X of the TFEU. A prima facie comparison of these two sections with Title XI of the Treaty on European Community (Amsterdam version) gives the impression that it is almost an identical copy of the former Treaty. However, it cannot be seen in isolation. It needs to be viewed in conjunction with the two earlier parts of the Constitution and, at present, with Articles 2, 3 and 6 of the TEU. These provisions deal with the values and objectives of the Union and define how the Union relates to *fundamental rights*.

The question is whether this new way of framing largely unchanged competences puts the social dimension of the European Union in a different light. In this contribution, I want to explore whether the distinction as well

[1] J-C Piris, *The Lisbon Treaty* (Cambridge: Cambridge University Press, 2010) p 71.

[2] See, inter alia, B Bercusson, *European Labour Law*, 2nd edn (Cambridge: Cambridge University Press, 2009) 217–55 and 715–37; M de Vos and B de Wolf, 'The Treaty of Lisbon and social policy: a tempest in a teapot?' (2010) 22 *EELC*; F Dorssemont, 'La dimension sociale de l'Union européenne après la Constitution' *Semaine sociale Lamy*, Supplément 'Comment réussir une Europe élargie', *Semaine Sociale Lamy*, 25 April 2005 89–95; ATJM Jacobs, 'The social Janus head of the European Union: social market economy versus ultraliberal policies' in J Wouters, L Verhey and P Kijver (eds), *European Constitutionalism beyond Lisbon* (Antwerp: Intersentia, 2009) 111–28; J Kenner, 'The Constitution that never was: is there anything worth salvaging from the wreckage?' (2005) *Industrial Relations Journal* 541–67; M Schmitt, 'La dimension sociale du traité de Lisbonne' (2010) *Droit social* 682–95; I Schoemann, 'Le Traité de Lisbonne: L'Europe sera-t-elle enfin plus sociale?' (2010) 1 *ETUI Policy Brief* and P Syrpis, 'The Treaty of Lisbon: Much Ado … But About What?' (2008) 37 *Industrial Law Journal* 219–35.

as the relation between *values* and *objectives* might provoke a shift in the 'balance' between fundamental (social) rights and fundamental economic freedoms.

II. FROM THE TREATY ON THE EUROPEAN UNION (MAASTRICHT VERSION, 1992) TO THE LISBON TREATY (2007): VALUES SPEAKING EVER LOUDER THAN OBJECTIVES

Ever since the Treaty on European Union (Maastricht version, 1992), 'objectives' have been put forward.[3] The objectives concerned were, inter alia,

> to promote economic and social progress which is balanced and sustainable, in particular through the creation of an area without internal frontiers, through the strengthening of economic and social cohesion and through the establishment of economic and monetary union, ultimately including a single currency in accordance with the provisions of this Treaty.

A. Values

The Treaty on European Union (Maastricht version) did *not* refer explicitly to 'values'. Many recitals in the Preamble of the Treaty did refer to 'principles' which have been qualified as 'values' in subsequent versions of the Treaty on European Union.[4] These principles have been 'confirmed' and qualified as 'desirable'.

It is worth considering that the creation of a common or internal market and a monetary union is *not* approached as a primary objective in Article B of the TEU (Maastricht). The creation of a common or internal market is a means to reach a more far-reaching objective, namely balanced and sustainable economic and social progress. This instrumental approach to the establishment of a common market as a means to an end is mirrored by ex-Article 2 TEC.[5]

[3] See Article A TEU (Maastricht).

[4] '*[C]onfirming* their attachment to the principles of liberty, democracy and respect for human rights and fundamental freedoms and of the rule of law, *desiring* to deepen the solidarity between their peoples while respecting their history, their culture and their traditions, *desiring* to enhance further the democratic and efficient functioning of the institutions so as to enable them better to carry out, within a single institutional framework, the tasks entrusted to them' (italics added).

[5] Article 2 TEC: 'The Community shall have as its task, by establishing a common market and an economic and monetary union and by implementing common policies or activities referred to in Articles 3 and 4, to promote throughout the Community a harmonious, balanced and sustainable development of economic activities, a high level of employment and of social protection, equality between men and women, sustainable and non-inflationary growth, a high degree of competitiveness and convergence of economic performance, a high level of protection and improvement of the quality of the environment, the raising of the standard of living and quality of life, and economic and social cohesion and solidarity among Member States'.

The notion of 'values' appeared as late as the adoption of the Constitutional Treaty (CT). The distinction between 'values' as opposed to 'objectives' was made abundantly clear by the use of *rubricae* (the headings underneath the Articles) and by the fact that 'values' were consecrated prior to the establishment of objectives. In the Lisbon version of the TEU, these 'rubricae' have disappeared and the wording of Article 3 as such *ceases* to refer *expressis verbis* to 'objectives'. As a result, the Lisbon version of the TEU now explicitly refers to values in the body of the common provisions and does *not* make any explicit reference to 'objectives', either in the body or in the Title of the Common Provisions. This evolution is an inversion of the initial situation.

The Constitutional Treaty refers to values which were already referred to in the Preamble of the former TEU: 'liberty', 'democracy', 'respect for human rights and fundamental freedoms' and 'respect for the rule of law'. Furthermore, the Constitutional Treaty and the Lisbon Treaty innovate by adding other values. These are respect for human dignity, equality and respect for the rights of persons belonging to minorities. Furthermore, both the Constitutional and the Lisbon Treaty indicate that 'These values are common to the Member States in a society in which pluralism, non-discrimination, tolerance, justice, solidarity and equality between women and men prevail'. During the Convention, the Working Group XI 'Social Europe'[6] did not manage to get 'social justice' inserted in that list, although the idea of 'social justice' was mentioned as one of the European Union's *objectives* from the very first draft. The final version of the Constitution as well as the Lisbon Treaty do contain a reference to the principle of equality, which the Group had advocated,[7] but its calls for a reference to *gender* equality were not heeded by the Convention. The Intergovernmental Conference (IGC) altered this Article to accommodate the Group's wishes.[8]

The structure of Article 2 is enigmatic. Prima facie, it creates a contrast between the high ranking 'values' on which the European Union is explicitly founded and other concepts (among which solidarity) which are used to

[6] In order to look at the main problem areas of the European Constitution in detail 10 working groups were set up within the Convention, very much in line with the problem areas identified in the Laeken conclusions. The question of the social dimension did not feature in those conclusions, and was not seen as sufficiently important to warrant such a focus group. No significant attention is given to the issue in either the terms of reference or the activities of the working groups. It was only at a very late stage in the work of the Convention that Working Group XI 'Social Europe' was set up. The Working Group on Economic Governance and a few members of the Convention had pressed for a detailed discussion of 'social questions', or 'Social Europe' at a plenary session. What happened at that session led the President, Giscard d'Estaing, to announce the setting up of Working Group XI 'Social Europe'.

[7] Article I-2 CT mentions the prohibition of discrimination. The Working Group referred to 'equality, particularly between men and women'.

[8] CIG 81/04, p 7.

describe the qualities of a (civilised) society common to the Member States. In my view, the value of 'solidarity' is of the same nature and quality as the other values mentioned. For this reason, it has been integrated in this fundamental provision. Therefore, it would be erroneous to disqualify 'solidarity' as a value within the meaning of Article 2 TEU. Such an interpretation runs counter to the fact that the Preamble of the Charter of Fundamental Rights of the European Union (CFREU) qualifies 'human dignity, freedom, equality and solidarity' as the 'indivisible and universal values' on which the European Union is founded. Furthermore, solidarity is intertwined with the fundamental rights rubricated in the CFREU under the heading of 'Solidarity'. Hence, it would run counter to 'respect for human rights' within the meaning of Article 2 TEU *not* to value solidarity. Last but not least, the Oxford English Dictionary defines a value in terms of *desirability*. The Preamble of the TEU describes the deepening of the solidarity between the peoples of the European Union as the ultimate object of desire.

In this respect, it can be argued that solidarity is a value which is at the core of the EU and hence an important tool for interpretation.[9]

B. Objectives

As far as *objectives* are concerned, both the Constitutional Treaty and the Lisbon Treaty have underlined objectives which are extremely relevant for the development of EU labour law. These are 'a highly competitive social market economy, aiming at full employment and social progress', 'social exclusion and discrimination', the promotion of 'social justice and protection', 'equality between women and men' and 'solidarity between generations'.

From the very first draft of the Constitutional Treaty the Union's objectives included 'full employment', a step up from the 'high level of employment' referred to in the text of the TEU (Maastricht). The 'full employment' approach is very much in line with the equally maximalist ILO Declaration of Philadelphia.[10] It is regrettable that the 'right to work' (*le droit au travail*) was not included in the CFREU, which recognises the 'right to engage in work' (*le droit de travailler*) as well as 'the freedom to choose an occupation'. The 'right to work' and the 'right to engage in work' stem from two very different traditions. The right to work implies a relationship between a subject and an object. The notion 'work' (*travail*) in such a formula does

[9] On this, see Veneziani (ch 5 in this volume).

[10] See, inter alia, the Declaration of Philadelphia. Although Article 1 ESC recognises 'a right to work', this Article formulates a slightly more nuanced ambition of the 'the achievement and maintenance of as high and stable a level of employment as possible, with a view to the attainment of full employment'.

not refer to 'workforce', but to a 'job opportunity'. The CFREU merely recognises a marginal aspect of this basic right, which is the right to have access to the labour market.[11] The latter is just an aspect of the freedom to work (*liberté du travail*). The emphasis is on the development of innate human capital. Freedom to work merely implies that the authorities refrain from action in order to allow citizens to work or not to work. The workforce is inseparable from the individual. It is not an external job opportunity. The inescapable impression is that the right to engage in employment is being used as a sop to appease advocates of the right to work.

The wording of Article III-209 CT (*cf* Article 151 TFEU) seems equally off-balance, with this 'preamble' to the section on 'Social Policy' still referring to 'high employment'. The same applies to Article III-117 CT (*cf* Article 9 TFEU).

The Working Group XI had called for efficient and high-quality social services and services of general interest to be included among the objectives,[12] probably because it feared that such services would come under pressure from the common market. The proposal was not accepted.

The provision related to objectives does not refer only to social objectives, but to the establishment of an internal market. As evidenced by the infamous *Laval Quartet*,[13] economic objectives can clash with social objectives. Since economic objectives are intrinsically linked to fundamental freedoms, whereas social objectives are related to fundamental rights, these clashes end up affecting the relationship between fundamental freedoms and fundamental rights.

The question arises whether Article 3 TEU provides a clue to handling these clashes. In such an approach, the relationship between objectives is studied in isolation of other provisions of the TEU. The semantics of the isolated provision urge the interpreter to 'balance' these objectives. Thus, instead of referring to a market economy, the provision refers to a *social* market economy. Furthermore, the idea of economic, social and territorial *cohesion* is expressed, and notions of *sustainable* development and *balanced* economic growth are highlighted.

The idea of a balance model which is being suggested does not shield social objectives, let alone the domestic social policies of the Member

[11] Article 15(1) and (2) Charter of Fundamental Rights of the European Union (CFREU).

[12] See on the same subject the speech by E Gabaglio on 24–25 June 2002 and CONV 799/03. See also the attention given to these services in the CFREU Chapter IV, Article 36. See also Article III-122 CT. The IGC amended this Article in order to safeguard the Member States' independence with regard to the establishment of such services. The services did not feature in Section I of the Draft Constitution.

[13] *Laval Quartet:* Case C-438/05 *ITF v Viking Line ABP* [2007] ECR I-10779; Case C-341/05 *Laval v Svenska Byggnadsarbetareförbundet* [2007] ECR I-11767; Case C–346/06 *Dirk Rüffert v Land Niedersachsen* [2008] ECR I-1989 and Case C-319/06 *Commission v Luxembourg* [2007] ECR I-4323.

States against competing economic objectives and the economic freedoms consecrated by the TEU and TFEU. The outcome of the balance exercise is highly unpredictable.

C. Priority of Values in Relation to Objectives

In my view, a more 'holistic' reflection on the relationship between values and objectives could be more helpful to safeguard social objectives as well as workers' rights. First, there is no reason to suggest that values as such need to be sacrificed to the objectives of the Union. On the contrary, Article 3(1) TEU provides for a hierarchical order between values as primary and other objectives as secondary.[14] Furthermore, a lot of the objectives listed in Article 3 can be conceptually related to the values enshrined in Article 2 TEU. Thus, the references to values such as non-discrimination, freedom, justice and solidarity in fact reappear in Article 3 TEU. In my view, as evidenced by the structure of the Constitutional Treaty, the values are intertwined with the issue of citizenship, whereas the objectives relate to the Union. Taking a rational approach, citizenship rights cannot be sacrificed to the objectives of an organisation.[15] In fact, citizenship—hence, the values on which the Union is based—constitutes a limit on the objectives of the Union and on the exercise of its powers.

The fact that values speak louder than objectives is also evidenced by the fact that the provision related to values, in contrast to the one related to objectives, is being sanctioned. As evidenced by Article 7 TEU, Member States are required to respect *in foro interno* the values enshrined in Article 2 TEU. This obligation is monitored by a preventive procedure in case of a 'clear risk of a serious breach by a Member State' and it is sanctioned in case of a 'serious and persistent breach' by a Member State.

The fact that some of the values can be sanctioned if a Member State does not respect them *in foro interno* contrasts with the way in which Member States are required to respect the 'fundamental rights' enshrined in the CFREU. According to Article 51 CFREU, the latter is applicable only to Member States in implementing Union law.

Although the objectives are not sanctioned as such, Article 9 TFEU does contain some 'general' or 'horizontal' clauses which urge the Union (that is, not the Member States *in foro interno*) to take some of these objectives into account. Thus, particular attention needs to be paid to the promotion of a high level of employment, the guarantees of adequate social protection, the fight against social exclusion and the aim of promoting equality between

[14] See: 'The Union's aim is to promote … its values'.

[15] Judged otherwise, social justice risks being sacrificed to what Supiot has called 'la marché total'. See: A Supiot, *L'esprit de Philadelphie* (Paris: Seuil, 2010) 179.

men and women and combating discrimination based on sex, racial or ethnic origin, religion or belief, disability, age or sexual orientation.

Recognising that values do speak louder than objectives might urge the Court of Justice of the European Union to distinguish between them when it has to consider genuine human rights, on the one hand and fundamental economic freedoms, on the other. In the *Schmidberger*,[16] *Laval* and *Viking*[17] cases the Court tends to refer in such a situation to conflicting 'interests' which have to be 'balanced'. Such a comprehensive qualification of interests as encompassing both human rights and fundamental economic freedoms devalues human rights. It disrespects the quintessential and qualitative distinction between the values underlying human rights and the objectives underlying fundamental economic freedoms.

Although the CFREU has indeed upgraded some fundamental economic freedoms to the status of 'fundamental rights', a distinction could be made between human rights within the meaning of Article 2 TEU and fundamental rights within the meaning of the CFREU. In sum, in interpreting EU Directives in the area of Social Policy the Court should take account of the constitutional values underlying these instruments, instead of interpreting them in light of the conflicting economic objectives of the European Union.

III. THE CFREU AND THE ISSUE OF VALUES

A. The CFREU as a Source of Fundamental Rights

No reflection on the values of the European Union can be undertaken without a thorough analysis of the CFREU. As indicated by Kenner,[18] there is an obvious overlap between the CFREU and the Constitutional Treaty in identifying the values concerned. The overlap is twofold. First, Article 2 TEU stresses the value of 'respect for human rights', whereas the CFREU contains a catalogue of 'fundamental rights'. The semantic difference between both categories is slightly puzzling. Furthermore, within the CFREU a relationship between fundamental rights and major concepts is established by way of *rubricae* under which fundamental rights are allocated.

These *rubricae* relate to 'dignity', 'freedom', 'equality', 'solidarity', 'citizenship' and 'justice'. With the exception of citizenship, these *rubricae* all feature in Article 2 TEU.

The question thus arises whether the CFREU as a concrete illustration of EU values is a helpful tool to strengthen the social dimension of the European Union to the detriment of conflicting economic objectives.

[16] Case C-112/00 *Schmidberger* [2003] ECR I-5659.
[17] See above (n 13).
[18] Kenner (n 2) p 548.

The inclusion of fundamental rights improves the conceptual framework of European labour law. Earlier, Boonstra, referring to Betten, referred to the various functions that fundamental social rights fulfil.[19] They provide a framework for assessing the actions of the EU institutions, and they can serve as a statement of principles which the Member States undertake to observe. As far as the Member States are concerned, the CFREU is relevant only insofar as they implement Union law. In principle, fundamental social rights form a basis for the competences of the European institutions and, where appropriate, for the creation of Union law. However, this function was ruled out by the CFREU, in structural terms. Boonstra refers to an interesting fourth function: fundamental social rights protect 'national systems against the dominance of European economic objectives'.[20] In my view, the relevance of the last function has been sufficiently highlighted by the infamous *Laval* quartet.

The fact that a number of these fundamental rights are not elaborated at all—or only barely elaborated—in secondary Union law is *not* a good enough reason not to incorporate these rights. Internal contradictions can arise between fundamental social rights and common market principles. The exemptions and restrictions provided for in the Articles of the Treaty which enshrine economic freedoms are not in themselves enough to shield domestic labour law against interference due to the economic freedoms.

The historical assumption that the social dimension of the European Union does not need to be strengthened because social policy is a field in which the Member States exercise their own sovereign judgment has proven to be erroneous.[21] Sovereignty is inevitably curtailed wherever the social policy pursued by the Member States conflicts with the economic principles of the common market. Hence, the partial 'mutism' of EU law in the field of social law always comes with strings attached. Despite its commitment to subsidiarity, such a mutism effectively undermines the sovereign power of the Member States to pursue a social policy.

There have been a number of significant cases in which the Member States' social policy has been challenged, with varying degrees of success, on grounds of economic law. National legislation on days off,[22] the ban on

[19] K Boonstra, *Fundamenten voor een Sociaal Europa* (The Hague: Boom Juridische Uitgevers, 2003) 32–33.

[20] Ibid 31.

[21] See the seminal analyses of S Deakin, 'Labour law as market regulation' in P Davies, A Lyon-Caen, S Sciarra and S Simitis (eds), *European Community Labour Law* (Oxford: Oxford University Press, 1996) 63–93 and S Giubboni, *Social Rights and Market Freedom in the European Constitution* (Cambridge: Cambridge University Press, 2006) 290. See recently S Giubboni, 'Social rights and market freedom in the European Constitution: a re-appraisal' (2010) 2 *European Labour Law Journal* 161–84, as well as Deakin (ch 1 in this volume).

[22] CJEU, Case C-145/88 *Torfaen Borough Council* [1989] ECR 3851; Case C-312/89 *Conforama* [1991] ECR I-997.

night work for women,[23] national collective bargaining,[24] the ban on job procurement by private companies[25] and the protection of certain labour markets have all come under fire in the past.[26] One could admit prior to the *Laval Quartet* that the Court of Justice had found perfectly reasonable solutions from a labour law point of view. What is still worrying, however, is that these solutions were argued on purely economic grounds that were at odds with the standards and values that had inspired the national legislatures. The *Laval Quartet* changed that perspective. In *Viking* and *Laval* an attack was launched on fundamental workers' rights; whereas *Rüffert*, *Viking* and *Commission v Luxembourg* tend to reverse the classical paradigm of labour law as setting a 'floor of rights' instead of a 'ceiling'. Broadening the conceptual framework offers greater guarantees of a more balanced approach to social issues. It also gives Member States more ammunition to safeguard domestic social policy and legislation against the detrimental effects of negative integration propagated by the Court. For this reason, many distinguished labour lawyers have rightly praised the adoption of the CFREU and its integration into the TFEU.[27]

B. The CFREU as a Means of Combating Negative Integration

The prospects of the CFREU as a means of restricting 'negative integration' cannot be sufficiently underlined. The added value of incorporating funda-

[23] CJEU, Case C-345/89 *Stoeckel* [1991] ECR I-4047; Case C-158/91 *Lévy* [1993] ECR I-4287; Case C-421/92 *Habermann-Beltermann v Arbeiterwohlfahrt* [1994] ECR-I-6157.

[24] CJEU, Case C-67/96 *Albany International BV v Stichting Bedrijfspensioenfonds Textielindustrie* [1999] ECR I-5751; Case C-115/97, Case C-116/97, Case C-117/97 *Brentjen s'Handelsonderneming* [1999] ECR I-6025; Case C-219/97 *Maatschappij Drijvende Bokken BV* [1999] ECR I-6121; Case C- 222/98 *Van der Woude v Stichting Beatrixoord* [2000] ECR I-7111.

[25] CJEU, Case C- 41/90 *Höfner and Elser v Macroton* [1990] ECR I-1979.

[26] CJEU, Case C-22/98 *Becu* [1999] ECR I-5665; CJEU, Case C-179/90 *Merci Convenzionali v Siderurgica Gabrielli SpA* [1991] ECR I-5889; CJEU, Case C-154/89 *Commission v France* [1991] ECR I-659; CJEU, Case C-180/89 *Commission v Italy* [1989] ECR I-709.

[27] See also S Sciarra, 'Market freedom and fundamental social rights' in B Hepple, *Social and Labour Rights in a Global Context* (Cambridge: Cambridge University Press, 2002) 176. The author argues that the integration of fundamental social rights provides a healthy counterbalance to norms relating to the operation of the market. In the same vein, see Bercusson, *European Labour Law* (n 2) 384–99 and B Bercusson, 'Qu'attendre de la promotion de la Charte des droits fondamentaux par le Traité de Lisbonne' (2008) *Revue de droit du travail* 74–76. In a posthumously edited contribution, Yota Kravaritou welcomed the integration of the CFREU providing a prospect that the functioning of the common market and free competition could be reconciled with social rights: Y Kravaritou, 'Les chartes de l'Union européenne et les droits sociaux' in N Aliprantis (ed), *Les droits sociaux dans les instruments européens et internationaux* (Brussels: Bruylant, 2009) 55–74.

mental workers' rights into the TEU via the CFREU risks being hampered by the following three factors:

(i) The constitutionalisation of capitalist principles.
(ii) Inadequate formulation of social rights.
(iii) The perception of economic, social and cultural rights as second class rights.

Hence, it is important to know how to deal with these three intellectual challenges.

C. The Constitutionalisation of Capitalist Principles

The Constitutional Treaty tends to 'constitutionalise' the economic principles on which the single market is based. The position assigned to these principles in Title I (Definition and Objectives of the Union) is surprising. In clear contrast to the first draft,[28] the free movement of persons, goods, services and capital and freedom of establishment are upgraded to *fundamental freedoms.*[29] The use of the term 'fundamental freedoms' is in itself striking from the human rights point of view. In Article 6 of the Treaty on European Union (Maastricht version) this term had a clear human rights dimension, and the language used was very much in line with that of the ECHR. The human rights connotation of the term 'fundamental freedoms' gives the impression that 'fundamental freedoms' and 'fundamental rights' are interchangeable. This reading is at odds with the fact that fundamental freedoms are essentially a statement of the EU's objectives, while fundamental rights concern the EU's relationship with its citizens. For this reason, it can be argued that genuine fundamental rights should prevail.

In the present version of the TEU, the notion of 'fundamental freedoms' ceases to refer to principles of economic law, thus avoiding the idea that economic principles have been 'upgraded' to so-called fundamental freedoms. However, a closer reading of the CFREU urges the reader to remain 'vigilant'. The potential primacy of fundamental rights over market principles is diminished by the stealthy *upgrading* of a number of economic principles to full-fledged fundamental rights. For example, the freedom to conduct a business features under the heading 'Freedoms' in Article 16 CFREU.[30] The formulation of the 'right to choose an occupation' as well as

[28] CONV 528/03.

[29] Article I-4 CT. The inclusion of 'fundamental freedoms' in Title I occurs in CONV 724/03, dated 26 May 2003.

[30] In the same vein, see the critical observations of M Weiss, 'The politics of the EU Charter of Fundamental Rights' in B Hepple, *Social and Labour Rights in a Global Context* (Cambridge: Cambridge University Press, 2002) 88.

the 'the right to engage in work' contain references to the free movement of workers, the right of establishment and the right to provide services. The idea that the free movement of workers constitutes a 'fundamental right' was prefigured by an instrument of secondary EU law as early as 1968.[31] Constitutional recognition of the freedom to conduct a business is nothing new: the principle is enshrined in a number of European constitutions.[32] Article 41 of the Italian Constitution is the most developed example here. However, unlike the right to work this freedom is *not* classified as a fundamental principle, but is regarded as a *social function*.[33] Functions are traditionally distinguished from freedoms which are not linked to objectives. Freedoms protect aspects of human capital or innate abilities which individuals can use to achieve objectives spontaneously chosen. The recognition of the freedom to conduct a business in the CFREU is consistent with these constitutional traditions. It needs to be exercised 'in accordance with Union law and national law and practices'. Hence, the recognition is far from absolute.

The equal status given to the right to take collective action for workers and employers (and their respective organisations), which appears in Article 28 CFREU might also provoke some unease. Such an approach is consistent with Article 6 ESC, but it is at odds with the unequal recognition given to the right to collective action in many European constitutions.[34]

D. Inadequate Formulation of Social Rights

The fundamental social rights formulated in the CFREU offer no added value compared with a number of traditional lists of economic, social and cultural rights, failing to come up to the standard set by the Community Charter of Fundamental Social Rights of Workers and the European Social

[31] See the Preamble of the Regulation (EEC) No 1612/68 of the Council of 15 October 1968 on freedom of movement for workers within the Community: 'Whereas freedom of movement constitutes a *fundamental right* of workers and their families; whereas mobility of labour within the Community must be one of the means by which the worker is guaranteed the possibility of improving his living and working conditions and promoting his social advancement, while helping to satisfy the requirements of the economies of the Member States; whereas the right of all workers in the Member States to pursue the activity of their choice within the Community should be affirmed'.

[32] See in this connection Article 41 of the Italian Constitution, Article 12 of the German Constitution ('Basic Law') and Article 38 of the Spanish Constitution.

[33] Freedom to conduct a business is stated to be subordinate to 'utilità sociale'. It may also not be exercised in a manner that is harmful to safety, freedom and human dignity. The legislature is given the task of ensuring that public and private economic activity is carried out and coordinated with reference to those social objectives.

[34] In the French, Italian and Spanish Constitutions, for example, only the workers' right to strike is recognised. The Portuguese Constitution expressly prohibits lock-outs.

Charter, to which the Treaty on the European Community (Maastricht version), the TEU and the TFEU refer.[35]

The right to work is not included in the Charter, nor is the right to fair pay. The right to fair working conditions referred to in Article II-91 CT (Article 31 CFREU) does highlight the important issues of health, safety and dignity, including, more specifically, the issue of working time.

Thus, Kenner highlights that the CFREU could serve as a tool to challenge the infamous British opt-out with regard to maximum weekly working time.[36] Furthermore, the reference to 'dignity' in the text of Article 31 allows for a much broader interpretation of fair and just working conditions.

Industrial democracy does not get much further than the right to information and consultation. The right to codetermination—or participation—is not even mentioned. Information and consultation represents a narrower form of worker involvement. Directives on information and consultation are for this reason adopted by a qualified majority, whereas Directives relating to codetermination require unanimity. Many Directives relating to information and consultation clarify that the exercise of such a right cannot affect the managerial prerogative.[37] The CFREU thus fails to come up to the standard of the *acquis de l'Union* and to that of the Community Charter of fundamental social rights of workers.

E. The Perception of Economic, Social and Cultural Rights as Second Class Rights

The predominant approach these days is not to uphold the caricature of the traditional dichotomy between civil rights and economic, social and cultural rights as something corresponding to the distinction drawn between programmatic, unenforceable rights and enforceable '*Abwehrrechte*'. Economic, social and cultural rights are no longer regarded as second generation (or second class) fundamental rights. The question is whether the CFREU is consistent with this contemporary view. At first sight, the inclusion of civil rights, political rights and economic and social rights in a single instrument suggests that the two categories have equal status. In fact, the Preamble of the CFREU expresses the idea that the European Union is founded on the *indivisible,* universal values of human dignity, freedom,

[35] See in this connection Article 151 TFEU, the Preamble to the TEU and the Preamble to the CFREU.

[36] See Article 22 EU Working Time Directive 2003/88, and J Kenner, 'Economic and social rights in the EU legal order: the mirage of indivisibility' in T Hervey and J Kenner, *Economic and Social Rights under the EU Charter of Fundamental Rights* (Oxford: Hart Publishing, 2006) 21.

[37] See, for example, Point 2 of the Subsidiary Requirements provided for in the European Works Council Directive 94/45 and Part 2(c) of the SE Directive 2001/86.

equality and solidarity. The Preamble also re-affirms the rights enshrined in the instruments of the Council of Europe dealing with civil and political rights, as well as with social rights. However, the Lisbon Treaty, including the CFREU is often subjected to a different reading. Indivisibility is not always interpreted as giving identical status to social rights and to civil and political rights.

It is immediately striking that the EU merely seeks accession to the ECHR (Article I-9 CT and Article 6(2) TEU). No mention is made of accession to the European Social Charter on which the CFREU has based much of its substance.[38] The Draft Treaty on European Union approved by the European Parliament in 1984 scores considerably better. The so-called Draft Spinelli Treaty postulated the possibility of accession to the European Social Charter.[39] Neither Article I-9 CT nor Article 6(3) TEU refer to the ESC as a frame of reference for general principles of EU law—both provisions merely refer to the ECHR, taking the same line as the existing Treaties. The TEU suffers from the same problem, but the lack of any mention of the ESC in Article 6 TEU (on the Union's founding principles) is partly remedied by the Preamble, where the Member States confirm their support for the fundamental social rights set out in the ESC and the Community Charter.

The majority of the fundamental social rights in the CFREU come under the heading 'Solidarity'. Unlike such well-known headings as 'Freedoms' and 'Equality', this category might lack a certain Cartesian clarity in the eyes of a lawyer. The controversial classification of certain fundamental rights under this heading could amount to the perception that they are less relevant from a legal point of view. In fact, it is not at all clear why the freedom of collective bargaining, unlike the freedom to belong to a trade union, has not been included under the heading 'Freedoms'. The idea that fundamental social rights listed under the heading 'Solidarity' do not contribute to the notion of freedom and equality is an uncomfortable one, and detracts from the contribution that this tradition of basic rights has made to the development and credibility of both concepts. Last but not least, it seems highly questionable to us that human dignity should be thought of only in connection with the right to life, the right to human integrity, the prohibition of torture and inhuman or degrading treatment or punishment, and the prohibition of slavery and forced labour. The right to human dignity

[38] For a recent plea in favour of such an accession, see the contribution of O de Schutter, 'Le rôle de la Charte sociale européenne dans le développement du droit de l'union européenne' in O de Schutter (ed), *The European Social Charter: A Social Constitution for Europe* (Brussels: Bruylant, 2010) 95–146.

[39] See on this subject B Schulte, 'Titel VIIII' in H von der Groeben, J Thiesing and C-D Ehlermann, *Kommentar zum EU-/EG Vertrag* (Baden-Baden: Nomos Verlagsgesellschaft, 1999) 917, 936. The text of the Draft Treaty was published in [1984] OJ C 77.

is matricular;[40] all fundamental rights are derived from this notion. Thus, Article 31 relating to fair and just working conditions refers to 'dignity'.

The case against the equal status of the rights rubricated under 'solidarity' is often built on the enigmatic distinction in Article 51 CFREU between 'rights' and 'principles'.[41] Principles in this respect would not be awarded the same degree of enforceability. They need to be 'observed' rather than 'respected'. In my view, such a distinction is highly problematic. First, all the principles which are allegedly held to have a programmatic character have been phrased as rights. In fact, one of the rare examples of a 'right' enshrined in the CFREU which is qualified as a principle is the principle of equality. The mere fact that such a concept is qualified as a 'principle' is meaningless. Thus the former EC Treaty enshrined the 'principle' of equal pay of men and women for the same work as early as 1957. As the Court of Justice of the European Union (CJEU) argued in the famous *Defrenne* judgment,[42] the use of the word 'principle' in the Treaty cannot be used to challenge the direct effect of a Treaty provision. It is worth repeating the historic words of the Court in this seminal text:

> [I]t is impossible to put forward an argument against its direct effect based on the use in this article of the word 'principle', since, in the language of the Treaty, this term is specifically used in order to indicate the fundamental nature of certain provisions, as is shown, for example, by the heading of the first part of the Treaty which is devoted to 'Principles' and by Article 113, according to which the commercial policy of the Community is to be based on uniform principles.

IV. EPILOGUE: THE ACCESSION TO THE EUROPEAN CONVENTION ON HUMAN RIGHTS: A MEANS TO PROTECT VALUES AGAINST (ECONOMIC) OBJECTIVES

Due to the ratification of the Lisbon Treaty, the consolidated Treaty on European Union now provides that 'the Union *shall* accede to the European Convention for the Protection of Human Rights and Fundamental Freedoms'.[43]

The accession of the ECHR constitutes a more far-reaching step in the constitutional recognition of fundamental rights within the European Union. In my view, it goes beyond a recognition of fundamental rights as

[40] See in this connection the scope given to '*Menschenwürde*' at the top of the list of fundamental rights in the German *Grundgesetz*. The reference to the 'right to live in dignity' at the start of the Belgian list of fundamental rights in an Article that relates only to economic, social and cultural rights seems conceptually inappropriate.

[41] See on this interpretation the very critical observations of J Kenner (n 36) pp 14–24. See on this issue also M Weiss (n 30) pp 80–88.

[42] See CJEU, Case C 43/75 *Defrenne v Sabena* [1976] ECR I-455.

[43] Article 6(2) TEU.

mere general principles of EU law. In fact, Article 6(3) TEU *as such* already recognises such an impact of fundamental rights, as guaranteed by the European Convention on Human Rights. It goes beyond the effect of the reference to the CFREU within the TEU.

Due to the accession, the status of the fundamental rights enshrined in the ECHR will differ fundamentally from those enshrined in the CFREU. In fact, at best, the rights enshrined in the CFREU have the same legal value as conflicting fundamental freedoms enshrined in the EU Treaties. Furthermore, as indicated earlier, the CFREU itself has upgraded some of the fundamental freedoms which have the potential to conflict with fundamental (workers') rights. Thus, Article 15 CFREU has consecrated the freedom of establishment and the freedom to provide services as proper 'fundamental freedoms'. In *Viking* and *Laval*, both freedoms were considered to justify restrictions to the fundamental right to strike and the fundamental freedom of collective bargaining. Last but not least, Article 16 CFREU has consecrated the freedom to conduct a business. The only international court to interpret the CFREU will be the CJEU. For the CJEU, it will be one among other 'constitutional' principles to be taken into account.

In sum, in my view, the prospects that the TFEU reference to the CFREU might provoke a *shift* in the way the CJEU deals or even has to deal with potential conflicts between the right to strike and so-called fundamental (economic) freedoms are extremely weak.

The prospects stemming from accession to the ECHR of changing the economic constitution of the European Union or at least adding a flavour of social governance are more promising.[44] Accession to the ECHR might give some relief to the flat juxtaposition of fundamental freedoms and fundamental rights integrated into one CFREU. It puts genuine fundamental (workers') rights at the heart of the matter. Since the ECHR is corroborated by judicial supervision, it will force all European institutions, including the CJEU, to abide by the judgments delivered in Strasbourg. As opposed to Luxembourg, Strasbourg will not dwell on the question of whether human rights can restrict fundamental economic freedoms. It will assess whether and to what extent these fundamental economic freedoms can actually restrict genuine fundamental rights. It will force the European institutions to justify restrictions to citizens' rights, instead of forcing citizens to justify the exercise of their human rights.

[44] In the same vein, comparing the impact of the CFREU and the accession to the ECHR, see Syrpis (n 2) pp 233–34.

3

The Lisbon Treaty and the Charter of Fundamental Rights of the European Union

CSILLA KOLLONAY-LEHOCZKY, KLAUS LÖRCHER AND ISABELLE SCHÖMANN

FINALLY, THE CHARTER of Fundamental Rights of the European Union (CFREU) has become legally binding. This is probably the Lisbon Treaty's most important component with a social impact. Although this dimension of the Charter has already been explored in considerable detail,[1] an analysis is needed of the long way that remains to be traversed (section I) and of the many problems that will have to be solved (section II). Since it stands at the crossroads of 'rights' and 'principles', the Equality Title of the Charter is dealt with in more detail (section III).

I. HISTORY OF THE CHARTER OF FUNDAMENTAL RIGHTS

The year 2009 saw the ratification of the Lisbon Treaty following numerous serious setbacks that had dogged the process from the very beginning of the ratification process of the defunct Constitutional Treaty. Similarly, the EU Charter of Fundamental Rights that was adopted and promulgated by the Presidents of the European Commission, the European Parliament and the Council of the European Union at the summit held in Nice on 7 December 2000, has been finally integrated, in the slightly revised version of 12 December 2007, in the Reform ('Lisbon') Treaty. Having formed Part II of the Draft Treaty Establishing a Constitution for Europe, the EU Charter of Fundamental Rights is no longer an integral part of the Treaty of European Union in the Lisbon Treaty's version (TEU) but in the *Official Journal* publication it has been appended to the very end of the Lisbon

[1] B Bercusson (ed), *European Labour Law and the EU Charter of Fundamental Rights* (Baden-Baden, 2006).

Treaty, after the protocols, annexes and declarations. Nevertheless, as its principal novelty, Article 6(1) TEU states that 'The Union recognises the rights, freedoms and principles set out in the Charter of Fundamental Rights of the European Union of 7 December 2000, as adapted at Strasbourg, on 12 December 2007, which shall have the same legal value as the Treaties'.

Despite its contradictory, unclear, even questionable status in the hierarchy of norms[2] the Charter of Fundamental Rights has been incorporated into the primary law of the EU, following long-drawn-out and praetorian jurisprudence of the Court of Justice of the European Union (CJEU) based on the recognition of fundamental rights as general principles of Union law. Parallel to this, institutional and legislative developments progressively led to the elaboration of different Charters on compliance with and promotion of fundamental rights, the latest and most comprehensive of which is the Charter of Fundamental Rights. In addition, the method of the Convention gave birth to a very innovative, transparent document, described as a 'tangible witness of the superseding of "Europea mercatoria" by a political, social and ultimately human Europe'.[3] However, time will tell whether the Charter of Fundamental Rights lives up to the expectation it has raised, namely to install fundamental rights at the heart of the European Union as never before and to create a European area of fundamental rights, established on a new legal basis in the Lisbon Treaty.

A. Fundamental Rights in the Original Institutional Setting of the EEC/EC/EU

Initially, fundamental rights were not part of the institutional setting of the EEC/EC/EU, as the European Communities in the 1950s emphasised economic and functional integration. The Treaty of Paris, which established the European Coal and Steel Community (ECSC) and—after the failure, in 1954, of the European Defence Community (EDC)—the Rome Treaties reflect a sectoral and functionalist approach. This sectoral approach became a feature of the Rome Treaties establishing the European Atomic Energy Community (Euratom) and the European Economic Community (EEC). As a consequence, the founding Treaties were set apart from any basic law of a constitutional nature incorporating a solemn declaration on fundamental rights. Fundamental rights fell within the remit of the Council of Europe that placed them centre-stage through the adoption

[2] B Bercusson, 'The Lisbon Treaty and Social Europe' (2009) 10 *ERA-Forum* 87–105.

[3] B Lebaut-Ferrarese and M Karpenschif, 'La constitutionalisation de la Charte: un acte fondamental pour l'Union européenne' in C Philip and P Soldatos (eds), *La Convention sur l'avenir de l'Europe. Essai d'évaluation du project de traité établissant une Constitution pour l'Europe* (Bruylant, 2004) 125, 161.

of the European Convention on Human Rights (ECHR) in 1950 and the European Social Charter (ESC) in 1961. The economic approach adopted by the EEC/EC can be witnessed in several instances in which reference to fundamental rights was not invoked[4] or was resisted.[5] Although this factual repartition between the Council of Europe and the EEC/EC proceeded from the same belief that European integration can secure peace in Europe, this resistance to refer to fundamental rights in ECC/EC law and jurisprudence appeared to national courts and Member States as a potential threat to their national constitutions and the fundamental rights they refer to. In landmark rulings, the German and Italian constitutional courts[6] decided to check whether the EC had infringed the fundamental rights enshrined in their respective national constitutions.

In the absence of a European Bill of fundamental rights and facing such resistance, the CJEU gradually developed a 'narrative'[7] on fundamental rights in its case law in the 1970s, building on the application of general principles of Community law[8] based on common national traditions and on references to international texts ratified by Member States. The CJEU thus developed the notion that fundamental rights were an integral part of EU law in referring to a 'European' symbolic attachment to 'human rights' of the ECC/EC, based on constitutional traditions[9] of the Member States, and thus inherent in the Community legal order.

An additional source of inspiration of the praetorian CJEU jurisprudence on general principles of Community law is reference to international texts. In *Nold v Commission*,[10] the CJEU declared that international human rights treaties in which Member States collaborated, or of which they were signatories, also provided guidelines which should be followed within the framework of EU law. No measure could have the force of law unless it was compatible with the fundamental rights recognised and protected by

[4] For example, there was no initial reaction on the part of the six Member States to the intention of Spain under Franco to join the EEC. DC Thomas, 'Constitutionalization through enlargement: the contested origins of the EU's democratic identity' (2006) 13(8) *Journal of European Public Policy* 1196.

[5] CJEU case law considering that there was no community competence to deal with infringements of national constitutional principles: Case 1/58 *Stork* [1959] ECR 17 and Case *Sgarlata* 40/64 [1965] ECR 215.

[6] Bundesverfassungsgericht *Solange I* [1974] 2 CMLR 54, 549–50; *C-Frontini* (judgment of 27 December 1973), see (1974) *Common Market Law Report* 372.

[7] S Smismans, 'The European Union's fundamental rights myth' (2010) 48(1) *Journal of Common Market Studies* 45–66.

[8] CJEU Case C-29/1969 *Stauder* [1969] ECR 419; the case questioned the validity of a decision of the Commission, addressed to all Members, on making the reduced price sale of butter to some welfare beneficiaries dependent on revealing their name to the sellers; for more detail see (in particular in respect of 'principles') below section III.A.

[9] CJEU Case C-11/70 *Internationale Handelsgesellschaft* [1970] ECR 1125.

[10] Case C-4/73 [1974] ECR 491.

the Member States' constitutions. Furthermore, in *Rutili*[11] and in *Hauer v Land-Rheinland-Pfalz*,[12] the CJEU confirmed that the rights protected by the ECHR form part of Community law. Explicit reference to the Council of Europe's ESC, seen as the 'social counterpart' of the ECHR, as well as to other international treaties—such as ILO Conventions—appeared less often in the jurisprudence of the CJEU (*Defrenne*).[13] Instead, the common formulation used is the reference to various international treaties without further specific mention.

Indeed, it was the CJEU which first integrated the reference to ECHR into Community law and has since exerted overriding influence on their future interpretation and application.[14] However, as pointed out by Lenaerts and de Smijter (2001), the recourse to the ECHR led to a certain confusion and sometimes conflict in the protection of fundamental rights by different European courts (CJEU and European Court of Human Rights (ECtHR)).

International references have been referred to in Community law via the Treaties, although the EC itself was not, at the time, and is still not a party to the ECHR or to the ESC. While the European Parliament has favoured accession to the ECHR and the ESC,[15] the CJEU takes the view[16] that the EC lacks a legal basis for such action.[17] The Community Charter of the Fundamental Social Rights of Workers of 1989 ('Community Charter'), signed at the time by all the EC Member States except the United Kingdom, is an additional, if particular reference, as it is the first Charter elaborated by the European Community on fundamental (social) rights. This is neither a binding legal act of the EU, nor is it a Treaty among the signatory states binding under international law. It is merely a solemn declaration by the Heads of State or Government of the Member States and as such used as an interpretative guide to the provisions of the EC Treaty, since it is referred to in the Preamble of the TEU, as well as in Article 151 TFEU and reflects views and traditions common to the Member States and thus represents a declaration of basic principles which the EU and its Member States intend to respect.

Among scholars, the leading doctrine explains the introduction of references to fundamental rights in the European Treaties by the fact that European Community activity in the economic sphere and growing Member

[11] Case C-36/75 [1975] ECR 1219.

[12] Case C-44/79 [1979] ECR 321.

[13] Case C-149/77 [1978] ECR 1365.

[14] K Lenaerts and E De Smijter, 'The Charter and the Role of the European Courts' (2001) *The Maastricht Journal of European and Comparative Law* 90–101.

[15] European Parliament Resolutions of 1973, 1976 and 1989 (European Parliament, Resolution on the establishment of the Charter of Fundamental Rights: B5-0110/1999, [1977] OJ C 54/93.

[16] Opinion C-2/94 [ECR] I 1759 (28 March 1996).

[17] Since the entry into force of the Lisbon Treaty (1 December 2009) the European Union has been granted legal personality obliging it to accede to the ECHR (Article 6(2) TEU).

State cooperation within the EU in internal affairs and law are such that almost all aspects of EU citizens' lives are now affected by EU legal acts. Thus there appear(ed) to be a need for the individual to identify his or her fundamental rights, by which these acts are (were) gauged, not only in the constitution of his or her own country, but in EU primary law.[18] In addition, the social consequences of the creation of the Single European Market led to a need for the formulation and implementation of a comprehensive social dimension for the 1992 Commission programme. Furthermore, the praetorian jurisprudence of the ECJ, while developing general principles of Community law and referring to the ECHR, the ESC and the Community Charter of Fundamental Social Rights, did not provide sufficient transparency. Finally, the EU would gain more credibility when demanding that other countries respect human rights and obey the rule of law if it itself clearly based its activities on these principles. In 1977, the European Parliament, the Commission and the Council signed a Joint Declaration in which they committed themselves to promoting fundamental rights arising from the two sources identified by the Court.[19] In 1986, a further step was taken when, in the Preamble to the Single European Act, the Member States of the Community affirmed, for the first time in a European Treaty, their determination to 'work together to promote democracy on the basis of the fundamental rights recognised in ... the ECHR and the European Social Charter, notably freedom, equality and social justice'.

Interestingly, the reference to the ESC is absent from the Maastricht Treaty of 1992, although the Preamble reaffirmed Member States' 'attachment to the principles of liberty, democracy and respect for human rights and fundamental freedoms and of the rule of law', and Title I on common provisions, Article F(2) stated:

> The Union shall respect fundamental rights, as guaranteed by the European Convention for the Protection of Human Rights and Fundamental Freedoms signed in Rome on 4 November 1950 and as they result from the constitutional traditions common to the Member States, as general principles of Community law.

The reference to the ESC was not even mentioned in the Protocol on Social Policy which read: 'NOTING that eleven Member States ... wish to continue along the path laid down in the 1989 Social Charter; that they have adopted among themselves an Agreement to this end'. Furthermore, the correct reference should have read 'the Community Charter of the Fundamental Social Rights of Workers'.

[18] European Commission, Report of the Expert Group on Fundamental Rights, 'Affirming Fundamental Rights in the European Union—Time to Act' p 13 (February 1999)

[19] Joint Declaration by the European Parliament, the Council and the Commission concerning the protection of fundamental rights and the European Convention for the protection of human rights and fundamental freedoms, [1977] OJ C103/1.

This seems, however, to have been a short intermezzo, as the reference to the ESC reappeared in the Preamble of the Amsterdam Treaty of 1997 that stated in its third recital that the Members States: '[confirm] their attachment to fundamental social rights as defined in the European Social Charter signed at Turin on 18 October 1961 and in the 1989 Community Charter of the Fundamental Social Rights of Workers'. The reference is also to be found in the Title on Social Provisions, ex-Article 136 EC (now Article 151 TFEU):

> The Community and the Member States, having in mind fundamental social rights such as those set out in the European Social Charter signed at Turin on 18 October 1961 and in the 1989 Community Charter of the Fundamental Social Rights of Workers, shall have as their objectives the promotion of employment, improved living and working conditions, so as to make possible their harmonisation while the improvement is being maintained, proper social protection, dialogue between management and labour, the development of human resources with a view to lasting high employment and the combating of exclusion.

The reference to the ECHR appeared in ex-Article 6(2) EU (now Article 6(3) TEU):

> The Union shall respect fundamental rights, as guaranteed by the European Convention for the Protection of Human Rights and Fundamental Freedoms signed in Rome on 4 November 1950 and as they result from the constitutional traditions common to the Member States, as general principles of Community law.

However, the amendments introduced by the Maastricht Treaty in respect of recognition of fundamental rights and their integration into the Treaty were far from the proposal submitted to the European Commission by a 'Comité des Sages' in a report of 1996.[20] The Committee had suggested including in the Treaty a range of civil, political and social rights and duties to strengthen the sense of citizenship and democracy in the European Union by treating civil and social rights as indivisible, as well as the importance of formulating rights reflecting technological change and environmental concerns.

Rather than establishing a list of fundamental rights in the form of a Bill of Rights, the Amsterdam Treaty established a procedure to secure their protection (for example, in case of discrimination ex-Article 13 EC, now Article 19 TFEU) and empowering the CJEU to ensure that the European institutions respect fundamental rights (ex-Article 6(2) EU, now Article 6(3) TEU). A range of deficiencies and inconsistencies were pointed out in the report of the Expert Group on Fundamental Rights of 1999, among others the confusing and counterproductive system of references.[21] Furthermore, despite the fact that ex-Article 136 EC, now Article 151 TFEU, refers to the ESC and the Community Charter, the European Union is prevented from

[20] Smismans (n 7) pp 45–66.
[21] See above (n 18).

acting on its own to protect social rights traditionally protected by national constitutions, national law and international treaties, as ex-Article 137(6) EC, now Article 153(5) TFEU, explicitly excludes from the European Union's field of competence the right of association, the right to strike and the right to impose lock-outs. Finally, the selection of the references to a few international documents in the Treaties or by the CJEU often referring to the ECHR and other Conventions, bring confusion in respect of their legal status and practical impact. Such inconsistencies and deficiencies led the Expert Group on Fundamental Rights to conclude that the current system of references '[did not] secure equal respect for all fundamental rights'.[22]

B. The Process of Adoption of the Charter of Fundamental Rights

i. The First Convention and the Charter of Fundamental Rights

In this context, the European Council in Cologne in 1999 commissioned[23] a Draft Charter of Fundamental Rights of the European Union from a body composed of representatives of the Heads of State and Government and of the President of the Commission, as well as of members of the European Parliament and national parliaments, including representatives of the European Court of Justice as observers. Representatives of the Economic and Social Committee, the Committee of the Regions and social groups, as well as experts were given an opportunity to express their views. This body, constituted in December 1999, titled itself 'the European Convention' and was chaired by Roman Herzog. The objective was to present a Draft Charter at the European Council in December 2000, which would then be proposed to the European Parliament and the Commission. Together with the Council, they would then solemnly proclaim a European Charter of Fundamental Rights on the basis of the draft document.

The Convention adopted the draft on 2 October 2000 and it was duly proclaimed by the European Parliament, the Council of Ministers and the European Commission on 7 December 2000. At the same time, however, it was decided to defer making a decision on the Charter's legal status. This Charter is the end result of a special procedure, which is without precedent in the history of the European Union. Following the adoption in 1989 of the Community Charter, the Charter of Fundamental Rights sets out in a single text, for the first time in the European Union's history, the whole range of civil, political, economic and social rights of European citizens and all

[22] Ibid.

[23] Cologne European Council, 3–4 June 1999, Conclusions of the presidency. Annex IV—European Council decision on the drawing up of a charter of fundamental rights of the European Union. Available at: www.europarl.europa.eu/summits/kol2_en.htm#an4.

persons resident in the EU, covering dignity, freedoms, equality, solidarity, citizens' rights and justice, all based on the fundamental rights and freedoms recognised by the ECHR, the constitutional traditions of the EU Member States, the ESC, the Community Charter of Fundamental Social Rights of Workers and other international conventions to which the European Union or its Member States are parties. The question of the Charter's legal status and its integration into the Treaty was left to the general debate on the future of the European Union, despite the fact that the Charter was drafted 'as if' it were to become legally binding.[24] (The issue remained unresolved until the Lisbon Treaty entered into force in December 2009.)

ii. The Second Convention and the Constitutional Treaty

In December 2001, the Laeken European Council had recourse for the second time to the Convention procedure and launched the Convention on the Future of Europe, chaired by Valéry Giscard d'Estaing, in order to perform the ambitious task of writing the first ever European Constitution. The objective was to improve the efficiency of the European institutions in an enlarged European Union and to create 'a clear, open, effective, democratically controlled community approach', rendering the European Union more transparent and comprehensible for all European citizens. The Draft Treaty establishing a Constitution for Europe was presented at the Thessaloniki European Council on 20 June 2003 and should have served as a basis for a European Constitution, replacing the existing European Union Treaties with a single text, giving legal force to the Charter of Fundamental Rights. In fact, the 15 current and 10 future EU Member States adopted the final wording of the Constitution during an Intergovernmental Conference beginning in October 2003 and ending in May 2004, when the 10 new Member States were due to join the EU.

The Convention on the Future of Europe was divided into 11 working groups.[25] Working Group II was mandated[26] to examine the procedures for and consequences of any incorporation of the Charter into the Treaties, as well as the consequences of any accession by the Community/Union to the ECHR. In its final report,[27] Working Group II made recommendations first concerning the form of possible integration of the Charter, preferring by a large majority the insertion of the text of the Charter Articles at the beginning of the Constitutional Treaty. In a second range of recommendations

[24] COM(2000) 644 final, Communication on 'The legal nature of the Charter of Fundamental Rights of the European Union', para 7.

[25] See: european-convention.eu.int/doc_wg.asp?lang=EN.

[26] CONV 72/02 Brussels, 31 May 2002 (03.05). Available at: register.consilium.europa.eu/pdf/en/02/cv00/cv00072.en02.pdf.

[27] CONV 354/02 Brussels, 22 October 2002. Available at: register.consilium.europa.eu/pdf/en/02/cv00/cv00354.en02.pdf.

on certain legal and technical aspects of the Charter, Working Group II suggested drafting adjustments in the horizontal Articles (Article 51(1) and (2), new paragraphs (4), (5) and (6) in Article 52 CFREU to be found in the annex of the final report). Although such adjustments 'do not reflect modifications of substance',[28] it appeared that, while redundant, the adjustments are intended to strengthen the limited scope of application of the Charter, ensuring that the Charter respects the limits of the powers of the EU. These adjustments were introduced in the new version of the CFREU and included in the Draft Treaty establishing a Constitution for Europe. The latter was then the subject of an Intergovernmental Conference. Although the Treaty was adopted by the Heads of State and Government at the Brussels European Council on 17 and 18 June 2004 and signed in Rome on 29 October 2004, it was never ratified by all Member States. The Constitutional Treaty represented the latest stage in a reform process that broke down after French and Dutch voters rejected it in referendums in 2005. The Member States of the European Union thus abandoned the idea of a European Constitution which would have repealed the previous treaties, and returned to the traditional method of modifying a Treaty, amending the EC Treaty and the Treaty on European Union simultaneously.

iii. The Lisbon Treaty

Reflection on the reform process prompted the establishment of an Intergovernmental Conference in 2007. The resulting Reform Treaty was drawn up under the Portuguese presidency, unanimously ratified and signed at Lisbon, while the initial rejection of the Lisbon Treaty by referendum in the Republic of Ireland in June 2008 was reversed in October 2009 by a 67 per cent vote in favour of ratification. Therefore, with the ratification process completed, the way was clear for the entry into force of the Lisbon Treaty on 1 December 2009.

C. Interim Conclusions

While the approach adopted by the CJEU was to develop the notion of fundamental rights as an integral part of EU law, tensions appear when fundamental social rights are put in the balance with economic freedoms. When some authors see the EU Charter as 'tangible witness of the superseding of "Europea mercatoria" by a political, social and ultimately human Europe',[29] it seems that the CJEU's judges still have a paramount responsibility to

[28] Ibid p 4.
[29] Lebaut-Ferrarese and Karpenschif (n 3).

guarantee the protection of fundamental rights, the more so since an additional jurisdiction will enter the European sphere with the accession of the EU to the ECHR. With the EU Charter being legally binding one would expect that the protection of fundamental rights will be predominantly based on a written, exhaustive and stable text, rather than on the jurisprudence of the CJEU with its intrinsic defects (sometimes unstable, unpredictable, less intelligible and less accessible to the citizens).

II. THE EU CHARTER AND ITS APPLICATION AND INTERPRETATION

A. The EU's New Human Rights Dimension

The Lisbon Treaty creates a new dimension of human rights protection within which the CFREU plays the most important role but within which it also has to be placed. The most important introductory provisions set out the framework of the Union as a whole.

In this context, it should be recalled, from the outset, that the Preamble of the TEU confirms the attachment to the principles of liberty, democracy and respect for human rights and fundamental freedoms (fourth recital), and specifically the fundamental social rights (fifth recital).[30] Even more importantly, the 'respect for human rights' is a value on which the Union is based (Article 2 TEU) and one of the Union's aims is to promote its values (Article 3(1) TEU; see Dorssemont, chapter two in this volume). Within this framework, Article 6 TEU represents the core of human rights protection and its multilevel system. Paragraph 1 represents the most innovative dimension: the CFREU, which is made legally binding by having 'the same legal value as the Treaties'. Paragraph 2 contains the obligation to accede to the ECHR[31] and, finally—as an own source of EU law (at least understood as a source

[30] '[A]s defined in the European Social Charter signed at Turin on 18 October 1961 and in the 1989 Community Charter of the Fundamental Social Rights of Workers'. The same references to fundamental social rights are to be found in Article 151(1) TFEU.

[31] See also Protocol (No 8) relating to Article 6(2) of the Treaty on European Union on the accession of the Union to the European Convention on the Protection of Human Rights and Fundamental Freedoms and Protocol (No 30) on the application of the Charter of Fundamental Rights of the European Union to Poland and to the United Kingdom (see in this connection Case C-411/10 (*NS v Secretary of State for the Home Department*) and the respective preliminary question 7); see also Dorssemont (ch 2 in this volume). In the meantime, the draft text for an accession instrument has been elaborated by a Working Group (CDDH-UE): Draft Legal Instruments on the Accession of the European Union to the European Convention on Human Rights (containing the draft agreement on the accession of the EU to the Convention and the respective Explanatory report, provisional version, 24 June 2011, CDDH-UE(2011)016. Available at: www.coe.int/t/dghl/standardsetting/hrpolicy/CDDH-UE/CDDH-UE_documents_en.asp.

of legal guidance)[32]—paragraph 3 recalls the principles already contained in ex-Article 6(2) EU according to which fundamental rights as guaranteed by the ECHR and as they result from the constitutional traditions common to the Member States shall constitute general principles of Union law.[33]

It is within this framework that the CFREU has to be analysed.[34] From the outset, three fundamental points can be highlighted: (i) the importance of human rights in general and the absence of economic freedoms at this level in particular; (ii) the legal binding force of the CFREU; and (iii) the overall importance of the ECHR.

B. The CFREU's Horizontal Framework

The construction of the CFREU is based on the assumption that all rights (and principles) should be highlighted and made visible as much as possible; restrictions should not appear—as is the case in the ECHR—in relation to each right but in a condensed way and only at the end. The CFREU's text thus contains in six titles the substantive rights (and principles) in 50 Articles. It is only in the last part (Title VII) that all elements of application and interpretation for all the substantive provisions are defined (Articles 51–54 CFREU). Reinforced by the reference in Article 6(1)(3) TEU the latter are of a transversal character and therefore require a detailed analysis.[35]

i. Competences

In response to the main concerns surrounding the creation and adoption of the CFREU on the side of the Member States subparagraph 2 of Article 6(1) CFREU restricts its application to the existing competences of the Union under the Treaties by providing that the CFREU 'shall not extend in any way the competences of the Union as defined in the Treaties'. This principle had already been expressed by Articles 51(2) and 52(2) CFREU.[36] Therefore,

[32] See the Opinion of AG on 19 February 2009, Case C-8/08 *T-Mobile Netherlands*, fn 78 (in respect of the—not yet legally binding—CFREU).

[33] It should be recalled that fundamental rights are referred to also in specific fields such as area of freedom, security and justice (see Article 67 TFEU) and particularly in respect of fundamental social rights see above (n 30).

[34] Some of the commentaries on the CFREU were written before the entry into force of the Lisbon Treaty. They might therefore not have been able to take full account of this new framework (for example, PJ Tettinger (ed), *Europäische Grundrechte-Charta* (München, 2006). But more recent publications are also available (for example, J Meyer (ed), *Charta der Grundrechte der Europäischen Union*, 3rd edn (Baden-Baden: Nomos, 2011); HD Jarass, *Charta der Grundrechte der Euroäischen Union—Kommentar* (München: Beck, 2010).

[35] In the context of fundamental social rights Article 54 CFREU (abuse of rights) does not appear to require any further consideration.

[36] Interestingly, the CJEU has expressed the view that by referring to Article 51(1) and (2) CFREU it 'is called upon to interpret, in the light of the Charter, the law of the European

the existing competences have to be analysed in more detail.[37] One of the findings of this analysis is that—with the exception of the directly excluded matters (pay, the right of association, the right to strike or the right to impose lock-outs) mentioned in Article 153(5) TFEU—nearly all such rights are open to EU secondary legislation, notwithstanding any further conditions to be fulfilled (such as a unanimity requirement).[38]

According to this approach to competence any limitation of the legislative power of the EU[39] (and within that area limiting the legislative power of the Member States) concerning fundamental social rights would lead to a limitation of the effective application of fundamental social rights. However, a closer look at the source and nature of these rights, as well as the obligation to promote fundamental rights does not seem to permit any further limitation.

ii. Binding Force and Legal Value

The uncertainties accompanying the binding force of the 2000 Nice Charter have now been cleared by the Lisbon Treaty, since Article 6(1) TEU, gives the Charter (as adapted in 2007) 'the same legal value' as the Treaties. This brings the Charter to the level of primary EU law—also to be applied in the Member States as part of the national legal system.

Nevertheless, the third subparagraph of this provision—declaring that '[t]he rights, freedoms and principles in the Charter shall be interpreted in accordance with the general provisions in Title VII of the Charter governing its interpretation and application and with due regard to the Explanations referred to in the Charter, that set out the sources of those provisions'—gives rise to ambiguities with regard to the meaning of 'same legal value'. The respective provisions in Title VII (Articles 51–54) CFREU with a complex net of limitations—multiple levels, multiple approaches and multiple subject areas—will thus have to be examined in more detail.

iii. General Obligations

The rights (and principles) in the CFREU create obligations with a general character with regard to defined addressees.

Union within the limits of the powers conferred on it': CJEU, 5 October 2010—Case C-400/10 PPU *McB* (not yet reported) para 51.

[37] See Lörcher (ch 6 in this volume).

[38] See, in particular, Table 3: Social Fundamental Rights in the Charter of Fundamental Rights in the European Union (CFREU) and respective EU competences in the Treaty on the Functioning of the European Union (TFEU) Annex to ch 6 in this volume.

[39] See, in particular, Article 2(2) TFEU ('The Member States shall again exercise their competence to the extent that the Union has decided to cease exercising its competence').

a. Content

Article 51(1) CFREU requires that the addressees of the Charter's obligations 'respect the rights, observe the principles and promote the application thereof'. It follows from this definition that the CFREU is, in an overarching way, demanding not only 'respect' for but also the 'promotion' of fundamental rights. Therefore, it is not sufficient just to behave 'in conformity' with the CFREU [40] but to act positively in a way that ensures the best possible solution in respect of its application. This is all the more important in respect of fundamental social rights.

b. Addressees

From the outset, Article 51(1) CFREU defines that the institutions (Article 13 TEU), bodies, offices and agencies of the EU are the primary addressees of all obligations deriving from the CFREU. The Commission,[41] the Parliament[42] and the Council[43] have recently published their intention to effectively implement the CFREU, and the European Economic and Social Committee (EESC) is working on an opinion in this respect.[44]

A controversial issue is the impact of the CFREU on Member States. Article 51(1) CFREU's first sentence raises the main question: what does it mean for the Member States that the provisions are '*addressed* to' them, and '*only when* they are implementing Union law' (emphasis added) and 'with due regard for the principle of subsidiarity' (see Blanke, chapter seven in this volume). The reasonable interpretation would be that Member States (and their institutions, bodies, or, as the case might be, even private parties) *must* observe the Charter's provisions only when implementing Union law, whereas outside this area they are not obliged to but *may* observe those rights to the extent that their national system orders or allows them to do so. Explaining this result more clearly, this provision

[40] In its recent Communication 'Strategy for the effective implementation of the Charter of Fundamental Rights by the European Union' COM(2010) 573 final (19 October 2010), the Commission develops a framework for ensuring conformity with the CFREU 'as effectively as possible' but, generally speaking, neglects the promotional obligations and in particular fundamental social rights. In order to provide for a more concrete follow-up, the Commission has more recently published a Staff Working Paper, 'Operational guidance on taking account of fundamental rights in Commission Impact Assessments', SEC(2011) 567 final (6 May 2011).

[41] See above (n 40) and also European Commission (DG Justice, ed) 2010 'Report on the Application of the EU Charter of Fundamental Rights' (Brussels, 2011).

[42] European Parliament Resolution of 15 December 2010 on the situation of fundamental rights in the European Union (2009)—effective implementation after the entry into force of the Treaty of Lisbon (2009/2161(INI)).

[43] Council Conclusions on the role of the Council of the European Union in ensuring the effective implementation of the Charter of Fundamental Rights of the European Union (3071st Justice and Home Affairs Council meeting, 24–25 February 2011).

[44] EESC SOC/401 [2011] OJ C 376/74.

on binding force limits the obligations imposed on Member States by the Union, but does not limit or restrict the power of the Member States to 'address' either Charter rights or further human rights. It should be a ceiling for Union-imposed obligations, but only the floor for national human rights regimes.[45]

The Explanations to this provision seem to be clear and to confirm this interpretation. Further Explanations as well as some Court decisions appear to interpret the limits on the binding force of the Charter as limitations on the power of the Member States to acknowledge and respect human rights in line with their own traditions, national systems and—possibly—international obligations.[46]

iv. Interpretation

Before dealing more specifically with the legal concept underlying the interpretation of the CFREU contained mainly in Article 52 CFREU, it must be stated that those orientations are not to be understood in an exclusive way. They must be embedded—as a first layer—in the framework described above. The next layer refers to the 'normal' interpretation methods, such as '*effet utile*' and the references to the preambles (in the given context, the Preamble of the CFREU). Preambles are generally considered by the CJEU as a tool of interpretation.[47] The Preamble in question contains important principles. In particular, the second recital states that 'the Union is founded on the indivisible, universal values of human dignity, freedom, equality and solidarity' and thus underlines the principle of indivisibility of fundamental rights,[48] putting civil and political rights on the same level as fundamental social rights. Within this context, the main elements of Article 52 CFREU[49]—as a third layer—are to be considered.

[45] See, for example, J Heuschmid, 'Der Arbeitskampf im EU-Recht' in W Däubler (ed), *Arbeitskampfrecht*, Baden-Baden, 2011) § 11, paras 11ff.

[46] See the criticism of such a perception of the Charter by I de Jesús Butler and Olivier De Schutter, 'Binding the EU to International Human Rights Law' (2008) 27(1) *Yearbook of European Law* 277–320.

[47] Ample jurisprudence often in respect of the objective to be taken into account (see, for example, CJEU, 10 June 2010—Cases C-395/08 and C-396/08 *Bruno and Pettini* (not yet reported) paras 28ff; Case C-268/06 *Impact* [2008] ECR I-2483, paras 110ff).

[48] In respect of the Union's External Action Article 21(1) TEU refers to 'democracy, the rule of law, the universality and *indivisibility* of human rights and fundamental freedoms, respect for human dignity, the principles of equality and solidarity, and respect for the principles of the United Nations Charter and international law' (emphasis added).

[49] The first paragraph concerning the limitations is dealt with later (see 'Limitations' below, section II.B.v). Given the importance of the question of the relevance of the Explanations (para 7) the analysis of the interpretation framework in Article 52 CFREU starts with this provision.

a. References to the Explanations

During the whole process of the elaboration of the CFREU and further developments via the Constitutional Treaty to the Lisbon Treaty, the question of trying to define more clearly what could or would be the content of the rights in the CFREU played an increasingly important role. Whereas during the first Convention it was still disputed whether such a search for definitions would be necessary the compromise reached was that the existing 'Explanations' would in no way be legally binding but could serve as an indicative basis for a tool of interpretation. Their further development became more important. During the Constitutional Treaty discussions, a new paragraph 7 was added to Article 52 CFREU that now 'shall be given due regard'. In a slightly less stringent formulation ('with due regard') the Lisbon Treaty in Article 6(1)(3) TEU now takes up this principle. In the Court's words, the Explanations 'have to be taken into consideration for the interpretation of the Charter'.[50] But looking at the Explanations themselves, they demonstrate a less ambitious approach and recall in the Preamble that 'they do not as such have the status of law' and only that 'they are a valuable tool of interpretation intended to clarify the provisions of the Charter'. Therefore, the Explanations should only be seen as one of the elements which have to be taken account of in the interpretation process but are not the only means of interpretation. Explaining the legal value and function of the Explanations in the interpretation of the Charter, the whole document could be described more as a sort of a commentary rather than a legal instrument.

More specific questions require further consideration. The first relates to the 'the sources of those provisions' expressly mentioned in Article 6(1)(3) TEU. Besides the references to the ECHR, which will be dealt with later, it should be recalled that the sources of the social provisions of the CFREU are mainly the ESC and the Revised European Social Charter (RESC), also referred to in the Preamble.[51] The latter therefore form important tools for interpretation purposes. As a further important question it needs to be clarified to what extent the respective Explanations could themselves restrict the content of a given fundamental right. Since they are not legally binding and 'only' have to be given 'due regard' it does not appear possible that a restriction on fundamental rights could be based solely on the Explanations. Moreover, it has to be analysed 'by whom' due regard must be given to the Explanation. Referring to Article 51(1) CFREU one would suppose that the addressees of the Charter are the subject of the duty to pay 'due regard' to the Explanations. Surprisingly, however, Article 52(7)

[50] CJEU, 22 December 2010—C-279/09 *DEB Deutsche Energiehandels- und Beratungsgesellschaft* (not yet reported) para 32.

[51] See above (n 30).

CFREU refers to 'the courts of the Union and of the Member States'. This contradiction could be understood in terms of the way in which it reduces the legal impact of the Explanations.

b. References to the Treaties

The relations between fundamental rights enshrined, on the one hand, in CFREU and, on the other, now in the Treaties could raise substantial problems in case of different levels of protection. Paragraph 2 of Article 52 CFREU appears to provide for the priority of the latter. But the Explanations restrict the priority to 'rights which were already expressly guaranteed in the Treaty establishing the European Community' and refer to 'notably the rights derived from Union citizenship'. Following this approach, this question loses much of its impact in respect of fundamental social rights. Indeed, besides the equality of men and women in employment (ex-Article 141 EC, now Article 157 TFEU) no social right was found in the previous (or even actual) versions of the Treaties. Therefore, in principle[52] Article 52(2) CFREU does not exert a (restrictive) impact on social rights.

c. References to the ECHR

The predominant role of the ECHR in respect of the CFREU is demonstrated by several provisions, the most precise of which is paragraph 3 of Article 52 CFREU containing two main elements. In the words of the Explanations the first element could be described as a principle of 'consistency' between the two instruments to the extent that the CFREU contains rights which correspond to rights guaranteed by the ECHR. The second could be called the 'principle of the more favourable clause' in respect of EU law.[53]

If the first element would have to be understood in a restrictive way the second element would appear to be in direct contrast to it. How could a fundamental right guaranteed in both the ECHR and the CFREU, but interpreted on the basis of the ECtHR's case law in a restrictive way, be compatible with the CFREU's principle allowing for 'more extensive protection' than what is provided for in the ECHR? In order to better reconcile the two elements it is suggested that they should be understood in a procedural way. The first stage of examination would refer to the ECHR and the rights enshrined in it. They contain the absolute minimum. In the words of the Explanations, 'the level of protection afforded by the Charter may

[52] In the social field, para 2 might have an impact on the interpretation of Article 23 CFREU (equality between men and women), which is formulated in harmony with the concept of Article 157 (in particular, paras 3 and 4) TFEU.

[53] 'This provision shall not prevent Union law from providing more extensive protection.'

never be lower than that guaranteed by the ECHR'.[54] This is of the utmost importance, especially as this statement is accompanied by the clarification that it relates not only to the ECHR as such but also to its Protocols. Even more importantly, as stated in the Preamble of the CFREU and in the Explanations it relates also to the jurisprudence of the ECtHR. This is confirmed by the CJEU's case law. [55]

This examination becomes crucial taking into account the new era of the ECtHR's jurisprudence concerning fundamental social rights. Indeed, the Grand Chamber's judgment *Demir and Baykara*[56] has not only recognised the right to collective bargaining as enshrined in Article 11 ECHR (freedom of association) but it has also developed a comprehensive methodology of interpretation of the rights contained in the ECHR by referring to international (labour) standards such as the UN Covenant on Economic, Social and Cultural Rights, the respective ILO Conventions, the RESC and, interestingly enough, the CFREU itself. This approach has led the ECtHR also to accept that the right to strike is included in Article 11 ECHR.[57] But this methodology will also have important impacts on further rights, such as the right to a private and family life (Article 8 ECHR) and the prohibition of discrimination (Article 14 ECHR).[58]

Having thoroughly examined these minimum requirements, the second stage would investigate the extent to which EU law in general and the CFREU in particular provide for further protection.

d. References to National Constitutional Traditions

Fundamental rights based on the constitutional traditions common to the Member States 'shall be interpreted in harmony with those traditions' (paragraph 4). One might be tempted to read this in a restrictive way. Nevertheless, referring to the CJEU's case law,[59] the Explanations state that, under that rule, 'rather than following a rigid approach of "a lowest

[54] For the further consequences in relation to the limitations see below section II.B.v.

[55] See the Explanations, C-279/09 *DEB Deutsche Energiehandels- und Beratungsgesellschaft* (n 50) para 35 and Case C-400/10 PPU *McB* (n 36) para 53 ('the same meaning and the same scope ... as interpreted by the case law of the European Court of Human Rights'); see, for example, Heuschmid (n 45) paras 25 and 27.

[56] ECtHR (Grand Chamber) (12 November 2008), No 34503/97 *Demir and Baykara v Turkey*. See, for example, K Ewing and J Hendy, 'The dramatic implications of *Demir and Baykara*' (2010) 39(1) *ILJ* 1; K Lörcher, 'Das Menschenrecht auf Kollektivverhandlung und Streik—auch für Beamte (Zu den Urteilen ... *Demir und Baykara* und ... *Enerji Yapi-Yol-Sen*) (2009) *AuR* 299ff.

[57] ECtHR (21 April 2009), No 68959/01 *Enerji Yapi-Yol Sen v Turkey*.

[58] N Bruun and K Lörcher, 'Social innovation: the new ECHR jurisprudence and its impact on fundamental social rights in labour law' in I Schömann (ed), *Mélanges à la mémoire de Yota Kravaritou: a trilingual tribute* 335ff.

[59] For example, CJEU, Cases 44/79 *Hauer* [1979] ECR 3727 and 155/79 *AM&S* [1982] ECR 1575.

common denominator", the Charter rights concerned should be interpreted in a way offering a high standard of protection which is adequate for the law of the Union and in harmony with the common constitutional traditions'. In any event, analysing the fundamental rights which are—according to the respective Explanations—based on these traditions it becomes apparent that fundamental social rights as such are not touched.[60]

e. References to National Laws and Practices

Paragraph 6 states that '(f)ull account shall be taken of national laws and practices as specified in this Charter'. The Court has now referred to this provision for the first time in an important case concerning the right to collective bargaining. 'It is apparent from Article 28 of the Charter, read in conjunction with Article 52(6) thereof, that protection of the fundamental right to bargain collectively must take full account, in particular, of national laws and practices'.[61] The Explanations do not give any further orientation since they state only that paragraph 6 'refers to the various Articles in the Charter which, in the spirit of subsidiarity, make reference to national laws and practices'. This appears more to be a mere duplication without specific added content. Furthermore, it should be recalled that CJEU has interpreted such a reference to national legislation and/or practice as preventing Member States from making 'the existence of that right ... subject to any preconditions whatsoever'.[62]

f. Principles

In the past, the Court has referred to 'principles' (constitutional principles) common to the Member States as a firm, strong—unavoidable—source of rules, compulsory even in the absence of explicit mandatory rules. Now, conversely, paragraph 5 on principles is perhaps one of the most problematic 'horizontal' provisions.

In any event, the question of principles was one of the most hotly debated general questions. Now, the main definition in paragraph 5 (added in 2007) aims at restricting judicial powers explicitly to (secondary) 'acts'. Nevertheless, the core social rights (such as Articles 12 and 27–32 CFREU) are not touched on by this provision because they are considered to be rights

[60] Such definitions relate to CFREU's Article 10 (Freedom of thought, conscience and religion), para 2 (Media), Article 14 (Right to education) and Article 49 (Principles of legality and proportionality of criminal offences and penalties) and para 3 (principle of proportionality).

[61] CJEU, 15 July 2010—C-271/08 *Commission /Germany* (not yet reported) para 38. On Article 28 CFREU, see B Veneziani, 'Right of collective bargaining and action (Article 28)' in B Bercusson (ed), *European Labour Law and the EU Charter of Fundamental Rights* (Baden-Baden, 2006) 291ff.

[62] See Case C-173/99 *BECTU* [2001] ECR I-4881, para 53.

(from the wording and the content). In the same line, the Explanations themselves do not mention the core social rights.[63] Therefore, this restriction might be of less practical importance in respect of social rights but of more relevance concerning equality issues.[64] On the other hand, this provision shows that CFREU's 'rights' do not need implementation acts. Otherwise, this provision would be of no added value or any use.

v. Limitations

It is obvious and generally accepted that human rights cannot be exercised without limitations.[65] Legally speaking, there are a number of different concepts (for example, limitation, restriction, exception, interference). In order to better understand the CFREU's novelties it might be helpful to compare its concept with the one used by the ECHR and the ECtHR.

a. General Framework

Starting the legal analysis, it appears useful to quote the fundamental provision of Article 52(1) CFREU concerning permissible restrictions.

> Any limitation on the exercise of the rights and freedoms recognised by this Charter must be provided for by law and respect the essence of those rights and freedoms. Subject to the principle of proportionality, limitations may be made only if they are necessary and genuinely meet objectives of general interest recognised by the Union or the need to protect the rights and freedoms of others.

In addition to this definition, the CJEU's generally used approach should be recalled following which restrictions or limitations have to be interpreted narrowly.[66]

b. Condition 1 for a Permissible Restriction: Provided for by Law

When examining restrictions in respect of the condition 'provided for by law' for the first time under the CFREU's provisions the CJEU[67] saw no

[63] For example, Articles 25 (rights of the elderly) [in contrast to the word 'rights'], 26 (integration of persons with disabilities) and 37 (environmental protection). In some cases, an Article of the Charter may contain both elements of a right and of a principle, for example, Articles 23 (equality between men and women), 33 (family and professional life) and 34 (social security and social assistance) CFREU.

[64] For more detail see below section III.

[65] Even beyond the distinction between categories of human rights—such as absolute and relative—as already distinguished by the CJEU, the latter are limited by their social purpose. See CJEU Case C-112/00 *Schmidberger* [2003] ECR I-5659, para 80.

[66] For example, CJEU, 28 October 2010—C-72/09 *Établissements Rimbaud* (not yet reported) para 48.

[67] CJEU, 9 November 2010—Cases C-92/09 and C-93/09 *Volker und Markus Schecke* (not yet reported) para 66.

problem by accepting specific Articles of the regulation under review as sufficient in respect of the requirement 'provided for by law'. On the other hand, by referring also to Article 52(1) CFREU the Court[68] criticised the absence of a specific legal basis for allowing restriction in respect of procedural rights and, consequently, set aside a judgment of the General Court. In any event, the Court will have to deal with more difficult problems and will then have to base its judgments on the case law of the ECtHR.[69]

c. Condition 2 for a Permissible Restriction: Substantive Requirements

The substantive requirements for a permissible restriction of fundamental rights are twofold—'general interests' or 'rights of others'—but are embedded in more general requirements.

General Requirements ('Only if they are Necessary and Genuinely Meet Objectives')

To date, it appears that these requirements have not been taken very seriously. However, they should be considered at least as important as all the other elements because they add more and precise conditions. Furthermore, some conditions go beyond the provisions of the ECHR. In this respect, the first element is their general reinforcement by the introductory word 'only'. Thus, a strict examination is required. The second element concerns the qualification 'genuinely'. It is not enough simply to refer to certain objectives. Referring to other language versions,[70] it is apparent that this formulation requires an examination not only of the legal, but of the factual situation. In this context, it is reassuring that the Court appears to have also looked at the facts.[71]

First Permissible Objective: Objectives of General Interest Recognised by the Union

In this respect, the Explanations refer to CJEU case law, in particular the *Karlsson* case.[72] This is more than problematic as this judgment was developed in respect of non-discrimination but, in fact, was *not about the*

[68] CJEU, 1 July 2010—Case C-407/08 P *Knauf Gips / Commission* (not yet reported) para 91.
[69] See, for example, Jarass (n 34); Article 52 CFREU, para 65.
[70] German '*tatsächlich*', French '*effectivement*'.
[71] See CJEU, Cases C-92/09 and C-93/09 *Volker und Markus Schecke* (n 67) paras 69 and 70.
[72] CJEU, Case C-292/97 *Karlsson and Others* [2000] ECR I-2737, para 45. 'However, it is well-established in the case-law of the Court that restrictions may be imposed on the exercise of those rights ["principle of non-discrimination", see para 44], in particular in the *context of a common organisation of a market*, provided that those restrictions in fact correspond to objectives of general interest pursued by the Community and do not constitute, with regard to the aim pursued, disproportionate and unreasonable interference undermining the very substance of those rights' (Case 5/88 *Wachauf* [1989] ECR 2609, para 18) (emphasis added).

equal treatment of human beings in order to respect their equal dignity. Indeed, in this case, no nationals or other persons were concerned: it was an obligation of equal treatment between *Member States* under EU law and therefore not relevant for fundamental rights issues. Thus justification based on market (and agricultural policy) reasons might have justified *this differentiation*, but by no means restrictions on human rights or on the right to equal treatment in general. Such a restriction on the right to equal treatment—for economic policy reasons—would never be accepted under the various international human rights regimes. Thus—again—bringing up this particular case (especially as evidence of 'established case law') seems a shrewd choice of wording with the *aim of broadening the limitations* on human rights. But this aim appears to be even less achievable since the reference to this case is even less convincing bearing in mind that the judgment was rendered before the elaboration of the Nice Charter in 2000.

At first sight, the concrete examples of 'general interests recognised by the Union' given later by the Explanations could be considered more convincing as they refer to 'both the objectives mentioned in Article 3 of the Treaty on European Union and other interests protected by specific provisions of the Treaties such as Article 4(1) [TEU] and Articles 35(3), 36 and 346 [TFEU]'. Looking in more detail at these provisions the reference to Article 3 TEU appears normal as it contains the whole set of objectives of the Union (which must be understood within the framework of the values defined in Article 2 TEU—see Dorssemont, chapter two in this volume). But this is not the case with some of the further 'specific provisions'. Indeed, Article 4(1) TEU—stating that 'competences not conferred upon the Union in the Treaties remain with the Member States'—cannot be considered as an objective of 'general interest'. The reference to Article 35(3) TFEU is even less understandable, since paragraph 3 of the said Article does not exist. Only Article 36 TFEU containing a number of objectives[73] justifying restrictions on the freedom of goods and Article 346 TFEU concerning 'essential interests of its security' can be considered objectives of 'general interest'. The Court has accepted further specific Treaty provisions,[74] as well as those defined in the Preamble of the respective regulation[75] as defining 'general interests'.

However, probably the most important question remains to be solved: can all interests of whatever nature which are mentioned in the Treaties (or even in secondary legislation) be considered to be of 'general' interest? The first doubts arise from the normal understanding that a 'general interest' is

[73] For example, 'grounds of public morality, public policy or public security; the protection of health and life of humans, animals or plants; the protection of national treasures possessing artistic, historic or archaeological value; or the protection of industrial and commercial property'.

[74] Concerning the principle of transparency: Articles 1 TEU and 10 TEU and in Article 15 TFEU, see Cases C-92/09 and C-93/09 *Volker und Markus Schecke* (see n 67) para 68.

[75] CJEU, Cases C-92/09 and C-93/09 *Volker und Markus Schecke* (n 67) para 67.

something separate from individual, more economically oriented interests. The doubts in this respect are reinforced by further language formulations. Indeed, the French version with its reference to the '*intérêt général*' and even more the German version with its '*Gemeinwohl*' ('public wealth') would not seem amenable to interpretation in terms of economic interests (even if they are mentioned in the Treaties and are often seen as an overarching principle of EU law) to become the 'frontline fighters' against fundamental (social) rights by permitting any sort of (economically justifiable) restriction. This is all the more true when taking into account the non-economic oriented limitations which appear to prevail within the framework of the restrictions to rights guaranteed under the ECHR.[76]

Second Permissible Objective: Need to Protect the Rights and Freedoms of Others

Since there are many elements which could constitute 'general interests' it would appear that the second objective (rights and freedoms of others) would not become the biggest issue. But the first judgment in this respect shows that it is in particular in personal relationships that this objective might become relevant.[77]

d. Condition 3 for a Permissible Restriction: Principle of Proportionality

While it is a core concept of the limitations of human rights, there is little clarity about the concept and the elements of the comparison when proportionality is weighed. It is common ground that it has to be determined by the judicial bodies (including constitutional courts) assessing compliance with restrictions. The decisions by these bodies, referring to proportionality in a strict sense: appropriateness, necessity (see the link above to 'Condition 2' general requirements) and proportionality reveal at least some potential for the reasonable calculation of the proportionality reference.[78]

e. Condition 4 for a Permissible Restriction: Respect the Essence

The last condition in Article 52(1) CFREU is a sort of final safeguard. In the words of the Explanations, this concerns the 'very substance' of the rights[79]

[76] Looking at, for example, Articles 10(2) and 11(2) ECHR it would seem difficult to imagine (in particular individual) economic interests as 'legitimate aims' justifying restrictions; even in the only case where economic elements are mentioned (Article 8(2) ECHR) it is their general aspect in respect of the country as a whole ('economic well-being of the country'). See in this respect also below section II.B.v.f Condition 5.

[77] Case C-400/10 PPU *McB* (n 36) para 59 ('incompatible ... with the need to protect the rights and freedoms of others, within the meaning of Article 52(1) of the Charter').

[78] See, for example, Cases C-92/09 and C-93/09 *Volker und Markus Schecke* (n 67) paras 65 and 72ff (in respect of Articles 7 and 8 CFREU and the principle of proportionality referred to in Article 52(1) CFREU).

[79] Referring to the CJEU'S case law, see above (n 72).

concerned. But neither formulation solves the problem of the absence of a definition.[80] Thus, it might be difficult to predict the outcome of an examination.

f. Condition 5 for a Permissible Restriction: Conform with Minimum Requirements

As pointed out previously, Article 52(3) CFREU is to be considered a minimum requirement for interpretation purposes.[81] Since this provision is not integrated directly in the definition of permissible limitations in Article 52(1) CFREU the relationship between the two provisions must be examined. In this respect, the Explanations do not provide positive guidance; on the contrary, they create severe problems. Particularly strange is the text of the Explanations appended to Article 52(1) CFREU, regarding the scope of the limitations and the classification of the rights under the Charter.[82]

According to the Explanations, Article 52(3) CFREU, the principle of consistency[83] includes 'authorised limitations, [which] are the same as those laid down by the ECHR'. However, it is unclear what the 'inclusion' of 'authorised limitations' means here? Is this an additional authorisation, an encouragement to set limitations to Charter rights or merely a warning that, in respect of rights covered by Article 52(3) CFREU, authorised limitations must be in compliance with the strict criteria applied by the ECtHR?

The next paragraph of the Explanations to Article 52(3) CFREU seems to confirm this second interpretation.[84] Unfortunately however, the Explanations continue: '*without* thereby *adversely affecting the autonomy* of Union law and of that of the Court of Justice of the European Union' (emphasis added). This could be understood as a limitation on the strict requirements of the limitations, that is, subordinating even ECHR rights to the 'autonomy' of Union law and that of the Court. But the principle of 'autonomy' has to be put into the right perspective. First, it should be noted that the Treaties themselves do not refer to such a principle.[85] Furthermore, a similar concept in relation to the (EU's accession to the) ECHR is the principle of the 'specific characteristics' of Union law which is supposed to be protected by procedural safeguards and therefore not impeding ECHR's

80 See as an example of application CJEU above (n 50) para 51, referring to the case law of the ECtHR.

81 See Condition 2 above, and concerning Article 53 CFREU, see below, section II.B.vi.

82 This contribution does not deal in particular with the derogation possibilities under Article 15 ECHR because in respect of social rights there so far have been no instances in which this possibility would be used.

83 See Condition 2 above.

84 'This means in particular that the legislator, in laying down limitations to those rights, must comply with the same standards as are fixed by the detailed limitation arrangements laid down in the ECHR, which are thus made applicable for the rights covered by this paragraph'.

85 Article 335 TFEU refers only to the Union's 'administrative autonomy'.

rights (and limitations).[86] Finally, the question of limitations cannot be solved in a different way than the questions of the content of the rights itself.

Looking more closely at the different formulations of the permissible restrictions in both instruments it appears obvious that they differ very much with regard to: the concept (CFREU: general approach for all rights; ECHR: individual approach for each right separately);[87] the formulation (CFREU: at least to a certain extent, wider approach based on 'general interests';[88] ECHR: more restricted and focused approach); and—as a consequence—in the level of protection. Therefore, it will be necessary to examine both and at the end to give priority to the solution offering more fundamental rights protection. Thus, as proposed above, it appears useful to start this test with the ECHR as a first step (Article 52(3) first sentence CFREU) and analyse afterwards the extent to which the CFREU provides for better human rights protection (Article 52(1) read in conjunction with Article 52(3) second sentence CFREU). In the affirmative, this (more protective) finding should prevail.

vi. Minimum Level of Protection

a. Article 53 CFREU as Ultimate Guarantee of Minimum Protection

As presented by the analysis above the interpretation process is complex and may result in setting different standards, depending on the source of the relevant right. This gives principal importance to the definition and clear indication of the minimum level of protection.

As first element, the *ECHR* has already been described as a *set of human rights standards mandatory for the EU and the Member States*. In addition, however, Article 53 CFREU contains more references to international standards as a minimum level of protection under the CFREU. The heading of the Article—'level of protection'—already indicates that that is the level of protection below which no interpretation of the provisions of the Charter itself (including the limitations) is possible. These *minimum standards*, going beyond EU law, cover *international standards*, if they are ratified by 'all' EU Member States. These clearly crystallised boundaries as well as the

[86] Article 1 Protocol (No 8) (n 31) refers to the 'specific characteristics of the Union and Union law', giving two examples ('in particular'): '(a) the specific arrangements for the Union's possible participation in the control bodies of the European Convention; (b) the mechanisms necessary to ensure that proceedings by non-Member States and individual applications are correctly addressed to Member States and/or the Union, as appropriate'. It does not appear possible to base an argument for priority in respect of Union law vis-à-vis the ECHR's rights on these procedural examples.

[87] This is all the more remarkable as Article 18 ECHR explicitly limits the use of restrictions on rights guaranteed under the Convention.

[88] See Condition 2 above.

title ('Level of protection') indicate that, within the interpretation process, the international standards create a floor of minimum standards. The reference to the ECHR (as already expressed in Article 52(3) CFREU, see above) is a further, clear confirmation of the interpretation of all sources mentioned in Article 53 CFREU as a minimum requirement. Finally, the Court seems to have followed this approach by putting the two elements of references to the ECHR in the same context.[89]

With regard to fundamental social rights, two levels of instruments require more specific consideration. First, the European level is defined by the 'social counter-part' of the ECHR: the RESC. Secondly, at the international level, the two main organisations in this respect are the UN and the International Labour Organisation (ILO).

b. Specific Role of (Revised) European Social Charter

In several respects, the (Revised) European Social Charter plays an important role in EU law.

Based on the ESC adopted 50 years ago, the RESC update of 1996 can probably be considered to be the most far-reaching protection of fundamental social rights at the international level. As already pointed out, the references to the ESC appear already in the fifth recital of the TEU as well as in Article 151(1) TFEU. Concerning the further development of the RESC, it is to be noted that, in its fifth recital, the Preamble of the CFREU refers to 'the *Social Charters* adopted by the Union and *by the Council of Europe*' (emphasis added). Furthermore, in many Explanations the RESC is mentioned as a source of the fundamental (social) rights.[90]

In general, it should be recalled that all EU Member States have ratified either the ESC or the RESC. Since the RESC extends the rights enshrined in the ESC, Article 53 CFREU leads to the conclusion that the ESC forms the absolute minimum level. That is most important in respect of Articles 5 and 6 ESC which guarantee trade union rights. Concerning the RESC, it means that wherever the Explanations refer to any provision of the RESC as a 'source' for a (social) right,[91] Article 6(1)(3) TEU would have to be understood at least as a sort of minimum level.

c. Specific Role of Further International Instruments

It is of the utmost importance that even the international level represents a sound basis for minimum social requirements. On the basis of Article 53

[89] Cases C-92/09 and C-93/09 *Volker und Markus Schecke* (n 67) para 51.
[90] See the references to the RESC in the Explanations concerning Articles 23, 25, 27, 30, 31, 33 and 34 CFREU.
[91] See ibid.

CFREU, it is clear that the following instruments have been ratified by all EU Member States and therefore form a minimum level of protection. At UN level the International Covenant on Civil and Political Rights (ICCPR) with the protection of freedom of association and, even more importantly, the International Covenant on Economic, Social and Cultural Rights (ICESR) should be highlighted. The same applies to the Convention on the Elimination of all forms of Discrimination Against Women (CEDAW) and the International Convention on the Elimination of All Forms of Racial Discrimination (ICERD). Interestingly, the Union recently ratified the Convention on the Rights of Persons with Disabilities (CRPD) and is therefore bound to it in the same way as the legal minimum in interpreting the CFREU's fundamental rights.

Within the framework of the ILO, at least nine conventions have been ratified by all EU Member States. The most important are the eight so-called 'core Conventions' concerning:

— Freedom of association (Conventions 87 and 98).
— Prohibition of forced labour (Conventions 29 and 105).
— Prohibition of child labour (Conventions 138 and 182).
— Non-discrimination (Conventions 100 and 111).

Furthermore, all EU Member States are also parties to Convention 81 concerning labour inspection. This will give the procedural safeguards of fundamental social rights an important 'backbone'.

In any event, it should be recalled that the ECtHR is already interpreting the ECHR's rights in light of the international instruments and the interpretation developed by the competent supervisory bodies.[92]

C. Interim Conclusions

Human rights are universal, 'congenital': they belonging to human beings as such—regardless of the legal force of their acknowledgement—and are indivisible.

To assess the extent to which the CFREU is satisfying the optimism connected to it as a *quasi*-constitutional declaration of fundamental rights, with special regard to social rights and the rights of the weak or whether, as a result of vacillation and uncertainties, the anticipations of more pessimist human rights protectors are being realised, it is necessary to pay attention to the inherent features of the human rights adopted by the Charter and to the consistency of inserting them in the specific and unique legal regime of the EU. What, in the end, is subordinated to what? The answer

[92] See above (n 56).

to this question will lie in the likelihood of progression or regression when comparing the possible and the real interpretation of the Charter with the previous 50 years of human rights protection under the EU legal system. Taking the new human rights dimension introduced by the Lisbon Treaty and, in particular, the CFREU seriously, there should be no doubt that it will impose constraint on an overall economic orientation for the EU.

III. A CONCRETE EXAMPLE: EQUALITY AS A RIGHT AND A PRINCIPLE

A. The Development of Equality as a Primary Principle Guaranteeing Fundamental Human Rights

Equality and non-discrimination have a special place among human rights and they have a special position in the Charter as well. Their special position is established by its dual character. First, it is a principle determining the content and exercise of all other fundamental rights and as such it is unequivocally acknowledged as a constitutive element of international human rights law. Secondly, it is a right of a specific kind, being a precondition of human dignity. This second meaning, the right to equal treatment, in contrast with the principle of equal treatment, is the subject of broad conceptual discussions.

Equality as a principle is reflected in all major human rights treaties:[93] they refer primarily and predominantly to non-discrimination as a 'horizontal' principle guaranteeing the equal enjoyment of all the rights enshrined in those treaties to all human beings, without distinction. In addition, some of them also guarantee equality before the law: that is, the right to equal application of the law, in other words equality in a narrow, formal sense. Protocol 12 annexed to the ECHR requires State Parties to secure equal enjoyment of any right set forth by law, as well as the avoidance of discrimination by any public authority on a significantly wider list of grounds than foreseen under Article 14 ECHR.[94]

The catalogue of prohibited grounds (protected attributes) varies considerably, although race/colour, sex, religious or other belief, national origin or language are normally included. Further prohibited grounds in the various

[93] First, the Universal Declaration of Human Rights, the UN International Covenant on Civil and Political Rights (ICCPR), the UN International Covenant on Economic, Social and Cultural Rights (ICESCR, both Conventions adopted in 1966, entered into force in 1976) and the ECHR.

[94] After a long and hard process of ratification the first judgment of the ECtHR applying Protocol No 12 (and finding a violation of it) was in the Grand Chamber judgment 22 December 2009—27996/06 and 34836/06—*Sejdić and Finci v Bosnia and Herzegovina*. See also Bruun and Lörcher (n 58) 335ff ('3. Equality, non-discrimination and Article 14').

catalogues might constitute an extended, still closed (exclusive) enumeration or an open-ended (or exemplifying) list of the attributes that are prohibited as grounds of differentiation.[95]

Besides these general human rights Conventions where equality is a 'horizontal issue' for all rights proclaimed, there are special Conventions under the aegis of the UN protecting and promoting the equality of particular groups (women, racial minorities, children or persons with disabilities)[96] or equal treatment in particular areas, pre-eminently employment.[97] Human rights scholars—when criticising the EU for the lack of a consistent human rights system corresponding to the standards and morals of these times—have raised expectations of bringing EU law more into compliance with the international human rights system: that is, bringing the most important international standards within EU law.[98]

The Charter of Fundamental Rights, in comparison to those international treaties, is a qualitatively different document. It preserves the double function of equal treatment and regulates it not only as a 'horizontal' principle of the application of a certain catalogue of rights, but is constituted also as an autonomous right, both in a narrower and a broader sense.[99] It prohibits discrimination on a wider scale list than any other international document, taking into consideration the development of the system of human rights and technological development as well. Beyond preserving the double meaning of equality, the Charter approaches and, indeed, constitutes equality as a complex, generic concept. Equality together with Dignity, Freedom and Solidarity constitute the main Titles of the Charter. They are all similarly multifaceted concepts and not only indivisible but inseparable

[95] While the 'open ended' lists that permit the disqualification of distinctions on 'any other' ground appear to grant extended protection of equality, a deeper view reveals that broadening the grounds, especially opening an infinite list of potentially prohibited grounds, may result in the listed grounds being taken to have relative value, making it particularly hard, among other things, to adopt positive measures. Furthermore, open-ended lists increase the need to set up a ranking of protected attributes, with special regard to the collision of such grounds.

[96] Such as CEDAW, CERD, ICRC and CRPD.

[97] ILO Conventions and Declarations, first, the Equal Pay Convention (No 100, adopted as early as in 1951) guaranteeing equal pay for work of equal value to women and the Discrimination (Employment and Occupation) Convention (No 111 adopted in 1958) on the elimination of discrimination in employment and occupation. (Both of these Conventions are included in the list of 'core conventions' declared by the ILO in 1998.)

[98] de Jesus Butler and de Schutter (n 46) pp 277–320.

[99] The distinction between fundamental rights in a narrower and a broader sense refers to the legal duties corresponding to the rights: while in a narrower sense the right is directly and individually enforceable via independent judicial bodies (court, tribunal or similar bodies), its meaning in a broader sense refers to rights that require measures of the State (government, Parliament) to establish institutions; they also mean a right guaranteed at a level from which the legislator may not step back without the risk of being confronted by a red light from the relevant Constitutional Court (or corresponding body). See LM Díez-Picazc and MC Ponthoreau, 'The constitutional protection of social rights: some comparative remarks' *EUI Working Papers* (Badia Fiesolana, 1992).

universal values;[100] at the same time, the conceptual constitutive pillars of the European Union place 'the individual at the heart of its activities'.[101]

The European Economic Community (EEC) was founded in 1957 with a clear economic purpose: to make possible the free movement of goods, services, capital and persons by establishing a common economic space and a common market. Protection of human rights—either civil and political freedoms or social rights—was not among the goals. Similarly, except for two elements, the non-discrimination principle was not part of the foundation. Equal treatment of nationals of Member States moving from one country to another with the aim of engaging in economic activity was guaranteed as an indispensable precondition of the free movement of persons and services. Besides this equality rule aimed at market integration, a single equality provision was enshrined in the Rome Treaty of 1957, the founding document of the EEC. Former Article 119 TEEC (now Article 157(1) and (2) TFEU) lays down the obligation to guarantee equal pay for equal work to men and women, also a market rule, the pre-condition for fair (equal) competition among countries with different systems of protection.[102]

The very first case in which the Court referred to respect for fundamental rights was *Stauder*, opening the case law characterised by repeated references to respect for fundamental rights—'inspired by the constitutional traditions common to the Member States'—that must be ensured by the Court of Justice, although this protection had to remain 'within the framework of the structure and objectives of the Community'.[103] Besides the repeated reference to 'fundamental human rights' and to 'principles' no concrete right or principle is mentioned in the case, which concerns the equality and privacy (personal data) of citizens.[104] Thus, *Stauder* not only represents an opening up to references to general principles and fundamental human rights, but an opening up to the ones most frequently addressed throughout the past four decades: protection of the fundamental principles of equality and privacy.

The creation of these fundamental principles and rights by the Court has been accompanied by mixed reactions. The predominant welcome was mixed with dissatisfaction over the lack of regulatory activity to fill the gap that was, after all, acknowledged by the Community itself through this jurisprudence. According to the criticism such judicial activism was

[100] See with regard to values Dorssemont (ch 2 in this volume).

[101] Preamble of the CFREU, second recital.

[102] The option taken in 1957: harmonising 'upwards' instead of expecting the Member State (in this case France) with a higher standard of protection to assimilate to those with lower standards could also be a model today.

[103] See *Stauder* (n 8) p 425.

[104] The case was about the interpretation of a regulation that required the 'identification' of beneficiaries of cheaper access to certain milk products and the issue was whether this might require the submission of names and certain personal data.

determined by the scope of the eventual cases brought before the Court. Thus, it was accidental and unpredictable regarding both scope and content. Furthermore, these principles could be used only to check the compliance of various national acts and Community acts with the human rights criteria behind the principles. Thus, it rather limited than developed and inspired the regulatory activity of the Community.[105] There have also been critical comments on the legitimacy of the Court's use of its authority to 'forge' such 'imaginary' rights, even if the Court mostly acted with considerable caution (thereby also setting a limit on the use of the general principles referred to and again raising criticisms from those who have been watching such judicial activism).[106] From almost all sides, therefore, there has been a growing need for a formal, legislative foundation for a European human rights system, leading to the adoption of the Charter of Fundamental Rights in 2000 and its 2007 amendment and integration into the system of the constituting Treaties as a document with the same binding force as the Treaties themselves.

B. Principles and Equality in the Charter

i. 'Principles versus Principles' Dispute

The Charter, while having solved a number of problems, also created a number of new ones, particularly regarding equality, namely, the distinction between the status of 'rights' and 'principles' in Article 52(5) CFREU, thereby originating dilemmas that affect Title III on Equality to the greatest extent from among the Titles of the EU Charter.

Whereas Article 6(1) TEU provides that the 'Union recognises the rights, freedoms and principles set out in the Charter', Article 51(1) CFREU stipulates that its addressees (institutions, bodies, offices and agencies of the Union as well as the Member States) have to 'respect the rights, observe the principles and promote the application thereof'. This linguistic variation would not imply any ranking itself. To the contrary, it seems to emphasise the promotion of the application of both. The hierarchical difference and

[105] See A Lyon-Caen and S Simitis, 'Community labour law: a critical introduction to its history' in P Davies, A Lyon-Caen, S Sciarra and S Simitis (eds), *European Community Labour Law: Principles and Perspectives. Liber Amicorum Lord Wedderburn of Charlton* (Oxford: Clarendon Press, 1996) 13–14.

[106] J Dutheil de la Rochere, 'Challenges for the protection of fundamental rights in the EU at the time of the entry into force of the Lisbon Treaty' (2010) *Fordham International Law Journal* 1777, also referring to T Tridimas, *The General Principles of EC Law*, 2nd edn (Oxford University Press, 1999) 204–05 and fns 9–11. Similarly critical of the recent activism (actually ultra vires decisions of the Court) are A Pliakos and G Anagnostaras, 'Who is the ultimate arbiter? The battle over judicial supremacy in EU law' (2011) 36(1) *European Law Review* 109–23. See also Lyon-Caen and Simitis, ibid.

consequent uncertainty follows only from the text of Article 52(5) CFREU and especially from the relevant Explanations.

Based on the assumption that there is a line between 'rights' and 'principles', qualifying principles merely as guiding ideas, binding only if put into legislative or executive acts, the first sentence of this paragraph reads merely as the authorisation necessary under EU law to put principles into legal norms, generating subjective rights and duties:

> The provisions of this Charter which contain principles may be implemented by legislative and executive acts taken by institutions, bodies, offices and agencies of the Union, and by acts of Member States when they are implementing Union law, in the exercise of their respective powers.

The reduction of the legal meaning of principles is included in the second sentence of Article 52(5) CFREU: principles 'shall be judicially cognisable only in the interpretation of such acts and in the ruling on their legality'. Essentially, this sentence is intended to prevent courts from doing what the Court of Justice has been doing for over 40 years (starting with *Stauder*): namely, basing their decisions on principles. In the context of those provisions of the Charter that are 'principles' courts would be permitted to do so only when they interpret or review acts implementing those principles. (To be clear: this requirement is different from the required link to Community law of the situation to which the Court applies the general principles.)

Thus, the concept of principles becomes perplexing. The drafters must have been aware of that there are 'general principles of fundamental rights' enshrined in Community law by the Court's case law, and that these fundamental principles have a pre-legal and guiding function for law making. That means that laws must be in correspondence with these principles, and the law made by either the Union or national legislators (within the context of EU law) will be checked against these principles. In that sense the lower value of principles and their dependence on actual (implementing) provisions of law may not be relevant to the 'general principles of fundamental rights'. Rather, the drafters of this paragraph might have had in mind 'principles' within the meaning of 'policy guidelines', goals to be achieved that, indeed, require implementing legislation or administrative law making.

Neither the text of Article 52(5) CFREU nor the Explanations help to clarify the boundaries of the two different uses of the concept and their interpretation, giving room for strong criticism and contradictory interpretations.[107]

[107] On the one hand, the principles seem 'structurally to resemble "general principles of Community law"'. (D Leczykiewicz, 'Effective judicial protection of human rights after Lisbon: should national courts be empowered to review EU secondary law?' (2010) 35(3) *European Law Review* 331).

The lengthy Explanations of this paragraph have three aims: first, to clarify what this differentiation means; secondly, to authenticate the distinction between rights and principles by reference to the case law of the Court and to the constitutional systems of the Member States; and thirdly, to provide orientation concerning which provisions in the Charter provide us with 'principles', thus having lower status than those containing rights.

The Explanations fail to clarify the meaning. Besides repeating the provisions of the Charter itself, it is only added that principles do not 'give rise to direct claims for positive action by the Union's institutions or Member State authorities'. This does not say anything because rights do not give rise to such claims, either. As to the authentication of the distinction between rights and principles, the Explanations address the distinction 'consistent' with the case law of the Court of Justice, 'notably case law on the "precautionary principle" in Article 191(2) of the [TFEU]', 'principles of agricultural law', 'scrutiny of the principle of market stabilisation and of reasonable expectations'. The exemplification only increases the smoke around the concept—and the supposed meaning by the Charter—of principles. These are indeed general principles; nevertheless it is hard to identify them with the principles of fundamental human rights and therefore to see the 'consistency' between the reduction of the juridical status of 'principles' and the case law of the Court of Justice.

ii. Concrete Examples

The examples given 'for illustration' and thereby to give orientation on what are merely principles in the Charter bring to the forefront the interpretation of equality as a general principle.

Altogether, six Articles are enumerated out of the total of 50, suggesting that the Explanations to the relevant Articles in the full list probably need to be checked too. This exemplification, taken together with the Explanations added to the various substantive provisions, reveal that (almost) the entire Equality Title III consists of mere principles (namely: Articles 20, 23, 24, 25, 26 CFREU—that is, five out of seven). A quick glance at the two Articles (21, 22) left in the 'Rights' category reveals that while, indeed, Article 21 CFREU regulates directly enforceable rights, it also regulates a frequently referred-to fundamental principle of EU law. Article 22 CFREU (cultural, religious, linguistic diversity),[108] although not qualified here as a 'principle', underlines the haziness of the rights/principles division of the Charter provisions, since it would be difficult to classify it under either of the two boxes. Article 23 CFREU (equality between women and men) permits that provisions 'may contain both elements of a right or of a principle', leaving

[108] 'The Union shall respect cultural, religious and linguistic diversity'.

in obscurity the extent to which these provisions might be, for example, 'judicially cognisable'.

iii. Interim Conclusions

In summary, the conflict between the fundamental principle of equal treatment and the interpretation of Article 52(5) CFREU given in the Explanations is obvious and suggestive. Not only because the peculiar Explanations to this paragraph on 'principles' puts (almost) the whole Title III on Equality into the category of principles, which, in the context of the Charter, apparently have only 'second class' status, but because this distinction and classification contradicts the established and conventional meaning of 'principles', especially in the context of equality, as established in the abovementioned international treaties, as well as in the case law of the Court of Justice. If the (lack of) clarity of the meaning of the classification of 'rights' and 'principles' remains as it is now under Article 52(5) CFREU and its Explanations, it may undermine the so far highly respected fundamental principle of equality and may result in a weakening of the position of these principles as against the legislative acts of the Member States, even when implementing Union law.

The short analysis given below attempts to prove that the provisions in question, especially the Explanations attached to them, are misleading, contradicting other provisions of the Charter (not to mention the Lisbon Treaty itself). Therefore, the text of the Explanations (thus, the distinction in Articles 51(1) and 52(5) CFREU as well) must be read in a highly differentiated way, and consequently the label 'principle' must also be regarded in a differentiated fashion. This may apply to all provisions concerning 'principles', but primarily the provisions of Title III on Equality.

C. The Relationship between the Principle of Equality and Legislative Acts

After discovering the contradiction between the different—in fact, opposite—meanings of 'principles' in Article 52(5) CFREU, on the one hand, and in the case law of the Court on the other, the question is what the impact of this conceptual conflict might be on the application of the classification under Article 52(5) CFREU. Would the resolution of the 'principles versus principles' dispute be able to preclude subordinating the principle of equal treatment to the classification under Article 52(5) CFREU?

Such subordination would evidently mean that implementation—and consequent judicial application—of the principle of non-discrimination would depend on the decision of the various EU and national institutions entitled to regulate and put the principles into formal norms. This would clearly mean a step back in terms of guaranteeing equality in Europe. Nonetheless, the argument that principles are weaker,[109] in general, than legislative norms (let alone constitutional norms), and that their prevalence in the Court's case law is the result of a necessity, connected to the lack of formal legislation on fundamental rights, seems to support this result and make the question at least justified.

The following section is intended to provide a summary view of the interaction between the application of the principle of equal treatment and the legislation of the Member States and the Union before the adoption of the Charter as a binding document and afterwards. The short review demonstrates that this general principle expressing the fundamental value of equality—a pre-condition of human dignity and also the dignity of society—is, even in legal terms, a strong source of concrete norms, rights and duties, with or without legislative rules since the early phases of the development of the European Union. At the same time, the principle is able to adjust itself flexibly to the goals and objectives, as well as the legislative developments of the Union, while not compromising its core substance.

i. The Court's Case Law before the Charter became Legally Binding

a. Pre-Equality Directives Case Law

As already mentioned, *Stauder* inaugurated not simply the history of Court references to general principles as sources of fundamental rights, but references to equality and privacy as general principles deriving from fundamental human rights.[110] Beyond this, it also signalled the different directions of the application of the general principles. Two elements—implied or hidden in *Stauder* but later becoming explicit and evident—deserve mention here.

The first is the link between the fundamental rights behind the principle of equality and the principle of uniform application of Union law. The implied fundamental principle in *Stauder* was equality between citizens falling under the personal scope of the same regulation. Later, in *Karlsson*, the Court made explicit reference to this connection.[111] *Karlsson* can be

[109] Leczykiewicz (n 107).

[110] See above III.A. This wording that designates 'fundamental human rights' as the sources of general principles now resembles the phrasing of Article 6(3) TEU ('Fundamental rights, [as guaranteed by the ECHR and as they result from the constitutional traditions of the Member States], shall constitute general principles of the Union's law'). The reasoning of the Court decisions does not consistently make the link between the two consistently in this way. Rather it refers to the '*respect* for fundamental rights' (emphasis added) that 'forms an integral part' of the general principles of law (CJEU *Internationale Handelsgesellschaft* (n 9) para 4).

[111] '[N]ational rules … must be reconciled with the need to apply Community law uniformly so as to avoid unequal treatment of traders'; Case C-292/97 *Karlsson and Others* (n 72) para 35.

mentioned as an emanation of *Stauder* in respect of the second element hidden in it.

The second factor, hidden already in *Stauder* and occurring on numerous occasions later, was the departure of the subject-matter of the case from the issue of human rights. The original role and place of equality in the Rome Treaty—the prohibition of discrimination with respect to nationality and the provision on equal pay for equal work for men and women—was merely the promotion of economic integration. No consideration of fundamental values and the dignity of the individual played a role, even though these two provisions of the Treaty had no connection whatsoever to the international human rights treaties guaranteeing equality. This was corrected later by the case law of the Court referring to the fundamental principle of equal treatment that aimed at the dignity of the human being. *Stauder*, the 'seed', *implied* both, and was followed by decisions that aimed either at the protection of the fundamental human rights of persons[112] or at mere market integration, with less involvement of the dignity of the persons affected being in the focus of the international human rights systems, or cases in which both were at stake.

While this analysis tried to distinguish the two elements—the 'market integration' element and the 'human dignity' element—in the European development of the principle of equal treatment, it must be added that in most cases they are inseparable, although perhaps the emphasis is sometimes more on one than on the other. Thus, they certainly have not been—and could not have been—separated in Court decisions and have been promoted without distinction, thereby contributing to the growing significance of this principle over the years.

b. Pre-Charter Case Law

The first regulatory manifestation of the principle of equal treatment is to be found in the title and provisions of Directive 76/207/EEC, entitled 'on the implementation of the principle of equal treatment for men and women' (in employment). It might be considered to support the idea expressed in Article 52(5) CFREU, namely the supremacy of formal regulation over principles. However, such an interpretation of the enactment of the principle has been demonstratively contradicted by the Court. Among others, in the *P v S and Cornwall County Council* decision.[113] The Court declared, in response to an argument aimed at restricting the scope of the Directive, that 'the directive is simply the expression, in the relevant field, of the principle of equality, which is one of the fundamental principles of Community law',

[112] Case C-404/92 *X v Commission* [1994] ECR I-4780.
[113] Case C-13/94 *P v S and Cornwall County Council* [1996], para 18.

making clear its view of the order of precedence between the principle and the regulation. A similar view is expressed in the *Grant* case, here already emphasising the 'limited field of application' of the Directive, in contrast to the general scope of the fundamental principle of equality.[114]

Since the 2000s, the extremely broad principle of equal treatment has been applied on various grounds, provided that there was a comparable situation. In *Spain v Commission*, the Court declared a classic and important abstract principle: 'the principle of equal treatment or non-discrimination requires that comparable situations must not be treated differently and that different situations must not be treated in the same way unless such treatment is objectively justified'.[115] This broad formulation of equal treatment has, over time, been repeated in a number of decisions fleetingly extending the scope of the principle of equal treatment in an almost unlimited fashion.[116] While such an extended concept of equality may tend to weaken the assessment of situations of severe discrimination on the grounds of historical stereotype(s) and prejudice, these decisions have strong merit in having promoted the creation of a massive, solid and reinforced presence of the principle of non-discrimination in the Community with a broad and general coverage by the end of the twentieth century.

The year 2000 saw the adoption of the equality Directives on the basis of the authorisation provided by ex-Article 13 EC (now Article 19 TFEU),[117] the so-called 'Article 13 Directives' and, of equal rank, the adoption of the Charter of Fundamental Rights. Thus, from 2004 in certain aspects, and from 2007 within the broad scope of Title III of the EU Charter, the principle of equal treatment has had regulatory sources that could be referred to when assessing the compliance of equality regulations with Community law. This was supposed to make reference to general principles of equal treatment unnecessary.

As a 'last minute' case before the expiry of the implementation date in respect of the Equality Directive 2000/78, in the *Mangold* case[118] the general principle of equal treatment prevailed over the traditional interpretation and

[114] Case C-249/96 *Grant* [1998], para 41.

[115] Case C-304/01 *Spain v Commission* [2004], para 31.

[116] In Case C-304/01 (n 115) the 'comparable situation' was the size (length) of sea going vessels with regard to a derogation from a limitation under Regulation (EC) No 1162/2001; in Case C-210/03 *Swedish Match* [2004] there were tobacco products that were 'not in the same situation' (see paras 70 and 71); and finally Case C-344/04 *International Air Transport Association and Others* [2006] ECR I-403, refers to this abstract principle of equal treatment (para 95), and the situations of airline undertakings (para 96), of means of transportation (para 97) and of airline passengers suffering cancellation or long delay (para 98) are compared.

[117] Para 1 giving authorisation to legislate on discrimination on certain grounds: 'Without prejudice to the other provisions of the Treaties and within the limits of the powers conferred by them upon the Union, the Council ... may take appropriate action to combat discrimination based on sex, racial or ethnic origin, religion or belief, disability, age or sexual orientation'.

[118] Case C-144/04 *Mangold* [2005] ECR I-9981.

implementation rules of the Community. Going further than in previous case law, the Court referred also to international instruments as underlying sources of the principle of non-discrimination,[119] in addition to the 'constitutional traditions common to the Member States'.[120]

ii. *The Court's Case Law since the Charter became Legally Binding*

Contrary to certain expectations, the Court continued its reference to the firm basis of general principles after the adoption of the Charter as a binding document by the Lisbon Treaty.

The reference to general principles is now confirmed and accompanied by references to the provisions of the Charter, in particular to Article 21 (on the prohibition of discrimination) and Article 23 CFREU on the equality of women and men. Interestingly, there are fewer references to Article 20 CFREU, the general equality provision. Nevertheless, the primary status of general principles in the judicial decisions of the Court has, to date, not changed in the wake of the Lisbon Treaty's attribution of binding force to the Charter. The Court has continued to refer to them as autonomous sources of law, sometimes autonomous sources of Union rules, generating the equality provisions themselves.

In the *Kücükdeveci* judgment, adopted shortly after the entering into force of the Lisbon Treaty,[121] the reasoning of the Court implies a sort of ranking among the three sources of the prohibition on discrimination on the ground of age. First, it declares 'the existence of a principle of non-discrimination on grounds of age which must be regarded as a general principle of European Union law prohibiting age discrimination'. Directive 2000/78 is mentioned in the second place, as an instrument that 'gives specific expression to that principle',[122] and thirdly, it mentions ('it should be noted') the Charter that, under Article 6(1) of the TEU, 'has the same legal value as the Treaties' and, in its Article 21(1), prohibits age discrimination as well.[123]

119 Ibid para 74.

120 Ibid. This latter reference, according to the strong criticism of the Court in academic and high judicial circles, lacks grounds, considering that the majority of the Member States have no regulation on the prohibition of age discrimination. See, for example, Pliakos and Anagnostaras (n 106) 112–13. (It might be worth noting that under Article 23 RESC on the right of elderly persons to protection, indeed, only a small minority of the Member States could demonstrate that they have explicit prohibition of discrimination on the ground of age, either in the Constitution or in lower level legislation.)

121 Case C-555/07 *Kücükdeveci* (January 2010) on compliance of national legislation with Directive 2000/78/EC prohibiting age discrimination.

122 Ibid para 21, underlining that the Directive does not in itself lay down the principle of equal treatment in the field of employment and occupation.

123 Ibid para 22. See also Pliakos and Anagnostaras (n 106) p 114.

In the most recent case, *Test-Achats ASBL*[124] (on gender differentiated actuarial calculation of insurance premiums and benefits), the Court continues to refer to the 'constitutional traditions common to the Member States, as general principles of Community law' as the source of the fundamental rights (as guaranteed by the ECHR), underlying the disputed Directive, 2004/113/EC, on the equal treatment of women and men in the area of services.[125] The reference to the Charter—incorporating those fundamental rights, deriving from the general principles—is dictated (also) by considering that the fourth recital of the Directive refers to the Charter, Articles 21 and 23.

The relatively modest case law adopted on the application of the principle of equality since the entering into force of the Lisbon Treaty shows that the force of this general principle continues to permeate existing regulations without regard to Article 52(5) CFREU. It might also be of interest and exert influence when the individual provisions of Title III are applied and analysed in CJEU case law.

D. Rights and Principles provided for by Title III of the EU Charter

Title III on Equality contains seven Articles, from 20 to 26: equality before the law (20); non-discrimination (21); cultural, religious and linguistic diversity (22); equality between women and men (23); the rights of the child (24); the rights of the elderly (25); and the integration of persons with disabilities (26). The obviously eclectic type and nature of the provisions (rights, principles, social goals) may, in their totality, target a certain level of social equality and cohesion, but concrete definition of such a level depends very much on the meaning given to them by the institutions, authorities, administrative and judicial bodies responsible for their application and implementation.

i. Article 20 CFREU: General Principle of Equal Treatment

Article 20 CFREU declares that '[e]veryone is equal before the law'. This provision is, essentially, the long-awaited regulatory expression of the fundamental and general principle of equal treatment, the most decisive and broad among the principles of fundamental rights constituted by the Court of Justice first in *Stauder* and consistently in the subsequent 40 years or so.

While the provision of Article 20 CFREU establishes a directly justiciable right of individuals to the equal application of the law, it also lays down

[124] Case C-236/09 *Association belge des Consommateurs Test-Achats* (1 March 2011).
[125] Ibid para 16.

a 'principle'. This nature of the provision cannot be interpreted within the reduced meaning attributed to principles by Article 52(5) CFREU. Rather, this principle may support the assumption that the framers of the Charter might have in mind two different kinds of principles—'principles' and 'general principles' (or 'basic principles')[126]—even if the Explanations are not clear, let alone the definition of the two concepts.

According to the Court's view, (expressed in *Chatzi*) the fundamental nature of 'the principle of equal treatment, which is one of the general principles of the European Union law', is 'affirmed'—that is, not created—in Article 20 of the Charter. The Court also repeated its consistently followed interpretation that this principle 'requires that comparable situations must not be treated differently and that different situations must not be treated in the same way unless such treatment is objectively justified'.[127] Illustrating this requirement, the Court refers to *Sturgeon and Others*,[128] in which the principle of equal treatment is applied in the case of airline passengers (comparing the situation of those whose flight was cancelled to those whose flight was delayed three hours or more). In *Akzo*,[129] in which the principle of equal treatment was applied by comparing the situation of 'in-house' and external lawyers, finding that the two categories—despite certain similarities in their status—are differently situated (regarding the level of their independence), the principle of equal treatment in this case required different treatment.[130] That—if drawn under Article 20 CFREU—shows the extent of the scope attributed to this principle: it is to be applied to unreasonable differentiation on any ground or unreasonable equalisation of any different situation.

ii. Article 21 CFREU: Prohibited Grounds of Discrimination

Article 21 CFREU is based on the earlier list of prohibited grounds of discrimination in ex-Articles 12 and 13 EC (now Articles 18 and 19 TFEU) prohibiting discrimination on the ground of nationality (ex-Article 12 EC,

[126] The Explanations declare that this provision 'corresponds to a general principle of law which is included in all European constitutions and has also been recognised by the Court of Justice as a basic principle of Community law'. Adding to the puzzles produced by the Explanations, while there are numerous decisions of the Court—in part referred to above—involving the clear application of the principle of equal treatment, the examples brought forth by the Explanations to illustrate the recognition of principles by the Court are (in part made unavailable through the database of the Court) unrelated to human rights, and instead deal with economic regulation of agricultural products, such as Case C-292/97 *Karlsson and Others* (n 72). The latter is also referred to by the Explanations to Article 51(2) CFREU, and needs some conceptual extension to classify it as an equal treatment case.

[127] Case C-149/10 *Chatzi* [2010], paras 63 and 64.

[128] Joined Cases C-402/07 and C-432/07 *Sturgeon and Others* [2009] ECR I-10923.

[129] Case C-550/07 P, *Akzo Nobel Chemicals* [2010] (not yet reported).

[130] Ibid paras 56, 58 and 59.

now Article 18 TFEU) and on the grounds of sex, racial or ethnic origin, religion or belief, disability, age or sexual orientation. While in the Treaties non-discrimination on the ground of nationality—an indispensable pre-condition of the free movement of persons and services—has been of primary significance apart from any human rights consideration, admission of the specific grounds of discrimination has been the result only of a later stage of development.

Article 21(1) CFREU prohibits discrimination on certain specified grounds. Its paragraph (1) prohibits discrimination 'on any ground such as sex, race, colour, ethnic or social origin, genetic features, language, religion or belief, political or any other opinion, membership of a national minority, property, birth, disability, age or sexual orientation'. This catalogue is not only far wider than the list of protected attributes than in Article 19 of TFEU (ex-Article 13 of TEC), but exceeds the grounds regulated in Article 14 ECHR. Taking Protocol 12 to the ECHR the scope of the protection is similar, but Article 21 CFREU goes beyond that list by the addition of genetic features and disability.[131] The relationship of this provision to the narrower Article 19 TFEU[132] needs explanation. Although Article 21(1) CFREU is undoubtedly about rights, the Explanations routinely repeat that, while Article 19 TFEU 'confers power on the Union to adopt legislative acts … to combat discrimination', Article 21(1) CFREU does not create any such power; it only prohibits discrimination on those wide grounds when the institutions and bodies of the Union themselves are exercising powers conferred under the Treaties, and when Member States are implementing Union law.

The consequence of the obvious distinction has been demonstrated by the Court in the *Bartsch* case in connection with age discrimination. The principle of non-discrimination on the grounds of age, as repeatedly emphasised by the Court, is a fundamental principle of Union law[133] on which the Framework Directive 2000/78 prohibiting discrimination in employment on certain grounds is based. However, it is to be applied in any context of the application of Union law, but has not been considered mandatory in this case (exclusion from entitlement to a survivor's pension under an occupational private pension scheme, allegedly in an age discriminatory way).[134]

[131] It is notable that mention of Protocol 12 is cautiously avoided, although the Explanations to 51(3) explicitly define that 'reference to the ECHR covers both the Convention and the Protocols to it', despite the fact that it is already in force and applied by the European Court of Human Rights. See also above (n 1).

[132] Covering sex, racial or ethnic origin, religion or belief, disability, age or sexual orientation only with regard to authorisation to combat discrimination.

[133] Cases C-144/04 *Mangold* [2005] ECR I-9981 at 75, and C-555/07, *Kücükdeveci* [2010], paras 43, 55 and 56.

[134] Case C-427/06 *Bartsch* [2008] ECR I-7245, paras 18 and 25.

Article 21(2) CFREU prohibits discrimination on grounds of nationality. As provided for by this provision, nationality is a protected attribute (only) within the scope of application of the Treaties and without prejudice to any of their specific provisions, in compliance with its former application. Since Article 18 TFEU confers the right on the European Parliament and the Council to adopt rules to prohibit such discrimination, the legal nature of Article 21(2) CFREU is not questioned. This right therefore seems to correspond fully to the original principle of non-discrimination on the ground of nationality—being part of the market integration of Community law since the Treaty of Rome.

Nevertheless, the reversed order—putting nationality after the general list of grounds as a specific item—permits the presumption that this prohibition is now part of the human rights system of the Union and not purely or primarily an instrument of promoting integration. If so, in the future it might be applicable not only in the context of the free movement of persons, but in general, and therefore not only to nationals of other Member States, but to Member States' own citizens—in contrast to the interpretation of this provision only under Article 18 TFEU (ex-Article 12 EC). Such an interpretation seems reasonable and might also have huge implications for economic and labour rights.

iii. Article 22 CFREU: Cultural, Religious and Linguistic Diversity

Article 22 declares that the Union shall respect cultural, religious and linguistic diversity. On the face of it, this text appears merely declaratory and to contain no legal rights or duties. Nevertheless, the Explanation to Article 52(5) CFREU refrains from labelling them 'principles', and since they are not rights either, this provision adds a question mark to the categorisation of the Charter's provisions in Article 52. Being based on Article 6 TEU—and even more being connected to Article 17 TFEU as well as to Article 167(1) and (4) TFEU—Article 22 CFREU is connected to mandatory objectives of the Union, that can and shall be promoted, through actions such as those (incentive measures, recommendations) indicated in Article 167(5) TFEU.[135]

The fundamental guarantee of the diversity addressed in Article 22 CFREU is, of course, the legally enforceable prohibition of discrimination on the wide range of grounds enumerated in Article 21(1) CFREU. Article 22 CFREU is

135 According to Article 167(5) TFEU, in order to contribute to the achievement of the objectives of Article 167 TFEU, the European Parliament and the Council, acting in accordance with ordinary legislative procedure and after consulting the Committee of the Regions, shall adopt incentive measures, excluding any harmonisation of the laws and regulations of the Member States. The Council, on a proposal from the Commission, shall also adopt recommendations.

able to guarantee that the already existing diversity in European countries[136] would result in much more than simple tolerance and guaranteed equality; rather it could contribute to the development and enrichment of society in the long term.

iv. Article 23 CFREU: Equality between Men and Women

Article 23 CFREU does not add to and does not change existing provisions on equality between men and women. In its two paragraphs the first provides for the right to equal treatment in 'all areas', in other words including but not limited to employment. In its second non-numbered paragraph, Article 23 CFREU provides that [t]he principle of equality shall not prevent the maintenance or adoption of measures providing for specific advantages in favour of the underrepresented sex'. This is a shortened—and thereby even more unfortunate—version of Article 157(4) TFEU, which is a more specific and nuanced provision on permitting Member States to adopt or maintain measures that are—somewhat dubiously—perceived as 'exceptions' or 'derogations' from the principle of equal treatment. This phrasing obscures the fact that, within the meaning of the fundamental principle of equal treatment, different situations must not be treated in the same way (as used consistently by the Court). What is permitted is thus primarily the due consideration of existing differences and not (exceptionally permitted) unequal treatment.[137]

v. Articles 24–26 CFREU: Specific Groups

Articles 24, 25 and 26 CFREU (protection of the rights of the child, the elderly and persons with disabilities) have something in common that is also shared by the previous Charter provisions. This is their double and mixed character. Regarding each of the three groups of persons the provisions of the Charter show that the protective, paternal approach is combined with respect for and promotion of the equal freedom and dignity of the individuals belonging to those groups.

[136] See R Blanpain, 'Diversity, equality and integration. An introductory study' in R Blanpain (ed), *Diversity, Equality and Integration. Beyond the Law. A Comparative Study* (Vander Broele Publishers, 2008) 16–18 and 28–30.

[137] A further comment might be made on the mistaken perception of a situation deriving from the simplified phrasing of the Charter: 'underrepresented sex'. Underrepresentation in certain positions and situations might be a result of a socially advantaged position that does not justify specific advantages, whereas the overrepresented sex might need compensation for the disadvantages that result in overrepresentation in certain positions. This provision of the Charter—which does not differ much in Article 157(4) TFEU—is based on a mistaken symmetrical approach to the issue of sex discrimination. See D Schiek, 'A new framework on equal treatment of persons in EC law?' (2002) 8(2) *European Law Journal*, especially 309.

This double character is reflected in a concentrated way in the first paragraph of Article 24 CFREU, which includes protection and care of children, as well as children's freedom to express their views and their right that their views should be taken into consideration when decisions are made concerning them.

This combination, reflected by the three paragraphs in question here, also represents a paradigm of development in time. The earlier predominant paternal approach that was based rather on protective (guarding, sheltering) and social-assistance type measures permeating the national and (few) international provisions dealing with protection of these three groups have gradually given way to a more freedom-oriented human-rights approach, targeted first at the removal of barriers obstructing these persons from freely making decisions regarding their life and living conditions, from everyday living through choice of profession and occupation to an independent family and private life. The change is well demonstrated by the adoption of the 1989 UN Convention on the Rights of the Children (CRC: the most ratified convention in the world), the 2007 CRPD—both Conventions demonstrating the abovementioned shift.

Similarly, the new or rephrased provisions of the 1996 RESC reflect this shift from care and shelter (necessarily always subject to limitations) to an approach that is aimed at promoting the fullest possible autonomy for persons with difficulties in creating it for themselves. The change from the benign and helpful, but today considered less dignifying attitude in Article 15 ESC (1961) that guaranteed '[t]he right of physically or mentally disabled persons to vocational training, rehabilitation and social resettlement', the new title of Article 15 RESC (1996) guarantees '[t]he right of persons with disabilities to independence, social integration and participation in the life of the community'. Similarly, Article 25 CFREU is based on Article 23 RESC, a new provision, granting the elderly the right to remain full members of society for as long as possible, to choose their lifestyle freely and to lead independent lives in their familiar surroundings for as long as they wish and are able, and when living in institutions the appropriate support must respect their privacy and participation in decision making.

While the three provisions might appear to frame mere 'principles' within the secondary meaning used by Article 52(5) CFREU—that is, soft guidelines and benevolent desires to be realised depending on the will of the law-making powers (with eternal reference to the scarcity of means)—the teeth of such 'soft' norms when coupled with the principle of equal treatment—within the full meaning developed by the Court—is shown by the *Chatzi* decision on the right to receive an increased parental leave payment in case of twins. While the Court declined to consider this case as an equal treatment case under Article 24 CFREU, it added the following:

> Observance of the principle of equal treatment, which is one of the general principles of European Union law and whose fundamental nature is affirmed in

Article 20 CFREU, is all the more important in implementing the right to parental leave because this social right is itself recognised as fundamental by Article 33(2) CFREU. This principle requires that comparable situations must not be treated differently and that different situations must not be treated in the same way unless such treatment is objectively justified.[138]

IV. CONCLUSIONS

The peculiar situation of an increasingly important and powerful supranational entity without a fundamental rights framework for its citizens has come to an end: the legally binding Charter of Fundamental Rights puts the Union 'back on earth' and opens up new dimensions in respect of the Union as a whole.

The analysis of the sometimes very difficult process, starting from the beginning, via elaboration, adoption, 'adjustment' and ratification to the decisive point of entry into force of the Charter, as well as of the complex system of references and interdependencies within the Charter, the Treaties, international instruments and so on, and the important example of equality as one of the main pillars of the Union's fundamental principles bordering on concrete fundamental rights, has shown how many elements have to be taken into account when trying to give the fundamental (social) rights a real content and impact in everyday situations.

The Charter's effective implementation will depend on the permanent and extensive use of its provisions in political debates and probably even more in strategic litigation. This contribution hopefully offers a useful approach.

[138] See *Chatzi* (n 127) paras 63 and 64.

4

*How the Horizontal Social Clause can be made to Work: The Lessons of Gender Mainstreaming**

PASCALE VIELLE

THE NEW ARTICLE 9 of the Treaty on the Functioning of the European Union (TFEU) requires the EU institutions and the Member States to assess all their policies, laws and activities in light of their implications for the achievement of social goals. In combination with the Charter of Fundamental Rights and the future accession of the EU to the Convention for the Protection of Human Rights and Fundamental Freedoms, it may contribute to a fundamental reorientation of EU legislation and jurisprudence towards social aims. The implementation of gender mainstreaming over the last ten years enables identification of the key factors required if horizontal European policies are to succeed. The experience of gender mainstreaming shows in particular that, in order to develop its full potential, the new Horizontal Social Clause will require firm commitment on the part of all European actors involved in the fields of employment, social protection, the fight against social exclusion, education and training and human health. Subject to impetus by a strong political will, Article 9 has the potential to prompt significant redirection of the most liberal European policies towards social ends and to contribute to the emergence of a European social model.

I. INTRODUCTION

The Treaty of Lisbon, amending the Treaty on European Union and the Treaty establishing the European Community, was signed on 13 December

* This text has been adapted from a paper for the conference 'Alternatives to flexicurity: new concepts and approaches', M Keune and A Serrano (eds), organised by the ETUI, the University of Amsterdam (AIAS/HSI) and the Industrial Relations School (UCM) (in collaboration with the TRANSOC Institute) (Madrid, Escuela de relaciones laborales, 6–7 May 2010).

2007 and came into force on 1 December 2009. The section entitled 'Treaty on the functioning of the European Union' contains the following new provision, widely referred to as the 'Horizontal Social Clause':

> Article 9
>
> In defining and implementing its policies and activities, the Union shall take into account requirements linked to the promotion of a high level of employment, the guarantee of adequate social protection, the fight against social exclusion, and a high level of education, training and protection of human health.

The first commentators on the social dimension of the Treaty, when they do not lament the inbuilt ineffectiveness of this Article, given the extremely limited extension of the EU's social competences,[1] accord it no more than marginal significance.[2] As related by the European Commission, the story of the social clause is a tale of enshrinement in the Treaty of a practice of 'intelligent regulation' developed by the Commission itself since 2002.[3] It was indeed in that year that the Commission put in place an integrated Impact Assessment (IA) procedure designed to examine the economic, social and environmental effects of its policy proposals. This procedure was subsequently applied in 2005 in the context of the European employment strategy and the Lisbon strategy. In 2009, following an external assessment of the IA, the guidelines for intelligent regulation were amended,[4] and the IA was extended to cover all legislative initiatives. The Lisbon Treaty came into force in the same year. In 2010 the Belgian Presidency launched a debate on strengthening the social dimension of the IA in the context of the Horizontal Social Clause. The Commission, taking the view that IA already suffices to meet its new obligation under the Lisbon Treaty, henceforth stresses the need for the Member States themselves to adopt appropriate processes geared to similar ends.[5]

[1] B De Witte, A Trechsel, D Damjanovic, E Elquist, J Hien and P Ponzano, 'Legislating After Lisbon, New Opportunities for the European Parliament' (EUDO Observatory on Institutional Changes and Reforms (2010).

[2] See, for example, I Schömann, 'The Lisbon Treaty: a more social Europe at last?' (2010) 1 *ETUI Policy Brief*.

[3] See the European Commission site: ec.europa.eu/enterprise/policies/better-regulation/impact-assessment/index_en.htm, and Belgian Presidency of the European Union, background paper: The horizontal social clause and social mainstreaming in the EU—The Horizontal Social Clause as a call for intensified cooperation and exchange of knowledge through the Commission's Impact Assessment (3ème Forum sur les Services sociaux d'intérêt général (SSIG), Brussels, Belgian Federal Public Service Social Security, 26–27 October 2010): www.socialsecurity.fgov.be/eu/docs/agenda/26-27_10_10_sia_en.pdf).

[4] European Commission (2009), Impact Assessment Guidelines que l'on peut trouver sur le site: ec.europa.eu/governance/impact/commission_guidelines/docs/iag_2009_en.pdf.

[5] See M Kühnemund, 'Social impact assessment as a tool for mainstreaming social inclusion and social protection concerns in public policy in EU Member States' in E Marlier and D Natali (eds), *Background document prepared for the international conference on EU coordination in the social field in the context of Europe 2020: Looking back and building the*

Over and above this narrative couched in a technocratic register inspired by private management practices,[6] it is nonetheless important to point out that the social clause is rooted in a fundamentally progressive vision of the purpose of public policies. Such a vision finds expression, for example, in the theoretical works of Amartya Sen and his practical contribution, within the United Nations framework, to a 'human development index'; or in the highly instructive pursuit, since 1995, of gender mainstreaming within both the United Nations and the European Union.

What the Horizontal Social Clause actually asserts is the primacy to be accorded to social goals in EU activities and policy-making, and this includes those fields where 'hard' economic considerations appear to reign supreme. The new provision is worded so as to apply to all the European institutions (Parliament, Council, Court of Justice,[7] Commission, committees involved in the Lisbon or Europe 2020 process,[8] etc), as well as to the Member States. Each of these actors is henceforth required to ensure that the clause is appropriately implemented within the sphere of its own responsibilities.

In the field of hard law the new clause protects from annexation by the laws of economics several fields of social action of quintessential significance in relation to what might be called the 'European social model'.[9] In the field of soft law, the Horizontal Social Clause could, appropriately handled, allow the Lisbon and Europe 2020 process to become relatively exempt from application of the economic convergence criteria; it could even entail subjecting the various economic fields to the test of their compatibility with the social purposes of the Treaty as enshrined in the new clause. It is, however, up to the European institutions and social actors to recall and draw attention to the demands stemming from the new provision and to propose appropriate institutional mechanisms that will ensure its effectiveness. Interestingly enough, the Social Protection Committee lost no time in taking the measure of the potential offered by the Horizontal Social Clause.[10]

future, organised by the Belgian Presidency of the Council of the European Union with the support of the European Commission (14–15 September 2010, La Hulpe, Belgium) pp 68–75.

[6] See on the Commission website: Social impact assessment, background: ec.europa.eu/enterprise/policies/better-regulation/impact-assessment/background/index_en.htm.

[7] While it may indeed not be possible to deduce from it any direct effect, either horizontal or vertical—which means that an individual cannot derive rights from this clause and demand their implementation, either by a Member State or by another individual—the Court of Justice should in principle refer to it in the framework of its classical teleological interpretation method.

[8] Thus, at the request of the Belgian EU Presidency, the EPSCO Council has already begun to give thought to how to step up social mainstreaming in the wake of the horizontal social clause. See: www.eutrio.be/pressrelease/informal-meeting-epsco-council-social-security-and-social-inclusion.

[9] For the same purpose, it is also possible to refer to the EU Charter of Fundamental Rights or to a future ratification by the EU of the European Convention on Human Rights.

[10] Contribution by the Social Protection Committee finalised at its meeting on 18 May 2010 and presented in the run-up to the EPSCO Council meeting on 7 and 8 June 2010, Council of the European Union, memorandum, Brussels, 21May 2010 (27.05) (OR. en) 9964/10SOC 358.

In theory, therefore, it is possible, on the basis of Article 9 of the TFEU, to supply the European Social Question—on the European as much as the national level—with answers that transcend the traditional scope of social policy implementation and social law. This is true whether one speaks of the personal and material scope and targets of social policies, or of the instruments, actors and government levels whereby, by whom and at which they are implemented.

In order to indicate how such an approach might be implemented, I shall base my considerations on the Horizontal Social Clause's 'elder sister', namely, the gender mainstreaming clause, introduced by the Amsterdam Treaty, in order (1) to show that it is indeed possible, under certain conditions, to develop horizontal policies on the scale of the EU, and (2) to identify the potential benefits and likely pitfalls associated with the horizontal social clause in light of the experience of the gender mainstreaming clause.

From a legal standpoint, three arguments may be put forward to justify the comparison with gender mainstreaming. The first argument is textual: the wording of the Horizontal Social Clause is, *mutatis mutandis*, very similar to that of the gender mainstreaming clause. The second argument is contextual: the Horizontal Social Clause was introduced into the Treaty just after the gender mainstreaming clause and just before the environmental clause. The third argument pertains to a common articulated structure which, in these fields, establishes links between the law—a formal guarantee of fundamental rights—and public policies for the achievement of substantive goals (genuine equality, social justice).

This third argument deserves further development given its extreme importance for understanding the function of the Horizontal Social Clause within the overall rationale of the reforms introduced by the Lisbon Treaty. Gender mainstreaming was conceived and came into being as a result of the observed incapacity of 'hard' law to ensure substantive equality between men and women. Once the effectiveness of law in *formally eliminating discrimination* had been demonstrated, it was necessary to implement a strategy suitable for *promoting the material equality of situations*. Accordingly, the United Nations, in 1995, adopted the Beijing strategy to complement the Convention on the Elimination of all forms of Discrimination Against Women (CEDAW—1979) and a few years later, a gender mainstreaming strategy was enshrined in the Amsterdam Treaty to complement the provisions of European law that prohibited discrimination between women and men. While individuals may claim effective rights only under Article 157 TFEU (on the prohibition of discrimination) and its derived Directives, the gender mainstreaming clause requires the European institutions and Member States to assign egalitarian aims to all their activities and policies. Similarly, the Horizontal Social Clause can be understood only when viewed in conjunction with the new Treaty provisions that, on the one hand, enshrine the European Charter of

Fundamental Rights, and, on the other, oblige the EU to accede to the European Convention on Human Rights (Article 6(2) TEU).[11] These latter provisions recognise formal rights—to which individuals can or will be entitled to lay claim in the law courts—whereas the Horizontal Social Clause requires the EU and its Member States to assess the consequences of their activities and policies from the standpoint of the effective realisation of certain of these rights.

II. GENDER MAINSTREAMING: A PARTIAL AND REAL—BUT INSUFFICIENTLY WELL KNOWN—INSTANCE OF SOCIAL PROGRESS

The Amsterdam Treaty, which came into force on 1 May 1999, amended Article 3 of the European Community Treaty. After the enumeration of the policies that may be conducted at European level, Article 3 henceforth states: '2. In all the activities referred to in this Article, the Community shall aim to eliminate inequalities, and to promote equality, between men and women'.

In conjunction with Article 2 of the same Treaty, this clause establishes a legal base for the gender mainstreaming strategy at the level of the European Union. It commits the institutions to the devising and conduct of active policies to promote gender equality, over and above the mere elimination of discrimination. It is impossible not to be struck by its close similarity to the Horizontal Social Clause.

When the idea of introducing gender mainstreaming into European policies was enshrined in the Amsterdam Treaty, it was not a brand new concept. It was at the Fourth World Conference on Women, which met in Beijing in 1995 under United Nations auspices, that the concept had first found formal expression, even if it had not yet received a name. At this gathering 189 countries adopted the Beijing Platform, setting up a programme for equality between women and men in 12 critical fields of action. In the accompanying declaration, the governments undertook 'to implement the following Platform for Action, ensuring that a gender perspective is reflected in all our policies and programmes'. In the wake of this declaration, the European Commission, on 21 February 1996, adopted a communication in which it undertook to 'incorporate equal opportunities for women and men into all Community policies and activities'.[12] It was in

[11] See, for example, Schömann (n 2). Official talks on the European Union's accession to the ECHR started on 7 July 2010.

[12] COM(96) 67 final of 21 February 1996.

this communication that the first explicit definition of gender mainstreaming was to be found:[13]

> This involves not restricting efforts to promote equality to the implementation of specific measures to help women, but mobilising all general policies and measures specifically for the purpose of achieving equality by actively and openly taking into account at the planning stage their possible effects on the respective situations of men and women ('gender perspective'). This means systematically examining measures and policies and taking into account such possible effects when defining an implementing them (…) The systematic consideration of all the differences between the needs of women and men in all Community policies and actions, this is the basic feature of the principle of 'mainstreaming' which the Commission has adopted.

A. Areas

Even if its results are not always apparent, even if they vary from one field to another, gender mainstreaming has contributed, without any doubt whatsoever, to improving equality between women and men in the European Union. In 2009 the Swedish Presidency reported its assessment of 15 years of Community implementation of the Beijing Platform.[14] While an examination of European policies reveals a somewhat limited impact of gender mainstreaming in relation to the Lisbon Process and the European structural funds,[15] major efforts and progress are to be observed in the areas of research policy, external relations, development aid, humanitarian aid, as well as in the framework of the process of EU enlargement. As a means of ensuring less fragmentary progress, the report recalls the importance of systematically subjecting all EU policies and activities to a gender test. However uneven the outcome so far, the development and institutionalisation of gender mainstreaming have enabled the gender dimension of numerous European and national public policies to be revealed and have served to ensure that the aim of promoting substantial equality between women and men remains on the political agenda.

[13] It is to be noted that in 1998 the Commission was to adopt the Council of Europe's definition: 'Gender mainstreaming is the (re)organisation, improvement, development and evaluation of policy processes, so that a gender equality perspective is incorporated in all policies at all levels and at all stages, by the actors normally involved in policy-making'.

[14] *Beijing + 15: The Platform for action and the European Union*, Report from the Swedish Presidency of the Council of the European Union, 2009.

[15] On this point see also P Vielle et al, 'L'égalité des genres et conciliation travail famille' in B Vanhercke, G Verschraegen, P-P Van Gehuchten and Y Vanderborght (eds), *L'Europe en Belgique, la Belgique dans l'Europe, Configuration et appropriation des politiques sociales* (Louvain-la-Neuve, Academia-Bruylant, 2010).

With reference to these 15 years during which gender mainstreaming has been implemented, the key factors of success can today be identified. With the noteworthy and unfortunate exception of the Court of Justice, gender mainstreaming methods and structures have been put in place by all the European institutions. However, for ease of presentation, the illustrations that follow will be taken from the experience of the Commission alone.

B. Structures

Research has stressed that the existence of a motivated, committed and cooperative 'velvet triangle'—made up of (1) political and administrative institutions, (2) civil society, and (3) scientific expertise—forms the backcloth of the implementation of an effective gender mainstreaming strategy.[16] These ingredients are found within the European context. The Commission, for its work in this sphere, relies on the 'Commissioners' group on fundamental rights, anti-discrimination and equal opportunities' (2004) to enhance consistency among the Commission's activities in these fields in accordance with (former) Article 3 of the Treaty. The 'interservice group on gender equality' (1995) is composed of representatives of all the DGs and is responsible for developing gender mainstreaming in all the Commission's activities and programmes and for contributing to the annual report on equality. The 'equality and anti-discrimination group', responsible for overseeing transposition of European Directives in the Member States, also provides coordination for a network of bodies responsible for equality in the different Member States (EQUINET), oversees the uniform implementation of equality Directives and encourages the exchange of best practices. But it is the 'equal opportunities unit' that forms the administrative pivot of this whole group of bodies and supplies the necessary impetus by developing the promotion of general and specific gender mainstreaming measures. In this task it is assisted by the 'advisory committee for equal opportunities', composed of representatives of the Member States, the European social partners and civil society—including the European Women's Lobby (EWL)—which provide help in devising and implementing equality policies. The role of civil society is decisive here: the EWL and the social partners—with financial support from the Commission—are valuable interlocutors in prompting debate, in initiating and implementing equality policies. The 'high-level group'—an informal group composed of representatives from the Member States responsible for gender mainstreaming

[16] A Woodward, 'Building Velvet Triangles: Gender and Informal Governance' in T Christiansen and S Piattoni, *Informal Governance in the European Union* (Cheltenham, Edward Elgar, 2004).

on the national level—is the forum for planning the strategic follow-up to gender mainstreaming, including the highly political task consisting in the development of indicators and preparation of the annual report on equality presented each year by the Commission to the European Council and European Parliament.

C. Instruments

The implementation of gender mainstreaming requires, in addition, the availability and development of a series of *specific instruments*. These include a methodology for the assessment in terms of gender—*ex ante* and ex post—of the situations covered by the European programmes, policies and activities; the development of a battery of statistics and indicators broken down by sex and presented from a gender standpoint; and quality research conducted for the purpose of diagnosing inequality and its causes. The 'roadmap for equality between women and men' (2006–10), which has replaced the earlier 'five-year action programmes', is a concentrate of the Commission's efforts on these aspects of the government of gender mainstreaming. In future, however, it will be the recently set up 'European gender institute' that will take charge of the development and dissemination of tools to be used by the European institutions and Member States for strengthening the gender mainstreaming strategy.

Financial support is essential for encouraging and accompanying the European and national actions in the priority fields, from research on specific topics to the implementation of pilot schemes, through awareness-raising, information and training initiatives. This financial support comes from two sources: from the integration of the gender dimension into all the European financial funds, on the one hand, and from the adoption of specific budgets closely linked to the five-year action programmes for equality (or, since 2006, the 'roadmap for equality') on the other.

Finally, the introduction of a gender mainstreaming dimension must not be allowed to entail neglect of the *continuation of specific measures to promote women* in a series of vitally important areas. It is thus that the Commission conducts affirmative actions, for example in the fields of research or female entrepreneurship.

The history of Article 3(2) of the EC Treaty in the version of the Amsterdam Treaty and of gender mainstreaming in Europe reveals the potential and the limits of horizontal clauses on the European level. It thus offers a wealth of experience and numerous lessons for the possibilities of concrete implementation of a Horizontal Social Clause.

III. TOWARDS A FORM OF SOCIAL MAINSTREAMING? TAKING THE HORIZONTAL SOCIAL CLAUSE SERIOUSLY

We have seen that an assessment of experience to date in relation to the gender mainstreaming clause is somewhat mixed.[17]

A. Differences between Gender and Social Horizontal Clauses

The Horizontal Social Clause presents some similarities with gender mainstreaming, but also some significant differences. The first such difference relates to its subject matter which is more diversified and complex than the concept of gender equality. In this case, it is a question of simultaneously mainstreaming concerns associated with employment, social protection, human health, education and training. Unlike gender equality (present since 1957 in Article 119 of the Treaty of Rome),[18] several of these topics are subject to only very limited EU competence. However, as we have seen, it is the activist stance of the 'equality actors' that has enabled the value of gender equality, as a *general principle*, to be gradually asserted, in spite of the fact that the original formulation of this principle in the Treaty is confined to the matter of equal pay. It is, however, important not to underestimate the scale of the difficulties entailed by the diversity of the social clause goals. The difficulties stem not only from the diversity of the actors concerned, but from the diversity of the—sometimes contradictory—interests, priorities and solutions which these actors pursue. To overcome these difficulties, it might perhaps be appropriate to put the Horizontal Social Clause to the test, in the first instance, in areas which, without being peripheral to the European institutions' missions, do not relate to their core business (like competition, for example). Such areas might include, for example, energy, mobility, training, new information and communication technologies, etc.

This difficulty would seem to be further exacerbated when it is considered that Article 9 is one of several horizontal clauses included in the TFEU and that the aims of some of the others (eg environment, consumers) might well conflict with social objectives.

Another difficulty, stemming this time from the wording of the social clause, relates to the fact that employment appears to be considered from a quantitative standpoint alone. While this is actually not the case (see hereafter: 'the content of the horizontal social clause'), the European institutions—the Court of Justice in particular—would have to be prepared to bend the letter of the law and deploy persuasive arguments to maintain that

17 See Vielle et al (n 15).

18 Ancestor of the current Article 157 TFEU.

a 'high level of employment' entails a qualitative as well as a quantitative dimension. This certainly represents a strategic challenge for European actors concerned to promote the quality of employment. It is a question, indeed, of preventing a situation where a restrictive interpretation of this formulation would, for example, compromise the possibility of achieving progress in the ECJ's case law, or might exacerbate the deregulation of labour law in the discussions on flexicurity.

Unlike gender mainstreaming, the insertion of a social mainstreaming provision in the Treaty was not the outcome of an already existing strong political will on the part of the European institutions. For the social clause to deploy its full potential is clearly going to require a political commitment sustained over time and at the highest level, in the wake of the initiative taken by the Belgian Presidency. All the different actors and institutions concerned must together decide to appropriate this new spirit of the Treaty which represents a Copernican revolution in relation to the initial purposes of the European Union and requires a reorientation of the whole policy corpus towards the wellbeing of European citizens. In this respect, a rapid communication from the Commission, along lines similar to the gender mainstreaming communication of 1996, and specifying the meaning and scope of the social clause, would represent a useful contribution to its effectiveness. What is more, the European social actors, with the support of the institutions, must also espouse the social clause, and develop their activism in the direction of its implementation.

B. The Content of the Horizontal Social Clause[19]

On closer examination, the horizontal clauses (Articles 8–12 of the TFEU: gender equality, social aims, environmental aims, non-discrimination and consumer protection) appear to constitute the missing link between, on the one hand, the general social aims mentioned in the TEU (in particular in Article 3) and, on the other, the competences of the EU as stated in the TFEU. They thus serve to establish consistency between the activity of the EU and its fundamental missions.

Paragraph 3 of Article 3 TEU is worded as follows:

> '3. The Union shall establish an internal market. It shall work for the sustainable development of Europe based on balanced economic growth and price stability, a highly competitive social market economy, aiming at full employment and social progress, and a high level of protection and improvement of the quality of the environment. (...)

[19] My warm thanks go to Professor Niklas Bruun for his valuable suggestions in relation to this point.

> It shall combat social exclusion and discrimination, and shall promote social justice and protection, equality between women and men, solidarity between generations and protection of the rights of the child'.

Article 9 TFEU systematically echoes several of these demands and aims to ensure convergence of all EU powers in support of the aims of Article 3. It establishes a reference standard for the institutions in respect of not only their social policy competences (Articles 151ff for legislation, Articles 145ff for employment, and Articles 162ff for the European Social Fund) but also of all their other competences taken as a whole.

Close attention to the wording reveals, however, a semantic shift in relation to each of the areas mentioned. Thus, 'full employment' (Article 3, paragraph 3, TEU) translates in Article 9 TFEU into a 'high level of employment'. The Belgian Presidency of the EU did not omit to point out in 2010 that the notion of 'high level' in Article 9 was to be understood in a qualitative as well as a quantitative sense, recalling the importance of the 'quality of employment' (a notion enshrined some ten years earlier in the European employment strategy thanks to the same Belgian Presidency). According to a similar analysis, the transition from a 'high level of protection' (Article 3 TEU) to 'adequate social protection' (Article 9 TFEU) constitutes a reference to the Lisbon Strategy and the open method of coordination which establishes a contrast between the notions of 'sustainability' and 'adequacy', the first of which refers to the economic viability of social protection systems—and hence their financing—and the second to the adequacy of benefits in relation to the needs that they are intended to meet. It will be noted with interest that Article 151 TEU (which henceforth has to be interpreted in light of Article 9) refers merely to 'proper social protection'.

While Article 9 is intended to apply to both hard and soft law, it is a familiarity with the latter that provides a key to the particular shapes and meanings underlying its formulation. The whole history of the Lisbon process has been characterised by a strong tension between the social content and procedures, on the one hand, and those that are economic in nature, on the other. If Article 9 TFEU is read in light of the open coordination methods, the choice of wording will be understood as an unequivocal reference to a determination to redress the balance in favour of socially directed purposes.

C. Concrete Obligations in Respect of the Commission

i. Structures

Any horizontal policy requires considerable commitment and input on the part of the European civil service. To ensure that the social clause really does result in genuine change, it will be necessary to provide civil servants with training in social matters (or to appoint civil servants already in possession of the requisite specialisation) in all the Commission DGs. A special unit—ideally within the General Secretariat—should be created to spearhead and coordinate this effort, as well as internal concertation groups. Such coordination is currently non-existent, such that some social policies conducted within the employment and social affairs DG are developing quite at odds with one another. One example of a lack of synergy is to be found in the area of combining family and working life, an endeavour to which the bodies in charge of equality have been devoting considerable efforts but which has been quite neglected in the drafting of working time Directives, while a gender approach is also missing from the new version of the Maternity Directive.

ii. Methodology

The development of a rigorous methodology applicable to the horizontal approach is indispensable. Either this must be entrusted to an appropriate existing external body, for example, the Dublin Foundation, or a new one must be set up specifically for the purpose. Such a body would be responsible for awareness-raising and for the training of national and European actors and institutions, for the collection of statistics and devising of indicators and all the other tools required to ensure effective processes and procedures (ex ante and ex post assessment methodologies, support for research in specific areas intended to identify the critical fields for intervention, networking of actors, etc).

iii. Consultation and Concertation Requirements

The process of consultation and exchange between the European institutions and all the actors involved in and affected by the formation and implementation of social policies must be institutionalised, with the aim of achieving a properly consolidated epistemic community able to focus on all issues relating to the achievement of social progress. This raises, however, the question of how to identify the actors in possession of the relevant expertise, a matter that is far from having been resolved to judge from the Commission's IA guidelines or the IA fiches already completed. In light of the experience of gender mainstreaming, the actors concerned must—in our own view—include, at least, the social partners, as well as representatives of civil society—as already institutionalised or subject to further requisite institutionalisation—on the European level in the fields covered by the clause. Each of the actors in question must then first agree to take part in the process and subsequently undertake to contribute to a cooperative and constructive effort with the other categories of actors affected by the clause. On the gender question, the experience of the fight against domestic violence is edifying in this respect. A number of women's organisations (the 'traditional' actors in the gender sphere) had refused, in the first instance, to cooperate with the grassroots actors invited to define and evaluate the policies, whose legitimacy in the field they contested and who, they feared, would weaken their strategic position by depriving them of their monopoly on consultation. Experience showed, on the contrary, that it is important for the effectiveness and legitimacy of ongoing policies to have all these actors present around the table and also that their respective positions are actually strengthened by the experience of developing cooperation and joint efforts in the field.

Taking into account the new provision of Article 152 TFEU, it would appear very helpful if the very specific (and therefore very distinct from other NGOs) role of the social partners in general and the trade unions in particular (at the European level mainly the European Trade Union Confederation (ETUC)) would not only be recognised but—taking into account the specific obligation—promoted.

The process of consultation and concertation must take on a horizontal character (the full range of affected and involved European actors: institutions, social partners, NGOs active in the social clause fields) but the vertical dimension is equally important. One of the key factors of the success of gender mainstreaming is to be found precisely in this vertical integration: the European institutions are supported at one and the same time by the United Nations and by the Member States and they, in return, support these two decision-making levels. A similar dynamic—some traces of which are already apparent in the Commission negotiations with the ILO on common job quality indicators, or in the Lisbon process with the Member States—remains to be invented and put into practice in social matters.

iv. Areas

The ex ante and ex post ('social test') evaluations must be generalised across the full range of European economic and social policies. The Lisbon process must be revisited, as much in terms of procedures as of substance, in order to better reflect the new balance between economic and social policies required by the horizontal clause.

Ambitious research programmes must be conducted to analyse the evolution of the social situation in Europe, identifying priority questions, understanding the causes of social problems and exploring ways of solving them. This requires the systematic integration of the fields covered by the social clause in the European framework research programmes (incorporation of social aspects in the content of calls for tender, but also consideration of the social impact of the research being subsidised), in parallel with the specific individual research programmes on social matters.

Programmes to identify the priority actions to be conducted and the results to be achieved by specific deadlines must be drawn up by the Commission. In conjunction with this step, the structural funds must undergo revision in accordance with the clause's priorities and must be complemented by specific funds intended to initiate and support projects in the most critical fields and which will allow the conduct of specific research projects to focus on these issues, the provision of awareness-raising and training programmes, support for the actors concerned and the encouragement of pilot actions.

Finally, the EU must continue the development of legislation and social policies in those areas where it has specific competences. Such legislation and policies must serve as both foundation and cement in building the new horizontal social approach.

It is subject to these demanding but imperative conditions that the Horizontal Social Clause can be used to give a new chance to a genuine 'European social model' based on the gearing of all policies, both economic and social, towards the purpose of the wellbeing and social security (in the broadest sense of the term) of all EU citizens. It is equally in light of these considerations that a careful analysis must be conducted of the complex processes put in place by the Commission in the IA framework, and of the IA fiches that have already been produced.[20]

D. Concrete Obligations in Respect of the Court of Justice

The *Laval* and *Viking* cases served to demonstrate what most European labour law experts had foreseen: in the absence of recognition and guarantee by the European Treaties of fundamental social rights (recognised as among the most fundamental by the International Labour Organisation[21] and by all the Member States), the Court of Justice, faithful to its teleological approach, interpreted, for instance, the right of free collective bargaining or the right to strike as restrictions on the economic freedoms guaranteed by the Treaty. It thus set out to test whether these expressions of fundamental social rights were in compliance with the Treaty, going so far as to assess whether they were necessary, proportionate and appropriate for achievement of the goals they were intended to serve. In this way, Member State citizens had imposed on them a legal order that made their fundamental rights subordinate to their compatibility with the economic goals of

[20] See the Commission website: ec.europa.eu/enterprise/policies/better-regulation/impact-assessment/index_en.htm.

[21] ILO Declaration on Fundamental Principles and Rights at Work and its Follow-up, Adopted by the International Labour Conference at its Eighty-sixth Session, Geneva, 18 June 1998 (Annex revised 15 June 2010).

the Treaty. *L'ordre juridique qui s'imposait dès lors aux citoyens des Etats membres subordonnait leurs droits fondamentaux à leur compatibilité avec les objectifs économiques du Traité.*[22]

With respect to Article 3(2) of the EC Treaty in the version of the Amsterdam Treaty in which the principle of gender mainstreaming was first enshrined, it cannot but be observed that this Article has exerted no more than a limited influence on the case law of the Court of Justice which has developed principally through recourse to Articles recognised as entailing direct effect (in particular Article 119 of the Treaty of Rome). And yet, international law is witness to the fact that joint recourse to hard and soft law can serve to influence the direction taken by case law.

The adoption of the Treaty of Lisbon should thus, in future, serve to point the Court's decisions in a new direction. In conjunction with the Charter of Fundamental Rights and the European Convention on the Protection of Human Rights and Fundamental Freedoms, the Horizontal Social Clause represents an appeal to the Court to interpret—more than has been the case in the past—European law in light of more clearly affirmed social goals and fundamental rights. In situations like the *Laval* or *Viking* cases, it is henceforth with regard to their impact on the level (both qualitative and quantitative) of employment, on adequate social protection, on training or on human health, that the Treaty Articles should be interpreted by the Court.

The ongoing negotiations with the Council of Europe for accession of the EU to the Convention should, what is more, encourage the Court to interpret Article 9 itself in light of this Convention. It is indeed hard to conceive that the EU, in the context of the negotiations, should fail to move in the direction of making its own legislation and jurisprudence consistent with that emanating from the Council of Europe. This additional teleological key should be used to flesh out and lend additional weight to Article 9 so as to enable prevention of an inappropriate shift in its interpretation (towards quantity rather than quality of employment or towards the sustainability of social protection systems rather than their adequacy).

IV. CONCLUSIONS

As is frequently pointed out, the original purpose of the Treaty of Rome was principally economic in nature. Article 2 of that Treaty stated that:

> It shall be the aim of the Community, by establishing a Common Market and progressively approximating the economic policies of Member States, to promote

[22] 'The legal order that was imposed upon Member State citizens made their fundamental rights subordinate to their compatibility with the economic goals of the Treaty.'(trans)

throughout the Community a harmonious development of economic activities, a continuous and balanced expansion, an increased stability, an accelerated raising of the standard of living and closer relations between its Member States.

The European Economic Community established a Customs Union and was required to guarantee four main pillars: the free movement of persons, services and capital, as well as freedom of competition.

The structure of the Treaty of Rome formed the matrix for subsequent Treaties. Apart from the aspects connected with free movement of workers—which, from the outset, was to be understood as the guarantee of the free movement of an economic production factor and not as recognition of a fundamental human right—the history of social Europe has had to be written within the confines of this original mould, which made it difficult to delimit an area of autonomy—whether national or European—for labour law, social policy or social protection. In this context, the *Defrenne II* ruling which gives full effect to the sole substantially social Article of the Treaty (Article 119 on equal pay for men and women) is to be regarded as a notable exception. The Court of Justice indeed acknowledged this provision as a 'foundation of the Community' whereas the Member States referred to the economic purpose underlying its inclusion in the Treaty (to limit the international competitive disadvantage of sectors with a high density of female labour which practised equal treatment).[23]

The Maastricht Treaty opened the way to potential emancipation of European social law from the standpoint of the spirit of the Treaties for it enshrines, among other things, the possibility for the European social partners autonomously to draw up binding social law provisions. Other forms of progress in the social sphere—albeit less significant and sometimes little more than window-dressing—are to be found in subsequent Treaties: extension of the possibility of adopting social provisions by majority vote (yet excepting the most sensitive questions like social protection, pay or strikes), inclusion of a specific Title on Employment, or establishment of a convergence process in a range of essential social policy fields, in particular that of social protection.

[23] CJEC 43/75, Judgment of the Court of 8 April 1976, *Gabrielle Defrenne v Société anonyme belge de navigation aérienne Sabena*: 'first, in the light of the different stages of the development of social legislation in the various Member States, the aim of Article 119 is to avoid a situation in which undertakings established in states which have actually implemented the principle of equal pay suffer a competitive disadvantage in intra-Community competition as compared with undertakings established in states which have not yet eliminated discrimination against women workers as regards pay; secondly, this provision forms part of the social objectives of the Community, which is not merely an economic union but is at the same time intended, by common action, to ensure social progress and seek the constant improvement of the living and working conditions of their peoples, as is emphasized by the preamble to the Treaty (...) this double aim, which is at once economic and social, shows that the principle of equal pay forms part of the foundations of the Community'.

And yet, the hegemony enjoyed by the economic freedoms, and which has, since 1957, become tantamount to a constitutionally valid tenet within Europe, has led, slowly but surely, to a situation in which on the one hand the only social policies conducted at European level are those liable to contribute to the economic aims of the Treaty and, on the other, the rules of national social law are regarded as market 'rigidities' or obstacles to the European economic freedoms.

With the Lisbon Treaty, in conjunction with the EU Charter of Fundamental Freedoms—with its numerous limits—or, more securely, with the EU accession to the European Convention on Human Rights, the Horizontal Social Clause henceforth affirms the primacy of the social purpose of EU policies and actions, even in the 'hardest' economic fields. The clause is binding on all the European institutions, which means, of course, on the Commission and the Council, but also on the European Parliament and Court of Justice. It thereby serves to place several emblematic social policy areas safely beyond the reach of economic law.

The social actors must from now on revise their legal strategies in light of the Horizontal Social Clause and remain permanently on the watch in order to issue reminders of its demands, not in social questions alone, but in all other areas of EU competence. This requires that these actors expand their own spheres of competence and intervention to embrace new fields, in particular the economic policy areas in which the EU has competence. For example, information and communication technologies, or energy, mobility, or banking law, all exert an influence on employment, social protection and human health. In these fields the EU will in future need to issue legislation that takes account of the implications of Article 9. The different participatory bodies (like the Economic and Social Committee) whose role it is to become involved in the legislative processes will thus need to seize every opportunity to demand that the Horizontal Social Clause be taken into account when legislation and standards are being drawn up in these areas. At the same time, there will be numerous and regular opportunities to invoke the Horizontal Social Clause in the national courts and the Court of Justice in order to reiterate the social aims of the Treaty, including on those occasions when the economic freedoms enshrined in this same Treaty are the subject of examination.

Accordingly, it is not only up to the institutional actors but also the social partners and civil society to take up the Horizontal Social Clause and to exploit its potential to the full for the purpose of constructing, finally, a genuine 'European social model'.

5

The Role of the Social Partners in the Lisbon Treaty

BRUNO VENEZIANI

I. INTRODUCTION: SOLIDARITY AS A NEW TOOL FOR INTERPRETATION

THE NEW INSTITUTIONAL framework requires a profound modification of the European culture and a new attitude to reshaping the European social model. The European Employment Strategy, initiated by the Delors White Paper on 'Growth, Competitiveness, Employment' in 1993 and made operational by the Essen Council in 1994, marked a turning point in the development of concerted action to tackle EU problems as part of a broader economic strategy, calling for an 'open and solidaristic' new economic culture.[1]

Solidarity as a value underlines the slow growth of the trade union movement and it is at the root of all systems of labour law. It is included in the EU's Charter of Fundamental Rights (hereinafter: EU Charter or CFREU) as Title IV and in a (never legally binding) Treaty establishing a Constitution for Europe signed in Rome on 29 October 2004 (hereinafter: Constitutional Treaty, Article I-2) as a value applying to both national and, above all, European society. It is also a meaningful component of the unitary concept of European citizenship, constructed on the basis of 'social citizenship', which defines the condition of the European citizen as a *socius* both in the *polity* and in the labour market and *welfare* contexts. A more comprehensive concept of European citizenship entails civil rights (freedom, equality), political rights (participation in democratic life) and social rights (welfare and solidarity).[2]

[1] COM(94) 333 final, 'European Social Policy: A Way Forward for the Union—A White Paper'.

[2] AA.VV, *A Manifesto for Social Europe* (Brussels: ETUI, 2001).

II. EUROPEAN SOCIAL CITIZENSHIP

European social citizenship has multiple meanings linked to the *status* of worker, both as an individual and as a member of a group, requiring a set of norms and principles defending its identity in a more general *milieu* of European legal order.[3]

The Constitutional Treaty of 2004 provided for freedom, democracy (already existing in Article 6 TEU), dignity and equality. The European Union is now a large legal framework in which pluralism, non-discrimination and solidarity are deeply embedded as labour law and social policy values in the new 'European dictionary'. Social justice has been included—as suggested by Group XI on 'Social Europe'[4]—in the list of 'horizontal' values relevant to the European social model (Article 3(3) point 2 TEU; generally on values and objectives see Dorssemont, chapter two in this volume).

Most of those values are closely interwoven with labour law, social policy and industrial relations: dignity and equality compose the 'genetic code' of the individual employment relationship, while democracy, pluralism and solidarity describe the essential core of collective labour relations. Both demand strong engagement and responsibilities from the social partners in conditioning the political decisions and legal activity of European political bodies. The strategic role of values is to guide the Union's legal and economic planning with regard to its objectives, as described in a lexical 'crescendo' in Article 3 TEU (ex-Article 2 TEU): the EU '*shall combat*' social exclusion and discrimination and '*shall promote*' 'social justice and protection, [as well as] equality between women and men'.

To 'combat' and to 'promote' indicate strong commitments. Semantic variations are important but not sufficient to renew an institutional mechanism included in the previous Article 2 TEU: the new formulas contain a Utopia—full employment—and a promise—to promote social justice. But it is important to stress that the social partners and industrial relations in general within the context of a new version of the TEU reshaped in Lisbon in December 2009 are no longer completely neglected, even though a clear philosophy—recalling the Union's Sustainable Development Strategy agreed by the European Council in Göteborg in 2001—was based on the principle that the economic, social and environmental effects of all policies should be examined as an integrated strategy which requires the efforts of *all actors* in the labour market and industrial society.

The final result is an affirmation of social objectives as equal and not subordinate to economic ones: the idea of a 'social market economy' goes

[3] See also COM (2010) 603 final, 'Dismantling the obstacles to EU citizens' rights'.

[4] CONV 516/1/03 REV 1, Final report of Working Group XI on Social Europe, p 8.

back to the Lisbon Summit, where it was laid down as a strategic objective for the European Union for 2010.

It is important to stress that the overall architecture of the two Treaties of 2009 is inspired by the principles and values provided for by Article 2 TEU and Articles 7(1), 13 and 49 TEU as 'a parameter of legitimacy' of actions and interpretations on the part of all EU institutions. Solidarity is one of the values inspiring Title I (Article 2) of the TEU and Part Three Title X on Social policy of the Treaty on the Functioning of the European Union (TFEU). And it is such as binding tool of analysis of the legal context that its infringement by a Member State can expose it to the warning and sanction procedures of *ex*-Article 7 TEU and Article 354 TFEU.[5]

This is the way chosen to enforce politically what is considered a core of fundamental rights dealing with a clear and precise object.[6]

The new reform of the Treaties adopted in Lisbon in 2009, finally, achieves the objective of a legally binding framework of fundamental rights by declaring the EU Charter legally binding. Article 6(1) TEU changes the wording of the previous Article 6 EU. The change is significant. The Union is now obliged to 'recognise' and no longer merely 'respect' the rights, freedoms and principles set out in the EU Charter. The Charter 'shall have the same legal value as the Treaties', which means that rights and principles provided for in it have the same legal nature and strength as the rights, freedoms and principles already recognised in the Union legal system.

In particular, the role of trade unions is regulated *directly* because it is rooted in and defined by: Article 12(1) CFREU on freedom of association; (Article 5 (Revised) European Social Charter (R)ESC)); and Article 28 CFREU on the rights to collective bargaining and collective action (Article 6 (R)ESC). Both provisions guarantee the exercise of rights at 'appropriate levels' and the Explanations to the EU Charter explicitly include the European level.

Furthermore, the TEU *indirectly* corroborates the promotion of the social partners, stating (Article 6(2)) that the Union shall accede to the European Convention for the Protection of Human Rights and Fundamental Freedoms (ECHR) and that fundamental rights—as guaranteed by the ECHR and as they result from constitutional traditions common to the Member States—'shall constitute general principles of Union Law' (Article 6(3) TEU). We should note the more cautious, but no less meaningful reference made by the Treaties in the fifth recital of the Preamble of the TEU ('confirm … the attachment') as well as ('having in mind') in Article 151(1) TFEU, both referring to the fundamental social rights of the European Social Charter (Turin 1961

[5] As stated in the comment to Article 2, CONV 528/03, Annex II.
[6] Ibid.

[revised in 1996]) and the Community Charter of Fundamental Social Rights of Workers (Strasbourg 1989; hereinafter: Community Charter).

III. THE SOCIAL DIALOGUE AND THE ROLE OF THE SOCIAL PARTNERS

A. The Strategic Role of Social Dialogue

The first stage on which the social partners can appear at European level coincides with the first revolutionary transformation of the institutional structure of social law and policy of the Maastricht Treaty.[7] The history of *social dialogue* goes back to 1987 when the Single European Act introduced the 'golden formula' of social dialogue: 'The Commission shall endeavour to develop the dialogue between management and labour at European level which could, if the two sides consider it desirable, lead to relations based on agreement' (ex-Article 118b TEEC), as specified further in 2003 after the Maastricht, Amsterdam and Nice amendments (ex-Article 139 EC, now Article 155 TFEU).

Today, the Lisbon Treaty in Article 152 TFEU reproduces the formula used in the Constitutional Treaty 2004 (Article I-48).

The statement is quite clear and must be interpreted in light of the overall philosophy of Title II of the TEU dedicated to 'Provisions on democratic principles'.

Article 152 TFEU recognises explicitly the functions of collective autonomy at Union level and the strategic role of social dialogue in strengthening democracy within the supranational context. Both collective autonomy and social dialogue represent a parameter of 'democratic equality', in other words, the right of citizens to 'receive equal attention from the Union's institutions, bodies, offices and agencies' (Article 9 TEU).

Civil, political and social representativeness require an auxiliary role for the EU institution as indicated in Article 11 TEU where a broad concept of democracy is included, together with a provision that the European Commission 'shall carry out broad consultations with the parties concerned in order to ensure that the Union's actions are coherent and transparent' (Article 11(3) TEU).

According to the new Article 13 TEU, the Union institutional framework 'shall aim to promote its values, advance its objectives, serve its interests, those of its citizens and those of Member States and ensure the consistency, effectiveness and continuity of its policy and actions' (Article 13(1) TEU.

[7] B Bercusson, 'Institutional reform and social and labour policy' in AA.VV, *Manifesto* (n 2) p 111.

It seems only consistent that the involvement of the social partners at EU level must be analysed and interpreted in this renewed context, taking into account, first, that all 'social objectives and aims' of the EU are contained in Article 3(3) TEU.

Furthermore, the EU has a shared competence with the Member States in the matter of social policy and social cohesion (Article 4(2)(b) and (c) TFEU) and also 'supporting' competence in vocational training (Article 6(e) TFEU; see Lörcher, chapter six). According to the new provisions of Part one Title II ('having general application') of the TFEU, the Union 'in defining and implementing its policy and activity' (Article 9 TFEU; see Vielle, chapter four) in the field of its competence is obliged by a social horizontal clause to respect two principles: (i) consistency between its policy and activity and objectives (Article 7 TFEU) and (ii) social responsibility (Article 9 TFEU).

B. The New Article 152 TFEU

The new Article 152 TFEU must be seen and analysed in light of the new legal and institutional philosophy of the Lisbon Treaty process. First, it is placed in Part Three Title X of the TFEU on Social Policy and it represents, in the field of labour law, trade union law and welfare systems, the values of representative democracy in the social field (social democracy) and participation (social dialogue). In other words, it expresses the idea that the 'collective autonomy' of social partners is a protagonist of a reshaped legal system as a whole, in which all collective rights and actions (collective bargaining and action, freedom of association, participation) have acquired full legal status. These are rights clearly guaranteed by a legally binding source of law (Article 6(1) TEU in respect of the EU Charter) which can be used as a parameter of legitimacy for all actions of the European institutions.

In this context, Article 152 TFEU contains:

(a) The right of the social partners to be recognised and promoted by the Union.

(b) An obligation on the Union to facilitate dialogue between the social partners and to respect their autonomy. The role of the Union is strongly emphasised because the Lisbon reform extends functions (that is, 'recognition and promotion') from the Commission—as indicated in Article 154 TFEU (ex-Article 138 EC)—to all Union bodies and institutions now engaged in roles not only 'passive' ('respecting' a right), but also 'proactive or promoting' ('facilitating') dialogue in general, also so that 'dialogue may lead to contractual relations, including agreements' (Article 155(1) TFEU).

Articles 12, 27 and 28 CFREU provide for a dense legal network of collective actions protecting at Union level the dignity of workers and solidarity, as indicated in Article 2 TEU and in specific Titles of the EU Charter (Titles I and IV) 'which shall have the same legal value as the Treaties' (Article 6(1) TEU).

C. The Autonomy of Social Partners

The rule of 'autonomous social dialogue' is the legal source for private collective powers to build up an independent system of industrial relations, also at international and Union level.

Article 152 TFEU must be understood in its relationship with the existing provisions on employment (Title IX) and social policy (Title X). In Title X it is placed after the aims of EU social policy (Article 151 TFEU, ex-Article 136 EC), but before the provision on legislative competences (Article 153 TFEU, ex-Article 137 EC). It seems that the scope of Article 152 TFEU is not restricted to the areas in which the Union has legislative competence because Article 9 TFEU—as a new horizontal (mainstreaming) social clause (see Vielle, chapter four in this volume)—provides for the first time that social aims must be taken into account in respect of all policies and activities.

The so-called passive obligation to 'recognise' the role of collective autonomy is in principle related to protection of the situation prior to the Lisbon Treaties. It does not appear possible that any Union institution will reduce the procedural and material impact of the social partners in general. Article 152 TFEU 'recognises' the pre-existing *acquis communautaire* (Part Three Title X (Social Policy)) and the value of the autonomy of the social partners (Articles 153, 154 and 155 TFEU), so that the first obligation has a specific aim of not reducing the intensity and breadth of the following actions:

(a) Promoting their consultation at Union level.
(b) Adopting measures to facilitate their dialogue.
(c) Ensuring balanced support for the social partners.
(d) Consulting the social partners on the possible direction of Union action.
(e) Consulting the social partners on the content of proposals.
(f) Accepting their opinions or, where appropriate, a recommendation, to be forwarded to the Commission.
(g) Providing for possible autonomous initiatives of the parties to launch the bargaining process for an autonomous agreement.
(h) Adopting a decision to implement agreements concluded at European level at the joint request of the signatory parties.

The autonomy of the actors interferes with the procedures of the legislative process, with regard to both the submission of a proposal and the decision on its contents.

The mechanism openly recognised in Article 152 TFEU with regard to social dialogue and EU law based collective agreements is a key element of European social strategy. Its history shows the successes and defeats of the golden formula and also how this legal device was employed alternatively in following an autonomous procedure: framework agreements on teleworking (2002); work-related stress (2004); harassment and violence at work (2007) and inclusive labour markets (2010); or via a legal path: parental leave (1995)[8] and revised version (2010),[9] part-time (1997)[10] and fixed-term workers' rights (1999).[11] The sectoral dialogue suggests a positive judgement on the efficiency of the mechanism: European agreements on the reduction of risk (agriculture 2005) and on the organisation of working time (maritime 1998, railways 1998 and airline transport 2000),[12] agreement on fundamental social rights in the European commerce sector (1999) and a sectoral framework on child labour in the footwear industry (1998) are the output of the process. The social partners are also active in various ways delivering joint opinions, memoranda and recommendations.[13]

An important role for employees' and employers' federations is acknowledged in the Lisbon process, taking the form of regular 'social affairs summits' on the occasion of the spring European Council, at which the social partners have the opportunity to express their opinions on the issues at stake.

The practice was based on the Tripartite Social Summit for Growth and Employment[14] which has now been institutionalised at the level of primary law (Article 152(2) TFEU) as one way of implementing the right to recognition and promotion.

The name given to this new institution seems to cover all the different areas: employment and economic growth. The tripartite body is strongly oriented to social policy and employment, giving support in particular to social dialogue.

[8] Directive 96/34/EC of 3 June 1996 on the framework agreement on parental leave concluded by UNICE, CEEP and the ETUC, [1996] OJ L 145/4.

[9] Directive 2010/18/EU of 8 March 2010 implementing the revised framework agreement on parental leave concluded by BUSINESSEUROPE, UEAPME, CEEP and ETUC and repealing Directive 96/34/EC, [2010] OJ L 68/13.

[10] Directive 97/81/EC of 15 December 1997 concerning the framework agreement on part-time work concluded by UNICE, CEEP and the ETUC—Annex: framework agreement on part-time work, [1998] OJ L 14/9.

[11] Directive 1999/70/EC of 28 June 1999 concerning the framework agreement on fixed-term work concluded by ETUC, UNICE and CEEP, [1999] OJ L 175/43.

[12] European Commission, 'Industrial relations in Europe', editorial 2000 in M Biagi (ed), *Towards a Model of Industrial Relations?* (Deventer-Boston: Kluwer, 2001) 22.

[13] R Blanpain, 'The European Union and employment law' in R Blanpain and C Engels (eds), *Comparative Labour Law and Industrial Relations in Industrialized Market Economies* (Deventer-Boston: Kluwer, 2001) 174; European Commission, *Industrial Relations in Europe* (Brussels: EU, 2004) ch 3, and European Commission, *European Sectoral Social Dialogue—Recent Developments* (Brussels: EU, 2010) Part II.

[14] Decision 2003/174/EC: Council Decision establishing a Tripartite Social Summit for Growth and Employment, [2003] OJ L 70/31.

Here the public components (Council and Commission) are not driving forces but play the role of *primus inter pares* in all concertation procedures. In fact, it has been stated that public EU powers have the function 'to facilitate' management and labour 'by ensuring balanced support for the parties' (Article 154(1) TFEU).

The Tripartite body must 'ensure ... continuous concertation between the Council, Commission and social partners' and 'enable the social partners at European level to contribute ... to the various components of the integrated economic and social strategy'.

The involvement is intended to contribute also—but not only—to the 'sustainable development dimension'.[15] The political aim is also clear: the range of topics to be dealt with is vast as it involves economic and social strategy—from the macro-economy to employment, labour law and industrial relations. This choice is consistent with the political perspective of the Commission, according to which both bipartite and tripartite dialogues 'contribute to better cohesion and to building consensus by stimulating cooperation between levels of industrial relations players, which helps to develop trust and mutual understanding'.[16]

IV. THE SOCIAL PARTNERS AND THE LEGAL CONTEXT

The obligation to promote the role of the social partners includes a really wide and continuous effort which leads to the 'dynamic' character of the provision. As a general rule, it should face the crucial question: is the *legal* recognition of the role of the unions and employers' associations in the current *legal* context still satisfactory?

The impression is that the legal outcome, contained in the rather sober sentences of the Treaties, is not completely coherent with the abovementioned role played by the social partners and social dialogue to date.

In fact, the meaning of 'autonomy' is emphasised by the European judges in evaluating the social dialogue as a 'substitute of the European Parliament in the decision-making process'. In other words, the social dialogue (and the parties which are co-regulators at European level) has the function to 'democratise Union life'.[17] The fundamental principle of democracy (Article 2 TEU) requires that the participation of the people in law-making processes be otherwise assured[18] and the judges have concluded that, in order to make sure that the requirement of democracy is complied with, participation must be

[15] Decision 2003/174/EC, Article 2.

[16] COM(2004) 557 final, 'Partnership for change in an enlarged Europe—Enhancing the contribution of European social dialogue', Annex I, p 12.

[17] Case T-135/96 *UEAPME v Council and Commission* [1998] ECR II-2335; M Schmitt, 'La dimension sociale du Traité de Lisbonne' (2010) 6 *Droit Social* 694ff.

[18] Case T-135/96 *UEAPME v Council and Commission* [1998] ECR II-2335, para 89.

guaranteed in alternative ways, in this case by the social partners stipulating the agreement to which the Council—on the Commission's proposal—provides a legal basis.

A. Some Contradictions

It must be observed that the autonomy of the social partners has been compromised by the additional supervision requirement on the Commission, the Council and the Court[19] concerning the quality (representativeness) of the actors.

This is an unresolved problem in general, and which could be resolved, first, if Article 152 TFEU is interpreted in light of the EU Charter 2000–07 in terms of a reinforced role for management and labour in building a true system of industrial relations, as called for by the European Trade Union Confederation (ETUC).[20] The precondition is guaranteeing respect for transnational trade union rights—that is, the right of association and strike action at European level—amending Article 153(5) TFEU, as was also proposed by some members of Working Group XI on Social Europe 'as a logical consequence of the recognition of the autonomy of action of management and labour'.[21]

Secondly, another possible approach is to interpret Article 152 TFEU as a tool for 'anchoring the role and rights of the European social partners as co-regulators and their involvement in EU related decision-making procedures, in general as regards consultation and concertation, in all issues concerning their direct responsibilities'[22] and enlarging their competences.[23] A third road might be to reinforce the structural identity of the social dialogue providing for the establishment of a 'permanent European social partner infrastructure' to secure and develop institutionalised consultation and negotiation with them.[24]

The basic philosophy is still to promote and enhance horizontal subsidiarity, which poses the problem of the identity of co-regulators. The issue is hotly contested between the trade unions and the employers' associations.

The idea of autonomy implies freedom of the mechanism from any outside interference and the independence of the parties involved in the procedure.

[19] B Bercusson, 'Democratic legitimacy and European labour law' (1999) *Industrial Law Journal* 28.

[20] ETUC Executive Committee, 'A Constitutional Treaty for a Social and Citizens' Europe' (9–10 October 2002).

[21] CONV 516/1/03 REV 1 (n 4) para 68.

[22] ETUC Executive Committee, 'A Constitutional Treaty' (n 20) p 5.

[23] CONV 516/1/03 REV 1 (n 4) para 68.

[24] ETUC Executive Committee, 'A Constitutional Treaty' (n 20) p 5.

The Commission has adopted a realistic and pragmatic approach favouring the status quo on the grounds that 'a substantial body of experience' was already in place—the legacy of the democratic life of the Union—among ETUC, UNICE and the European Centre of Employers and Enterprises (CEEP). The Commission concluded in a study[25] that the diversity of practice in the different Member States is such that there is no single model that could be replicated at European level and different Members' national systems. But the Commission has tried to draw up some criteria for the purpose of consultation and has suggested that organisations should: (i) be cross-industry or relate to specific sectors or categories and be organised at European level; (ii) consist of organisations which are themselves an integral and recognised part of Member State social partners' structures and with the capacity to negotiate agreements and including representatives of all Member States as far as possible; and (iii) have adequate structures to ensure effective participation in the consultation.[26]

The European Economic and Social Committee (EESC) Opinion on the Commission's Communication proposed two alternative criteria: (i) to designate as representative EU-level social partners those organisations recognised by national social partners deemed representative by national law and practice; and (ii) the social partners at EU level are to be selected with regard to the nature of the process and the outcome of EU social dialogue. These would indicate transnational criteria linked to national partners and organisational capacity.[27] But the Commission was so respectful of the so-called 'autonomy of the parties' that it concluded that only the organisations themselves would be able to develop their dialogue and negotiating structure[28] and suggested leaving it to the social partners to decide who satisfies the criteria.[29]

B. More Effective 'Social Governance'

According to the Commission, social dialogue is the 'ideal instrument for the harmonious development of the Commission's social policy'[30] and, at

[25] COM(93) 600 final, 'Communication concerning the application of the Agreement on Social Policy' presented by the Commission to the Council and the European Parliament, Annex 3.

[26] COM(93) 600 final, 'Communication' (n 25), Annex 2, and COM(98) 322, Annex 1, in A Neal, *Cases and Materials*, vol 1 (Kluwer, 2002) 69–70.

[27] OJ 1994, C 397/40 para 2.1.12.

[28] COM(93) 600 final, 'Communication' (n 25) para 26.

[29] COM(96) 448 final, 'Development of the Social Dialogue at Community Level', para 17; COM(98) 322 final, 'Adapting and Promoting the Social Dialogue at Community level', para 18. A Neal, *Cases and Materials* (n 26) p 53; for a complete survey of the issue coordinated, at the request of the Commission, by the Institute des Sciences du Travail—Université Catholique de Louvain—see the Report on the representativeness of social partner organisations, Louvain, 1999, Part I.

[30] Commissioner Flynn cited in 'Social dialogue—The situation in the Community in 1995' (1995) 2 *Social Europe* 5.

the same time, it might also be a source of legitimacy for all parties involved in the law-making process at the Union level. An agreement between the social partners and the European Parliament on a framework of negotiating rules and principles would satisfy the 'sufficient representativity' test, preserving the autonomy of the social partners.[31]

This is a precondition for strengthening the overall architecture of the industrial relations system—consultation, information and collective bargaining—which could be developed in order to cope with a vast range of current issues: competitiveness and innovation with social cohesion, wage responsiveness, social inclusion and protection, training and lifelong learning, working conditions and work organisation, new forms of employment, working time management and the reconciliation of work and family life.

The proposals emerging from the 'Report of the High Level Group on Industrial Relations and Change in the European Union'[32] are intended to improve the role of the European level of collective relations with several instruments: interaction between EU and national and local level, for instance, if the European level identifies strategic issues to be addressed at decentralised levels; interaction between bipartite and tripartite processes at the European level enhancing both processes; interaction between the sectoral and inter-professional levels; and the creation of a new committee at the highest political level, close to the European spring councils, to rationalise and simplify consultation and concertation procedures.[33]

The philosophy underlying this reform project is implied in the general expression '*social governance*', in terms of which unions and employers' associations redefine the content of their traditional and private strategies in a 'public manner assuming wider responsibilities touching matters of general interest': the Irish Social Pact highlights that participation and inclusion are 'twin' goals and the Dutch Accord places the policies of employers and unions in the context of an 'activating labour market policy'.[34] The strategy can be exported at European level enlarging the scope of social dialogue to issues such as immigration, non-discrimination and ageing and the participation of civil society actors.

V. FEATURES AND PROBLEMS OF AUTONOMOUS SOCIAL DIALOGUE

Despite the trade unions' suggestions and the 'material constitution'—represented by the *acquis communautaire*—the road followed by the Lisbon

[31] Bercusson, 'Democratic legitimacy' (n 19) p 170.

[32] European Commission, 'Report of the High Level Group on Industrial Relations and Change in the European Union' DG Employment and Social Affairs, 2002.

[33] Ibid p 5

[34] Ibid p 6.

reform has been only partially satisfying. It seems like an 'interrupted discourse' with the social and labour law institutions acting on the European scene.

The *rationale* of the Lisbon Treaties' social democracy is a third piece in a coherent mosaic of a general idea of democracy.[35]

In the area of EU collective relations, the recognition of the social partners' role in primary law is much more than wishful thinking: it has legal force, in a twofold sense. From a juridical point of view it imposes a legal obligation on the EU with regard to collective private powers, while from a political perspective it affirms the role of EU institutions as a third neutral actor in the Community legal order.

A. Interpreting Article 152 TFEU

Article 152 TFEU hypothesises a pluralistic dimension of the framework of industrial relations at EU level and the relevance of its autonomous quality. It takes into account how the EU has changed over the past few years, proposing a new economic model—a social market economy—and enriched legal devices (horizontal subsidiarity and negotiated legislation, European collective agreements, European Works Councils, social dialogue) within a new political context: social governance and partnership.

It would therefore have been a good idea to include a more explicit statement in Article 152 TFEU in favour of promoting the role of the EU in recognising and facilitating a European industrial relations system supported above all by transnational trade union rights (information and consultation, freedom of assembly and association and so on). It is possible in any case to derive indirectly the recognition of a transnational dimension of collective actions via interpretation of the EU Charter.

In this perspective, it is possible to make sense of all the neutral words used in the lexical context of the Article, whose sober formulation requires first of all clarification about the actors. With regard to the social partners, the reference to 'the role … at its [that is, the EU] level', implies of course both already existing and future activities to be performed on the EU stage in the field of their concern (as indicated in Articles 153, 154 and 155 TFEU) and covering the traditional and historical features of an industrial relations model (consultation, co-regulation, collective negotiation, social dialogue).

With regard to the obligation of the EU to 'facilitate' social dialogue, historically it stems from the practice of involving social partners in economic

[35] CONV 516/1/03 REV 1 (n 4) para 7 contains the general principle of the explicit recognition of the social partners.

governance procedures, as suggested by the Macroeconomic Dialogue (Cologne 1999), the Luxembourg Employment Strategy (since 1997) and the social summit at European Council meetings.

B. How can one 'Facilitate' Dialogue and 'Respect the Autonomy' of the Social Partners?

The obligation to 'facilitate' has the internal limit of 'taking into account' also the 'diversity of national systems'. That means respecting also the autonomy of national social partners when they are implementing EU legal provisions and obligations. The obligation to respect may concern a vast range of activities—both external and internal to the 'zone' of freedom of the social partners as actors of the dialogue—which the EU could perform.

The word recalls the expression used in Article 154(1) TFEU where the duty of the Commission is laid down as 'ensuring balanced support for the parties'. The public commitment is inserted into a macro-consultation procedure on the possible direction of EU action within the framework of the direct interests of the social partners, as it is 'social policy'.

A systematic interpretation suggests that Article 2 TEU—by affirming a general principle of promoting the EU as a pluralistic and democratic society—illustrates the new 'constitutional' culture and imposes a larger obligation on its institutions, not only giving 'balanced support' to the parties, but 'respecting their autonomy'.

The strong principle fixed as a rule of primary law by Article 152 TFEU underlines the contradictory manner in which the Commission has in the past fulfilled its commitment to 'facilitate' the autonomous efforts of the management and labour within the dynamic process of the dialogue.[36]

On the one hand, it consists in external support for a procedure which is supposed to be the private affair of the social partners, although it needs a favourable attitude on the part of the EU. The relevant authorities can express themselves in various ways:

— By *welcoming* the wish of management and labour to pursue a 'more autonomous' dialogue to achieve the Lisbon objectives.
— By *encouraging* the use of all possibilities provided by many Directives with regard to issues to be fleshed out through negotiations at all relevant levels.
— By *stepping up* the support for bipartite social dialogue and by improving its visibility.
— By *assisting* the social partners in following up their text by promoting the sharing of experiences in follow-up activities.

[36] COM(2004) 557 final, 'Partnership' (n 16).

- By *reinforcing* financial support for joint follow-up actions by the European partners.
- By *encouraging* them to make greater use of peer review techniques inspired by the Open Method of Coordination (OMC).

On the other hand, the Commission seemed to temper its enthusiasm with regard to the ability and capacity of collective autonomy to build up a system of collective labour relations oriented towards EU law and principles.

The Commission seemed to draw a picture which is not in harmony with the dynamic relations between EU governing bodies and collective private powers, according to Title X on Social Policy.[37]

The new framework lays down a procedure inspired by the idea of the overwhelming presence of public institutions within the parties' initiative and their 'autonomous agreements'; in other words within an area traditionally reserved for collective forces.[38]

Two types of limit are imposed on the development of a dynamic and genuine industrial relations system. The *procedural* limits are represented by corresponding powers of the Commission:

- To *undertake* an ex-ante assessment of autonomous agreements before publishing them and to inform the EU Parliament and Council of Ministers.
- To *evaluate*—while giving precedence to monitoring initiated by the social partners themselves—upon the expiry of the implementation and monitoring period the extent to which it has contributed to the achievement of the EU's objectives.
- To *consider*, in the case of a negative judgement, the possibility of putting forward a proposal of a legislative act.
- To *exercise*, at any point, including the implementation period, the right of initiative if it guesses that the social partners are delaying the pursuit of Community objectives.

Substantial limits to autonomous agreements show how Commission intends to balance the dynamic between its prerogatives and the regulating role of the social partners. It underlines how preference should be given to the implementation of Council decisions:

- When fundamental rights or important political options are at stake.
- Where the rules must be applied in a uniform fashion in all Member States and the coverage must be complete.

[37] COM(2003) 843 final, 'Communication concerning the re-examination of Directive 93/104/EC concerning certain aspects of the organization of working time' (Brussels, 30.12.2003).

[38] COM(2004) 557 final, 'Partnership' (n 16) para 4.4.

— When autonomous agreements are not appropriate for the revision of previous Directives adopted by the Council and the European Parliament through the normal legislative procedure.

C. Limits to Social Autonomy?

Procedural and substantial limits seem to contradict the proclaimed and reiterated respect for the role of collective freedom. The Commission has no intention of playing a secondary role within the collective bargaining process, despite the rather emphatic and rhetorical deference foreshadowed in the 12 August 2004 Communication. Sentences such as 'fully recognises the negotiating autonomy of social parties', 'while respecting the principle of autonomy', 'while giving precedence to the monitoring undertaken by the social parties themselves' and 'while recognising the broad scope of the social competences' (4.4) have the flavour of mere 'ceremonial (ritual) clauses'.

Articles 154 (ex-Article 138 TEC) and 155 (ex-Article 139 TEC) TFEU seem to be considered by the Commission as 'empty boxes' to be filled with procedural powers and substantive regulations—not expressed by the present EU legal system—and in some way as infringing a bipartite dialogue considered and qualified as 'autonomous'. According to the last reform (Lisbon Treaty) the European Parliament has the right to be informed but no formal power to suggest amendments to an agreement (Article 155(2) TFEU); the Commission does not have express power to interfere in the implementation and monitoring period of the agreement which is a task of collective parties deeply interested in reaching the objective of their negotiating strategy. The Commission neither has distinct discretionary power to exercise a right of initiative 'at any time, including during the implementation period' or to do so on the ground that the agreement does 'not succeed in meeting the Community objectives'.[39]

The envisaged model represents a serious threat to the autonomy of social dialogue. The freedom of the partners and solidarity seem more conditioned by substantive limits: who judges when political options are so important that they must restrict the scope of competences of social partners or which rights are to be considered fundamental? Should management and labour not be allowed to bargain on the right to strike, collective bargaining structure and association? Who decides the meaning of 'social market economy' and what are appropriate legal measures (legislation or collective agreements) for achieving this goal?

[39] Ibid.

A correct approach to the rationale of Article 152 TFEU could give an adequate response to these open questions using the method of systematic interpretation and '*effet-utile*' which links the same Article to the legal recognition of the freedom of collective autonomy clearly proclaimed in Title IV of the EU Charter.

VI. SOCIAL PARTNERS AND EUROPEAN EMPLOYMENT STRATEGY

The Lisbon Summit 2000 agreed on a strategic goal for the Union for the decade in an effort to promote: 'more and better jobs and greater social cohesion'.[40]

Part Three Title IX TFEU reproduces the overall strategy without changes. Ex-Title VIII EC and ex-Article 125 EC (now Article 145 TFEU) mirror and formalise the Essen process and the emerged European Employment Strategy. The position of employment policy, close to economic policy (Title VIII TFEU), both embedded in the general Part Three (Union Policies and internal actions), still reflects the economic 'mortgage' which has conditioned the social policy culture since the Community's beginning. Employment and related strategies are still complementary to economic strategies, despite the fact that 'full employment' is proclaimed as one of the EU's objectives (Article 3(3) TEU) and a social market economy is an ideological pillar of its internal culture.

A. More Centralised Control of the Labour Market

The lack of any linkage between economic and employment strategy is not made good, as has been suggested by the ETUC Executive Committee, by proposing employment mainstreaming as part of the Broad Economic Policy Guidelines; rather the latter must be 'consistent with the employment guidelines adopted pursuant to [ex-]Article 128'[41] EC (now Article 148 TFEU).

The formula adopted in Article 146(1) TFEU (ex-Article 126 EC) reverses the terms of the sequence and priority given to economic guidelines on employment issues which 'shall be consistent with the broad guidelines adopted pursuant to Article 121(2) TFEU'. The real protagonist of the scene is the Council acting on a recommendation from the Commission (Article 121(2) TFEU).

[40] Lisbon Presidency Conclusions, para 5, confirmed by the Commission in its 'Social Policy Agenda 2000–2005' COM (2000)379 final, 28 June 2000, section 1-2 in A Neal, *European Labour Law and Social Policy*, vol I (Deventer-Boston: Kluwer, 2002) 255.

[41] ETUC Executive Committee, 'A Constitutional Treaty' (n 20) p 8.

The entire architecture of the European Employment Strategy (EES) is inspired by the idea of centralised control of the labour market as part of the economic performance of the European single market,[42] so that under the Council the 'employment title is founded on a decentralising conception of subsidiarity in which the Union enables and the member states deliver'. The procedure includes, after the reform decided in Lisbon, also the Parliament (Article 149 TFEU, ex-Article 129 EC), although the Commission still has the role of a supporting player.[43]

However, it essentially marginalises the role of social dialogue and gives the social partners merely a right to be consulted by the Employment Committee (Article 150(2) TFEU). The Committee is a centralised mirror of the national labour market and all its tasks concern proactive functions:

— Advisory status to promote coordination between Member States on employment and labour market policy.
— Monitoring both the employment situation and policy in Member States and the EU.
— Without prejudice to Article 240 TFEU, formulating opinions at the request of either the Council or the Commission or on its own initiative, as well as contributing to preparation of the Council's proceedings referred to in Article 148 TFEU.

B. A Limited Role for the Social Partners

The role of the players in the EES is designed in a contradictory way, reading the dense rules dealing with the Employment Title (Articles 145–150 TFEU). In fact:

— The coordination of strategies for employment and for promoting an efficient labour market belongs both to the EU and the Member States, based on a—correct—analysis that the completion of the internal market is under pressure from globalisation, enterprise and sectoral restructuring and diversification of national and regional labour markets.
— The procedure is bottom-up: employment is a matter of *common concern* of the Member States and the EU, whose task is to develop 'a coordinated strategy' to promote employment and improve the quality of the workforce.

[42] R Pena-Casas, 'European employment and social inclusion policies amidst the crisis: an opportunity for the future?' in C Degryse (ed), *Social Developments in the European Union 2009* (Brussels: ETUI, 2010) 9.

[43] J Kenner, *EU Employment Law. From Rome to Amsterdam and Beyond* (Oxford and Portland, OR: Hart, 2003) 388.

— The engine for employment policy remains primarily the national level, although the EU is to encourage cooperation between Member States (Article 147(1) TFEU (ex-Article 127 EC).

Furthermore, EU law recognises that at national level the social partners' responsibility is important, having 'regard to national practices' (Article 146(2) TFEU). This sentence contains a realistic acknowledgement of the historical role of the unions as 'owners' of the labour market strategy and controllers of workforce flows and skills.

The contradiction is striking for two reasons. First, attention must be paid to the Council's statement that '[t]he effective implementation of the employment guidelines requires active participation of social partners, at all stages, from designing policies to their implementation'.[44] A second reason is the model of *social pacts*, widespread in most European countries since the beginning of the 1990s, dealing with employment and competitiveness. They constitute an innovative approach to bipartite or tripartite bargaining strategy.[45]

Despite this appreciation of trade unions' responsibilities the EU neglects a more active role for the social partners within the so-called OMC established in 1997 and now encapsulated in the TFEU (Articles 148–50, ex-Articles 128–130 EC). Their ancillary position is described in terms of a mere duty of the Employment Committee to 'consult management and labour' (Article 150(2) TFEU). Compared with the qualified objective that the Union should bring about 'full employment' (Article 3 TEU), the mechanism to achieve this objective is extraordinary fragile in the absence of social partnership which could ensure a preventive social consensus on European decision-making. In fact, the intervention of the social partners as protagonists is placed at the end of the entire OMC procedure; they do not take part in the phases of adoption of conclusions by the European Council, consultation concerning the implementation of national employment policies and of adoption of guidelines which the Member States must take into account.

Here is an 'open space' for the EU in fulfilling its positive obligations stemming from Article 152 TFEU to 'promote' a proactive role for the social partners, whose right is provided for by Article 12 CFREU.

It would have been more consistent with national trade union traditions and with their responsibilities—clearly envisaged in the consultation procedure enshrined in Article 154 TFEU—to allow both actors in the labour

[44] Council Decision of 22 July 2003 on guidelines for the employment policies of the Member States, 2003/578/EC, [2003] OJ 197/13.

[45] E Leonard and P Renan, 'Jobs, jobs, jobs: ambivalence of concerted change for employment in Europe' (2004) 4 *Transfer* 560.

market to be present, in a more institutionalised way, at the moment of decision 'on the possible direction of EU action' (Article 154(2) TFEU).

The lack of courage shown in reshaping the institutional apparatus of OMC can be explained on the basis of a number of political considerations, such as the subordination of employment guidelines to monetary and economic guidelines (Stability Pact), the tendency to reach a forced compromise between national self-interest and the pride of national clubs as managers of labour and the centralistic option of governing supranational bodies. This trend was strongly emphasised by the recent financial crisis which generated a significant rise in income inequality and poverty.

The debates at EU level reveal the real obstacles to overcome. A Commission Communication (mid-January 2003) indicates a vast range of priorities but no links are established between employment and social protection.[46]

C. EU Commission: Ambiguities and Good Intentions

The delicacy of the subject matter is proved by the circumstance that discussion inside the Convention's Working Group XI on Social Europe did not touch on the integrity of the model as established at the Lisbon 2000 European Council and welcomed the efficiency and usefulness of the method.[47] A change in the role of the actors was not considered, despite the strong emphasis put on this in the Commission Communication of September 2002,[48] taking into account, among the priorities adopted at the Barcelona European Council, the need 'to reinforce the role and responsibility of the social partners in implementing and monitoring the guidelines'.[49]

The past history of the Employment Guidelines indicates that the Commission has encouraged direct social partner involvement—and not only at national level—in supporting the employment pillar. The words used mirror a semantic seesaw between hesitancy and regression, foreshadowing the lack of a legally defined role for collective autonomy. On the one hand, parties are 'called on' to conclude a framework agreement to create jobs devoted to training, work experience and apprenticeships[50] and on

46 P Pochet, 'The European employment strategy at the crossroads' in *Social Developments in the European Union* (Bruxelles: ETUI, 2003) 87.

47 CONV 516/1/03 REV 1 (n 4) para 40.

48 Commission Communication, 'The European social dialogue, a force for innovation and change' COM(2002) 341 final; Commission Communication, 'Adapting and promoting the social dialogue at Community level' COM(1998) 322 final.

49 Presidency Conclusions, Barcelona European Council, 2002, p 11.

50 Commission Guidelines for 1998 COM(97) 497 final, point III, Employability.

the other hand they are 'exhorted' to quickly conclude agreements on the modernisation of work organisation.[51]

The Commission has reiterated that the European Council in Santa Naria de Feira (June 2000) invited the social partners to 'play a more prominent role in defining, implementing and evaluating the employment guidelines'.[52]

In this perspective the social partners 'should negotiate and agree to improve education and lifelong learning for adults and to promote the adaptability of workers'.[53] There must also be a commitment at the European level where the social partners are invited to define their own contributions and to monitor, encourage and support efforts undertaken at national level.[54]

This perspective is less ambiguous when the Commission recognises that the social 'partnership at all appropriate levels is crucial for the modernisation of the organisation of work and the promotion of the adaptability of undertakings and their employees'.[55]

It seems clear that the European Employment Strategy requires a broad involvement at institutional level and a specific commitment of all actors with social responsibility in governing and protecting social citizenship: better governance is above all social governance, demanding a direct contribution from the 'social partners and other relevant actors'.[56]

In the same perspective, the Commission has considered a 'global partnership' involving EU institutions—including 'our social partners'[57]—to move towards a common goal, clearly recalling the constitutional vision of Article 3(3) TEU (social progress, full employment and competitive social market economy) and to deliver 'stronger, lasting growth and creating more and better jobs'.[58]

The objectives are ambitious and the intentions worthy if we bear in mind that it requires a reshaping of some features of labour law and labour market institutions: attracting more people into employment, modernising social protection systems, improving adaptability of workers and labour market flexibility and investing in human capital through education and training.

[51] COM(97) 676 final.

[52] 'Proposal for a Council Decision on guidelines for Member States' employment policies for the year 2001' COM(2000) 548 final, 'Proposal for a Council Decision', recital 7.

[53] COM(2000) 548 final (n 52), Annex lit. B.

[54] COM(2000) 548 final (n 52), Annex lit. C.

[55] COM(2001) 512 final, 'Recommendation for a Council Recommendation on the Implementation of Member States' Employment Policies', recital 19.

[56] COM(2002) 621 final, p 109.

[57] COM(2005) 24, 'Working together for growth and jobs—A new start for the Lisbon strategy' p 3.

[58] Ibid p 7.

The institutional mechanism is in the hands of the social partners and the Member States: the 'new idea' is that the strategy must be taken forward through a changed partnership between Member States and the EU, with the full involvement of management and labour, from the top to local level.

However, despite the proclaimed intentions—refocused by the Commission in its strategic programme for 2005–2009[59] and underlined by the values laid down as ideological bases of its reform (prosperity, solidarity and security)—the institutional mechanism to boost the economy (growth) and labour law (employment) is still lacking a social partner presence at the EU level.

The Commission openly expresses the idea that to enhance reforms it is necessary to 'tak[e] on board ... all the various players' at national level.[60] With regard to the EU level, the Commission has 'the central role of initiating policy and ensuring implementation [working] closely with the Parliament and Council, as well as drawing on the expertise of the other institutions, such as the European Economic and Social Committee [and] the Committee of the Regions'.[61]

At this top level, the social partners are nevertheless absent from the crucial phases of the whole procedure of the formation of the EES and their role consists simply of 'draw[ing] up their own multi-annual Lisbon programme for growth and jobs using powers granted to them under the Treaty'.[62]

This power has now been granted by Article 152 TFEU.

VII. SOCIAL POLICY AND SOCIAL PARTNERS

A. A Cooperative System of EU Industrial Relations

More generally, the new European culture is expressed by the Commission Communication referring to the idea of social dialogue contributing to 'building *consensus*'.[63] Any sustainable reform requires investment in 'political capital' and efforts to develop intelligent and effective institutions, indispensable for which is a genuine partnership for change on the part of European and national social partners.[64]

This political strategy implies an effort to resolve two main problems on which its success strongly depends: (i) the presence of institutional

[59] COM(2005) 12 final, 'Europe 2010: A Partnership for European Renewal. Prosperity, Solidarity and Security'.

[60] COM(2005) 24, 'Working together' (n 57) p 14.

[61] Ibid p 15.

[62] Ibid p 31.

[63] COM(2004) 557 final, 'Partnership' (n 16) p 12.

[64] Ibid p 6, para 2.4.

mechanisms to build up a genuine and cooperative system of industrial relations at European level and (ii) the competences in the 'social policy field' of the European social partners in the new Treaties.

For the purpose of this analysis, the points of departure are as follows:

(a) The common concerns of the EU and the Member States; that is, the social policy objectives provided for by Article 151(1) TFEU (ex-Article 136(1) EC): promotion of employment, improved living and working conditions, proper social protection, dialogue between social partners, development of human resources and combating exclusion.
(b) The idea that all the abovementioned objectives can be reached by 'procedures provided for in the Treaties', Article 151(3) TFEU (ex-Article 136(3) EC).

The Lisbon reform has introduced 'only tiny improvements'[65] in the field of social competences between the EU and the Member States and a limited role for the social partners. The range of social policy issues is vast and touches all aspects of labour law and industrial relations, while employment—intended as a strategy for managing the labour market in all its complexity—has received particular attention in a different section of the TFEU as a specific area (Part Three Title IX).

Labour law and industrial relations therefore suffer from this artificial framework dealing separately with subjects that share the same historical and legal roots in all European countries.

However, the institutional mechanisms for promoting social policy in the Treaties reflect the idea that social policy is a matter of shared competence between the EU and Member States.[66]

In fact, to achieve its social policy objectives, the EU 'supports and complements' national activities throughout: (i) the legislative procedure of the European Parliament and the Council to encourage cooperation between Member States (improving knowledge, developing exchanges of information and best practices promoting innovative approaches end evaluating experiences), in other words, using the OMC, already envisaged as a method to support cooperation in the field of employment and labour market (Article 149 TFEU); and (ii) Directives and minimum requirements for gradual implementation adopted by the European Parliament and the Council with regard to issues indicated in Article 153(1) TFEU (letters *a* to *i*) which, in principle, covers all aspects of labour law and industrial relations.

It sounds odd in this perspective that social actors seem to be excluded from a procedure dealing with important topics historically managed and regulated also by trade unions and employers' confederations.

[65] See Lörcher (ch 6 in this volume).

[66] All members of Working Group XI 'felt that social matters should remain an area of shared competence', CONV 516/1/03 REV 1 (n 4) para 27.

In fact, the exclusive motor of the procedure is European law and an ancillary role is played by the Economic and Social Committee which participates in the formation of 'ordinary legislative procedure' (Article 153(2) TFEU).

B. OMC and the Social Partners

A more detailed analysis of the final report of the Convention's Working Group XI and point (b) of Article III-210 of the Constitution 2004—now Article 153 TFEU—can open up a rather different perspective and generate different conclusions. Of course, the Group stressed:

— The role of the OMC as an instrument 'which supplements legislative action' by the Union but 'under no circumstances replaces it'.[67]
— Its nature: its incorporation into the Constitution—and now into the Treaties—as a non-legislative measure.[68]
— Its function: the need to bestow transparency and democracy on its structure and to clarify its procedures by designating the actors and their respective roles.[69]

However, on two points the draft final report was quite clear in opening up space for a more active role for the social partners. First, according to the view that OMC is an instrument for achieving the Union's objectives it can be implemented where the Union does not have legislative competence and where its competence in the area of sectoral competence is not enshrined in the Treaty or 'where the Union has competence only for defining minimum rules, in order to go beyond these rules'.[70]

The second point deals with the procedure for implementing the method: decisions by Member States within the Council, conclusions of the European Council, initiatives of the Commission, notification of the European Parliament, consultation of national parliaments and local authorities and 'the social partners when the OMC is applied to the social field'.[71]

These suggestions are mirrored in the rationale of Article 152 TFEU and consider the wide breadth of the principle, namely that the OMC can be used also in the social field, as it is mirrored within Article 153(2)(b) TFEU which specifies that the European Parliament and Council 'may adopt, in the

[67] CONV 516/1/03 REV 1 (n 4) para 43.
[68] Ibid para 42.
[69] Ibid para 44.
[70] Ibid para 43.
[71] Ibid. In the Preliminary draft report (WG XI WD 038 Rev.1) the model of such a clause was presented by Professor Vandenbroucke, p 15, para 13.

field referred to in paragraph 1(*a*) to (*i*), by means of directives, minimum requirements'.

If one wants to read Article 153 TFEU in this light we can conclude that the OMC can only change *in melius* the minimum requirements promoting higher standards in all topics referred in (1)(*a*) to (*i*). The OMC can operate entirely freely in the last two fields where there is no provision for legislative minimum standards: combating social exclusion (*j*) and modernisation of social protection systems (*k*).

These two fields are those most frequently exposed to the wind of crisis and do not escape the constraints of EMU and the economic turbulence that affects the substance of labour law rights and welfare protection (see Bruun, chapter eight in this volume). Here the recognition of the legal nature of the EU Charter can sustain collective autonomy in the field of employment policy at two levels: (i) the participation of the social partners in the procedural steps of OMC and (ii) the use of rules of the Charter as legal parameters of decisions taken both by the Union and the Member States implementing the OMC.

VIII. OMC AND SOCIAL DIALOGUE

It is clear that the OMC is not a substitute for all legal instruments envisaged by the Treaties, including those stemming from social dialogue agreements. But it does not exclude possible links between the OMC architecture (guidelines, indicators, exchange of practice, monitoring and evaluation and national plans) and social dialogue mechanisms because both instruments operate within the same area of social policy, where unions and employers' confederations and their members have direct, relevant interests: industrial relations (right of association and collective bargaining), terms and conditions of employment (working time, atypical work) and welfare systems.

That is why, moreover, the Convention's Working Group XI on Social Europe took the view that the role of employees' and employers' organisations, already included in the Treaties, 'should be recognised, facilitated and—as far as possible—enhanced with horizontal subsidiarity'. The Group also agreed[72] that the role should have been formally specified in Title VI of the Constitutional Treaty. The last suggestion has not been followed, however, and now also Article 302(2) TFEU (ex-Article 259(2) EC) provides only for a possible consultative role of the social partners foreshadowed by the rather vague formula according to which the Council 'may obtain the opinion of the European bodies which are representative of the various economic and social sectors'.

[72] CONV 516/1/03 REV 1 (n 4) para 66.

The correct implementation of the positive obligations deriving from Article 152 TFEU consists in respecting the procedural requirement to really fair, correct and timely information and consultation.

Which are the links between OMC and social governance?

Two types of links between OMC and social dialogue are possible: substantial and procedural. The first (substantial) link means that processes and measures of OMC in social policy should be replicated in the form of framework agreements deriving from social dialogue at EU level,[73] implemented at Member State level throughout the formula 'in accordance with the practices and procedures specific to management and labour and the Member States' (Article 155(2) TFEU, ex-Article 139(2) EC). The second (procedural-institutional) link is suggested by the Communication from the Commission which 'encourages the social partners to make greater use of peer review techniques inspired by the open method of coordination for following up these texts, for example by setting targets (quantitative, where feasible) or benchmarks, and regularly reporting on progress made towards achieving them'.[74]

It seems clear that framework agreements belong to the category of transnational tools,[75] in other words private 'autonomous agreements'—such as the framework agreements mentioned above and on a European licence for drivers performing a cross-border service (2004).[76] The social partners are legally responsible for implementing and monitoring them and the signatory parties shall exert influence on their members to implement it. In fact, an autonomous agreement can also deal with procedural provisions whereby European partners set up a peer committee to make recommendations to their members for follow-up, involving regular evaluation of the progress made towards achieving their objectives and cooperation with public authorities. Such agreements can contain the exchange of good practice and mutual learning and, as process-oriented texts, 'sometimes help to prepare the ground for future [Union] legislation'.[77]

The emphasis on autonomy and innovation with regard to relations between the social partners has been underlined with the same intensity by the Commission.[78]

[73] B Bercusson, 'The Charter of Fundamental Rights and Constitution of the European Union' in B Bercusson (ed), *European Labour Law and the EU Charter of Fundamental Rights* (Baden-Baden: Nomos, 2006) 482ff.

[74] COM(2004) 557 final, 'Partnership' (n 16) para 4.3.

[75] European Commission (ed), Expert Group, 'Transnational Collective Bargaining: Past, Present and Future, Final Report' 2006, p 13.

[76] See: ec.europa.eu/employment_social/dsw/public/actRetrieveText.do?id=8787.

[77] COM(2004) 557 final, 'Partnership' (n 16) p 16.

[78] Ibid p 4 (Introduction); see also 3.1.

A. Strong Legal Support for the Social Partners

The evolution described supports the efforts of the Commission to achieve better governance at all levels, including the EU level. The analysis is correct but it contrasts sharply with the fragile legal web of rules which should sustain efficient and concrete actions on the part of management and labour in the supranational dimension.[79] Today, the recognition of a collective bargaining right at supranational level, as laid down in Article 28 CFREU, is a strong legal device governing the activities of the social partners at EU level, which operates jointly with Article 152 TFEU.

Ex-Article 137(5) EC still survives in Article 153(5) TFEU, even though it was at the core of the debate in the Convention's Working Group XI. The exceptions provided for dealing with the quality of rights concerned—that is, their political (right of association, right to strike and to lock out) and economic (pay) nature—in some ways are closely linked to national and European systems of industrial relations. Article 153 TFEU explicitly excludes the adoption of measures on those rights, using the procedure provided for within the framework of the same Article. But it does not rule out the possibility of adopting measures under other provisions of the Treaties. The Article seems to limit *only partially* EU competence over the matter in question and nothing excludes that a different set of rules can be used to deal with the same matters. As stated by Working Group XI:

> Although [ex] Article 137(5) [EC] rules out the adoption of a uniform minimum requirement on pay, it does not rule out the possibility of adopting measures under other provisions of the Treaty, even if these measures have an impact on pay. The result is that a number of Community instruments contain provisions on pay.[80]

B. Transnational Collective Labour Rights and the EU Charter

The EU Charter—now legally binding—could have an impact on this problem. The nature of its insertion (reference in Article 6(1) TEU to a text published in the 'C' [Communications] part of the OJ) and the quality of its rights and principles testify to the quasi-constitutional status of the Charter. This new placement means that:

— The primacy of EU law with regard to national legal orders of the Member States 'only when they are implementing Union law' (Article 51(1) CFREU) has been restated.

[79] Transnational Collective Bargaining Group (n 75) p 13.
[80] CONV 516/1/03 REV 1 (n 4) para 28.

— A new coordination of its rules—that is, concerning labour law and industrial relations—with the remaining part of the Treaties text, including those dealing with the Title IV on Solidarity, is required.

The Convention's Working Group II confirmed that the incorporation does not alter the equilibrium of competences between the EU and the Member States, but it also said that

> the fact that certain rights concern areas in which the Union has little or no competence to act is not in contradiction to it, given that, although the Union's competences are limited, it must respect all fundamental rights wherever it acts and therefore avoid indirect interference also with such fundamental rights on which it would not have the competence to legislate.[81]

At the moment, a more appropriate instrument could be social dialogue as an original tool of improved consultation and the implementation of horizontal subsidiarity.

But to allow social dialogue and industrial relations to freely develop at EU level provision should be made to ensure the full recognition of a set of transnational trade union rights.

There are several arguments in favour of recognition of a transnational right to strike as strongly supporting the social partners' strategy at EU and national level (see Kollonay-Lehoczky, Lörcher and Schömann, chapter three in this volume). In the era of the globalisation and internationalisation of markets companies are relocating their production in different states and artificially dividing into a number of discrete corporate entities or 'buffer companies' to avoid labour law and industrial relations institutions (collective representation of the workforce, collective bargaining and strong trade unions). In other words, the changing face of the economy threatens the solidarity which is part of the genetic code of labour law and all defensive legal devices.

The right to strike in theoretical terms is a political weapon insofar as it provides workers with an opportunity to participate in the industrial, economic and political life of society as whole. This is shown by those European countries in which the legal—constitutional—recognition of the freedom (and right) to engage in industrial conflict is essentially linked to freedom of association.[82] It is also true that the ILO Committee on Freedom of Association has stated that 'a declaration of the illegality of a national strike protesting against the social and labour consequences of the government's

[81] CONV 354/02, 'Final report of Working Group II' p 5 (2).

[82] ATJM Jacobs, 'The law of strikes and lock outs' in Blanpain and Engels (eds), *Comparative Labour Law and Industrial Relations in Industrialized Market Economies* (n 13) 585; R Ben Israel, *International Labour Standards: The Case of Freedom of Strike* (Deventer: Kluwer, 1988) 26; T Novitz, *International and European Protection of the Right to Strike* (Oxford: OUP, 2003) 55ff.

economic policy and the banning of the strike constitutes a serious violation of freedom of association'.[83]

From the viewpoint of industrial relations, however, the weapon of industrial action is coordinated not only within the framework of the collective bargaining process, but more generally in a larger socio-political perspective: the bigger and more interwoven are the interests implied in the continuous process of market integration, the more urgent it is to respond with adequate legal means supporting all kind of union powers at national as well as, of course, at European level.

'There is a greater scope for cross-border solidarity action, that is, action in support of another strike against another employer'[84] and of course recourse to such action is legitimate as far as the secondary action is legally recognised in the respective country. The principle has been expressed clearly by the ILO Committee of Experts, which stated that 'a general prohibition on sympathy strikes could lead to abuse and workers should be able to take such action, provided the initial strike they are supporting is in itself lawful'.[85]

It is true that legislation in only a few Member States makes specific reference to international disputes and conditions for their lawfulness.

Greek law 1264/82 (Article 19(1)) recognises explicitly a right to strike on the grounds of solidarity in support of workers in different companies or establishments belonging to the same multinational firm as the workers coming out in sympathy. But the outcome of the dispute must have an immediate impact on the economic and professional interests of Greek workers and it must be approved by the relevant national labour confederations.[86] The Trade Union and Labour Relations (Consolidation) Act 1992 (TULRCA) of the United Kingdom, on the other hand, recognises that a trade dispute may exist under English law even though it relates to matters occurring outside the UK (section 244(3) TULRCA): the principle ruling the action is the same as the previous example, which is that British workers must be 'likely to be affected', in respect of one or more of the matters specified in the law (section 244(1) of TULRCA), by the outcome of the dispute overseas. In addition, however, a more stringent condition is that both British and overseas workers 'must share the same employers'.

Of course, this last condition is more restrictive in the UK—where the law refers to 'the employer under contract of employment' (section 224(2)

[83] ILO, Freedom of Association: Digest of decisions and principles of the Freedom of Association Committee of the Governing Body of ILO, 5th revised edn (Geneva, 2006) para 542.

[84] Novitz, *Right to Strike* (n 82) p 12.

[85] ILO, 'Freedom of association and collective bargaining. General survey of the reports on the freedom of association and protection of the right to organise', Convention 1948 (no 87) and 'The right to organise and collective bargaining convention', 1949 (no 98), Report III (part 4B), International Labour Conference, 81st Session, 1994, Geneva, 1994a, para 168.

[86] Y Kravaritou, 'Greece, National Report' in EUC (ed), *The Regulation of Working Conditions in the Member States of the European Union*, vol II (Luxembourg, EC, 1998) 67.

TULRCA)—than the one used by Greek law, that is, 'enterprises controlled by the same multinational'.[87]

The evolution of the European economic integration process underlines that the last English condition ('same employer') seems inadequate to protect modern labour conflicts which involve different qualities and quantities of interests, functions, identities and subjects (Societas Europaea, transnational enterprises, multinational holdings, multi-employer strategies, transnational collective bargaining structure, European employment policies and institutions, such as social dialogue). It also seems inadequate to use the golden formula of 'community (or affinity) of interests' between workers involved in the primary action and those supporting them with secondary action, as required in southern European countries to ascertain the lawfulness of sympathy strikes.[88]

This old device, used in the past to regulate social phenomena, gives rise to dilemmas with regard to the assessment of the lawfulness of foreign conflict: to use the criteria prevailing in the foreign country in question or national criteria or something in between, as happens in some judicial decision in Nordic countries, such as Sweden, but also in Germany. In other words, the view that cross-border solidarity strikes within groups of companies are acceptable as long as they do not breach the duty of the parties to a collective agreement to maintain industrial peace as long as the agreement lasts.[89]

The formula of the affinity of interests needs to be read in light of a European dimension—not only in purely economic terms—and the value of solidarity must be interpreted as intended in the EU Charter. The answer with regard to the lawfulness of solidaristic collective action at European level can be found by taking into account all the elements supporting the idea of an international strike as co-essential to a new European framework of industrial relations.

The expression 'affinity of interests' therefore needs to be read in light of the new European dimension of industrial relations institutions as they have been enriched recently. The kinds of interests involved concern, among other things:

(a) The functioning of European works councils.
(b) The problems raised by the Posted Workers Directive.
(c) The functioning of social dialogue.
(d) The development of an EU collective agreement.

[87] See Council of Europe (ed), European Committee of Social Rights (ECSR), *Conclusions XIV-1* (Article 6 §4, United Kingdom, p 804ff) ruling that taking action only against 'their' employer makes impossible for the trade unions to take action, inter alia, against the company which is their true 'employer' but which may hire the workers through an intermediary company'.

[88] N Bruun and B Veneziani, 'The right or freedom to transnational industrial action in the European Union' in ETUI, *A Legal Framework for European Industrial Relations* (Brussels: ETUI, 1999) 80.

[89] Ibid p 82.

(e) Multinational companies closing plants at both national and EU level.
(f) An enterprise crisis affecting workers in one area but also affecting another area.

International and EU confederations have called for legal intervention at EU level, but UNICE is against it.[90]

More recently, new international relations with regard to production and marketing have enhanced the importance of transportation and seem to have given impulse to the legal regulation of international solidarity action.[91]

Recent examples include: *Viking*,[92] *Laval*,[93] *Rüffert*[94] and *Commission v Luxembourg*.[95]

These represent clear-cut examples of social dumping and the paradox with regard to the *Viking* and *Laval* cases is that strike action is protected by the Finnish and Swedish constitutions as a right. The strength of this guarantee runs the risk of being weakened at EU level, even though in all countries it constitutes an essential part of the life and vitality of collective labour.

Once more, two common market objectives, both provided for in the TFEU, are in conflict: the free movement of services (Article 56 TFEU ex-Article 49 EC) and the right of establishment (Article 49 TFEU ex-Article 43 EC), on one side, and social policy objectives guaranteeing decent living and working conditions and proper social protection (Article 151 TFEU), on the other. In the previous cases *Albany*, *Brentjens* and *Drijvende Bokken*, as well in the later *Pavlov* and *Van der Woude*,[96] the two opposed market institutions were collective agreements and competition rules: the decision expressed the view that the former were protected from the latter.

But the five cases quoted above represent the start of a new era: the contrast is between employers' economic freedoms and the principle of solidarity, a typical 'Gordian knot' which national judges were not prepared to cut, accepting that collective industrial action is protected in the same way in

[90] European Parliament (ed), DG Research, 'Strikes and secondary industrial action in the EU member states', Working Paper no 8, Luxembourg, 1995, p 26. See also J Atleson, 'The voyage of Neptun Jade. Transnational labour solidarity and the obstacle of domestic law' in J Conaghan, RM Fischl and K Klare (eds), *Labour Law in an Era of Globalization* (Oxford: OUP, 2002) 379.

[91] P Germanotta and T Novitz, 'Globalisation and the right to strike: the case for European-level protection of secondary action' (2002) 18(1) *IJCLLIR* 69.

[92] Case C-438/05 *Viking* [2007] ECR I-10779.

[93] Case C-341/05 *Laval un Partneri* [2007] ECR I-11767.

[94] Case C-346/06 *Rüffert* [2008] ECR I-1989.

[95] Case C-319/06 *Commission v Luxembourg* [2008] ECR I-4323.

[96] Cases C-67/96 *Albany* [1999] ECR I-5751; C-115–117/97 *Brentjens* [1999] ECR I-6025; C-219/97 *Drijvende Bokken* [1999] ECR I-6121 [2000]; C-180–184/98 *Pavlov* ECR I-6451 and C-222/98 *Van der Woude* [2000] ECR I-7111.

the EU legal order, in which a new culture prevails today. The Community Charter (No 13), the EU Charter, ILO Conventions and the (Revised) Social Charter of the Council of Europe (1961 and 1996), although not all legally binding, sustain the right to collective action.

The so-called 'Monti Regulation', aimed at preventing the free movement of goods from being obstructed by the actions of private individuals, clearly states that it 'may not be interpreted as affecting in any way the exercise of fundamental rights as recognised in Member States, including the right to strike' (Article 2).[97]

The statement is not sufficient to give the transnational right to industrial conflict full citizenship in the EU legal system. One cannot exclude that some cases might involve collective interests more frequently in the future so that the European trade union movement has proposed inserting a last sentence into Article 2 of the Regulation: 'These rights may also include the right or freedom to take other actions covered by specific industrial relations systems in Member States'. This is in the direction of the suggestion clearly expressed in the recent 'Monti Report'.[98]

C. How to Build Social Consensus at EU Level

The emerging idea in the European *milieu* is that the EU authorities are engaged in 'building consensus' at EU level, encouraging close cooperation between the social partners, improving social dialogue 'by enhancing the synergies between the various sectors as well as between the European cross-industry and sectoral levels in the relevant area (lifelong learning, work organisation) or company level (environmental responsibilities) linked to employment issues'.[99] The current model of European industrial relations includes a mix of past legal ('formal' legal Community social order) and informal *acquis* ('material' or 'substantive' Community social order).

The whole set of information and participation rights has been guaranteed by law in a historically meaningful sequence: European Works Council (EWC) Directive (1994);[100] Directive on employee involvement in the

[97] Council Regulation (EC) No 2679/98 of 7 December 1998 on the functioning of the internal market in relation to the free movement of goods among the member states, [1998] OJ L 337/8 (the 'Monti Regulation'); see also S Clauwaert, *International/Transnational Primary and Secondary Collective Action* (Brussels: ETUI, 2001) 9.

[98] M Monti, 'A new strategy for the single market—At the service of Europe's economy and society', Report to the President of the European Commission, 9 May 2010, p 70.

[99] COM(2004) 557 final, 'Partnership' (n 16).

[100] Directive 94/45/EC of 22 September 1994 on the establishment of a European Works Council or a procedure in Community-scale undertakings and Community-scale groups of undertakings for the purposes of informing and consulting employees, [1994] OJ L 254/64.

European company (2001),[101] to be read together with the Statute on the European company containing rules on company law;[102] Directive on the minimum framework for information and consultation at national level (2002).[103]

The legislative model has its own dynamic based on underlying values contained in the EU Charter[104] and the Commission is committed to ensuring that the Charter will be taken into account 'when EU policies are drawn up'[105] and—even more strongly—'to make the fundamental rights provided for in the Charter as effective as possible. The Union must be exemplary in this respect.'[106]

The 'material' system of industrial relations is represented by the full variety of policy instruments which mirrors all types of social dialogue mechanism (joint opinions, declarations, rules of procedure, process-oriented texts, codes of conduct, policy orientation) expressed by the autonomous dynamism of social partners at all European levels.

Today, the coexistence between two different provisions in the same legal order is striking: Article 153(5) TFEU forbidding the enactment of European laws on the rights to conflict and association and Articles 12 and 28 CFREU promoting the same rights as the fundamental rights of workers.

Both rights, in fact, are intended to be applicable 'at all levels', in other words also at Union level, as also affirmed by the Explanations relating to the Charter prepared under the Presidium of the Convention (see Kollonay-Lehoczky, Lörcher and Schömann, chapter three). They state that the scope of the provisions of Article 12 CFREU is 'wider [than that of the ECHR] since they apply at all levels, including European level'.[107]

The Explanations with regard to Article 27 CFREU in supporting this interpretation recall 'the considerable Union *acquis*' in both fields, as underpinned by legal texts.[108]

[101] Directive 2001/86/EC of 8 October 2001 supplementing the Statute for a European company with regard to the involvement of employees, [2001] OJ L 294/22.

[102] Regulation (EC) No 2157/2001 establishing a Statute for a European company (SE), [2001] OJ L294/1.

[103] Directive 2002/14/EC of 11 March 2002 establishing a general framework for informing and consulting employees in the European Community, [2002] OJ L 80/29.

[104] M Weiss, 'The dynamic of the EU social model' in AA.VV, 'Work in global economy', Papers and Proceedings of International Symposium (Tokyo, 1–3 December 2003, Bit, Geneve) 161.

[105] COM (2010) 608 final, 'Towards a Single Market Act' p 19.

[106] COM(2010) 573 final, 'Strategy for the effective implementation of the Charter of Fundamental Rights by the European Union' p 3.

[107] Explanation, Article 12 [2007] OJ C 303/22.

[108] Explanation, Article 27—Workers' right to information and consultation within the undertaking [2007] OJ C 303/26 referring to Articles 154 and 155 TFEU, Directives 2002/14/EC (n 103), 98/59/EC (collective redundancies), 2001/23/EC (transfers of undertakings) and 94/45/EC (n 100).

IX. THE CHALLENGES TO SOCIAL PARTNER AUTONOMY

The language of social democracy has not been increased at all stages of the constitutional itinerary where it would be more appropriate and logical to involve the social partners in all fields of their concern and competence: monetary policy, as made by European Central Bank, as well as macroeconomic and social policies. International comparative surveys demonstrate how fruitful and widespread is the involvement at the top level of social partners in different fields.[109] Furthermore, despite some political dependence and criticism of their formal nature 'after a decade or so of experience, it can be concluded that tripartite consultation has demonstrated its resilience and become a constant feature in the new Member States'.[110]

A. The Antinomy within the Treaties

The starting point for complaining about the absence of a provision regarding a more institutionalised presence of the social partners is the internal contradiction in the 'book of Union laws', where the EU, among other objectives, identifies both a 'highly competitive social market economy' (Article 3(3)(1) TEU) and 'the principle of an open market economy with free competition' (Article 119(1) TFEU, ex-Article 4(1) EC).

In the whole EU legal edifice the contrast between the two rules is striking, unless one takes the view that the former provision represents a mere aspiration, and that Article 119 TFEU mirrors how the Union actually is. But if so, how is it possible to explain why the social actors suddenly disappear from fields in which they are strongly interested as far as the impact on labour relations of economic choices is concerned? They are deeply involved regarding both macroeconomic and labour market strategies, as shown by the close link between the two policy spheres in Part Three TFEU: Title VIII 'Economy and Monetary Policy' on the one side and Titles IX 'Employment' and X 'Social Policy' on the other—in the same revised Treaties.

It would be consistent with the proposed constitutional rationale of the 'Provision on democratic principles' (Title II TEU) and coherent with a symmetrical political strategy in all parts of the architecture to use Article 152 TFEU to promote the role of collective private powers at Union level:

— In the coordination of economic policy (Article 119 TFEU) and employment strategy (Article 147 TFEU, ex-Article 127 EC).
— In consultations preceding the adoption of EU legislation (Article 153 TFEU, ex-Article 137 EC) concerning the establishment of measures

[109] European Commission (ed), DG Employment and Social Affairs, 'Industrial relations in Europe' (Brussels, 2004) 51.
[110] Ibid 50ff.

to encourage cooperation between Member States and proposing Directives providing for minimum requirements in all fields of collective and individual labour relations.

— In consultations preceding the delivery of opinions by the Commission on social policy (Article 156 TFEU, ex-Article 140 EC) and measures (including EU legislation) on the application of the principles of equal opportunities and gender equality (Article 157(3) TFEU, ex-Article 141(3) EC).
— In consultations preceding the adoption of EU legislation on vocational training (Article 166(4) TFEU, ex-Article 150(4) TEC).

Despite the consistent accumulation of real experiences and the *acquis*, the emphatic proclamation of the autonomy of social dialogue seems seriously challenged by the project of an *Interinstitutional agreement on better law-making between the European Parliament, the Council and the Commission.*[111]

The interaction between social private collective powers and the decisions of EU bodies—now considered a normal source of regulation of social and labour law issues in Article 154 TFEU (ex-Article 138 EC) and Article 155 TFEU (ex-Article 139 EC)—represents, according to the same project, an anomaly of the normal law-making process (paragraphs 3–15). Social dialogue is not considered a factor of 'better coordination of the legislative process' (paragraphs 3–9). The social partners are ignored as possible actors to be consulted both in 'pre-legislative consultation' procedures (paragraph 26) and with regard to 'choice of legislative instrument and legal basis' (paragraphs 12 and 14), unless one takes the view that consultation with the social partners is envisaged in the provision in which the Commission is obliged, in referring its legislative decisions to the European Parliament and the Council, to 'take into account the results of any consultation' (paragraph 12). In any case, the reason for this option is probably that the combined presence of public power and private actors at the same 'law-making table' constitutes a heterodox system for producing norms and legal provisions.

European social dialogue and agreements reached under it are classified as 'alternative methods of regulation', belonging to the sub-category of 'co-regulation and self regulation'. In other words, social dialogue (and its outcome) are like a 'separate brother' compared with the 'regular' normative procedure.

[111] Concluded by the Council, Commission and European Parliament on 16 December 2003, [2003] OJ C 321/1.

But the challenge to the role of social dialogue lies in several points of the Interinstitutional Agreement which potentially restrict its autonomy. They consist in substantive conditions (in paragraph 17) in respect of:

- Procedure: 'The Commission will ensure that any use of co-regulation or self-regulation is always consistent with Community law'.
- Actors: The same use 'has to meet the criteria of transparency (in particular the publishing of agreements) and representativeness of the parties involved'.
- Content: 'these mechanisms will not be applicable where fundamental rights or important political options are at stake or in situations where the rules must be applied in a uniform fashion in all Member States'.

The exclusion of fundamental rights is understandable because of their 'constitutional' quality, which is not to be submitted to a public–private law-making procedure. But the exclusion of 'important' political options and situations requiring 'uniformity' of compliance with the rules, which could include matters relevant in the labour market and social policy, potentially limits the autonomy of the procedure.

In fact, both exclusions require delicate interpretation and provide scope for discretionary power on the part of the political body involved in the co-regulation procedure and negotiations, insofar as paragraph 17 of the Interinstitutional Agreement stipulates substantive conditions for the outcome of social dialogue.

Furthermore, social dialogue must: (a) 'represent added value in the general interest' and (b) 'does not affect the principles of competition or the unity of the internal market'.

Both conditions explain an extraordinary contradiction within the new European culture of industrial relations reform and contrast sharply with the idea of the promotion and facilitation of collective autonomy which Article 152 TFEU injects into the whole EU body.

B. Social Partners and the Interinstitutional Agreement

Nevertheless, 'general interests' and 'principles of competition' are the *idola tribus* of the EU legal culture, despite the fact that the Court of Justice of the European Union has affirmed and described collective agreements as an area exempted from competition law.[112] Those principles are strongly embedded in the Community legal structure and require new and reinforced protection at the top political level.

112 See cases *Albany*, *Brentjens* and *Drijvende Bokken* (n 96).

Co-regulation is still a way of entrusting the attainment of legislative objectives to private parties (also but not exclusively the social partners) whose agreements must comply with the provisions laid down in Part Three Title X TFEU. But according the Interinstitutional Agreement this trust is subject to conditions which might transform an autonomous procedure into a rigid and centralised model. In fact, Parliament and Council control the co-regulative procedure, having (paragraphs 18 and 19): (a) discretionary power to decide that the basic legislative act may 'include a provision for a two-month period of grace following the notification of a draft agreement to the European Parliament and the Council' (paragraph 20(3)); (b) discretionary power to suggest amendments if in their opinion the agreement does not meet the objectives laid down by the legislative authority; (c) discretionary power to object to the entry into force of that agreement; and (d) discretionary power to ask the Commission to submit a proposal for a legislative act.

This mechanism distributes powers and prerogatives according to a logic completely different from that accepted in the Treaties.

Since the Lisbon reform the European Parliament has had a more active presence than in the past. In fact, it acts in the area of social policy with the Council, adopting 'measures to encourage cooperation between Member States' (Article 153(2)(a) TFEU) and, 'by means of directives, minimum requirements for gradual implementation' (Article 153(2)(b) TFEU.

In both cases the Parliament operates 'in accordance with ordinary legislative procedure' (Article 153(2) TFEU), but it is absent from the web of rules concerning the co-regulation model and has no power to suggest amendments to an agreement or objections to its entry into force. The minor change is a provision on the mere right of the Parliament to be informed about the adoption by the Council of regulations or decisions proposed by the Commission implementing agreements concluded at Union level (Article 155(2) TFEU).

It is easy to understand that the reason for the change is the attempt to put right the absence from democratic procedure of this strong source of legitimacy.

C. A Dominant Role for the Commission?

The quality of the right and its content—a simple information—underlines the political will of the EU to not affect or alter the voluntarism inherent the mechanism proposed in Articles 154 and 155 TFEU. Both Articles show the auxiliary role played by the public bodies involved in the overall procedure essentially in taking 'any relevant measure to facilitate their dialogue by ensuring balanced support for the parties' (Article 154(1) TFEU). The Commission has no power to refuse to propose the agreement for decision by the Council if there has been a 'joint request of the signatory parties'. It cannot submit an alternative 'proposal for a legislative act' nor do so on the grounds that it does not 'meet the objectives laid down by the legislative authority'.

The procedure suggested by the Commission in its Communication goes back to 1993 and it is more cautious in respecting the efforts made by the social partners in reaching agreement:

> By virtue of its role as guardian of the Treaties, the Commission will prepare proposals for decisions to the Council following consideration of the representative status of the contracting parties, their mandate and the 'legality' of each clause in the collective agreement in relation to [Union] law, and the provisions regarding small and medium sized undertakings set out in [ex-]Article 138(2) [EC, now Article 154(2) TFEU]. At all events, the Commission intends to provide an explanatory memorandum on any proposal presented to the Council in this area, giving its comments and assessment of the agreement concluded by the social partners. Where it considers that it should not present a proposal for a decision to implement an agreement to the Council, the Commission will immediately inform the signatory parties of the reason for its decision.[113]

The text assumes that there is no *legal* provision authorising the role of sentinel of Treaty or any *legal* rule supporting the scrutiny of the content of the agreement or *authorised* power to stop the procedure.

Otherwise, the interaction between public bodies and collective autonomy would become unbalanced with regard to a possible reopening of social dialogue because of amendments proposed by European Parliament or Council.

According to the Interinstitutional Agreement the true judge of the social dialogue is the Commission which could refuse or reject the agreements already concluded and substitute them with a legislative act. Furthermore, the same instrument may be used by the Commission to intervene to replace the practices or agreement, 'at the request of the competent legislative authority' (paragraph 23).

More accurately, the Communication of 1993 stated:

> If the Council decides, in accordance with the procedures set out in the last subparagraph of [ex-]Article 139 (2) [EC, now Article 155(2) TFEU] not to implement the agreement as concluded by the social partners, the Commission will withdraw its proposal for a decision and will examine, in the light of the work done, whether a legislative instrument in the area in question would be appropriate.[114]

Proposals under the Interinstitutional Agreement are an attempt to transform into a rule of law what in the past was intended to be a mere political judgement. According to the Agreement, the Commission is the only institution

[113] COM(93) 600 final, 'Communication' (n 25) para 39.
[114] Ibid para 42.

charged with the huge task of deciding whether self-regulation '[contributes] to the attainment of the EC Treaty objectives and [is] being compatible with its provisions' and on the 'added value of commitments'. It must also scrutinise what normally pertains to autonomous social dialogue and voluntary agreements, such as 'the representativeness of the parties concerned, sectoral and geographical coverage' (paragraph 23).

The proposal seems to me to try to limit the autonomy of social partners, which must be protected from outside incursions in their internal structure and dynamism.

In fact the social partners have strongly affirmed their intention to safeguard the prerogatives attained within the legal framework of the European Union. The Joint contribution by the social partners to the Laeken European Council (13 December 2001), in which they jointly and strongly reaffirmed their 'specific role' in tomorrow's Europe, and their wish 'to develop a work programme for a more autonomous social dialogue' (paragraph 1) can be considered to be their manifesto. The same attitude has been stressed unilaterally by UNICE both in its strong reaction to the Commission's 2004 Communication,[115] asserting that only the social partners can shape social dialogue and that the Commission is 'dominated by an excessively administrative and interventionist conviction which contradicts the logic of industrial relations'.[116] Both statements recall that the Protocol on subsidiarity and the International Agreement of 1993 set out specific obligation for all institutions of the Union and that the Commission 'must consult widely before proposing legislation'.[117]

X. CONCLUSIONS

The Lisbon Treaty is a potential resource enabling the social partners to enlarge their role in labour law and industrial relations at all EU institutional levels. The key elements of a renewed strategy are Article 152 TFEU and the EU Charter, now legally binding for the EU. A new kind of 'social governance' must be embedded in the *acquis* and interpreted in light of the rights and duties provided for by the values of dignity and solidarity. These values now belong to the new EU legal culture and they represent a common feature of all constitutional traditions of Member States in the fields of individual and collective labour law and welfare.

[115] COM(2004) 557 final, 'Partnership' (n 16).

[116] UNICE, *Prise de position de UNICE sur la Communication de la Commission sur le dialogue social du 12 août 2004*, paras 2–4 in UNICE, 'The Voice of Business in Europe' 25.11.2004: www.unice.org/3/LCPDHPA DGADAIDLMHNFPFKMGPDBK9DPYBN93V71KM/UNICE/docs/DLS/2004-02106-FR.pdf.

[117] COM (2009) 504 final, 'Report on subsidiarity and proportionality'. 16th Report on better law making covering the year 2008 (Brussels, 25.9.2009) para 2.2.

In this context, the autonomy and freedom of the social partners must be seen and promoted by the Union. Article 152 TFEU provides for a specific legal obligation for all EU institutions insofar as the social partners are involved at all levels of social and institutional governance, as indicated not only in Articles 154 and 155 TFEU, but in all areas with a social impact. Consultations with EU institutions and at the Tripartite Social Summit require complete and timely information. Social dialogue needs more stringent legal support, possibly an obligation to bargain. Respect for the autonomy of the social partners as co-legislators implies a negative obligation for the Union not to alter the content of agreements.[118]

[118] See Recommendations in XI, Appendix.

Part II

The Social Framework or Substance of the Social Dimension (Instruments)

6

Social Competences

KLAUS LÖRCHER

What must ... be tolerated is a tendency ... to effectively interpreting competences.

(German Federal Constitutional Court, Judgment of 30 June 2009 on the Treaty of Lisbon, paragraph 237).

I. INTRODUCTION

THE SCOPE AND distribution of competences between the European Union and its Member States reveal the present state of European integration. The distribution of competences is at a crossroads with regard to European development.

Not surprisingly, therefore, competences were at the very heart of the debates within the framework of the (second) Convention on the Future of Europe. Following the adoption of the EU Charter of Fundamental Rights (CFREU), which had been elaborated by the first Convention, but before the final act of the enlargement process in May 2004, Member States were anxious to clarify more precisely the division of competences between the Union and the Member States. The 'Laeken mandate' given to the second Convention[1] had expressly requested 'a better division and definition of competence in the European Union'.[2]

The importance of the issue of competences was indicated by the establishment of two Working Groups, the first on 'subsidiarity' (Working Group I)[3] and the second on 'supplementary competences' (Working Group V),[4] both tasked with looking for possible solutions to questions concerning

[1] See generally S Clauwaert and K Lörcher, 'The European Trade Union Confederation (ETUC) and the draft EU Constitutional Treaty in M Jørgensen, J Baerentsen and J Monks (eds), *European Trade Union Yearbook* 2003/2004 (Brussels: ETUI) pp 157ff.

[2] See the Laeken Declaration on the Future of the European Union: european-convention.eu.int/pdf/LKNEN.pdf.

[3] See: european-convention.eu.int/doc_register.asp?lang=EN&Content=WGI.

[4] See: european-convention.eu.int/doc_register.asp?lang=EN&Content=WGV.

competences. In contrast—and of particular concern, as well as symbolic significance—was the fact that the Working Group on 'Social Europe' (Working Group XI)[5] was the last to be established by the Convention, despite the fact that social policy was an area of dispute in general in the Convention and, in particular, raised questions of social competences.

The Lisbon Treaty has not altered the principles foreseen in the Constitutional Treaty which themselves had envisaged no substantive change in respect of the previous competence provisions. But it has strengthened to a large extent the desire of Member States to limit the extension of the Union's competences as much as possible.

II. GENERAL ISSUES

The question of competences is close to the very heart of the European Union. Historically, the EU was established on the foundation of the European Economic Community (EEC) Treaty. This determined the predominantly economic profile of the Community during the first decades of its existence. Looking back on its evolution over more than half a century, reaching a new level with the entering into force of the Lisbon Treaty, the question arises of what role social competences have played or will play in the future.

The answer very much depends on the conception of the nature of the EU in general, and, in particular, conceptions of its social competences vis-à-vis those of the Member States.

A. Conceptions of Social Competences

Three approaches reveal different conceptions of social competences, primarily in terms of their relations to economic competences. These conceptions also, to a certain extent, reflect a perspective on the historical evolution of the EU:

(i) *Secondary* to economic competences: social competences are conceived of as inherent and inevitable in market integration, but social competences are not positively relevant to nor actively engaged by the EU; this approach could describe the first decades of the EEC.

(ii) *Equal* to economic competences: EU social competences are conceived of as aiming to balance or combat the negative social consequences of market integration; in practice, this balance is far from being

[5] See: european-convention.eu.int/doc_register.asp?lang=EN&Content=WGXI.

achieved. But from a policy viewpoint, the economic and the social dimensions of the EU should be on an equal footing.

(iii) *Superior* to economic competences: EU social competences are conceived of as the foundation of the European social model; they determine the dominant profile of the EU as a Social Union.

These different conceptions may be tested against the background of the historical evolution of EU competences in the social field. But from the very outset, it is obvious that the third conception is far away from being accepted or appearing acceptable and therefore not operational at all.

B. The Need for Social Competences at the EU Level: Labour Policy as Exemplar

The tendency towards the expansion of the EU's social competences is often criticised, either from a political point of view (Member States lose the power to act in a major policy area which is seen by the public in Member States largely as their domain) or from an economic viewpoint (EU social regulation is an obstacle to economic growth). This critique neglects the fact that the social policy competences of Member States are potentially overwhelmed, and their practical exercise effectively blocked, in a competitive European common market, with the serious threat or consequence of 'social dumping'.[6]

With regard to EU competences this implies certain minimum and specific legal policies:

— A legal framework enabling Member States to use their competences to require respect for social standards in the form of a 'most favourable labour standards clause'.
— Common (harmonised) binding labour standards, taking labour costs out of competition.
— Transnational regulation of multinational enterprises; including through collective bargaining, rights with regard to collective action and free movement of labour in a transnational labour market.

[6] See the discussion about the Services Directive 2006/123/EC and its implications, particularly for labour law and, not least, the judgments in the cases *Viking* (Case C-438/05 *International Transport Workers' Federation and Finnish Seamen's Union* [2007] ECR I-10779 ('Viking Line')); *Laval* (Case C-341/05 *Laval un Partneri* [2007] ECR I-11767; *Rüffert* (Case C-346/06 [2008] ECR I-1989) and *Commission v Luxembourg* (Case C-319/06 [2008] ECR I-4323).

The exercise of the EU's social competences in the past has given rise to legislation in which the first policy is acknowledged.[7] Astonishingly, however, the second policy does not appear to be a priority on any agenda.[8]

The Union needs sufficient competences in the social policy area. The Union must then be enabled to and in practice exercise these competences in order to achieve the social values (Article 2) and objectives embodied in Article 3(3) TEU (see Dorssemont, chapter two in this volume), Article 9 TEU (see Vielle, chapter four in this volume) and Article 151 TFEU. Only then would equality between the economic and social dimensions of the Union be guaranteed.

III. THE HISTORY OF SOCIAL COMPETENCES

A. Pre-Lisbon Developments

The history of social competences might be summarised as an evolution towards increased competences, although this should not be equated with their effective use. On the one hand, this evolution has been linked to an overall trend towards the expansion of EU competences in general; on the other hand, the expansion of specifically social competences was a consequence of the perceived need to balance economic competences. The underlying conception of the European Economic Community involved a neglect of social questions—at least as far as Community-level developments were concerned. Nonetheless, in a number of stages, and always related to political developments, the EU nevertheless obtained a wide range of social competences.[9]

The Convention on the Future of Europe was confronted by the major question of how competences should and could be clarified. This was done mainly in Part I of the Constitutional Treaty, dealing with more fundamental questions.[10] With respect to specific social competences, Working Group XI on Social Europe concluded 'in general that the existing competences are adequate', but suggested further clarification and proposed 'that specific extensions to existing competences in the area of public health should be envisaged as well as a possible redrafting of [ex-]Article 16 [EC (now Article 19 TFEU; see Jacobs, chapter nine in this volume)] in order to

[7] With the important substantive exception in the *Laval* case when the CJEU turned a social minimum into a maximum standard.

[8] See, for example, the agenda of the CJEU. The cases *Steen I* (C-332-90, [1992] ECR I-341) and *Steen* II (C-132-93, [1994] ECR I-2715) concerned the right to strike and free movement of persons, yet the Court refused to deal with the issues because there was no real cross-border movement.

[9] See Appendix Table 1: From Article 118 TEEC to Article 153 TFEU.

[10] Besides competences ia aims, institutions etc.

further enable EU legislation in the field of services of general interest'.[11] Attempts to reduce unanimity requirements in order to stimulate the functioning of the legislative machinery on social policy by excluding vetoes were unsuccessful.[12] In the end, only minor changes were made by the Constitutional Treaty to the existing Treaty provisions, such as a new legal basis for services of general economic interest.[13] The following the 'Lisbon' Intergovernmental Conference (IGC) introduced even more restrictive provisions compared with the Constitutional Treaty:

— Social security of migrant workers: a new clause was added restricting qualified majority voting in the event that fundamental aspects of the social security system would be affected.[14]
— Services of general economic interest: Member States' competences were strengthened.[15]

B. The Lisbon Treaty: Limitative Approach

The general principle regarding changes in relation to the Constitutional Treaty (which itself had already produced important restrictions) seemed to be: 'We have reached a compromise, but let us make all elements perfectly clear in order to prevent in particular the CJEU from any possibility of an "expansive" jurisprudence'. This strategy had a threefold impact on the Lisbon Treaty. First, important general framework provisions were amended,[16] which will not be dealt with here. The second—and probably the most important dimension—related to competences. The third impact was on certain specific provisions, in particular sensitive ones, such as common foreign and security policy matters; but only issues with a social impact will be dealt with here. Nevertheless, it should not be overlooked that at least some minimal improvements were made.

With regard to the second (restrictive) dimension, provisions aimed at restricting the Union's competences were reinforced. The new Article 4(1) TEU provides that 'competences not conferred upon the Union in the Treaties remain with the Member States'. In the same line of thinking,

[11] See final report (p 2): register.consilium.eu.int/pdf/en/03/cv00/CV00516-re01en03.pdf (4 February 2003).

[12] See, for example, the amendment in this respect proposed by Emilio Gabaglio, General Secretary of the ETUC.

[13] See CONV 850/03 (18 July 2003) then Article III-6.

[14] CIG 86/04 (25 June 2004) then Article III-21.

[15] CIG 86/04 (25 June 2004), then Article III-6; addition: without prejudice to the competence of Member States, in compliance with the Constitution, to provide, to commission and to fund such services.

[16] For example, the CFREU was 'expelled' from the Treaties' text itself and remained a separate document.

Article 48(2) TEU now explicitly states that proposals for amendments to the Treaties 'may, *inter alia*, serve ... to reduce the competences conferred on the Union in the Treaties'. The definition of the principle of conferral was given a more restrictive content by adding the word 'only' in Article 5(2) TEU.[17] Any extensive interpretations of competences coming from the CFREU were to be avoided by the new Article 6(1)(2) TEU.[18] Surprisingly, the role of national parliaments which to date had been understood as possible controllers of the principle of subsidiarity were now given an active obligation in this respect (Article 12(b) TEU).[19] Last but not least, a Protocol on the exercise of shared competence (Protocol No 25) explicitly provides (with reference to Article 2(2) TFEU) that 'when the Union has taken action in a certain area, the scope of this exercise of competence only covers those elements governed by the Union act in question and therefore does not cover the whole area'.

Concerning the third dimension dealing in particular with social issues, it is worth noting that the recognition of the role of social partners was changed from Part I, Title VI ('Democratic life of the Union') as Article I-48 to the Social Policy Title as Article 152 TFEU (see Veneziani, chapter five in this volume).

From a general perspective, only tiny improvements in respect of the general framework or the social policy field can be discerned. It is worth mentioning that a new Protocol (No 26) on Services of General Interest was introduced (see Jacobs, chapter nine in this volume). What should probably only be considered an adaptation (without being a substantive improvement) is the inclusion of the 'objectives' in Article 13(2) TEU describing the framework of action of the Union's institutions.

IV. THE (NEW) FRAMEWORK FOR COMPETENCES IN GENERAL

The main work done by the Convention in respect of competences was a better definition of the fundamental principles, but above all the new categorisation of competences. Although not in the form envisaged by the Convention and the Constitutional Treaty the form which it acquired in the Lisbon Treaty substantially follows these lines.

[17] 'Under the principle of conferral, the Union shall act *only* within the limits of the competences conferred upon it by the Member States in the Treaties to attain the objectives set out therein' (emphasis added).

[18] 'The provisions of the Charter shall not extend in any way the competences of the Union as defined in the Treaties.'

[19] 'National Parliaments contribute actively to the good functioning of the Union: ... (b) by seeing to it that the principle of subsidiarity is respected in accordance with the procedures provided for in the Protocol on the application of the principles of subsidiarity and proportionality'.

A. Fundamental Principles (Articles 5 TEU and 2 TFEU)

i. The Limits of Competences: The Principle of Conferral

The starting point is the basic 'principle of conferral', already included in Article 1(1) TEU.[20] It is reproduced in Article 5(1) TEU[21] and described in more detail in paragraph 2 of that Article[22] as the first of the fundamental principles limiting the competences and, as a counterpart, stressing that competences not conferred on the Union remain with the Member States. This principle is further strengthened by Article 4(1) TEU.

It is interesting to note, however, that certain of the following provisions do not adopt this approach and, instead, refer to the Treaties conferring competences.[23] These different approaches might be explained by different stages of the discussion within the Convention.[24] However, this is not sufficient for the reconciliation of these different formulations in interpreting the Treaties. One solution might be to look at concrete problems to see the extent to which different formulations produce different answers. In the—most likely—few cases of such differences emerging, a more in-depth analysis interpreting the Treaties would be required to show which approach should prevail, bearing in mind that the fundamental principle is included in Article 1(1) TEU.

The second major issue is the direct link to 'objectives they have in common'. First, it has to be clarified that the objectives are not only common to the Member States, but the Union. Therefore, this reference is not, of course, restricted to the objectives in Article 3 TEU but, specifically for social issues, also includes the social policy objectives in Article 151 TFEU (ex-Article 136 EC). This link is all the more important when it comes to the competences potentially available under the flexibility clause (Article 352 TFEU, ex-Article 308 EC).[25]

ii. The Use of Competences: The Principles of Subsidiarity and Proportionality (Article 5(3) and (4) TEU)

Based on previous developments of the principles of subsidiarity and proportionality as regards the use of competences already included in the

[20] 'By this Treaty, the HIGH CONTRACTING PARTIES establish among themselves a EUROPEAN UNION, hereinafter called "the Union", on which the Member States confer competences to attain objectives they have in common'.

[21] 'The limits of Union competences are governed by the principle of conferral'.

[22] 'Under the principle of conferral, the Union shall act only within the limits of the competences conferred upon it by the Member States in the Treaties to attain the objectives set out therein. Competences not conferred upon the Union in the Treaties remain with the Member States'.

[23] See below, section IV.B.ii.a.

[24] In February 2003, the formulation was still 'conferred upon it by the Constitution' (see CONV 528/03 Article 8 (now Article 5(2) TEU).

[25] See below, section IV.B.v.

Maastricht Treaty, the Constitution's 'fundamental principles' elevate these to an even more important role. In this respect, the Protocol on the application of the principles of subsidiarity and proportionality, which already existed, is strengthened by the role of the national parliaments, whose representatives in the Convention accounted for nearly half its membership.

This directly affects competences because this Protocol allows for the possibility of challenges to legislative acts on the grounds of infringement of the principle of subsidiarity (see Blanke, chapter seven in this volume).[26]

B. Categories of Competences (Articles 2–6, 352 TFEU)

With the definition of the categories of competences the Convention achieved one of the main goals of its mission: to 'clarify the competences'. All further developments will very much depend on the clarity of these definitions. Article 2 TFEU gives an overview of the main categories.[27]

First and foremost, it is important to note that, for the main areas of exclusive and shared competences in Article 2(1) and (2) TFEU, the Treaties and not the Member States (as in Article 1 TEU) confer competences on the Union. This was expressly debated in the Convention.[28] The approach adopted can thus be seen as an argument against excessively restrictive interpretations vis-à-vis Union competences in general.

There is no definition of the 'open method of coordination', despite this being much requested by several Members of the Convention.[29] That too leaves a whole set of questions unresolved.

i. Exclusive Competences (Articles 2(1) and 3 TFEU)

In the field of social policy there is no real exclusive competence of the Union. However, it should be borne in mind that at least two clearly exclusive competences of the EU have a direct impact on social issues:

(i) The establishing of the competition rules necessary for the functioning of the internal market.

(ii) Common commercial policy.

[26] Protocol (No 2) on the Application of the Principles of Subsidiarity and Proportionality, Article 8 with reference to the procedures in Article 263 TFEU.

[27] See Appendix Table 2: Overview of competences.

[28] Bearing in mind that 'Constitution' has been replaced by 'the Treaties', see CONV 601/03 para 19 ('several amendments had called for a further express mention of the fact that the Union's powers flow directly from competences transferred by the Member States') and para 21 ('certain members': 'it was not the Constitution which was conferring competences on the Union, but rather the Member States "in" the Constitution'), CONV 624/03 para 1.

[29] But see Article 5(3) TFEU: 'The Union may take initiatives to ensure coordination of Member States' social policies'.

At one stage of the discussions in the Convention, the Presidium had proposed a wider competence for the internal market.[30] This was reduced in order to confine it to the 'rules on competition' (Part III, Title VII, Chapter 1). Under this heading, Articles 101–109 TFEU (ex-Articles 81–89 EC) lay down the rules applying to undertakings, as well as aid granted by Member States. These are a continual threat to public services (see Jacobs, chapter nine in this volume). As such, they are of great relevance to the fundamental social right of access to services of general economic interest (Article 36 CFREU),[31] as well as other Articles dealing with social security and social assistance (Article 34 CFREU) and health care (Article 35 CFREU).

Following the same logic, the common commercial policy (Articles 206ff TFEU, ex-Articles 131ff EC) has become another threat to public services, which are increasingly under threat of liberalisation.

ii. Shared Competences (Articles 2(2) and 4 TFEU)

a. General

The quality of 'shared' competence is the most important aspect of competences in the social field.

The Convention discussed whether the notion of 'shared' competence correctly describes the content of this category. This debate continues.[32] The substance of the critique relates to the express 'pre-emption clause' in Article I-12(2). This excludes the exercise of competences by Member States to the extent that the Union has exercised its competence.[33] Admittedly, this debate about concepts will probably not assist in the solution of practical problems because, in very general terms, it is clear that the Union *and* the Member States have and exercise competences in these areas, the extent of which is defined in the relevant provisions.

Social policy is explicitly defined as an area of 'shared competence' (Article 4(2)(b) TFEU) 'for the aspects defined in this Treaty'. The same phrase was added to the area of 'common safety concerns in public health matters' (Article 4(2)(k) TFEU). The aim appears to be not to expand competences in the social field by allowing any extension of competences via the

[30] 'The Union shall have exclusive competence to ensure the free movement of persons, goods, services and capital, and establish competition rules, within the internal market, and in the following areas:'. CONV 528/93– (6 February 2003).

[31] See also Protocol (No 26) on Services of General Interest, see Jacobs (ch 9 in this volume).

[32] See, for example, R Streinz, C Ohler and C Hermann, *Der Vertrag von Lissabon zur Reform der EU* (München, 2008) p 72 ('*Ettikettenschwindel*', labelling swindle).

[33] 'The Member States shall exercise their competence to the extent that the Union has not exercised, or has decided to cease exercising, its competence'. See the description of the general debate in M Nettesheim, 'Kompetenzen', in A von Bogdandy (ed), *Europäisches Verfassungsrecht* (Berlin, 2003) 449–52.

CFREU—an objective also sought by Article 51(2) CFREU and even more explicitly in Article 6(1)(2) TEU ('The provisions of the Charter shall not extend in any way the competences of the Union').

Shared competence regarding the internal market (Article 4(2)(a) TFEU) has implications for the important competences on free movement of workers. It implies a principle of non-discrimination not only in respect of labour law,[34] but social security law.[35] Similarly, the freedom to provide services is a well-known case of overlap as a result of the debate on, for example, a framework legislative act, in particular, for services of general economic interest. Without a direct legal basis, as now foreseen in Article 14 TFEU, as well as its complementary Protocol (No 26) on Services of General Interest, internal market competence would have remained the only possibility. Again, the consequences of internal market laws for the 'working environment' continue to be one of the arguments for maintaining or introducing national legislation.[36]

b. Pre-emption Clause (Article 2(2) TFEU)

Article 2(2) TFEU provides that, in the case of shared competences: 'The Member States shall again exercise their competence to the extent that the Union has decided to cease exercising[37] its competence'. Although the main message of this provision seems to be directed in favour of the Member States' competences it contains on the other hand that the EU exercise of competence pre-empts the area: Member States are precluded from exercising competence in the area already regulated by the EU.

First, it should be noted that the EU secondary legislation requires its transposition by Member States mainly by legislating—with the important qualification in the social policy field that European laws and framework laws 'shall not prevent any Member State from maintaining or introducing more stringent protective measures compatible with the Treaties' (Article 153(4) second indent TFEU, ex-Article 137(4) second indent EC). As far as social legislation adopted under other Articles is concerned, it is mostly the Recitals[38] or final clauses[39] which contain such 'most favourable clauses'.

[34] See, in particular, Regulation 1612/68 (Articles 7 and 8).

[35] See, in particular, Regulations 1408/71 (now 883/2004) and 574/72 (now 987/2009).

[36] See Article 114(4) and (5) TFEU, ex-Article 95(4) and (5) EC.

[37] Although this alternative does not seem important in the social policy field for the time being, it might well become so.

[38] See, for example, Recital 28 of Council Directive 2000/78/EC of 27 November 2000 establishing a general framework for equal treatment in employment and occupation, [2000] OJ L 303/16 (adopted under Article 13 EC, now Article 19 TFEU): 'This Directive lays down minimum requirements, thus giving the Member States the option of introducing or maintaining more favourable provisions'.

[39] See, for example, Article 7 ('More favourable provisions') of Council Directive 91/533/EEC of 14 October 1991 on an employer's obligation to inform employees of the conditions

The minimum requirements in European framework laws, on the other hand, prohibit lower standards in the Member States. Therefore, the pre-emption clause cannot prevent (better) national implementation legislation which is of the utmost importance for better national fundamental rights vis-à-vis CFREU's rights protection.

The difficulty which arose with regard to the problem of defining the 'extent' to which the competence was exercised is now clarified by the Protocol (No 25) on the exercise of shared competence by explicitly restricting the scope of the exercise (only) to the area covered. Therefore, it would be difficult to argue, for example, that the title of a Directive on its own would allow for the pre-emption effect.

A more esoteric question is whether the pre-emption doctrine could also apply to EU social dialogue agreements. Do agreements adopted at EU level preclude Member State regulation, including by the social partners in the Member States? Since there is no definition of their legal quality[40] indicating the contrary, it appears clear that the pre-emption clause only applies if and to the extent they are implemented by Directives (Article 155(2) TFEU, ex-Article 139(2) EC). In any event, these agreements contain minimum requirements, allowing Member States to go further in the protection of workers.

c. The Choice of Legal Basis

Even within the 'shared competences' category, social policy matters are treated in a different manner (in particular, in respect of the unanimity requirement). The question thus arises of which legal basis is appropriate. For example:

— Different instruments with the same legal basis and explicitly linked: the European Company (SE) Regulation 2157/2001[41] and the SE Directive 2001/86/EC,[42] both based on ex-Article 308 EC (now Article 352 TFEU).

applicable to the contract or employment relationship, [1991] OJ L 288/32: 'This Directive shall not affect Member States' prerogative to apply or to introduce laws, regulations or administrative provisions which are more favourable to employees or to encourage or permit the application of agreements which are more favourable to employees'.

[40] Article III-212(2) of the Constitutional Treaty (CT) characterised social dialogue agreements as 'non-legislative acts' which were defined in Article I-35(2) by referring to 'European regulations and decisions'.

[41] Council Regulation (EC) No 2157/2001 of 8 October 2001 on the Statute for a European company (SE) [2001] OJ L 294/1.

[42] Council Directive 2001/86/EC of 8 October 2001 supplementing the Statute for a European company with regard to the involvement of employees, [2001] OJ L 294/22.

— One instrument with different legal bases: working time in road transport[43] based on ex-Articles 71 and 137(2) (now Articles 91 and 153(2) TFEU).[44]

Generally speaking, according to the CJEU's[45] settled case law, the choice of a legal basis for a measure must rest on objective factors which are amenable to judicial review. Those objective factors include, in particular, the aim and the content of the measure.[46] If examination of a Union act shows that it has a twofold purpose or twofold content, and if one of these is identifiable as the main or predominant one, whereas the other is merely incidental, the Union act must be founded on a single legal basis; that is, the one dictated by the main or predominant purpose or content.[47] Only exceptionally, if it is established that the act simultaneously pursues a number of objectives, which are indissociably linked, without one being secondary and indirect in relation to the other, may such an act be founded on various corresponding legal bases.[48] Furthermore, the Court has made it clear that other Articles of the Treaty may not be used as a legal basis in order to circumvent the express exclusion of harmonisation laid down in ex-Article 129(2) EC[49] (now Article 149 TFEU).

iii. The Coordination of Economic and Employment Policies (Articles 2(3) and 5 TFEU)

This category of competences was debated for quite some time during the Convention, which tried to find a coherent basis for a number of disparate activities. At present, Member States are under an obligation to coordinate their economic and employment policies within the arrangements provided for by the Union 'as determined by this Treaty' (Article 2(3) TFEU).

[43] Directive 2002/15/EC of the European Parliament and of the Council of 11 March 2002 on the organisation of the working time of persons performing mobile road transport activities [2002] OJ L 80/35.

[44] See the CJEU's judgment of 9 September 2004 (Joined Cases C-184/02 and C-223/02—*Spain and Finland v EP and Council* [2004] ECR I-7789) where the Court only examined and accepted the first legal basis (ex-Article 71 EC, now Article 91 TFEU), leaving open the question of whether ex-Article 137(2) EC (now Article 153(2) TFEU) would also apply.

[45] See a brief overview in Nettesheim (n 33) pp 473–477.

[46] See, in particular, Case C-269/97 *Commission v Council* [2000] ECR I-2257, para 43, and Case C-36/98 *Spain v Council* [2001] ECR I-779, para 58.

[47] See, inter alia, Case C-42/97 *Parliament v Council* [1999] ECR I-869, paras 39 and 40, and Case C-36/98 *Spain v Council*, [2001] ECR I-779, para 59.

[48] 10 December 2002 (Directive 2001/37/EC on the manufacture, presentation and sale of tobacco products concerning the legal basis—Articles 95 EC and 133 EC) Case C-491/01 *British American Tobacco Investments and Imperial Tobacco*, para 94, by referring to Opinion 2/00 [2001] ECR I-9713, para 23.

[49] 5 October 2000 (Case C-376/98 *Germany* [2000] ECR I-8419) on Directive 98/43/EC (Advertising and sponsorship of tobacco products and the problem of the legal basis, in particular ex-Article 100a TEC (now Article 114 TFEU)) para 76.

However, while Article 5(3) TFEU provides that the Union 'may' take initiatives to ensure coordination of Member States' social policies, no such reference is to be found in Article 2(3) TFEU.

Does this mean that coordination initiatives may be taken by the Union outside the TFEU? There are several reasons for answering this question in the affirmative. First, there is no such restriction in the text; on the contrary, the formulation is very broad. Secondly, the context shows that the provisions on economic[50] and employment[51] policies are based primarily on coordination (mainly through guidelines), whereas in social policy provisions, minimum standards legislation plays the important role. Finally, this general approach is justified by the fact that there is no coordination obligation.

Bearing in mind that there are two important provisions which deal with the coordination of social policy in the TFEU, mainly Article 153(2)(a) TFEU (ex-Article 137(2)(a) EC) and Article 156 TFEU (ex-Article 140 EC), a further question arises. May social policy questions which do not appear in the Section on 'Social Policy' (and, consequently, are not covered by Article 156 TFEU (ex-Article 140 EC)) be coordinated under this provision? This might be the case for (elements of) certain rights included in the CFREU, such as:

— The rights of children (Article 24).[52]
— The rights of the elderly (Article 25).[53]
— The integration of persons with disabilities (Article 26).
— Placement services (see Article 29).[54]

To the extent that the TFEU does not provide for explicit coordination measures, Article 5(3) TFEU offers the Union the option to take the relevant initiatives.

iv. Areas of Supporting, Coordinating or Complementary Action (Articles 2(5) and 6 TFEU)

Following as it does the general coordination provision in Article 5(3) TFEU in respect of social policy, there is some doubt regarding the specific relationship to this of social policy as an area for coordination in Article 6 TFEU. At least two areas are specified which relate to social matters: protection and improvement of human health (Article 6(a) TFEU)[55] and

50 Part III, Title VIII, Chapter 1, Articles 120 *et seq* TFEU (ex-Articles 98 *et seq* EC).
51 Part III, Title IX, Articles 145 *et seq* TFEU (ex-Articles 125 *et seq* EC).
52 But at least certain elements will be covered by Articles 6(e), 165 and 166 TFEU.
53 Different competences might be relevant: Article 153(1)(c), (h) and (j) TFEU.
54 Some aspects will fall under the social security competence in Article 153(1)(c) TFEU.
55 See in Part III, Article 168 TFEU.

vocational training (Article 6(e) TFEU).[56] In order to avoid problems, it will be necessary to regard these two areas as '*leges speciales*' in respect of Article 5(3) TFEU. This is supported by the express derogation in Article 168(4) TFEU from Articles 2(5) and 6(a) TFEU, allowing for harmonisation measures in certain areas of public health.

Concerning other areas mentioned, the framework for supporting, coordinating or complementary action remains limited in at least two respects:

— There is to be no superseding of the Member States' competence in these areas (Article 2(5)(1) TFEU).
— There are to be no legal harmonisation measures (Article 2(5)(2) TFEU).

v. The 'Flexibility Clause' (Article 352 TFEU)

This provision may be regarded as one of the 'core issues' of the entire Convention exercise. Together with Article 95 EC (internal market), it was referred to in the Laeken Declaration[57] in the context of 'competence creep':

> Lastly, there is the question of how to ensure that a redefined division of competence does not lead to a creeping expansion of the competence of the Union or to encroachment upon the exclusive areas of competence of the Member States and, where there is provision for this, regions. How are we to ensure at the same time that the European dynamic does not come to a halt? In the future as well the Union must continue to be able to react to fresh challenges and developments and must be able to explore new policy areas. Should Articles 95 and 308 of the Treaty be reviewed for this purpose in the light of the '*acquis jurisprudentiel*'?

In the social policy field, ex-Article 235 TEC (then ex-Article 308 EC, now Article 352 TFEU) was quite often used when social competences did not exist, or existed only to a very limited extent.[58] Its impact should not be underestimated. More recently, the European Company Statute Regulation and the associated employee participation Directive were both adopted on the basis of ex-Article 308 EC.[59]

In the final text of the Constitutional Treaty (Article I-18 CT) and consequently in the Lisbon Treaty, the substance of this provision has been maintained and even extended in respect of all policy areas 'defined in the

[56] See Articles 165 and 166 TFEU (bearing in mind the further reference to vocational training in Article 156(1) 3rd indent TFEU).

[57] 'The Future of the European Union', 15 December 2001. See above (n 2).

[58] In the fields of equality between men and women: equal pay and equal treatment Directives (75/117, 79/7) and restructuring of enterprises: collective redundancies (75/129) transfer of undertakings (77/187), protection of workers in cases of insolvency (2002/74/EC amending Directive 80/987).

[59] See above, section IV.B.ii.c and nn 41 and 42.

Treaties'.[60] Nevertheless, far-reaching procedural requirements have been added, mainly to do with the subsidiarity principle: the Commission is obliged to inform the national parliaments in order to give them the possibility to monitor '*ex ante*' the application of this principle (see Blanke, chapter seven in this volume).

A further new element is the prohibition of harmonisation 'where the Treaties exclude such harmonisation' (Article 352(3) TFEU). On the one hand, this formulation is a regression in comparison to ex-Article 308 EC. On the other hand, without this provision, it would not be surprising if national parliaments were to react with a 'veto' if harmonisation were excluded by the Treaties. However, this legal basis was invoked for a new proposal in order to 'circumvent' the prohibition. This is relevant not only to supporting, coordinating or supplementing action (Article 2(5)(2) TFEU), but whenever harmonisation is expressly excluded.[61]

Quite a different problem is the non-application of Article 153 TFEU (which provides the legal basis for EU Directives) to measures concerning 'pay, the right of association, the right to strike or the right to impose lock-outs' (Article 153(5) TFEU). If legislative measures in these areas of the social policy field are excluded under Article 153 TFEU, is it possible that harmonisation in these same areas could be based on use of the flexibility clause in Article 352 TFEU?

It seems fairly clear that Article 153 TFEU does not 'exclude harmonisation' as such with respect to these policy areas. This is indicated by the fact that Article 153 TFEU is the equivalent of ex-Article 137 EC in the substantially revised form in which it was redrafted by the Treaty of Nice. The redrafting included a significant change to ex-Article 137(2) EC. A new element was the clause explicitly excluding 'harmonisation' which was added—and is now in Article 153(2)(a) TFEU—with respect to 'measures designed to encourage cooperation'. In contrast, no such prohibition of harmonisation was applied with respect to what is now Article 153(2)(b) TFEU, which concerns European framework laws establishing 'minimum requirements'.

Harmonisation and minimum standards are thereby distinguished. Rightly so, as, in principle, there are great differences between the two. Harmonisation means equal conditions; minimum standards allow for a great variety of conditions above a defined level. The justification for treating these two approaches differently is that they imply quite different

[60] The further new procedural provision introduced by the Lisbon Treaty does not concern social matters since the new para 4 relates to common foreign and security policy. The addition of a specific reference to the special legislative procedure (new sentence 2 introduced in para 1) will nevertheless have an impact on the social legislation in the areas in which this procedure is required (Article 153(2)(3) TFEU, ex-Article 137(2)(3) EC). See below, section VI.A.i.b.

[61] See, for example, Article 153(2)(a) TFEU.

degrees of intervention in Member States' legislation. Harmonisation implies a substantial impact; minimum standards, much less of an impact. The conclusion is that Article 352(3) TFEU does not in itself preclude the adoption of appropriate measures on minimum standards in the areas of social policy excluded by Article 153(5) TFEU: 'pay, the right of association, the right to strike or the right to impose lock-outs'.

Of course, only important considerations would support the adoption of such measures. But if the Union is bound by the obligation that it, inter alia, 'recognises and promotes the role of the social partners' (Article 152(1) TFEU), it is quite conceivable that legislative measures to implement this obligation could and should be based on Article 352 TFEU (ex-Article 308 EC), bearing in mind, in particular, the objective stated in Article 151(1) TFEU (ex-Article 136(1) EC) of promotion of dialogue between management and labour. Similarly, it follows that the legal basis for decisions of the 'Tripartite Social Summit', which as the new provision stipulates 'shall contribute to social dialogue' (Article 152 TFEU) need no longer be confined to the disputed ex-Article 202 second indent EC.[62]

Apart from the areas specified in Article 153(5) TFEU (ex-Article 137(5) EC), there are other unforeseen areas of social policy which may emerge from which legislation is excluded by this Article. The abovementioned legislation on the European Company illustrates how there may well arise new challenges for which Article 352 TFEU will provide the possibility for legislative action.

vi. External Competences

In respect of cooperation with international organisations as well as ratification of international instruments there are general provisions. The social policy cooperation with the UN, the ILO and the Council of Europe could be based on Article 220 TFEU. But a more specific provision in the social field (as in Article 167(3) TFEU for cultural policy issues) would have been preferable, taking into account the specificities of those organisations (in particular, the tripartite structure of the ILO). In general terms, it would appear possible to ratify all instruments falling within the (internal) competence of the EU, taking account of the opinion of the CJEU on the ILO Conventions[63] or the (Revised) European Social Charter (RESC)[64] on

[62] See COM(2002)341 final (Proposal for a Council Decision establishing a Tripartite Social Summit for Growth and Employment): 'Having regard to the Treaty establishing the European Community, and in particular Article 202 thereof'. The new formulation of Article 16(1) TEU concerning the powers of the Council would no longer serve as a possible legal basis (nor could Article 290 TFEU be used as a basis for a Council Decision).

[63] Opinion of the CJEU of 19 March 1993—Opinion 2/91—ILO Convention No 170 concerning safety in the use of chemicals at work.

[64] O De Schutter, 'L'adhésion de l'Union européenne à la Charte sociale européenne révisée' EUI Working Paper LAW No 11 (2004). See in this sense also European Parliament resolution

the basis of Articles 216 and 218 TFEU. One major step has been taken by the ratification of the UN Convention on the Rights of Persons with Disabilities;[65] the next step is the accession to the ECHR.

V. THE (NEW) FRAMEWORK FOR SOCIAL COMPETENCES

It has already been pointed out that there have been few improvements with regard to social competences: ex-Article 137 EC has become Article 153 TFEU (with some slight changes). One might conclude that there is no need to deal with this provision in more detail. However, the framework has changed and, therefore, some elements may now have to be looked at from a different perspective.

First, the social ambitions of the Union are expressed on at least three different levels: (i) in the values and objectives of the Union (Articles 2 and 3 TEU) (see Dorssemont, chapter two in this volume); (ii) the mainstreaming clauses concerning social, gender and anti-discrimination objectives (Articles 8–10 TFEU) (see Vielle, chapter four in this volume); and (iii) more concretely the specific social objectives (Article 151 TFEU) as well as the recognition and promotion of the role of the social partners at EU level (Article 152 TFEU) (see Veneziani, chapter five in this volume and the Recommendations in the Appendix).

Secondly, the new framework for social competences includes one further major element: the CFREU (Article 6(1) TFEU). This incorporates, for the first time, explicitly legally binding fundamental social rights (see Kollonay-Lehoczky, Lörcher and Schömann, chapter three in this volume). Although this is a qualitatively new element, it should be borne in mind that, in substance, there was already a basis for taking fundamental social rights into account: the reference in ex-Article 136 EC (now Article 151 TFEU) to:

- The European Social Charter, 1961.
- The Community Charter of the Fundamental Social Rights of Workers, 1989.

of 19 May 2010 on the institutional aspects of the accession of the European Union to the European Convention for the Protection of Human Rights and Fundamental Freedoms (2009/2241(INI) on the question of ratification of the European Social Charter (ESC)and Revised European Social Charter (RESC) (para 30: 'accession by the Union to the ECHR constitutes an essential first step which should subsequently be complemented by accession by the Union to, inter alia, the European Social Charter, signed in Turin on 18 October 1961 and revised in Strasbourg on 3 May 1996, which would be consistent with the progress already enshrined in the Charter of Fundamental Rights and in the social legislation of the Union').

[65] The instrument of ratification was deposited on 23 December 2010 (although some 10 Member States have not yet ratified it). It should be noted that the respective 'Council Decision of 26 November 2009 concerning the conclusion, by the European Community, of the United Nations Convention on the Rights of Persons with Disabilities' ([2010] OJ L 23/35) was adopted before the entry into force of the Lisbon Treaty.

These instruments constitute the foundation of the fundamental social rights now in the CFREU. The significance of this is that the exercise of the Union's competences must contribute also to achieving these fundamental social objectives in legislation and, consequently, also in practice.

A. Explicit (Direct) Legislative Competences

Debate in the two Conventions on the question of competences often concerned the issue of fundamental social rights. Examples are the debates on Article 52 CFREU in the first Convention, and on Article 4 TFEU in the second Convention: shared competences concerning the express restriction concerning social policy.[66]

From the outset, it should be noted that the Treaties do not provide a general competence to adopt secondary legislation in respect of fundamental rights. The only new specific legal basis is to be found in Article 6(2) TEU and Article 218(6)(a)(ii) TFEU for the Union's accession to the ECHR.[67]

For this reason, it is essential to analyse in more detail the relationship between the various fundamental social rights and the Union's competences in the social policy field. A general overview reveals the extent to which Union competences can be used to implement most fundamental social rights through secondary legislation.[68]

Following the structure of the CFREU three main areas may be examined:

(i) Freedom (Title II).
(ii) Equality (Title III).
(iii) Solidarity (Title IV).

Some more specific problems remain, which are dealt with in relation to these three areas.

First, when explicit competences are absent from the social policy field, the examination must be extended to other areas of EU competence, the most important being the internal market. It may be recalled, from the outset, that quite a number of important social policy Directives have this legal

[66] Article 4(2)(b) TFEU: 'social policy, for the aspects defined in this Treaty'.

[67] Article 6(2) TEU: 'The Union shall accede to the European Convention for the Protection of Human Rights and Fundamental Freedoms. Such accession shall not affect the Union's competences as defined in the Treaties'. See Opinion 2/94 on Accession by the Community to the ECHR, [1996] ECR I-1759, paras 27–35, where the Court found no general power of the Community to enact rules on fundamental rights but at the same time recalled that respect for fundamental rights, as general principles of Community law, is a condition of the lawfulness of Community acts. See also Kollonay-Lehoczky, Lörcher and Schömann in this volume (ch 3, section II.A).

[68] See Appendix Table 3: Social fundamental rights in the EU Charter and EU competences in the TFEU.

basis. One area taken from Title II which could perhaps be considered to be adapted for use in future as the legal basis of the internal market (Article 114 TFEU, ex-Article 95 EC) might be Article 15(1) CFREU: 'Everyone has the right to engage in work and to pursue a freely chosen occupation'.

Secondly, there are a number of examples of areas, mainly in the Equality Title (III),[69] for which the TFEU does not explicitly attribute any competence. Could the 'flexibility clause' (Article 352 TFEU) be used to legislate in these areas? This would seem logical: if there are no specific competences and if the objectives of the EU are to be attained, it is for the 'flexibility clause' to fill the gap in competences.[70]

Furthermore, the development of secondary social legislation shows how much it was necessary to use this legal basis.[71] The main argument against this approach is that it would be an extension of competence, which is prohibited by Article 51(2) CFREU, denying 'any new power or task for the Union' if not provided for in other Parts of the Treaties. But Article 352 TFEU, as one of the fundamental competences, aims to allow for at least some flexibility in respect of future developments. Before making an assessment in a specific case, the circumstances would have to be explored to see whether the appropriate conditions for taking advantage of the flexibility clause in that case were fulfilled.

Thirdly, there is the case in which competences have been excluded explicitly. This is the case in respect of the use of one of the most important competence provisions in the Solidarity Title (IV) , namely Article 153(5) TFEU (ex-Article 137(5) EC), in particular, the right to strike. This provision confronts both collective rights Articles 12 and 28 CFREU (in particular, the right to strike). This is a controversial issue. The main argument for a restrictive interpretation of Article 153(5) TFEU lies in its wording ('This Article shall not apply'). The implication is that it does not preclude the Union taking action under other Articles of the Treaties, including Article 352 TFEU.

Even in cases in which no explicit legislative competences exist, fundamental social rights have an impact on legislation: they must not be restricted by secondary EU legislation. The main example is the so-called 'Monti Regulation', Council Regulation No 2679/98 on the functioning of the internal market in relation to the free movement of goods among the Member States,[72] in which it was deemed necessary to include an Article ensuring that the regulation is without prejudice to the fundamental rights, notably the

[69] See above, section IV.B.iii.
[70] See above, section IV.B.v.
[71] See above (n 58).
[72] [1998] OJ L 337/8.

right to strike.[73] It appears that in this regulation the Council has recognised explicitly the point that its acts, as well as Member States' actions implementing them, must *respect* even such fundamental rights as the right to strike on which it arguably might not have *competence to legislate*.[74] In principle, the same approach has been adopted in the Services Directive 2006/123.[75]

Another example quoted during the debate in the second Convention (but not directly related to the legislation competences) was the organisation of a competition for the recruitment of staff by a Community institution to be held on a Jewish holiday, which could impinge on the freedom of religion of potential participants. It was this situation that led the CJEU to recognise freedom of religion as part of the fundamental rights in Community law.[76]

B. 'Open Method of Coordination' (OMC)

The 'Open Method of Coordination' (OMC) was not discussed in depth by the Convention but postponed until the end of the discussions, when the Presidium proposed adding important elements of the OMC to four policy areas, one of which was social policy.

The origins of the OMC are to be found in the European Employment Strategy, introduced by the Treaty of Amsterdam as new Title VIII of the EC Treaty, 'Employment' (ex-Articles 125–130 EC, now Articles 145–150 TFEU) and, to a certain extent, were also in the Social Chapter with regard to social exclusion.[77]

In the social policy field, the Treaties now contain three references to the OMC:

(i) In the most general terms, in Article 5(3) TEU.[78]
(ii) In Article 153(2)(a) TFEU.
(iii) In Article 156 TFEU.

[73] See Article 2: 'This Regulation may not be interpreted as affecting in any way the exercise of fundamental rights as recognised in Member States, including the right or freedom to strike. These rights may also include the right or freedom to take other actions covered by the specific industrial relations systems in Member States'. See also Recital No 4: 'Whereas such measures [ie measures which the Member States are obliged to take under the regulation with a view to facilitating the free movement of goods in their territory] must not affect the exercise of fundamental rights, including the right or freedom to strike'.

[74] See WG II WD 3.

[75] Article 1(7): 'This Directive does not affect the exercise of fundamental rights as recognised in the Member States and by Community law. Nor does it affect the right to negotiate, conclude and enforce collective agreements and to take industrial action in accordance with national law and practices which respect Community law'.

[76] Case 130/75 *Vivien Prais v Council*, [1976] ECR 1589.

[77] Article 137(2)(3) EC. But see the amendments introduced by the Treaty of Nice, now in Article 137(2)(a) EC.

[78] See above, section IV.B.iii.

Only the second of these, Article 153(2)(a) TFEU, provides for 'measures' including all sorts of acts

> to encourage cooperation between Member States through initiatives aimed at improving knowledge, developing exchanges of information and best practices, promoting innovative approaches and evaluating experiences, excluding any harmonisation of the laws and regulations of the Member States.

Recourse to legislation in these cases will be justified by the 'most democratic' principle (the ordinary legislation procedure in Article 294 TFEU), with co-decision of the European Parliament, as well as the principle of legal certainty. In contrast, Article 156 TFEU refers to certain comparable actions: 'exchange of best practice', 'evaluation', but, instead of the ordinary legislative procedure, '[t]he European Parliament shall be kept fully informed' (Article 156(2) TFEU).

VI. SPECIFIC SOCIAL COMPETENCES

The Union's social competences cover a very large area. Some are not perceived as competences because they are excluded from Union legislation. This is an error. They remain EU competences irrespective of the form in which they are exercised. Nevertheless, the evolution of European social law reveals an emphasis on legislative competences. It may be that, in future, 'soft' law will become more important.

A. Legislative Competences

As already mentioned, there should be a close link between (social) competences and the fundamental social rights in the CFREU. With the possible exception of the specific problem of 'pay, the right of association, the right to strike' (Article 153(5) TFEU), most of the (work-related) fundamental social rights in the CFREU fall within the legislative competences of the Union in the TFEU and, therefore, could lead to Directives.[79]

i. The General Provision (Article 153 TFEU)

The most important provision is Article 153 TFEU, which covers a wide range of legislative competences for Directives. Astonishingly, the competences may also be exercised in the form of regulations, although in this case 'excluding any harmonisation of the laws and regulations of the Member States' (Article 153(2)(a) TFEU).

[79] See Appendix Table 3: Social fundamental rights in the EU Charter and EU competences in the TFEU.

Some procedural points should be highlighted, although they are not new in substance.

a. Ordinary Legislative Procedure

First, the ordinary legislative procedure in respect of Directives applies to the areas provided for in Article 153(2)(b) TFEU (ex-Article 137(2)(b) EC) in respect of the following fields mentioned in Article 153(1) TFEU:

- Improvement in particular of the working environment to protect workers' health and safety (a).
- Working conditions (b).
- Information and consultation of workers (e).
- Integration of persons excluded from the labour market (h).
- Equality between women and men with regard to labour market opportunities and treatment at work (i).

Secondly, legislation in all forms ('measures') is possible under Article 153(2)(a) TFEU (ex-Article 137(2)(a) EC) in all the social policy fields mentioned in paragraph 1 of this provision, including the abovementioned areas, those covered by a special legislative procedure with unanimity requirements[80] and also the following:

- Combating social exclusion (j).
- Modernisation of social protection systems (k).[81]

However, the exercise of competence under Article 153(2)(a) TFEU (ex-Article 137(2)(a) EC) includes the major restriction: 'excluding any harmonisation of the laws and regulations of the Member States'. Rather, it is limited in a variety of ways to 'measures designed to encourage cooperation between Member States'.

b. Special Legislative Procedure

Since social legislation remained a very sensitive issue throughout the debates in the Convention, it is not really surprising that in the end the ordinary legislative procedure remained (Article 153(2)(3) TFEU, ex-Article 137(2)(2) EC) so as to require unanimity in the Council (while attributing to the European Parliament only a consultative role) in respect of:

- Social security and social protection of workers (c).
- Protection of workers where their employment contract is terminated (d).

[80] See above, section VI.A.i.b.

[81] Without prejudice to point (c) on social security and social protection of workers (Article 153(1)(c) TFEU, ex-Article 137(1)(c) EC).

— Representation and collective defence of the interests of workers and employers, including codetermination (f).
— Conditions of employment for third-country nationals legally residing in Union territory (g).

However, this was combined with the possibility of a unanimous decision by the Council to apply the ordinary legislative procedure (with qualified majority voting), the so-called 'passarelle clause' (Article 153(2), subparagraph 4 TFEU, ex-Article 137(2), subparagraph 2 EC). The most sensitive issue remains under the unanimity requirement (without a 'passarelle clause'): social security and social protection of workers. But it should be noted that Article 48(7) TEU offers the so-called 'simplified revision procedure', with the involvement of national parliaments.

c. Implementation via Collective Agreements

The possibility for implementing Directives via collective agreements in the Member States remains vital, in particular, for the Nordic labour relations systems (Article 153(3) TFEU, ex-Article 137(3) EC)—the so-called 'Christophersen clause'). The possibility of collective agreements in the Member States implementing European social dialogue agreements which had been implemented through decisions in accordance with Article 155(2) TFEU (ex-Article 139(2) EC), was newly introduced.[82]

ii. The Specific Provisions

Only the most important specific social competences will be mentioned.

a. Services of General Economic Interest (SGEI) (Article 14 TFEU)

This issue is dealt with in detail in another chapter of this book.[83] With regard to competence issues, it may be noted that this is a new legislative competence (compared with ex-Article 16 EC). Moreover, Article 14 TFEU provides that, within this competence, the Union and the Member States 'shall take care that such services operate on the basis of principles and conditions, in particular economic and financial conditions, which enable them to fulfil their missions'.

It is particularly surprising that it is not a Directive, but that only 'regulations ... shall establish these principles and set these conditions'. One question is whether this restriction to regulations affects the scope of EU competences, or only the legal instruments which may be used. As a

[82] Thanks to a late amendment to Article III-210(4).
[83] See Jacobs (ch 9 in this volume).

provision of general application, the impression is of a horizontal clause applicable to all policy fields, without as such widening the scope of the EU competence. In any event, a regulation might implement Article 36 CFREU: 'The Union recognises and respects access to services of general economic interest' as one central feature of the relevant 'principles and conditions'.

b. Non-discrimination (Article 19 TFEU, ex-Article 13 EC)

In respect of non-discrimination, Article 19 TFEU reflects the content of ex-Article 13 EC. However, it was possible neither to introduce qualified majority voting (apart from the 'incentive measures' referred to in Article 19(2) TFEU), nor to expand the scope of the competence beyond the existing grounds of discrimination ('sex, racial or ethnic origin, religion or belief, disability, age or sexual orientation'). This raises a particular problem in relation to Article 21(1) CFREU, which prohibits discrimination on additional grounds: colour, social origin, political or any other opinion, membership of a national minority, property, or birth). The flexibility clause (Article 352 TFEU, ex-Article 308 EC) could offer a solution.

c. Social Security of Migrants (Article 48 TFEU, ex-Article 42 EC)

The unanimity requirement of ex-Article 42 EC was an important issue debated by the Convention. It was decided that Article 48 TFEU would allow the ordinary legislative procedure to 'adopt such measures in the field of social security as are necessary to provide freedom of movement for workers'. However, along with some other issues, the IGC inserted provisions allowing some veto powers into Article 48(2) TFEU.

d. Equality between Men and Women (Article 157(3) TFEU, ex-Article 141(3) EC)

Ex-Article 141(3) EC, introduced by the Treaty of Amsterdam, was taken up by the Convention, and the envisaged change in language[84] has been dropped by the Lisbon Treaty which reverts to the old formulation (but introduces the reference to the ordinary legislative procedure). The latest Directives concerning equal treatment and working conditions (Directive 2002/73/EC as well as the recast Directive 2006/54) were both based on ex-Article 141(3) EC (now Article 157(3) TFEU), rather than the other possibility of ex-Article 137(1) EC (now Article 153(1)(i) TFEU).

[84] Instead of ex-Article 141(3) EC ('The Council ... shall adopt measures'), Article III-214(3) CT provided 'European laws or framework laws shall establish measures'. Concerning the consequences in respect of 'autonomous agreements', see below, section VI.B.

One specific question is whether Article 157(3) TFEU (ex-Article 141(3) EC) affects EU competence regarding positive action (paragraph 4). Can the EU adopt measures of positive action under Article 157(3) TFEU (ex-Article 141(3) EC) which go *beyond* the limited scope permitted to Member State measures on positive action by its paragraph 4? There is no indication in the wording that these Articles imply mutually exclusive competences for EU legislation in this area. Instead, Article 157(4) TFEU (ex-Article 141(4) EC) could be interpreted as a 'minimum requirement' (as in Article 153(2)(b) TFEU, ex-Article 137(2)(b) EC) or as a 'most favourable clause' (as in Article 153(4) second indent TFEU, ex-Article 137(4) second indent EC III-210(5)(b)). The overriding importance which the Treaties attach to sex equality issues without any restriction, beginning with Articles 2 and 3(3) TEU through to Article 23 CFREU and Article 8 TFEU, supports this interpretation. In particular, Article 23, second sentence CFREU read in conjunction with the obligation to promote fundamental rights (Article 51(1) CFREU) makes it even more obvious that this would not only cover Member States, but also the EU.[85]

e. Public Health (Article 168(4) TFEU, ex-Article 152(4) EC)

Some aspects of the fundamental social right to health care (Article 35 CFREU) could be dealt with in all legislative forms ('measures'), such as high standards of quality and safety for medicinal products and devices for medical use. But those areas do not have a direct influence on workplace-related matters.

B. 'Autonomous Agreements' (Article 155(2) TFEU, ex-Article 139(2) EC) outside the Scope of Article 153 TFEU (ex-Article 137 EC)

Under the Constitutional Treaty, as under the EC Treaty and now again under the Lisbon Treaty, the same question is raised: how much scope is there for autonomous agreements concluded by the social partners under Article 155 TFEU (ex-Article 139 EC) to include matters outside the competences defined for the EU institutions under Article 153(1) TFEU (ex-Article 137(1) EC)?

The structure of Article 155(2) TFEU (ex-Article 139(2) EC) appears to clearly distinguish two alternatives: one set of competences within (decisions adopted by the Council 'in matters covered by Article 153' TFEU), and the other, not so limited, outside the scope of Article 153 TFEU. This

[85] See for more details in respect of equality Kollonay-Lehoczky, Lörcher and Schömann in this volume (ch 3, section III.)

contextual argument should suffice to confirm that the autonomous social dialogue is not limited by Article 153 TFEU.[86]

One counter-argument is that, in accordance with Article 5(1) TEU, a distinction may be made between the '*limits* of Union competences' and the '*use* of Union competences'. EU competences may be *used* or exercised by the social partners, but the social partners cannot *extend* their limits. This counter-argument is less than convincing because the TFEU confers on the Union a wide range of social competences beyond the scope of Article 153 TFEU, some of which have been described in this chapter.[87] The clear formulation in Article 155(2) TFEU is consistent with this possibility.

Another, equally important question is, *if* such agreements *are* possible, within the scope of Article 153(1) TFEU or even outside its scope, do such agreements have a *specific legal status under EU law*? The argument is that, as explicit competence is allocated to the EU social partners by Article 155 TFEU to conclude agreements, the resulting agreements have legal effects *going beyond merely private law agreements*. The problem is to define exactly what these legal effects are. One indication is in Article 155(2) TFEU (ex-Article 139(2) EC): 'Agreements concluded at Union level shall be implemented'. This imposes an EU legal obligation to implement the agreements on both the social partners in the Member States and the Member States.

Although the wording of Article 155(2) TFEU (ex-Article 139(2) EC) does not refer to Directives or regulations but only to decisions (of the Council) as an implementation method, the practice clearly is related to the implementation by Directives[88] which has been upheld by the CJEU.[89] Therefore, one might assume that any form of legislative act could be used (by a decision) at least as long as the legal basis to which it refers permits such a legislative act. Looking more precisely to Article 153 TFEU it might be assumed that the 'measures' referred to in paragraph (2)(a) could include, for example, regulations (bearing in mind that harmonisation is excluded).

[86] See B Bercusson, *European Labour Law*, 1st edn (Butterworths, 1996) ch 35, pp 546–48.

[87] See above, section VI.A.ii.

[88] One of the latest examples is Council Directive 2010/18/EU of 8 March 2010 implementing the revised Framework Agreement on parental leave concluded by BUSINESSEUROPE, UEAPME, CEEP and ETUC and repealing Directive 96/34/EC, [2010] OJ L 68/13, based on Article 155(2) TFEU.

[89] See CJEU, Case C-537/07 *Gómez-Limón Sánchez-Camacho* [2009] ECR I-6525, para 34 ('As the Court has held that case law can be applied to agreements which, like the framework agreement on parental leave, are the product of a dialogue, based on [ex-]Article 139(1) EC, between management and labour at Community level and which have been implemented in accordance with Article 139(2) EC by a directive of the Council of the European Union, of which they are thus an integral component (see Impact, paragraph 58, and Joined Cases C-378/07 to C-380/07 *Angelidaki and Others* [2009] ECR I-[3071], paragraph 195)').

The next question is whether it may be argued that Article 155(2) TFEU does not prevent the Council from adopting regulations or decisions to implement social dialogue agreements on matters outside the scope of Article 153(1) TFEU. The wording appears at first glance to prevent such a possibility. Even the very structure of the (ordinary) legislative procedure (co-decision by the European Parliament) would have to be understood as preventing a Council decision outside the 'matters covered by Article 153 [TFEU]'. Nevertheless, taking also into account the obligation to promote the role of the social partners, the Commission would have to have very weighty reasons not to present a legislative proposal (for example, the two (anti-)discrimination provisions in Articles 19(1) or 157(3) TFEU) if the social partners concluded an agreement.

VII. POSSIBLE FUTURE DEVELOPMENTS

In particular in respect of the CFREU, the question of social competences at the EU level will remain a controversial issue; not simply in respect of vertical and horizontal subsidiarity, but in respect of the question of whether and to what extent the (enlarged) EU will be able to solve social problems via legislation or any other Union act.

As already pointed out, the TFEU offers a wide range of competences which are far from being fully exploited. Conversely, in recent years, practically no new Directives in the social field have been adopted (apart from, in particular, the anti-discrimination legislation and the Temporary Agency Work Directive 2008/104).[90] The reasons are well known: it is not only the express exclusion of competences in Article 153(5) TFEU and the unanimity requirement in important areas, but above all the lack of political will which prevents new EU social legislation in general.

The question which remains concerns the extent to which the Lisbon Treaty has remedied this situation. It should be recalled that already at national level a constitution in general or a specific competence provision will not in itself create an absent political will. At the European level this would be even less probable. Nevertheless, extending the areas of competence, putting all social competences under the system of qualified majority voting and, last but not least, reducing the express exclusions in Article 153(5) TFEU (ex-Article 137(5) EC) would offer a better framework for making fundamental social rights (more) effective and thus possibly contributing to the creation of the requisite political will.

[90] [2008] OJ L 327/9. The revised Parental Leave Directive (see n 88) only implements a framework agreement by the social partners.

A. Within the Framework of Existing Competences

This approach seems to be easier to follow.

i. Extension of Qualified Majority Voting and Co-decision Procedure

At first glance, the easiest approach might seem to be the extension of the qualified majority voting procedure. The 'passarelle clause' would already allow—in three areas[91]—passing from the unanimity requirement to a qualified majority voting procedure (still by unanimous decision) without any amendment of the Treaties. Within the existing competences, an extension of the qualified majority voting procedure to all areas would seem much easier than enlarging those competences.

In political terms, one might be tempted to overestimate these possibilities to a certain extent because the main obstacle to adopting secondary legislation seems to be removed. But examples show that social legislation was adopted unanimously (the Anti-discrimination Directives based on ex-Article 13 EC, now Article 19 TFEU), even if there was no political enthusiasm.[92] On the other hand, even in the case of Directives adopted under qualified majority rules Member States often tend reach consensus by compromises in order to avoid (majority) decisions, an approach which in reality very much resembles the approach in the unanimity decision cases. Nevertheless, the extension of qualified majority voting would certainly help ease the adoption of social secondary legislation.[93]

ii. Extension of Minimum Standard Legislation

In two areas the TFEU (as the Constitutional Treaty) foresees only the open method of coordination (in Article 153(1)(j) and (k) together with (2)(a) and (b) TFEU): combating social exclusion and modernisation of systems of social protection. The first area is closely related to the fundamental social right of social security and social protection (Article 34(3) CFREU) and therefore should be integrated in the catalogue of competence for minimum standard legislation. The other aspect—which might even be used against

[91] See above, section VI.A.i.b.

[92] In particular, Council Directive 2004/113/EC of 13 December 2004 implementing the principle of equal treatment between men and women in the access to and supply of goods and services, [2004] OJ L 373/37, which was very much disputed and nevertheless adopted unanimously.

[93] The German Federal Constitutional Court states that 'in this respect the approval by the representative of the German government always requires a law within the meaning of Article 23 [(1)] sentence 2, and if necessary sentence 3, of the Basic Law', BVerfG, 30 June 2009, 2 BvE 2/08, para 319: www.bverfg.de/entscheidungen/es20090630_2bve000208en.html). In practice, this might turn out to become an insurmountable hurdle for the use of the 'passarelle clause'.

acquired social rights—should remain as it stands, especially because it very much impinges on national social (security) systems.

B. New Explicit Social Competences

In order to avoid at least some of the interpretation problems referred to above (for example, the relationship to Article 352 TFEU) new explicit competences could help. It should be recalled, however, that this question was on the table from the very beginning of the discussions of the social dimension of the Constitution. Therefore, it might be helpful to look in more detail at the discussions held in Working Group XI on this topic.

i. Removal of Limitations by Deleting 153(5) TFEU (ex-Article 137(5) EC)

One important problem was the express exclusion of certain competences in Article 153(5) TFEU (ex-Article 137(5) EC). Although several Members of the Convention (including the observer representing ETUC) had asked for the deletion of this paragraph,[94] Working Group XI as a whole 'was unable to reach agreement on the question of amending the exceptions in [ex-]Article 137(5)' EC (now Article 153(5) TFEU).[95] This deletion would—under weighty political circumstances—allow reacting directly to threats to, for example, pay or the right to strike.[96]

ii. New Explicit Competences (on the hypothesis of a deletion of Article 153(5) TFEU)

Any demand for new social competences should start by analysing the fundamental social rights for which no (explicit) competence is foreseen in the TFEU.[97] From the outset, two areas are left aside:

(i) The right to education (Article 14(1) CFREU), which is considered to be more of a cultural right, largely separate from the more social aspects (for example, the right to vocational training).
(ii) Respect for entitlements to social security benefits (Article 34(1) CFREU), insofar as it is related to the modernisation of social protection systems (Article 153(1)(k) TFEU), a problem which has been dealt with previously.[98]

[94] 'Proposition d'amendement à l'article III.99 (ex-Article 137 TCE)'.
[95] CONV 516/1/03 REV 1, para 28.
[96] Concerning possible references to Article 352 TFEU, see above section IV.B.v.
[97] See Appendix Table 3: Social fundamental rights in the EU Charter and EU competences in the TFEU.
[98] See above, section VII.A.ii.

The main areas without an explicit EU competence remain:

(i) The right to engage in work and to pursue a freely chosen or accepted occupation (Article 15(1) CFREU); but it could be argued that at least certain elements (such as its internal market dimension (see section V.A) or the protection against unfair dismissal) are covered.
(ii) The grounds of non-discrimination (Article 21(1) CFREU) not included in Article 19 TFEU (that is, social origin, political or any other opinion, membership of a national minority, property, birth).
(iii) The legal, economic and social protection of families (Article 33(1) CFREU) insofar as it is not covered by Article 153(1)(c) TFEU (which provides a competence for 'social protection').
(iv) Combating social exclusion and poverty (Article 34(3) CFREU) where harmonisation legislation is excluded in Article 153(2)(a) TFEU.

An extension of competences in order to cover all the grounds for non-discrimination is necessary in order to harmonise these provisions, especially since there is nothing to justify different treatment between the grounds of non-discrimination.

The other areas seem to be more complex. They very much concern general employment and social policy issues which might not be easy to legislate at the European level. Furthermore, the subsidiarity principle (see Blanke, chapter seven in this volume) might be invoked in the political debate. In any case, even if there were a new explicit competence it might be difficult to exercise because of the limitations provided for in Article 5(3) and (4) TEU.

On the other hand, it should be borne in mind that there are also areas of fundamental social rights which have not been included in the Charter, such as the right to decent remuneration.[99] Although it might be desirable to empower the EU institutions for secondary legislation new competences in these respects seem even less probable.

VIII. CONCLUSIONS

The Lisbon Treaty offers, for the first time, a systemic account of the Union's competences by evaluating in particular the consequences of the new general framework on (social) competences. The social competences are now to be interpreted within this new general framework. In particular, a framework of competences governed by the Union's new values and objectives, and in light of the fundamental social rights in the CFREU. This wider framework offers new prospects for the Union's exercise of social

[99] See Article 4(1) ESC.

competences. But they are limited at least to a certain extent since most of the 'innovation' introduced by the Lisbon Treaty was in fact aimed at restricting the Union's competences, a line of thinking and action which was already developing during the Lisbon IGC, which diminished the outcome of the Second Convention.

Comparing the social competences with the economic competences of the Union, on the whole, it cannot be said that substantive improvements have been achieved; the two spheres are still not on the same footing. Nevertheless, it appears important at least to make use of all the (social) competences, in particular to give fundamental social rights an operational content.[100]

[100] See Appendix Table 3: Social fundamental rights in the EU Charter and EU competences in the TFEU.

ANNEX: Tables

Overview

ANNEX: Tables

Table 1: EU competences in the social policy field—From Article 118 TEEC to Article 153 TFEU

(The actual text of Article 153 TFEU in the Lisbon Treaty version is highlighted in **bold**)

	TEEC [Rome[1]] Article 118	TEEC [SEA[2]] Article 118a	TEC [Maastricht[3]] Social Agreement Article 2	EC [Amsterdam[4]] Article 137	EC [Nice[5]] Article 137	*Constitutional Treaty[6] Article III-210*	TFEU [Lisbon][7] Article 153	Comments
(1)	(2)	(3)	(4)	(5)	(6)	*(7)*	(8)	*(9)*
(a)	Without prejudice to the other provisions of this Treaty and in conformity with its general objectives, the Commission shall have the task of promoting close co-operation between Member States in the social field, particularly in matters relating to:	1. Member States shall pay particular attention to encouraging:	1. With a view to achieving the objectives of Article 1, the Community shall support and complement the activities of the Member States in the following fields:	1. With a view to achieving the objectives of Article 136, the Community shall support and complement the activities of the Member States in the following fields:	1. With a view to achieving the objectives of Article 136, the Community shall support and complement the activities of the Member States in the following fields:	*1. With a view to achieving the objectives of Article III-209, the Union shall support and complement the activities of the Member States in the following fields:*	**1. With a view to achieving the objectives of Article 151, the Union shall support and complement the activities of the Member States in the following fields:**	*In principle, Art 118 TEEC (1) has become Art 156 TFEU. Nevertheless, it still forms the basis for the development of EU competences.* *The very substantial changes relate to the 'upgrading' from (only) close cooperation between Member States (2) to direct legislative EU competences (3) which*

								have remained ever since and even been extended considerably (see below):
(b)		improvements, especially in the working environment, as regards the health and safety of workers, and shall set as their objective the harmonization of conditions in this area, while maintaining the improvements made.	— improvement in particular of the working environment to protect workers' health and safety;	— improvement in particular of the working environment to protect workers' health and safety;	(a) improvement in particular of the working environment to protect workers' health and safety;	*(a) improvement in particular of the working environment to protect workers' health and safety;*	**(a) improvement in particular of the working environment to protect workers' health and safety;**	*This new and first legislative competence (3) was caused by the social balancing of the Internal Market. But the wording was far reaching ('improvements … of the working environment'), whereas it appeared limited in end to safety and health.*
(c)	— employment;							*[see Art 156 TFEU and the developments in respect of Title IX TFEU 'Employment']*
(d)	— labour law and working conditions;		— working conditions;	— working conditions;	(b) working conditions;	(b) *working conditions;*	**(b) working conditions;**	*In the impressive list of new legislative competences this was probably the most important innovation because it covers in principle the whole field of labour law.*
(e)	– basic and advanced vocational training;							*[see Art 156 TFEU and the developments in respect of Title XII 'Education, Vocational Training, Youth and Sport, in particular Art 166 TFEU']*

(*continued*)

Table 1 (*Continued*)

	TEEC [Rome[1]] Article 118	TEEC [SEA[2]] Article 118a	TEC [Maastricht[3]] Social Agreement Article 2	EC [Amsterdam[4]] Article 137	EC [Nice[5]] Article 137	*Constitutional Treaty[6] Article III-210*	TFEU [Lisbon][7] Article 153	Comments
(1)	(2)	(3)	(4)	(5)	(6)	*(7)*	(8)	*(9)*
(f)	— social security;		— *social security and social protection of workers;**	— *social security and social protection of workers;**	(c) social security and social protection of workers;	*(c) social security and social protection of workers;*	**(c) social security and social protection of workers;**	*Important limitations:* — *unanimity is required (see para. 2 subpara 3),* — *Member States can protect their systems (see para 4, 1st indent).*
(g)	— prevention of occupational accident, and diseases;	[see above]						*[see Art 156 TFEU and concerning legislative competences lit. a, see row (b)]*
(h)	— occupational hygiene;	[see above]						*[see Art 156 TFEU and concerning legislative competences lit. a, see row (b)]*
(i)			— *protection of workers where their employment contract is terminated;*[*8]	— *protection of workers where their employment contract is terminated;**	(d) protection of workers where their employment contract is terminated;	*(d) protection of workers where their employment contract is terminated;*	**(d) protection of workers where their employment contract is terminated;**	*Introduced by the Social Agreement (4) this competence requires unanimity ever since (see para. 2 subpara 3.)*
(j)			— the information and consultation of workers;	— the information and consultation of workers;	(e) the information and consultation of workers;	*(e) the information and consultation of workers;*	**(e) the information and consultation of workers;**	*The first (explicit) collective rights competence was introduced by the Maastricht Treaty (3).*

(k)			— *representation and collective defence of the interests of workers and employers, including co-determination, subject to paragraph 6;**	— *representation and collective defence of the interests of workers and employers, including co-determination, subject to paragraph 6;**	(f) representation and collective defence of the interests of workers and employers, including co-determination, subject to paragraph 5;	*(f) representation and collective defence of the interests of workers and employers, including codetermination, subject to paragraph 6;*	**(f) representation and collective defence of the interests of workers and employers, including co-determination, subject to paragraph 5;**	*Although the wording is far reaching important restrictions remain:* *— unanimity requirement (see para 2 subpara 3),* *— exclusion of competence in (para 5) which might take away most of its content.*
(l)			— *conditions of employment for third-country nationals legally residing in Community territory;**	— *conditions of employment for third-country nationals legally residing in Community territory;**	(g) conditions of employment for third-country nationals legally residing in Community territory;	*(g) conditions of employment for third-country nationals legally residing in Union territory;*	**(g) conditions of employment for third-country nationals legally residing in Union territory;**	*This competence is very much linked to Art 53 and 62 TFEU (eg, legal base for the Posting of Workers Directive 96/71/EC) and requires unanimity (see para 2 subpara 3); see within EU Art 46 TFEU*
(M)			— the integration of persons excluded from the labour market, without prejudice to Article 127 of the Treaty establishing the European Community (hereinafter referred to as 'the Treaty');[9]	— the integration of persons excluded from the labour market, without prejudice to Article 150;	(h) the integration of persons excluded from the labour market, without prejudice to Article 150;	*(h) the integration of persons excluded from the labour market, without prejudice to Article III-283;*	**(h) the integration of persons excluded from the labour market, without prejudice to Article 166;**	*The priority attributed to Art 166 TFEU reduces this competence at least to a certain extent.*

(*continued*)

Table 1 (*Continued*)

	TEEC [Rome[1]] Article 118	TEEC [SEA[2]] Article 118a	TEC [Maastricht[3]] Social Agreement Article 2	EC [Amsterdam[4]] Article 137	EC [Nice[5]] Article 137	*Constitutional Treaty[6] Article III-210*	TFEU [Lisbon][7] Article 153	Comments
(1)	(2)	(3)	(4)	(5)	(6)	*(7)*	(8)	*(9)*
(n)			— equality between men and women with regard to labour market opportunities and treatment at work.	— equality between men and women with regard to labour market opportunities and treatment at work.	(i) equality between men and women with regard to labour market opportunities and treatment at work;	*(i) equality between women and men with regard to labour market opportunities and treatment at work;*	**(i) equality between men and women with regard to labour market opportunities and treatment at work;**	*See the close link to Art 157 TFEU.*
(o)				*The Council, acting in accordance with the same procedure, may adopt measures designed to encourage cooperation between Member States through initiatives aimed at improving knowledge, developing exchanges of information and best practices,*	*(j) the combating of social exclusion;*	*(j) the combating of social exclusion;*	**(j) the combating of social exclusion;**	*This new element has been introduced by the Amsterdam Treaty. Harmonisation (via directives) is excluded (see para 2 subpara 1 lit. b.)*

				promoting innovative approaches and evaluating experiences in order to combat social exclusion.[10]				
(p)					*(k) the modernisation of social protection systems without prejudice to point (c).*	*(k) the modernisation of social protection systems without prejudice to point (c).*	**(k) the modernisation of social protection systems without prejudice to point (c).**	*No harmonisation via directives (see para 2 subpara1 lit. b.)*
(q	— the right of association, and collective bargaining between employers and workers.							*[see the explicit exclusion of competences in para 5]*
(r)	To this end, the Commission	[11]2. In order to help achieve the objective laid down in the first paragraph, the Council	2. To this end, the Council	2. To this end, the Council	2. To this end, the Council:	2. *For the purposes of paragraph 1:*	**2. To this end, the European Parliament and the Council:**	*In attributing legislative competences to the EU the shift from the Commission (1) to the Council (2) and Parliament with consultation requirements of the EESC (3) and the CoR (4) was necessary.*

(*continued*)

Table 1 (*Continued*)

	TEEC [Rome[1]] Article 118	TEEC [SEA[2]] Article 118a	TEC [Maastricht[3]] Social Agreement Article 2	EC [Amsterdam[4]] Article 137	EC [Nice[5]] Article 137	*Constitutional Treaty[6] Article III-210*	TFEU [Lisbon][7] Article 153	Comments
(1)	(2)	(3)	(4)	(5)	(6)	(7)	(8)	(9)
(s)	shall act in close contact with Member States by making studies, delivering opinions and arranging consultations both on problems arising at national level and on hose of concern to international organisations.				(a) may adopt measures designed to encourage cooperation between Member States through initiatives aimed at improving knowledge, developing exchanges of information and best practices, promoting innovative approaches and evaluating experiences, excluding any harmonisation of the laws and regulations of the Member States;	*(a) European laws or framework laws may establish measures designed to encourage cooperation between Member States through initiatives aimed at improving knowledge, developing exchanges of information and best practices, promoting innovative approaches and evaluating experiences, excluding any*	**(a) may adopt measures designed to encourage cooperation between Member States through initiatives aimed at improving knowledge, developing exchanges of information and best practices, promoting innovative approaches and evaluating experiences, excluding any harmonisation of the laws and**	*These cooperation initiatives are closely related to the activities described in (1) which have been transferred to Art 156 ut the 'old' list of peration areas has been — made more explicit in respect of labour law (see lit. d to g) and — extended (see lit h to k).*

						harmonisation of the laws and regulations of the Member States;	**regulations of the Member States;**	
(t)		acting by a qualified majority on a proposal from the Commission, in cooperation with the European Parliament and after consulting the Economic and Social Committee, shall adopt, by means of directives,	may adopt, by means of directives,	may adopt, by means of directives,	(b) may adopt, in the fields referred to in paragraph 1(a) to (i), by means of directives,	*(b) in the fields referred to in paragraph 1(a) to (i), European framework laws may establish*	**(b) may adopt, in the fields referred to in paragraph 1(a) to (i), by means of directives,**	*The most important EU exercise of social competences lies in the adoption of directives which is restricted nevertheless by* *— exclusion for (j) and (k)* *— unanimity requirement for (d), (d), (f) and (g).*
(u)		minimum requirements for gradual implementation, having regard to the conditions and technical rules obtaining in each of the Member States.	minimum requirements for gradual implementation, having regard to the conditions and technical rules obtaining in each of the Member States.	minimum requirements for gradual implementation, having regard to the conditions and technical rules obtaining in each of the Member States.	minimum requirements for gradual implementation, having regard to the conditions and technical rules obtaining in each of the Member States.	*minimum requirements for gradual implementation, having regard to the conditions and technical rules obtaining in each of the Member States.*	**minimum requirements for gradual implementation, having regard to the conditions and technical rules obtaining in each of the Member States.**	*The character of 'minimum requirement' is of utmost importance for the development of social policy measures by Member States. It is complemented by the explicit 'most favourable clause' in para 4, 2nd indent.*

(continued)

Table 1 (*Continued*)

	TEEC [Rome[1]] Article 118	TEEC [SEA[2]] Article 118a	TEC [Maastricht[3]] Social Agreement Article 2	EC [Amsterdam[4]] Article 137	EC [Nice[5]] Article 137	*Constitutional Treaty[6] Article III-210*	TFEU [Lisbon][7] Article 153	Comments
(1)	(2)	(3)	(4)	(5)	(6)	*(7)*	(8)	*(9)*
(v)		Such directives shall avoid imposing administrative, financial and legal constraints in a way which would hold back the creation and development of small and mediumsized undertakings.	Such directives shall avoid imposing administrative, financial and legal constraints in a way which would hold back the creation and development of small and medium-sized undertakings.[12]	Such directives shall avoid imposing administrative, financial and legal constraints in a way which would hold back the creation and development of small and medium-sized undertakings.	Such directives shall avoid imposing administrative, financial and legal constraints in a way which would hold back the creation and development of small and medium-sized undertakings.	*Such European framework laws shall avoid imposing administrative, financial and legal constraints in a way which would hold back the creation and development of small and medium-sized undertakings.*	**Such directives shall avoid imposing administrative, financial and legal constraints in a way which would hold back the creation and development of small and medium-sized undertakings.**	*It appears obvious that this restriction cannot prevent workers in SME from taking advantage of the basic rights (eg, safety and health) All Fundamental social rights have to be applied in full*
(w)	Before delivering the opinions provided for in this Article, the commission shall consult the Economic and Social Committee.		The Council shall act in accordance with the procedure referred to in Article 189c of the Treaty after consulting the Economic and Social Committee.	The Council shall act in accordance with the procedure referred to in Article 251 after consulting the Economic and Social Committee and the Committee of the Regions.	The Council shall act in accordance with the procedure referred to in Article 251 after consulting the Economic and Social Committee and the Committee of the Regions,	*In all cases, such European laws or framework laws shall be adopted after consultation of the Committee of the Regions and the Economic and Social Committee.*	**The European Parliament and the Council shall act in accordance with the ordinary legislative procedure after consulting the Economic and Social Committee and the Committee of the Regions.**	*The ordinary legislative procedure is defined in Art 289 TFEU. It is important to note that the EESC (Art 300 et seq TFEU) during the whole history of social competences was involved via consultation; for the consultation requirement for the Social Partners see Art 154 TFEU.*

(x)			3. However, the Council shall act unanimously on a proposal from the Commission, after consulting the European Parliament and the Economic and Social Committee, in the following areas: [see the 4 indents above rows (f), (i), (k) and (l) in italics with an *]	3. However, the Council shall act unanimously on a proposal from the Commission, after consulting the European Parliament, the Economic and Social Committee and the Committee of the Regions in the following areas: [see the 4 indents above rows (f), (i), (k) and (l) in *italics* with an *]	except in the fields referred to in paragraph 1(c), (d), (f) and (g) of this article, where the Council shall act unanimously on a proposal from the Commission, after consulting the European Parliament and the said Committees.	*3. By way of derogation from paragraph 2, in the fields referred to in paragraph 1(c), (d), (f) and (g), European laws or framework laws shall be adopted by the Council acting unanimously after consulting the European Parliament, the Committee of the Regions and the Economic and Social Committee.*	**In the fields referred to in paragraph 1(c), (d), (f) and (g), the Council shall act unanimously, in accordance with a special legislative procedure, after consulting the European Parliament and the said Committees.**	
(y)			— financial contributions for promotion of employment and job-creation, without prejudice to	— financial contributions for promotion of employment and				*To a certain extent this specific area was not very consistent with the otherareas of competence for directives ('financial contributions'). Furthermore,*

(*continued*)

Table 1 *(Continued)*

	TEEC [Rome[1]] Article 118	TEEC [SEA[2]] Article 118a	TEC [Maastricht[3]] Social Agreement Article 2	EC [Amsterdam[4]] Article 137	EC [Nice[5]] Article 137	*Constitutional Treaty[6] Article III-210*	TFEU [Lisbon][7] Article 153	Comments
(1)	(2)	(3)	(4)	(5)	(6)	(7)	(8)	(9)
			the provisions relating to the Social Fund.	job-creation, without prejudice to the provisions relating to the Social Fund.				*it is included(again to a certain extent) in Article 147(1) TFEU inserted already by the Amsterdam Treaty.*
(z)					The Council, acting unanimously on a proposal from the Commission, after consulting the European Parliament, may decide to render the procedure referred to in Article 251 applicable to paragraph 1(d), (f) and (g) of this article.	*The Council may, on a proposal from the Commission, adopt a European decision making the ordinary legislative procedure applicable to paragraph 1(d), (f) and (g). It shall act unanimously after consulting the European Parliament.*	**The Council, acting unanimously on a proposal from the Commission, after consulting the European Parliament, may decide to render the ordinary legislative procedure applicable to paragraph 1(d), (f) and (g).**	*This 'passerelle' clause opening the possibility to pass to the qualified majority voting is excluded for lit. c (social security and social protection).* *The unanimity requirement will not be easy to achieve (all the more in respect of the Judgment of the German Constitutional Court requiring the fulfilment of conditions for a constitutional amendment.*
			4. A Member State may entrust management and labour, at their joint request,	4. A Member State may entrust management and labour, at their joint	3. A Member State may entrust management and labour, at their joint request, with	*4. A Member State may entrust management and labour, at their joint request,*	**3. A Member State may entrust management and labour, at their joint**	*The so-called 'Christiophersen'-clause was introduced to take account of the different social systems, in particular in the Scandinavian*

			with the implementation of directives adopted pursuant to paragraphs 2 and 3.	request, with the implementation of directives adopted pursuant to paragraphs 2 and 3.	the implementation of directives adopted pursuant to paragraph 2.	*with the implementation of European framework laws adopted pursuant o paragraphs 2 and 3 tor, where appropriate, with the implementation of European regulations or decisions adopted in accordance with Article III-212.*	**request, with the implementation of directives adopted pursuant to paragraph 2, or, where appropriate, with the implementation of a Council decision adopted in accordance with Article 155.**	*countries. These systems are characterised by absence of legislation and very strong protection via collective agreements.*
			In this case, it shall ensure that, no later than the date on which a directive must be transposed in accordance with Article 189	In this case, it shall ensure that, no later than the date on which a directive must be transposed in accordance with Article 249	In this case, it shall ensure that, no later than the date on which a directive must be transposed in accordance with Article 249	*In this case, it shall ensure that, no later than the date on which a European framework law must be transposed, or a European regulation or decision implemented,*	**In this case, it shall ensure that, no later than the date on which a directive or a decision must be transposed or implemented,**	*The important 'counter'-part of the delegation to the social partners remains the obligation of the Member State secure the application in practice.*
			management and labour have introduced the necessary measures by agreement, the	*management and labour have introduced the necessary measures by*	*management and labour have introduced the necessary measures by agreement,*	*management and labour have introduced the necessary measures by agreement, the*	**management and labour have introduced the necessary measures by**	

(*continued*)

Table 1 (*Continued*)

	TEEC [Rome[1]] Article 118	TEEC [SEA[2]] Article 118a	TEC [Maastricht[3]] Social Agreement Article 2	EC [Amsterdam[4]] Article 137	EC [Nice[5]] Article 137	*Constitutional Treaty[6] Article III-210*	TFEU [Lisbon][7] Article 153	Comments
(1)	(2)	(3)	(4)	(5)	(6)	(7)	(8)	(9)
			Member State concerned being required to take any necessary measure enabling it at any time to be in a position to guarantee the results imposed by that directive.	*agreement, the Member State concerned being required to take any necessary measure enabling it at any time to be in a position to guarantee the results imposed by that directive.*	*the Member State concerned being required to take any necessary measure enabling it at any time to be in a position to guarantee the results imposed by that directive.*	*Member State being required to take any necessary measure enabling it at any time to be in a position to guarantee the results imposed by that framework law, regulation or decision.*	**agreement, the Member State concerned being required to take any necessary measure enabling it at any time to be in a position to guarantee the results imposed by that directive or that decision.**	
		3. The provisions adopted pursuant to this Article	5. The provision adopted pursuant to this Article	5. The provisions adopted pursuant to this Article	4. The provisions adopted pursuant to this article:	5. *The European laws and framework laws adopted pursuant to this Article:*	**4. The provisions adopted pursuant to this Article:**	*No change [The Constitutional Treaty had introduced references to the definitions of the legislative acts.]*
					— shall not affect the right of Member States to define the fundamental principles of their social security systems and must not	*(a) shall not affect the right of Member States to define the fundamental principles of their social*	**— shall not affect the right of Member States to define the fundamental principles of their social**	*Although this rather new element appears to be limited or at least linked closely to the social security competence (see para 1 lit. c), it might have an impact also to other areas of competence such as the inclusion*

					significantly affect the financial equilibrium thereof,	*security systems and must not significantly affect the financial equilibrium of such systems;*	**security systems and must not significantly affect the financial equilibrium thereof,**	*into the labour market (para 1 lit. h).*
		shall not prevent any Member State from maintaining or introducing more stringent measures for the protection of working conditions compatible with this Treaty.	shall not prevent any Member State from maintaining or introducing more stringent protective measures compatible with the Treaty.	shall not prevent any Member State from maintaining or introducing more stringent protective measures compatible with this Treaty.	— shall not prevent any Member State from maintaining or introducing more stringent protective measures compatible with this Treaty.	*(b) shall not prevent any Member State from maintaining or introducing more stringent protective measures compatible with the Constitution.*	**— shall not prevent any Member State from maintaining or introducing more stringent protective measures compatible with the Treaties.**	*This is the one of the most important elements of EU social policy: the 'most favourable clause'. Member States (and social partners within) remain free to develop better protection for workers.*
			6. The provisions of this Article shall not apply to pay, the right of association, the right to strike or the right to impose lock-outs.	6. The provisions of this Article shall not apply to pay, the right of association, the right to strike or the right to impose lock-outs.	5. The provisions of this article shall not apply to pay, the right of association, the right to strike or the right to impose lock-outs.	*6. This Article shall not apply to pay, the right of association, the right to strike or the right to impose lock-outs.*	**5. The provisions of this Article shall not apply to pay, the right of association, the right to strike or the right to impose lock-outs.**	*The exclusion of competences is restricted only to "(t)he provisions of this Article". Therefore, other legislative EU competences are not prohibited by this provision.*

(*continued*)

1 The Treaty of **Rome**—25 March 1957.
2 The **Single European Act**—Luxembourg –17 February 1986—Subsection III—Social policy—Article 21.

Table 1 (*Continued*)

[3] The **Maastricht** Treaty Provisions Amending the Treaty Establishing the European Economic Community with a View to Establishing the European Community—Maastricht 7 February 1992.

[4] Treaty of **Amsterdam** Amending the Treaty on European Union, the Treaties Establishing the European Communities and Related Acts—Official Journal C 340, 10 November 1997.

[5] Consolidated Version of the Treaty Establishing the European Community—Official Journal C 325 , 24 December 2002—Article amended by the Treaty of **Nice.**

[6] Treaty Establishing a **Constitution** for Europe —Official Journal of the European Union C 310, **16 December 2004** (the text of Article III-210 appears in *italics* because this Treaty has not entered into force).

[7] Consolidated versions of the Treaty on European Union and the Treaty on the Functioning of the European Union—**Treaty of Lisbon—***Official Journal C 83, 30 March 2010.*

[8] The text in *italics* * in rows rows (f), (i), (k) and (l) in the Maastricht (4) and Amsterdam (5) version refers para 3 (see row (x) where it is provided for a unanimity requirement).

[9] For the purpose of better comparison in the present table the order of the two last indents has been changed.

[10] In order to facilitate comparison, this subparagraph has been transferred from the original to this place (therefore it appears in *italics*).

[11] Has been amended by the Maastricht Treaty (see n 3): (33) The first subparagraph of Article 118a(2) shall be replaced by the following: '2. In order to help achieve the objective laid down in the first paragraph, the Council, acting in accordance with the procedure referred to in Article 189c and after consulting the Economic and Social Committee, shall adopt by means of directives, minimum requirements for gradual implementation, having regard to the conditions and technical rules obtaining in each of the Member States').

[12] Declaration on Article 2(2):

'The eleven High Contracting Parties note that in the discussions on Article 2(2) of the Agreement it was agreed that the Community does not intend, in laying down minimum requirements for the protection of the safety and health of employees, to discriminate in a manner unjustified by the circumstances against employees in small and medium-sized undertakings'.

Table 2: Overview of categories and areas of competences in the Treaty on the Functioning of the European Union (TFEU)

	Shared competence	Coordinate competence	Supportive competence	Unforeseen cases
PART ONE—PRINCIPLEs				
General provision (Art 2 TFEU)	Article 2 (2) TFEU (see Protocol No 25)[13]	Article 2 (3) TFEU	Article 2 (5) TFEU	
Content	2. When the Constitution confers on the Union a competence shared with the Member States in a specific area.	3. The Member States shall coordinate their economic and employment policies within arrangements as determined by Part III, which the Union shall have competence to provide.	5. In certain areas and under the conditions laid down in the Constitution, the Union shall have competence to carry out actions to support, coordinate or supplement the actions of the Member States.	
Pre-emption	[yes—to the extent of exercised competence; see also 'most favourable clause' in Article 153 para 4 2nd indent TFEU]	[no]	[no]	
Harmonisation	[minimum requirements]		[no]	
Specific provisions	Article 4 TFEU [Areas of shared competence]	Article 5 TFEU [Coordination of economic and employment policies]	Article 6 TFEU [Areas of supporting, coordinating or complementary action]	Article 352 TFEU [Unforeseen cases / flexibility clause]
Description of the areas of competences	1. The Union shall share competence with the Member States where the Treaties confer on it a competence which does not relate to the areas referred to in Articles 3 and 6.	1. The Member States shall coordinate their economic policies within the Union. To this end, the Council shall adopt measures, in particular broad guidelines for these policies.	The Union shall have competence to carry out actions to support, coordinate or supplement actions of the Member States.	1. If action by the Union should prove necessary, within the framework of the policies defined in the Treaties, to attain one of the objectives set out in the Treaties, and the Treaties have not provided the necessary

(continued)

Table 2 (*Continued*)

	Shared competence	Coordinate competence	Supportive competence	Unforeseen cases
		2. The Union shall take measures to ensure coordination of the employment policies of the Member States, in particular by defining guidelines for these policies. 3. The Union may take initiatives to ensure coordination of Member States' social policies.		powers, the Council, acting unanimously on a proposal from the Commission and after obtaining the consent of the European Parliament, shall adopt the appropriate measures. Where the measures in question are adopted by the Council in accordance with a special legislative procedure, it shall also act unanimously on a proposal from the Commission and after obtaining the consent of the European Parliament
				3. Measures based on this Article shall not entail harmonisation of Member States' laws or regulations in cases where the Treaties exclude such harmonisation.
Description of areas with social implications	2. Shared competence between the Union and the Member States applies in the following principal areas: (a) internal market; (b) social policy, for the aspects defined in this Treaty;		The areas of such action shall, at European level, be: (a) protection and improvement of human health; (e) education, youth, sport and vocational training;	

	(c) economic, social and territorial cohesion; (k) common safety concerns in public health matters, for the aspects defined in this Treaty.			
PART TWO—NON-DISCRIMINATION AND CITIZENSHIP OF THE UNION				
Services of general economic interest	Article 14 TFEU (see also Protocol No 26)			
Equality (nationality)	Article 18 TFEU			
Equality (sex, racial or ethnic origin, religion or belief, disability, age or sexual orientation)	Article 19 TFEU			
PART THREE—UNION POLICIES AND INTERNAL ACTIONS				
Freedom of movement of migrant workers	Title IV—Chapter 1, in particular — Article 46 TFEU			
Social security of migrant workers	— Article 48 TFEU			
Employment		Title IX (Articles 145 et seq TFEU)		
Social policy	Article 153 TFEU [see Tables 1 and 2]	Article 156 TFEU		
Equality (sex)	Article 153 para 1 lit. i TFEU Article 157 para 3 TFEU			

(continued)

Table 2 (*Continued*)

	Shared competence	Coordinate competence	Supportive competence	Unforeseen cases
Social protection policies (Committee)	(see also Article 153 para 1 lit. c TFEU	Article 160 TFEU		
European Social Fund		Title XI (Articles 162 et seq TFEU)		
Public health	Article 168 para 4 TFEU		Article 168 paras 1–3 TFEU	
Education			Article 165 TFEU	
Vocational training			Article 166 TFEU	

[13] See ch 6, III.B.

Table 3: Social Fundamental Rights in the Charter of Fundamental Rights in the European Union (CFREU) and respective EU competences in the Treaty on the Functioning of the European Union (TFEU)

Preliminary remarks:
This table is aimed at analysing the powers of the EU legislator to give the fundamental social rights a concrete content via secondary legislation. It also includes references to any other (non-legislative) competence in the respective field of a given fundamental social right.
At first, the content of the fundamental social right (2) is compared with the content of any EU competence in the respective field (4). In the further columns, it is examined which category of competence (including the 'Open Method of Coordination') is offered by the TFEU to make the fundamental right effective. The most important category is the legislative competence (5) which in the ordinary legislative procedure might—in practical terms— be limited in additional voting requirements (6).
Following explanations concerning the different columns might be helpful:

(1) Art	refers to the numbers of articles in the Charter of Fundamental Rights in the European Union (CFREU) for the following column:
(2) **Fundamental social rights**	quotes the content of the fundamental social rights contained in the EU Charter of Fundamental Rights (see Article 6(1) TFEU) in the order of the Articles
(3) Art	refers to the numbers of articles in the TFEU for the following column:
(4) **Competences** Content	quotes the substance of (any) competence in the matter the character of which is defined in the following columns:
(5) **Legisl** Art	refers to the TFEU Articles which provide for a competence for a **legislative** act (Article 289(3) TFEU) which is in the social rights field — normally a directive (Article 288(3) TFEU) — rarely a regulation (Article 288(2) TFEU)
(6) **Voting** Art	examines the TFEU Articles which define the ordinary legislative procedure (Articles 289(1) and 294 TFEU) in respect of **voting:** — in principle: qualified majority voting (QMV)

— ordinary legislative procedure: exemption: unanimity as provided for in specific cases (if this addition requirement may be led back to the QMV by a unanimous decision of the Council (so-called 'Passerelle Clause' Article 153(3)(2) TFEU) it is referred to as 'PC')

(7) **Comp** Art — defines the category of **competences** by referring to the specific articles (see also Table 3)
— shared competence (Articles 2(2) and 4 TFEU)
— coordinate competence (Articles 2(3), and 5 TFEU)
— supportive competence (Articles 2(4), and 6 TFEU)
— competence in unforeseen cases (Article 352 TFEU)

(8) **OMC I** Art — as **first** category for the **'open method of coordination'** all measures

(9) **OMC II** Art — as **second** category for the **'open method of coordination'** measures which are included in Social Policy Chapter (Article 156 TFEU)

(10) *Comments*: — summarises (in *italics*) the result of the analysis, ie, whether or not a legislative competences exists.

Art	Fundamental social rights Content	Art	Competences Content	Legisl Art	Voting Art	Comp Art	OMC I Art	OMC II Art	*Comments*
(1)	(2)	(3)	(4)	(5)	(6)	(7)	(8)	(9)	(10)
				TITLE II FREEDOMS					
8	**Protection of personal data** 1. Everyone has the right to the protection of personal data concerning him or her. 2. Such data must be processed fairly for specified purposes and on the basis of the consent of the person concerned or some other legitimate basis laid down by law. Everyone has the	16 (1)	1. Everyone has the right to the protection of personal data concerning them. …	16(2): 'rules'. directives and regulations					***Full** legislative competence.*

	right of access to data which has been collected concerning him or her, and the right to have it rectified. …								
12 (1)	**Freedom of assembly and of association** 1. Everyone has the right to freedom of peaceful assembly and to freedom of association at all levels, in particular in political, trade union and civic matters, which implies the right of everyone to form and to join trade unions for the protection of his or her interests. …	153 (1) (f)	(f) representation and collective defence of the interests of workers and employers, including codetermination, subject to paragraph 5	— [see 153 (5)][14]	—	—	153(2) (1)(a): 'measures'—no harmonisation	156 7th indent: right of association and collective bargaining	*Due to the reference to para 5 there is* ***no*** *legislative competence based on this Article. Very special circumstances might justify recourse to Art 352 TFEU.*[15]
14 (1)	**Right to education** 1. Everyone has the right to education and to have access to vocational and continuing training.	165 (2)	2. Union action shall be aimed at: — developing the European dimension in education, particularly through the teaching and dissemination of the languages of the Member States, — encouraging mobility of students and teachers, by encouraging inter alia, the academic recognition of diplomas and periods of study,	—	—	6(e) and 165(1)	165(4) 1st indent: 'measures'—no harmonisation; 165 (4) 2nd indent: Recommendations	156 3rd indent: basic and advanced vocational training	*In principle, for the cultural right to education there is* ***no*** *legislative competence, but for the more specific social (rights) aspect of vocational training a wide field of activities is foreseen.*

(*continued*)

Table 3 (*Continued*)

Art	Fundamental social rights Content	Art	Competences Content	Legisl Art	Voting Art	Comp Art	OMC I Art	OMC II Art	*Comments*
(1)	(2)	(3)	(4)	(5)	(6)	(7)	(8)	(9)	(10)
			— promoting cooperation between educational establishments, — developing exchanges of information and experience on issues common to the education systems of the Member States, — encouraging the development of youth exchanges and of exchanges of socio-educational instructors, and encouraging the participation of young people in democratic life in Europe, — encouraging the development of distance education, — developing the European dimension in sport, by promoting fairness and openness in sporting competitions and cooperation between bodies responsible for sports, and by protecting the physical and moral integrity of sportsmen and						

			sportswomen, especially the youngest sportsmen and sportswomen.						
15 (1)	**Freedom to choose an occupation and right to engage in work** 1. Everyone has the right to engage in work and to pursue a freely chosen or accepted occupation.	145	Member States and the Union shall, in accordance with this Title, work towards developing a coordinated strategy for employment and particularly for promoting a skilled, trained and daptable workforce and labour markets responsive to economic change with a view to achieving the aobjectives defined in Article 3 of the Treaty on European Union.	—	—	5(2): coordinate: 147(1)			***No** legislative competence; but a wide policy framework and great impact on other issue (see in this respect the 'Employment' Title IX Articles 145 et seq TFEU).*
15 (2)	2. Every citizen of the Union has the freedom to seek employment, to work, to exercise the right of establishment and to provide services in any Member State.	45	1. Freedom of movement for workers shall be secured within the Union. 2. Such freedom of movement shall entail the abolition of any discrimination based on nationality between workers of the Member States as regards employment, remuneration and other conditions of work and employment.	46: directives and regulations	46: QMV	4(2)(a): shared competence: internal market		—	*Since this right to seek employment is limited to 'citizen(s) of the Union', **full** legislative competence is guaranteed.* *[For the freedom 'to exercise the right of establishment and to provide services in any Member State' which are not considered to*

(*continued*)

Table 3 (*Continued*)

Art	Fundamental social rights Content	Art	Competences Content	Legisl Art	Voting Art	Comp Art	OMC I Art	OMC II Art	*Comments*
(1)	(2)	(3)	(4)	(5)	(6)	(7)	(8)	(9)	(10)
			3. It shall entail the right, subject to limitations justified on grounds of public policy, public security or public health: (a) to accept offers of employment actually made; (b) to move freely within the territory of Member States for this purpose; (c) to stay in a Member State for the purpose of employment in accordance with the provisions governing the employment of nationals of that State laid down by law, regulation or administrative action; (d) to remain in the territory of a Member State after having been employed in that State, subject to conditions which shall be embodied						*be social rights, see Chapters 2 and 3, ie, Articles 49 et seq and 56 et seq TFEU.]*

			in regulations to be drawn up by the Commission. 4. The provisions of this Article shall not apply to employment in the public service:						
15 (3)	3. Nationals of third countries who are authorised to work in the territories of the Member States are entitled to working conditions equivalent to those of citizens of the Union.	153 (1) (g)	(g) conditions of employment for third-country nationals legally residing in Union territory;	153(2) (1)(b): directives	153(2) (3): unanimity/ PC	4(2)(b): shared competence: social policy	153(2) (1)(a): 'measures'—no harmonisation	156 ('under this Chapter')[16]	***In principle*** *legislative competence but* — *unanimity required* — *difference between 'authorised to work' and 'legally residing'.*
TITLE III EQUALITY									
21 (1)	**Non-discrimination** 1. Any discrimination based on any ground such as sex,[17] race, colour, ethnic or social origin, genetic features, language, religion or belief, political or any other opinion, membership of a national minority, property, birth, disability,[18] age[19] or sexual orientation shall be prohibited.	19 (1)	1. Without prejudice to the other provisions of the Treaties and within the limits of the powers conferred by them upon the Union, the Council, acting unanimously in accordance with a special legislative procedure and after obtaining the consent of the European Parliament, may take appropriate action to combat discrimination	19(1): 'action': directives and regulations	19(1): unanimity	4(2): shared competence: general	19(2): 'measures'—no harmonisation	—	***Partly full, but partly no express*** *legislative competence for: social origin, political or any other opinion, membership of a national minority, property, birth;* ***possibly*** *use of* ***Art 352 TFEU.***

(continued)

Table 3 (*Continued*)

Art	Fundamental social rights Content	Art	Competences Content	Legisl Art	Voting Art	Comp Art	OMC I Art	OMC II Art	*Comments*
(1)	(2)	(3)	(4)	(5)	(6)	(7)	(8)	(9)	(10)
			based on sex, racial or ethnic origin, religion or belief, disability, age or sexual orientation.						
21 (2)	2. Within the scope of application of the Treaties and without prejudice to any of their specific provisions, any discrimination on grounds of nationality shall be prohibited.	45	2. Any discrimination based on nationality between workers of the Member States as regards employment, remuneration and other conditions of work and employment shall be prohibited. 4. This Article shall not apply to employment in the public service.	46: directives and regula-tions	46: QMV	4(2)(a): shared competence: internal market		—	***Full** legislative competence.*
		18 (1)	Within the scope of application of the Treaties, and without prejudice to any special provisions contained therein, any discrimination on grounds of nationality shall be prohibited.	18(2): rules': directives and regula-tions	18(2): QMV	4(1): shared competence: general			***Full** legislative competence.*
23	**Equality between women and men** Equality between women and men must be ensured in all areas, including employment, work and pay.[20]	153 (1) (i)	(i) equality between women and men with regard to labour market opportunities and treatment at work;	153(2) (1)(b): directives	153(2) (2): QMV	4(2)(b): shared competence: social policy	153(2) (1)(a): 'measures'—no harmonisation	156 ('under this Chapter')	***Full** legislative competence.*

	The principle of equality shall not prevent the maintenance or adoption of measures providing for specific advantages in favour of the under-represented sex.[21]								
		157 (3)	3. The European Parliament and the Council, acting in accordance with the ordinary legislative procedure, and after consulting the Economic and Social Committee, shall adopt measures to ensure the application of the principle of equal opportunities and equal treatment of men and women in matters of employment and occupation, including the principle of equal pay for equal work or work of equal value.	157(3): 'measures' directives and regulations	157(3): QMV	4(2)(b): shared competence: social policy		156 ('under this Chapter')	***Full** legislative competence.*
19 (1)			1. Without prejudice to the other provisions of the Treaties and within the limits of the powers conferred by them upon the Union, the Council, acting unanimously in accordance with a special legislative procedure and after obtaining the	19(1): 'action': directives and regulations	19(1): unanimity	4(2): shared competence: general	19(2): 'measures'—no harmonisation		***Full** legislative competence, but unanimity required.*

(continued)

Table 3 (*Continued*)

Art	Fundamental social rights Content	Art	Competences Content	Legisl Art	Voting Art	Comp Art	OMC I Art	OMC II Art	*Comments*
(1)	(2)	(3)	(4)	(5)	(6)	(7)	(8)	(9)	(10)
			consent of the European Parliament, may take appropriate action to combat discrimination based on sex.						
			TITLE IV SOLIDARITY						
27	**Workers' right to information and consultation within the undertaking** Workers or their representatives must, at the appropriate levels, be guaranteed information and consultation in good time in the cases and under the conditions provided for by Union law and national laws and practices.	153 (1) (e)	(e) the information and consultation of workers;	153(2) (1)(b): directives	153(2) (2): QMV	4(2)(b): shared competence: social policy	153(2) (1)(a): 'measures'—no harmonisation	156 2nd indent: labour law and working conditions	***Full** legislative competence.*
28	**Right of collective bargaining and action** Workers and employers, or their respective organisations, have, in accordance with Union law and national laws and practices, the right to negotiate and conclude collective agreements at the appropriate levels and, in cases of conflicts of interest, to take collective action to defend their interests, including strike action.	153 (1) (f)	(f) representation and collective defence of the interests of workers and employers, including codetermination, subject to paragraph 5;	153(2) (1)(b): directives	153(2) (3): unanimity/ PC	4(2)(b): shared competence: social policy	153(2) (1)(a): 'measures'—no harmonisation	156 7th indent: right of association and collective bargaining	*Due to the reference to para 5 there is **no** legislative competence based on this Article. Very special circumstances might justify recourse to Art 352 TFEU.*[22]

29	**Right of access to placement services** Everyone has the right of access to a free placement service.	153 (1) (c)	(c) social security and social protection of workers;[23]	153(2) (1)(b): directives	153(2) (3): unanimity	4(2)(b): shared competence: social policy	153(2) (1)(a): 'measures'—no harmonisation	156 4th indent: social security	***Partly** legislative competence to the extent that placement services are considered as being part of the social security system or organised as services of general interest.*
		14	Without prejudice to Article 4 of the Treaty on European Union or to Articles 93, 106 and 107 of this Treaty, and given the place occupied by services of general economic interest in the shared values of the Union as well as their role in promoting social and territorial cohesion, the Union and the Member States, each within their respective powers and within the scope of application of the Treaties, shall take care that such services operate on the basis of principles and conditions, particularly economic and financial conditions, which enable them to fulfil their missions.	14: regulations	14: QMV	4(1): shared competence: general			

(continued)

Table 3 (*Continued*)

Art	Fundamental social rights Content	Art	Competences Content	Legisl Art	Voting Art	Comp Art	OMC I Art	OMC II Art	*Comments*
(1)	(2)	(3)	(4)	(5)	(6)	(7)	(8)	(9)	(10)
			The European Parliament and the Council, acting by means of regulations in accordance with the ordinary legislative procedure, shall establish these principles and set these conditions without prejudice to the competence of Member States, in compliance with the Treaties, to provide, to commission and to fund such services.						
30	**Protection in the event of unjustified dismissal** Every worker has the right to protection against unjustified dismissal, in accordance with	153 (1) (d)	(d) protection of workers where their employment contract is terminated;	153(2) (1)(b): directives	153(2) (3): unanimity/ PC	4(2)(b): shared competence: social policy	153(2) (1)(a): 'measures'—no harmonisation	156 2nd indent: labour law and working conditions	***Full** legislative competence (but unanimity is required).*
	Union law and national laws and practices.								
31	**Fair and just working conditions** 1. Every worker has the right to working conditions which respect his or her health, safety and dignity. 2. Every worker has the right to limitation of maximum working hours, to daily and weekly rest periods and to an annual period of paid leave.	153 (1) (a)	(a) improvement in particular of the working environment to protect workers' health and safety;	153(2) (1)(b): directives	153(2) (2): QMV	4(2)(b): shared competence: social policy	153(2) (1)(a): 'measures'— no harmonisation	156 2nd indent: labour law and working conditions	***Full** legislative competence (only if one would include remuneration questions in this provision, a legislative competence would be excluded).*[24]

		153 (1) (b)	(b) working conditions;	153(2) (1)(b): directives	153(2) (2): QMV	4(2)(b): shared competence: social policy	153(2) (1)(a): 'measures'—no harmonisation	156 2nd indent: labour law and working conditions	*The possibly two different legal bases would pose no problem since all conditions are the same.*
32	**Prohibition of child labour and protection of young people at work** The employment of children is prohibited. The minimum age of admission to employment may not be lower than the minimum school-leaving age, without prejudice to such rules as may be more favourable to young people and except for limited derogations. Young people admitted to work must have working conditions appropriate to their age and be protected against economic exploitation and any work likely to harm their safety, health or physical, mental, moral or social development or to interfere with their education.	153 (1) (a)	(a) improvement in particular of the working environment to protect workers' health and safety;	153(2) (1)(b): directives	153(2) (2): QMV	4(2)(b): shared competence: social policy	153(2) (1)(a): 'measures'—no harmonisation	156 2nd indent: labour law and working conditions	***Full** legislative competence.*
33 (1)	**Family and professional life** 1. The family shall enjoy legal, economic and social protection.	153 (1) (c)	(c) social security and social protection of workers;[25]	153(2) (1)(b): directives	153(2) (3): unanimity	4(2)(b): shared competence: social policy	153(2) (1)(a): 'measures'—no harmonisation	156 4th indent: social security	***Partly** legislative competence in respect of 'social protection' (ambiguities concerning 'legal and economic protection').*

(*continued*)

Table 3 (*Continued*)

Art	Fundamental social rights Content	Art	Competences Content	Legisl Art	Voting Art	Comp Art	OMC I Art	OMC II Art	*Comments*
(1)	(2)	(3)	(4)	(5)	(6)	(7)	(8)	(9)	(10)
33 (2)	2. To reconcile family and professional life, everyone shall have the right to protection from dismissal for a reason connected with maternity and the right to paid maternity leave and to parental leave following the birth or adoption of a child.	153 (1) (b)	(b) working conditions;	153(2) (1)(b): directives	153(2) (2): QMV	4(2)(b): shared competence: social policy	153(2) (1)(a): 'measures'—no harmonisation	156 2nd indent: labour law and working conditions	***Full** legislative competence.*
34 (1)	**Social security and social assistance** 1. The Union recognises and respects the entitlement to social security benefits and social services providing protection in cases such as maternity, illness, industrial accidents, dependency or old age, and in the case of loss of employment, in accordance with the rules laid down by Union law and national laws and practices.	153 (1) (c)	(c) social security and social protection of workers;	153(2) (1)(b): directives	153(2) (3): unanimity	4(2)(b): shared competence: social policy	153(2) (1)(a): 'measures'—no harmonisation	156 4th indent: social security	***Full** legislative competence for 'social security with unanimity requirement (some ambiguityin respect of 'social assistance'/ 'social protection) but'*
		153 (1) (k)	(k) the modernisation of social protection systems without prejudice to point (c);	—	—	4(2)(b): shared competence: social policy	153(2) (1)(a): 'measures'—no harmonisation	156 ('under this Chapter')	***no** legislative competence in respect of modernisation of social protection systems.*
34 (2)	2. Everyone residing and moving legally within the European Union is entitled to social security benefits and social advantages in accordance with	48 (1)	The European Parliament and the Council shall, acting in accordance with the ordinary legislative procedure, adopt such measures in the field of	48(1): 'measures' directives and regula-tions	48(2): QMV/ veto[26]	4(2)(a): shared competence: internal market		—	***Full** legislative competence (also for 'social advantages' see Arts 45 and 46).*

	Union law and national laws and practices.		social security as are necessary to provide freedom of movement for workers; to this end, they shall make arrangements to secure for employed and self-employed migrant workers and their dependants: (a) aggregation, for the purpose of acquiring and retaining the right to benefit and of calculating the amount of benefit, of all periods taken into account under the laws of the several countries; (b) payment of benefits to persons resident in the territories of Member States.						
34 (3)	3. In order to combat social exclusion and poverty, the Union recognises and respects the right to social and housing assistance so as to ensure a decent existence for all those who lack sufficient resources, in accordance with the rules laid down by Union law and national laws and practices.	153 (1) (h)	(h) the integration of persons excluded from the labour market, without prejudice to Article 166;[27]	153(2) (1) (b): directives	153(2) (2): QMV	4(2)(b): shared competence: social policy	153(2) (1)(a): 'measures'—no harmonisation	156 4th indent: social security	*Since there is a clear relation to the labour market, there is only* ***limited*** *legislative competence.*

(*continued*)

Table 3 (*Continued*)

Art	Fundamental social rights Content	Art	Competences Content	Legisl Art	Voting Art	Comp Art	OMC I Art	OMC II Art	*Comments*
(1)	(2)	(3)	(4)	(5)	(6)	(7)	(8)	(9)	(10)
		153 (1) (j)	(j) the combating of social exclusion;	—	—	4(2)(b): shared competence: social policy	153(2) (1)(a): 'measures'—no harmonisation	156 ('under this Chapter')	***No** legislative competence.*
35	**Health care** Everyone has the right of access to preventive health care and the right to benefit from medical treatment under the conditions established by national laws and practices. A high level of human health protection shall be ensured in the definition and implementation of all Union policies and activities.	165 (4)	4. By way of derogation from Article 2(5) and Article 6(a) and in accordance with Article 4(2)(k) the European Parliament and the Council, acting in accordance with the ordinary legislative procedure and after consulting the Economic and Social Committee and the Committee of the Regions, shall contribute to the achievement of the objectives referred to in this Article through adopting in order to meet common safety concerns: (a) measures setting high standards of quality and safety of organs and substances of human origin, blood and blood derivatives; these measures shall not prevent any Member	165(4): 'measures': directives and regulations	165(4): QMV	In general: I-17(a): area of supporting, coordinating or complementary action	165(1)–(3)	—	***Limited** legislative competence because it exists only to a certain extent.*

			State from maintaining or introducing more stringent protective measures; (b) measures in the veterinary and phytosanitary fields which have as their direct objective the protection of public health; (c) measures setting high standards of quality and safety for medicinal products and devices for medical use.						
36	**Access to services of general economic interest** The Union recognises and respects access to services of general economic interest as provided for in national laws and practices, in accordance with the Treaties, in order to promote the social and territorial cohesion of the Union.	14	Without prejudice to Article 4 of the Treaty on European Union or to Articles 93, 106 and 107 of this Treaty, and given the place occupied by services of general economic interest in the shared values of the Union as well as their role in promoting social and territorial cohesion, the Union and the Member States, each within their respective powers and within the scope of application of the Treaties, shall take care that such services operate on the basis of principles and conditions, particularly economic and financial	14: regula-tions	14: QMV	4(1) shared competence: general	—	—	***Full** legislative competence appears to be given since only 'access' is guar-anteed and this is one main feature out of the more*

(*continued*)

Table 3 (*Continued*)

Art	Fundamental social rights Content	Art	Competences Content	Legisl Art	Voting Art	Comp Art	OMC I Art	OMC II Art	*Comments*
(1)	(2)	(3)	(4)	(5)	(6)	(7)	(8)	(9)	(10)
			conditions, which enable them to fulfil their missions. The European Parliament and the Council, acting by means of regulations in accordance with the ordinary legislative						
			procedure, shall establish these principles and set these conditions without prejudice to the competence of Member States, in compliance with the Treaties, to provide, to commission and to fund such services.						

(*continued*)

[14] '5. This Article shall not apply to pay, the right of association, the right to strike or the right to impose lockouts'. (see also Art 28 CFREU below)

[15] See also Article 152 TFEU and in particular the obligation to promote the role of the Social Partner at Union level.

[16] This is a wrong reference because no 'Chapter' exists any more in this respect; it can only relate to Title X 'Social Policy'.

[17] Not in the text: See also Article 23 CFREU below.

[18] Not in the text: Reference should be made also to Article 26 CFREU ("Integration of persons with disabilities") which appear to go, in principle, beyond non-discrimination rights in labour law.

[19] Not in the text: Reference should be made also to the protection of specific groups of persons:

- young persons: Article 24 CFREU ("The rights of the child") which appears to go, in principle, beyond non-discrimination rights in labour law and is therefore not dealt with here in detail, as well as Article 32 CFREU ("Prohibition of child labour and protection of young people at work") which is a major issue (see below),
- elderly persons: Article 25 CFREU ("The rights of the elderly") which also appears to go, in principle, beyond non-discrimination rights in labour law and is therefore not dealt with here in detail.

[20] Not in the text: see Article 157(1) and (2) TFEU.

[21] Not in the text: see Article 157(4).

22 See above Article 12(1) CFREU.

23 But see also Article 153(1)(k): 'the modernisation of social protection systems without prejudice to point (c)'.

24 See n 14.

25 But see also Article 153(1)(k): 'the modernisation of social protection systems without prejudice to point (c)'.

26 'Where a member of the Council declares that a draft legislative act referred to in the first subparagraph would affect important aspects of its social security system, including its scope, cost or financial structure, or would affect the financial balance of that system, it may request that the matter be referred to the European Council. In that case, the ordinary legislative procedure shall be suspended. After discussion, the European Council shall, within four months of this suspension, either:

(a) refer the draft back to the Council, which shall terminate the suspension of the ordinary legislative procedure; or

(b) take no action or request the Commission to submit a new proposal; in that case, the act originally proposed shall be deemed not to have been adopted'.

27 See above under Article 14 CFREU.

Abbreviations

Art	Article in the TFEU
Comp	(category of) competences (see Table 2I)
QMV	Qualified majority voting
Legisl	Legislation (power to legislate in respect of minimum standards or harmonised legislation)
OMC I	Open method of coordination I: mainly related to Art 153(2)(1)(a) TFEU including EUL and EUFL but without any harmonisation
OMC II	Open method of coordination II: mainly related to Art 156 TFEU
PC	'Passerelle Clause' (to pass from unanimity to QMV, see Article 153(4) TFEU)

7

The Principle of Subsidiarity in the Lisbon Treaty

THOMAS BLANKE

I. INTRODUCTION: THE CAREER OF THE PRINCIPLE OF SUBSIDIARITY IN EU LAW AND THE SHIFT FROM THE FRENCH MODEL OF EUROPEAN INTEGRATION TOWARDS THE GERMAN MODEL

THE PRINCIPLE OF subsidiarity regulates the exercise of powers in the EU. It determines whether the Union can take legal action or should leave intervention to the Member States. Article 5(3) TEU[1] provides the following definition of the principle of subsidiarity:

> Under the principle of subsidiarity, in areas which do not fall within its exclusive competence, the Union shall act only if and insofar as the objectives of the proposed action cannot be sufficiently achieved by the Member States, either at central level or at regional and local level, but can rather, by reason of the scale or effects of the proposed action, be better achieved at Union level.

For many years after the Treaty of Rome established the European Economic Community in 1957, the principle of subsidiarity played only a very minor role in Community law. The term 'subsidiarity' was itself unknown as a legal category. But this changed remarkably during the late 1980s, and formally and systematically as a result of the Treaty of Maastricht in 1992. That Treaty inserted into the EC Treaty the obligation for the Union to comply with the principle of subsidiarity in the exercise of its powers (ex-Article 3b(2) TEC).

One main reason for this shift lies in the transformation of the concept of European integration. This changed from the founding Treaty-based Economic Community, which aimed to create a regulated common market in specified spheres of the economy (goods, services, capital, labour) towards 'ever closer political union'. The emerging character of the European Union as a political entity (federal state?) placed the following question on the agenda

[1] Treaty on European Union and the Treaty on the Functioning of the European Union of 13.12.2007, consolidated version: OJ C 83/1 of 30.3.2010.

of the Treaties: how to share the legal, administrative and judicial competences between the central level of the Community and the Member States and the regions. The principle of subsidiarity was invoked as a concept serving to *counterbalance* the ongoing process whereby steadily more competences and powers were being assumed by the central European level.[2] This led to the shift of European integration from a 'French' vision to a 'German' vision:

> In a 'German' perspective which is essentially federal-oriented, a centre endowed with strong initiative capabilities and foreign representation placed individual members in competition among themselves, favouring an evolutionary process in which the more efficient define the common norms. This vision places the emphasis on the characteristics of initiative and control of the Commission, establishing by definition an alliance among 'strong' subjects acting within the administrative territory.[3]

But the relationship between the acquired legislative powers of the central EU institutions and the remaining competences of the Member States is only one reason for the growing relevance of the principle of subsidiarity in the EU. In this context one can say that the principle of subsidiarity has become, since the European Single Act and the Maastricht Treaty, one of the main pillars of the structure of the EU and of EU law. It became a constitutional principle and as such a principle of law. This principle decides on the exercise of powers between the central level and more decentralised levels of the Member States. 'Subsidiarity tackles the core of the problems of the Union's development, that of sovereignty'.[4]

This finds expression in the decisions of the German Constitutional Court regarding the Maastricht and the Lisbon Treaties.[5] In consequence of both decisions, the German Basic Law was amended with regard to European integration by reference to the principle of subsidiarity. First, in consequence of the Maastricht Treaty a new Article 23(1) was inserted in the German Basic Law that stated:

> With a view to establishing a united Europe, the Federal Republic of Germany shall participate in the development of the European Union that is committed to

[2] P Bianchi, 'Subsidiarity and its significance' in PJ Devine, Y Katsoulacos and R Sugden (eds), *Competitiveness, Subsidiarity and Industrial Policy* (Routledge, London and New York, 1996) pp 42ff, 43; Committee of the Regions (ed), *The Committee of the Regions and the implementation and monitoring of the principles of subsidiarity and proportionality in the light of the Constitution for Europe* (Luxemburg, 2006).

[3] *Cf* Bianchi (n 2) p 46.

[4] *Cf* Ibid p 43.

[5] BVerfG of 12.10.1993—Az: 2 BvR 2134—E 89,155 and BVerfG of 30.6.2009—Az.:—2 BvE 2/08, 2 BvE 5/08, 2 BvR 1010/08, 2 BvR 1022/08, 2 BvR 1259/08 and 2 BvR 182/09; see A Fiesahn, 'Bundesverfassungsgericht friert die europäische Demokratie national ein' (2009) (3) *KJ* pp 220ff.; see also: M Höpner, S Leibfried, M Höreth, FW Scharpf and M Zürn, 'Kampf um Souveränität? Eine Kontroverse zur europäischen Integration nach dem Lissabon-Urteil des Bundesverfassungsgerichts' (2010) (2) *PVS* pp 323ff.

democratic, social and federal principles, to the rule of law, and to the principle of subsidiarity, and that guarantees a level of protection of basic rights essentially comparable to that afforded by this Basic Law. To this end the Federation may transfer sovereign powers by law with the consent of the Bundesrat. The establishment of the European Union, as well as changes in its treaty foundations and comparable regulations that amend or supplement this Basic Law, or make such amendments or supplements possible, shall be subject to paragraphs (2) and (3) of Article 79.

Due to the decision of 30 June 2009 this Article 23 of the German Basic Law was further amended by paragraphs 1a and 2–7, which regulate in detail the cooperation between the two legislative chambers, that is, the German Bundestag and the Bundesrat, as well as the federal government in European matters.

The other reasons—of no less importance for the career of the principle of subsidiarity regarding the foundation of the EU—lie in the ambiguity of the EU's identity between a Union of States and a Union of Citizens.[6] This ambiguity, which finds expression, for example, in the different legislative powers of the Council of Ministers and the European Parliament, reflects a precarious equilibrium of political forces. On the one hand, the assumption of powers by a Union of States, mainly in the field of classic prerogatives of the executive such as foreign and security policy, must, on the other hand, be balanced by more powers given to the Union of Citizens.

This was the principal reason for the approval and proclamation of the European Union's Charter of Fundamental Rights at the summit at Nice on 7 December 2000. The power of citizens is not located only in the Parliament; it resides to a significant extent also in the guarantee of the fundamental rights of the citizens themselves.[7] It was in light of this aspect that it followed that the Charter of Fundamental Rights was to be inserted into the text of the Constitutional Treaty (CT) and, after its failure, was given the same legal value as the Treaties in the Lisbon Treaty (Article 6(1) TEU).

This acknowledgement and proclamation of the fundamental rights of the citizens of the EU also had at least as great an impact as the division of competences on the growing relevance of the principle of subsidiarity in the EU. Fundamental rights require universal validity. Fundamental rights at EU level require general acceptance—which could be seen as undermining the legal sovereignty of the EU Member States. The 'horizontal' provision laid down in Article 51(1) Charter of Fundamental Rights of the European Union (CFREU), which delimits the field of application of the fundamental rights 'to the institutions, bodies, offices and agencies of the Union with

[6] *Cf* J Schmierer, 'Die EU mit Verfassung. Ein offenes, doch begrenztes politisches Projekt' *Kommune* 1/05 pp 50ff.

[7] *Cf* K Fischer, *Der Vertrag von Lissabon*, 2. Aufl 2010, p 23.

due regard for the principle of subsidiarity and to the Member States only when they are implementing Union law', is the paradoxical result of this situation. It is a self-contradictory attempt to restrict the validity of universal principles.

Another widely acknowledged special expression of the principle of subsidiarity is the process and legal recognition of self-regulation in social matters[8] through the collective agreements of the social partners ('social dialogue'): so-called 'horizontal subsidiarity'.[9] This meaning of subsidiarity raises a central issue regarding the potential sources of EU law.[10] The Preamble of the TEU (Maastricht) of 7 February 1992[11] states: 'to continue the process of creating an ever closer union among the peoples of Europe ... decisions are taken as closely as possible to the citizen in accordance with the principle of subsidiarity'. But the scope of the principle of subsidiarity as applied to industrial relations and labour law is highly disputed. In fact, after the decisions of the European Court of Justice (CJEU) in the cases *Viking*, *Laval*, *Rüffert* and *Luxemburg* we have to note growing concerns about the future of Social Europe. The group of authors that regard Europe with scepticism is becoming more powerful than the Euro optimists. In Germany this position is represented, for example, by well-known authors of the Max Planck Institute for Social Research in Cologne (Scharpf,[12] Höpner[13] and Streeck,[14] but also by trade unionists—for example, Hans-

[8] See P Häberle, 'Das Prinzip der Subsidiarität aus der Sicht der vergleichenden Verfassungslehre' (1994) *AöR* p 169.

[9] B Bercusson, 'Maastricht: a fundamental change in European labour law' (1992) 23 *Industrial Relations Journal* pp 177ff; S Sciarra, 'Collective agreements in the hierarchy of European Community sources' in P Davies, A Lyon-Caen, S Sciarra and S Simitis (eds), *European Community Labour Law: Principles and Perspectives, Liber Amicorum Lord Wedderburn of Charlton* (Oxford, 1996) pp 202ff; O Deinert, 'Self-executing collective agreements in EC law' in M de Vos (ed), *A Decade beyond Maastricht: The European Social Dialogue Revisited* (The Hague, 2003) pp 33ff; see also Veneziani (ch 5 in this volume).

[10] O Deinert, 'Partizipation europäischer Sozialpartner an der Gemeinschaftsrechtsetzung' (2004) *RdA* pp 211ff, 217.

[11] OJ C 191 of 29.6.1992, p 1.

[12] F Scharpf, 'Der einzige Weg ist, dem EuGH nicht zu folgen', interview with political scientist Fritz Scharpf on the threats to the welfare state (2008) (7+8) *Die Mitbestimmung* p 18; see also the comments on this CJEU criticism in (2008) (9) *Die Mitbestimmung* pp 53ff and (2009) (3).

[13] M Höpner, 'Usurpation statt Delegation. Wie der EuGH die Binnenmarktintegration radikalisiert und warum er politischer Kontrolle bedarf', MPIfG Discussion Paper 08/12, December 2008; see also 'Das soziale Europa findet nicht statt' (2008) (5) *Die Mitbestimmung* pp 46ff.

[14] W Streeck and A Schäfer, 'Korporatismus in der Europäischen Union' in M Höpner and A Schäfer (eds), *Die politische Ökonomie der europäischen Integration* (Frankfurt, 2008) pp 203ff; see also W Streeck, 'European social policy after Maastricht: the social dialogue and subsidiarity' (1994) 15(2) *Economic and Industrial Democracy. An International Journal* p 155.

Jürgen Urban[15] und Frank Bsirske[16]—and others such as Alain Supiot[17] and Bernhard Nagel).[18] They argue partly in the tradition of the critics against the ratification of the draft EU Constitution in France and the Netherlands: according to this position the project of the EU in general is a neoliberal project with few social rights and without any reference to or prospect of building a welfare state. They argue that this general orientation of Europe as mainly a project oriented towards liberal markets also finds expression in the draft Constitution.

I think that this position is partly correct, partly false. Insofar as it is correct, it seems to be a realistic view of the EC Treaty as a concept of social inclusion through the expansion of markets. Insofar as it is false, I think that it is not a correct legal interpretation. The EU Charter of Fundamental Rights, which acquired legal status under the Lisbon Treaty (Article 6(1) TEU) includes many social rights which go far beyond what is recognised at national level and even the Lisbon Treaty foresees a new quality of Europe as a social state (*Sozialstaat*). But they are right: Europe will never be a social state in the traditional sense. Social adjustment remains with the Member States. However, I do not think that the political and intellectual concentration on Europe hinders the Member States in doing what is necessary in this field.[19]

Also disputed is the very foundation of its legitimacy. On the one hand, it is argued that legislation in the field of social policy is some kind of a state-delegated legal power. On the other hand, others consider that the social partners act in this field on the basis of a fundamental social right conferring on them a genuine legal capacity to act autonomously.[20]

The crucial point is whether regulation of social matters is primarily a state responsibility or not. If it is considered to be a state responsibility, then the principle of subsidiarity seems to be the right answer with regard to the fear that the state will be legally obliged to act in this field. This would have the effect of overburdening the state. The principle of subsidiarity serves to relieve the state in this respect.

[15] H-J Urban, 'Die Krise Europas und die Gewerkschaften. Zum Stand der europäischen Integration aus gewerkschaftlicher Sicht' in C Müller-Plantenberg and J Perelws, *Kritik eines technokratischen Europa* (Kassel, 2008) pp 107ff.

[16] F Bsirske, 'Politik der Entsicherung' (2008) (5) *Die Mitbestimmung* p 58.

[17] A Supoit, 'Europa im Griff der kommunistischen Marktwirtschaft' (2009) *Arbeit und Recht* p 151.

[18] B Nagel, 'Europäische Marktfreiheiten, Koalitionsfreiheit und Sozialstaatsprinzip' (2009) *Arbeit und Recht* p 155.

[19] See T Blanke, 'Europa sociale: un modello comune per evitare una corsa al ribasso?' (2009) 2 *Diritti—Lavori—Mercati* p 263.

[20] T Blanke, 'Sozialstaatsprinzip, Schutzpflichtgebot und Tarifautonomie. Ein Dialog mit Rudolf Wiethölters Recht-Fertigungs-Thesen' in C Joerges and G Teubner, *Rechtsverfassungsrecht* (Baden-Baden, 2003) pp 125ff.

The answers to the question of whether regulation of social matters is primarily a state responsibility vary widely among the Member States. The broad spectrum ranges from the liberal tradition of the UK, which attributes to the state a mainly passive social role based on non-intervention in this field, to the governmental tradition of France, which obliges the state to actively intervene to ensure a distinctive '*ordre public social*'. Germany leans more towards the French position. However, over the past two decades one can observe a slight but steady change towards the more liberal British view.

This finds expression in the changing conceptual foundation of the legitimacy of the industrial relations system and of the rights to collective bargaining and to conclude collective agreements. In the period after the Second World War, until the late 1980s, these were regarded mainly as state-delegated powers. Now they are considered to be based on personal market freedoms to conclude agreements. From this viewpoint, they are regarded as an independent and genuine competence, qualified as fundamental individual and social rights. As a consequence, the aspect of collective autonomy (and responsibility as well) is becoming more prominent in current interpretations than was the case in former times. The collective actors have a prerogative to act, and the state is obliged to respect this autonomy. The result is the contrary of the opposite option: the state itself is bound by the principle of subsidiarity.

II. SIGNIFICANCE OF THE PRINCIPLE OF SUBSIDIARITY IN THE EU MEMBER STATES AND ITS CONCEPTS

A. The Significance of the Principle of Subsidiarity in the EU Member States

The principle of subsidiarity has a very different significance in different EU Member States. In the majority, mainly in France[21] and the United Kingdom,[22] it is unknown as a principle of law or as a constitutional principle. With the exception of Austria, Belgium and Germany, EU Member States do not have federal structures. Nevertheless, the autonomy of local government is accepted in all EU Member States as a common principle. Furthermore, a stronger emphasis on the legally protected autonomy of regions can be ascertained in the recent past. Perhaps its strongest roots lie in the principle of subsidiarity in Germany (Article 23(1) GG), where it can be found in a

[21] J-P Puissochet, 'La Subsidiarité en droit Francais' in KW Nörr and T Oppermann, *Subsidiarität und Wirklichkeit* (Tübingen, 1997) pp 205ff.

[22] See H Lecheler, *Das Subsidiaritätsprinzip. Strukturprinzip einer Europäischen Union* (Berlin, 1993) p 55.

series of laws. Since the Treaty of Maastricht, it is also acknowledged as a principle in the EU. The principle of subsidiarity was inserted by the Treaty of Maastricht (ex-Article 3b(2) TEC,[23] ex-Article 5 EC, now Article 5 TEU), due to the influence of Germany and the United Kingdom, although for very different reasons.

B. Subsidiarity: 'Rights of Persons' versus 'Rights of Places'

The principle of subsidiarity has various sources.[24] In the liberal-democratic philosophy of state and law[25] the principle aims to protect the self-regulation of the emerging market society and the liberty of the citizen vis-à-vis the paternalistic overall competence of the absolutist authoritarian state.

In this liberal-democratic understanding, fundamental rights are primarily defensive rights of persons, providing individuals with a sphere of freedom for self-development in which, within a framework of general law applicable to everybody, they can act according to their subjective will. Citizens are perceived principally as 'market citizens'; their rights are related primarily to the freedoms of a market society: rights of property, freedom of contract, freedom of movement and the right of free access to the market.

In contrast to this, there is another relevant source of the principle of subsidiarity based on the so-called 'communitarian' tradition of modern societies. This emphasises the communitarian character of human beings and their existence based on a close social sphere (from family to tribe, from local authority to region) as a locus of ethical self-development. In this tradition, Catholic social doctrine regards the primary competence of the individual, and similarly of small and subordinated communities, as the highest social-philosophical principle.[26] In the communitarian version of social policy, this understanding of the principle of subsidiarity delimits competences between political and social institutions on both centralised and decentralised levels; in particular, with regard to the role of government and non-governmental institutions. Municipal self-administration, guarantees of regional partial autonomy and different kinds of federal structures are based on this communitarian understanding of subsidiarity.

[23] There were many preparations for this, mainly in Germany; see Häberle (n 8) p 169.

[24] For the roots of the principle of subsidiarity in the German history of the welfare state from the standpoint of the history of ideas, see the excellent article by C Sachße, 'Subsidiarität: Leitmaxime deutscher Wohlfahrtsstaatlichkeit' in S Lessenich (ed), *Wohlfahrtsstaatliche Grundbegriffe* (Frankfurt, 2003) pp 191ff.

[25] See, for example, D Ricardo, *Grundsätze der Volkswirtschaft und Besteuerung*, 3. Aufl., Jena 1923 and W von Humboldt, *Ideen zu dem Versuch, die Wirksamkeit des Staates zu bestimmen*, 1792.

[26] See the Encyclical 'Quadragesimo anno' of Pope Paul XI of 15.5.1931; for details of the historical tradition see Sachße (n 24).

The difference between these two social-philosophical concepts of subsidiarity is formulated by John Kincaid as '*rights of persons*' versus '*rights of places*'.[27] 'Rights of places' stands for the emphasis on municipal freedom of the communitarian model, while 'rights of persons' emphasises the individual freedom of the liberal model. Victor Vanberg[28] uses the distinction between 'exit' and 'voice' (based on AO Hirschman)[29] to characterise the two concepts. The liberal understanding of freedom (and subsidiarity) is assigned to the model of 'exit' options because it is based on the concept of arbitrary individual freedom (*individuelle Willkürfreiheit*). The communitarian understanding of freedom (and subsidiarity) relates to the model of 'voice' options since it deals with the creation of legally guaranteed rights to a say for small communities.

C. The Different Concepts of the Principle of Subsidiarity in Labour Law

These different philosophical sources of the principle of subsidiarity find expression also in the field of labour relations. A predominantly liberal concept in the US and the UK adheres to exit options (for example, hire and fire, termination at will), while a communitarian approach in Germany, Austria and the Netherlands seeks to integrate the labour force into the organisational structure of the company or undertaking via a multiplicity of voice arrangements (elected works councils, information and consultation procedures, codetermination and arbitration). The origins of the above-mentioned concept of 'horizontal subsidiarity' lie in this latter tradition of labour law. Social dialogue is regarded as a kind of social self-regulation. Through the variety of social dialogues and the resulting agreements, there emerges a specific social sub-system (the social sphere of the society). This encompasses a wide range of social practices in which the state is not to interfere, thereby respecting the principle of subsidiarity.

III. THE MEANING OF THE PRINCIPLE OF SUBSIDIARITY IN THE EU FROM THE TREATY OF MAASTRICHT TO THE TREATY OF NICE

It is striking that until the Single European Act came into force on 1 July 1987 the principle of subsidiarity was not mentioned in the EU. A special

[27] J Kincaid, 'Liberty, competition, and the rise of coercion in American federalism' in L Gerken (ed), *Competition among Institutions* (London, 1995).

[28] V Vanberg, 'Subsidiarity, responsive government and individual liberty' in KW Nörr and T Oppermann, *Subsidiarität und Wirklichkeit* (Tübingen, 1997) pp 253ff.

[29] AO Hirschman, *Exit, Voice and Loyalty—Responses to Decline in Firms, Organisations and States* (Cambridge, 1970).

provision for the primacy of Community competence only if the proposed objectives can better be achieved at Community level than at the level of the Member States was first formulated in the area of environmental law in Article 130r(4) TEEC,[30] but without explicitly mentioning the principle of subsidiarity.[31] Since then, the European Community has come to rely more and more on the principle of subsidiarity[32] to support its proposals in the area of social policy.

A. The Wording of the Treaty of Maastricht

The principle of subsidiarity was laid down officially as a principle of law for the first time in the Maastricht Treaty (Article 3b(2) TEC):

> In areas which do not fall within its exclusive competence, the Community shall take action, in accordance with the principle of subsidiarity, only if and insofar as the objectives of the proposed action cannot be sufficiently achieved by the Member States and can therefore, by reason of the scale or effects of the proposed action, be better achieved by the Community.

The importance of this principle is underlined by the fact that the contracting parties of the Maastricht Treaty affirm in the Preamble (No 12 of the recitals) that in the future Union 'decisions are taken as closely as possible to the citizen in accordance with the principle of subsidiarity'.

The wording of the principle of subsidiarity did not change very much between the different Treaties (Maastricht, Amsterdam, Nice and Lisbon). Article 5(3)(1) TEU now reads:[33]

> Under the principle of subsidiarity, in areas which do not fall within its exclusive competence, the Union shall act only if and in so far as the objectives of the proposed action cannot be sufficiently achieved by the Member States, either at central level or at regional and local level, but can rather, by reason of the scale or effects of the proposed action, be better achieved at Union level.

[30] This version of ex-Article 130r(4) TEEC was in force between 1987 and 1993. In 1993, this provision was separated from its original context in the environmental chapter and stated as a general rule in ex-Article 3b(2) TEC (becoming ex-Article 5(2) EC), *cf* L Krämer in H von der Groeben and J Schwarze (eds), *Kommentar zum Vertrag über die Europäische Union und zur Gründung der Europäischen Gemeinschaft*, vol 1 (Baden-Baden, 2003); preliminary remarks to Articles 174–176 EC, para 106; the German wording was as follows: insofar as the 'genannten Ziele besser auf Gemeinschaftsebene erreicht werden können als auf der Ebene der einzelnen Mitgliedstaaten'; *cf* EO Kempen, 'Subsidiaritätsprinzip, Europäisches Gemeinschaftsrecht und Tarifautonomie' (1994) *KritV* pp 13ff, 29.

[31] Bianchi (n 2) p 42.

[32] See Kempen (n 30) pp 13ff.

[33] The second subparagraph of this provision provides, furthermore, that: 'The institutions of the Union shall apply the principle of subsidiarity as laid down in the Protocol on the application of the principles of subsidiarity and proportionality. National Parliaments ensure compliance with the principle of subsidiarity in accordance with the procedure set out in that Protocol'.

Nevertheless, a remarkable change in the meaning of this principle has occurred.

B. The Relationship between the Principle of Subsidiarity and the Division of Competences

It was often observed that the definition of the principle of subsidiarity in Article 3b(2) TEC (now Article 5(3)(1) TEU) was unclear.[34] The Article made a sharp distinction between 'exclusive competences', where only the institutions of the Union had the power to act, and those areas of 'shared' or 'joint' or 'concurrent' competences, where the Member States could act only so long as the Union had not legislated. On the one hand, therefore, it was argued that there were no shared competences at all: 'in a long line of cases the Court has confirmed that once the Community has acquired legislative powers in a particular domain ... the Member States no longer have the power to legislate in the same field'.[35] The conclusion was, in consequence, that the principle of subsidiarity as defined in the Maastricht Treaty could not apply to any matter covered by the original EEC Treaty.

On the other hand, it was generally assumed that overall competence remained with the Member States. As stated in Article 5(2) EC[36] (formerly Article 3b TEC), the European Union 'shall act within the limits of the powers conferred upon it by this Treaty'. The Community was allowed to act only in accordance with the Treaty and its later amendments and supplements.[37] Therefore, it was asserted that only some cases indicate an exclusive competence of the Community. This is, for example, the case when future legislation in an area assigned to the Community could be endangered by the enforcement of national regulation.

The principle of subsidiarity applies *only* where the Union has *joint* competences. But the problem is that the Treaty—the original EEC Treaty and the following Treaties of Maastricht, Amsterdam and Nice—did not distinguish between exclusive and concurrent (now: shared) Union competences, and did not contain a list of matters falling within one or the

[34] AG Toth, 'The principle of subsidiarity in the Maastricht Treaty' (1992) 29 *Common Market Law Review* pp 1079ff, 1088f; G Lyon-Caen, 'Subsidiarité et droit social européen' (1997) 4 *Droit social* pp 382ff; Y Gaudemet, 'La subsidiarité en Europe: un principe ambigu et discutable' (November 2002) 280 *Futuribles* pp 5ff.

[35] Toth (n 34) pp 1079ff, 1084.

[36] Again, the wording has changed slightly. Now Article 5(2) TEU states: 'Under the principle of conferral, the Union shall act only within the limits of the competences conferred upon it by the Member States in the Treaties to attain the objectives set out therein. Competences not conferred upon the Union in the Treaties remain with the Member States'.

[37] See M Zuleeg in H von der Groeben and J Schwarze (eds), *Kommentar zum Vertrag über die Europäische Union und zur Gründung der Europäischen Gemeinschaft*, vol 1 (Baden-Baden, 2003) Art 5 EC Marginal pp 2ff.

other type of competence.[38] This situation has changed with Articles 2–6 of the TFEU: as was foreseen in the Constitutional Treaty (Article I-13), a catalogue of the categories and areas of the European Union competences was inserted.[39]

But the principle of conferral equally sets only *relatively* clear limits. The outlines become blurred by many unwritten competences.[40] These include the flexibility clause (Article 308 EC, now Article 352 TFEU), the principle of 'implied powers' (a competence based on the 'indivisible' connection of policies), the concept of '*effet utile*' in the decisions of the CJEU and the limits on national legislative action in the definition of the principle of subsidiarity itself: the Member States lose their overall competence 'insofar as the objectives of the proposed action cannot be sufficiently achieved by the Member States'.[41] This reference to the 'objectives of the proposed action' allows wider scope for different dynamic and function-oriented interpretations expanding Union competences but at the same time imposes very strict procedural requirements.

Other problems which arise from the definition of subsidiarity are the reference to the objectives being sufficiently achieved by the 'Member States' (without the additional qualification 'acting separately'), its relationship to the principle of proportionality (which prescribes that action taken by the Union, in terms of form and content, does not exceed what is required to achieve the objectives set out in the Treaties), and to what extent subsidiarity applies to Article 94 EC (now Article 114 TFEU) and to the 'gap-filling provision' of the 'flexibility clause' in Article 308 EC (now Article 352 TFEU).[42]

C. The Principle of Subsidiarity as a Guideline for the Exercise, not the Existence of Competences

Until the decision of the German Federal Constitutional Court on the Lisbon Treaty on 30 June 2009 it was widely acknowledged that the principle of subsidiarity does not regulate how competences may be distributed between

[38] See Toth (n 34) pp 1079ff; R Bieber, 'Subsidiarität im Sinne des EU-Vertrages' in KW Nörr and T Oppermann, *Subsidiarität und Wirklichkeit* (Tübingen, 1997) pp 165ff; for a different opinion, see HD Jarass, 'EG-Kompetenzen und das Prinzip der Subsidiarität nach Schaffung der Europäischen Union' (1994) *EUGRZ* pp 209ff, 214.

[39] Treaty on European Union (TEU) and the Treaty on the Functioning of the European Union (TFEU) of 13.12.2007, consolidated version: OJ C 83/1 of 30.3.2010, p 1; see Lörcher (ch 6 in this volume).

[40] *Cf* M ter Steeg, 'Eine neue Kompetenzordnung für die EU—Die Reformüberlegungen des Konvents zur Zukunft Europas' (2003) *EuZW* pp 325ff.

[41] Ex-Article 5(1) EC.

[42] See Toth (n 34) pp 1079, 1095, 1098.

the Member States and the Community, but rather serves as a guideline for the way in which the Community's competences should be exercised:

> It cannot create or confer competences on the Community and [ex] Article 3b [TEC, ex Article 5 EC; now Article 5 TEU] therefore cannot serve as a legal basis for a Community act, at least on its own. It can only be used to allocate the exercise of competences which have already been created by other provisions of the Treaty.[43]

It is a guideline for the *exercise* of competences,[44] and not for the *existence* of competences.[45]

The decision of the German Federal Constitutional Court of 30 June 2009 made a fundamental difference exactly on this point: following this decision, which applied primarily to Germany as an EU Member, one has to say that the principle of subsidiarity functions as a guideline for the existence of competences between the EU and the Member States.[46] The German Federal Constitutional Court states in Marginal 13: 'The Laeken Declaration on the Future of the European Union of 15 December 2001[47] laid down four objectives of the reform, the first of which was "A better division and definition of competence in the European Union"'.

This is, according to the German Federal Constitutional Court, also the line of the Lisbon Treaty: 'The Treaty of Lisbon pursues the objective of achieving more transparency concerning the division of competence between the Union and the Member States,[48] and it extends the European Union's competences'.[49]

The principle of subsidiarity functions as a basic rule for the decision of the German Federal Constitutional Court on the Lisbon Treaty:

> The Federal Constitutional Court reviews whether legal instruments of the European institutions and bodies, adhering to the principle of subsidiarity under Community and Union law (Article 5 [(2) EC]; Article 5 [(1)] sentence 2 and 5 [(3) TEU]), keep within the boundaries of the sovereign powers accorded to them by way of conferred power. Furthermore, the Federal Constitutional Court reviews whether the inviolable core content of the constitutional identity of the Basic Law pursuant to Article 23[(1)] sentence 3 in conjunction with Article 79 [(3)] of the Basic Law is respected. The exercise of this competence of review, which

43 Ibid p 1091.

44 See Zuleeg (n 37) Article 5 EC Marginal 25.

45 Bieber (n 38) pp 165, 175.

46 See A von Bogdandy, 'Prinzipien der Rechtsfortbildung im europäischen Rechtsraum. Überlegungen zum Lissabon-Urteil des BVerfG' (2010) *NJW* pp 1, 4: 'With this, the German Federal Constitutional Court quit the framework of the German Basic Law and takes the position of guardian of the EU treaties'.

47 Bulletin EU 12-2001, I.27 <Annex I>.

48 See Laeken, Declaration on the Future of the European Union of 15 December 2001, Bulletin EU 12-2001, I.27 <Annex I>.

49 Marginal 56.

> is rooted in constitutional law, follows the principle of the Basic Law's openness towards European Law [*Europarechtsfreundlichkeit*], and it therefore also does not contradict the principle of loyal cooperation (Article 4 [(3) TEU]); with progressing integration, the fundamental political and constitutional structures of sovereign Member States, which are recognised by Article 4 [(2) sentence 1 TEU], cannot be safeguarded in any other way. In this respect, the guarantee of national constitutional identity under constitutional law and the one under Union law go hand in hand in the European legal area.

Based on this understanding of the principle of subsidiarity, the German Federal Constitutional Court came to the decision that the EU should not exercise any unrestricted competence to extend competencies:

> The Member States are said to remain the 'masters of the Treaties' and are said not to have granted the European Union *Kompetenz-Kompetenz*. The principle of conferral is said to continue to apply. The use of the flexibility clause is said to be subjected to substantive requirements and procedural safeguarding mechanisms by the Treaty of Lisbon.[50]

It follows that the EU regulations based on Article 352 TFEU (ex-Article 308 EC) violate the German Basic Law.[51] The representative of Germany in the European Council may only declare their consent to such a regulation on the basis of a law.

This is valid also for the mechanisms of the Social State:

> The principle of the social state establishes the obligation on the part of the state to ensure a just social order. The state must fulfil this mandatory responsibility on the basis of a broad scope of discretion; for this reason, concrete constitutional obligations to act have only been derived from this principle in very few cases. The state must merely create the minimum conditions for a life of its citizens that is in line with human dignity. The principle of the social state sets the state a task, but it does not say anything about the means with which the task is to be accomplished in the individual case.[52]

> The requirements placed on the European Union under constitutional law as regards social integration or a 'social union' are clearly limited. It is true that pursuant to Article 23 [(1)] sentence 1 of the Basic Law, Germany's participation in the process of integration depends, *inter alia*, on the European Union's commitment to social principles. Accordingly the Basic Law not only safeguards social tasks for the German state union against supranational demands in a defensive manner but wants to commit the European public authority to social responsibility in the spectrum of tasks accorded to it.[53] What applies, however, also to the

[50] Marginal 150.
[51] Marginal 319.
[52] Marginal 257.
[53] See Heinig, *Der Sozialstaat im Dienst der Freiheit* (Mohr Siebeck, 2008) pp 531ff.

institutions of the European Union is that to be able to have an affect, the principle of the social state necessarily requires political and legal concretisation.[54]

In consequence of this decision all the mechanisms to extend the EU competences with regard to the use of the simplified Treaty revision procedure, the flexibility clause, the general (Article 48(7) TEU) and special bridging clauses (Article 31(3) TEU; Article 81(3)(2 and 3), Article 153(2)(4), Article 192(2)(2), Article 312(2)(2), Article 333(1) and (2) TFEU) and the so-called emergency-brake mechanism (Article 82(3), Article 83(3), Article 86(1)(2 and 3), Article 87(3)(2 and 3) TFEU) are declared to be violating the German Basic Law if not adopted in conformity with constitutional requirements:

> Amendments of the Treaties by which the content of the Basic Law is amended or supplemented or which make such amendments or supplements possible require the approval of two-thirds of the members of the German *Bundestag* and two-thirds of the votes of the *Bundesrat* (Article 23[(1)] sentence 3 in conjunction with Article 79[(2)] of the Basic Law).[55]

D. The Ideological Function of the Principle of Subsidiarity

With regard to the different legal traditions of the Member States, the importance of the principle of subsidiarity within the EU is undisputed and cannot be overestimated. Critics in French and British legal doctrine underline the ambiguous character of the principle and its complete lack of a concrete meaning.[56] Although it seemed to limit the competences of the European Community, in reality it was used to the contrary—and the wording of ex-Article 5(3) EC (now Article 5(3) TEU) allowed this—to expand the powers of the Union.[57] The relevance of the principle of subsidiarity, therefore, was mainly ideological: on the one hand, it served to create support for the ever expanding process of granting ever more competences to the Union and, on the other, it served to further the project of deepening cohesion in the EU by promising ever greater respect for the autonomy and sovereignty of the Member States.[58] In fact, although the principle of

[54] Marginal 258.

[55] Marginal 312.

[56] See Lyon-Caen (n 34) p 382; Gaudemet (n 34) pp 5ff; Toth (n 34) pp 1079ff; see also R Bieber, 'On the mutual completion of overlapping legal systems: the case of the European Communities and the national legal orders' (1988) *European Law Review* pp 147ff.

[57] This was explicitly foreseen in Article 3 of the 'Protocol on the application of the principles of subsidiarity and proportionality' attached to the Amsterdam Treaty of 1997; *cf* ter Steeg (n 40) pp 325ff, 328.

[58] This argument is supported, for example, by the statement of British Prime Minister, Blair: 'La subsidiarité est le mot qui sauve le traité des Maastricht' and the joint letter from French President Chirac and German Chancellor Kohl 'à la présidence britannique', in which

subsidiarity is often mentioned in decisions of the CJEU and in the Opinions given by the Advocates General[59] there isn't a single case declaring illegal an action taken by the European institutions due to violation of the principle of subsidiarity.[60]

Following the Protocol as formulated under the Constitutional Treaty and the Lisbon Treaty this problem of ambiguity of the principle of subsidiarity was eliminated. The formulation in Article 3 of the Protocol was reversed. It no longer foresees the possibility of expanding the activities of the Union but inserts mechanisms for strong *ex ante* control of legislative acts of the Union. In any case, the aim to create 'an ever closer Union', as foreseen in recital 11 of the TEC and 12 of the EC was strengthened; it is now part of Article 1(2) TEU.

French commentators also doubted whether the principle of subsidiarity is in conformity with the principle of democracy.[61] In this interpretation, the democratic principle gives exclusive legitimacy to create a compulsory legal order to the nation state, which has primacy in regulating the public and social order. This power is not given to decentralised, subordinated and intermediate institutions of the society, such as families, companies, communities, regions or associations.

Summarising the debate, one can conclude that the principle of subsidiarity plays an ever more important role in the Treaties of the EU. This manifestly conflicts with the fact of the ongoing process of the assumption of more and more competences by the Union. In reality, it does *not serve as a counterweight* to the presumption of an unwritten overall competence of the Union derived from functional considerations of market integration. The contrary is also the fact even if—taken literally—the principle of subsidiarity implies the requirement to respect the sovereignty of the Member States.

In particular, it is not possible to draw from it a commitment to either the abovementioned specific religious (Catholic) social ethic, or a federal structure of the EU. Rather, a liberal understanding serves as the lowest common denominator of its interpretation. This is supplemented by the principle of

it was indicated 'qu'il convient désormais "d'augmenter la capacité d'action et l'efficacité de l'Union européenne" et "d'accroître l'adhésion des citoyens à l' Europe", notamment en veillant à ce que les décisions soient prises "les plus près possibles des citoyens" ce qui suppose "la mise en oeuvre pratique du principe de subsidiarité"'; *cf* Gaudemet (n 34) pp 5, 10.

59 The website of the Court indicates more than 80 citations for the period between 2000 and 2004, *cf* for example, Case C-5/00 *Commission/Bundesrepublik Deutschland*, Opinion of Advocate General Geelhoed of 28.7.2001, Marginal 41 and Rs.C-229/00 *Commission/Finland*, Opinion of Advocate General Tizzano of 11.7.2002, Marginal 50.

60 ter Steeg (n 40) pp 325ff, 327.

61 See Lyon-Caen (n 34) pp 382ff.

municipal self-administration and, eventually, of social self-administration through the social partners.[62]

E. Strengthening the Application of the Subsidiarity Principle: The 1997 Protocol on the Application of the Principle of Subsidiarity and Proportionality

The weakness and the ambiguity of the principle of subsidiarity played a decisive role in driving attempts of the Member States to strengthen the application of the principle.[63] They succeeded by adding to the Amsterdam Treaty in 1997 a 'Protocol on the application of the principles of subsidiarity and proportionality' which stipulated stronger respect by the EU institutions for the principle of subsidiarity and introduced some first steps in monitoring the exercise of powers by the Community. Based on the provisions of this Protocol, for example, the German Government provided for an annual 'subsidiarity report'.[64] The aim of these reports is to assess the actions of the EU institutions, mainly legal measures, to verify whether they comply with the aims of the principle of subsidiarity. The result was usually positive: apart from a few individual complaints, the reports came to the conclusion that normally the requirements of the subsidiarity principle had been respected.

IV. THE PRINCIPLE OF SUBSIDIARITY IN THE CONSTITUTIONAL TREATY AND IN THE TREATY OF LISBON

A. The Results of the Working Group on the Principle of Subsidiarity in the Convention on the Future of Europe

The Convention on the Future of Europe established a Working Group (Working Group I) on the Principle of Subsidiarity.[65] The Working Group

[62] See Kempen (n 30) pp 13ff; for a different opinion *cf* Lyon-Caen (n 34) p 386: 'Il s'agit simplement de liberté contractuelle'.

[63] One remarkable example is Article 23(1) of the German Constitution (GG) which was amended in 1992 with the Treaty of Maastricht. The Article states that Germany contributes to the development of the EU based on democratic, social and federal principles and on the rule of law and which is bounded by the principle of subsidiarity. It is an interesting point that this amendment to the Constitution refers both to the federal structure and to the principle of subsidiarity. One must conclude that the two principles do not have the same content, even if in practice in the official '*Subsidiaritätsberichte*' of the German Government (see n 68) subsidiarity usually means respect for national rights and for those of the federal Member States.

[64] See (2001) *EuZW* p 111 (Subsidiaritätsbericht 1999, BT-Drs. 14/40717); (2002) *EuZW* p 3 (Subsidiaritätsbericht 2000, BR-Drs. 776/01); (2003) *EuZW* p 196 (Subsidiaritätsbericht 2001, BR-Drs. 814/02; Subsidiaritätsbericht 2004, BR-Drs.52/06 of 19.1.2006).

[65] CONV 71/02.

agreed on a series of proposals to improve the application and monitoring of the principle of subsidiarity.[66] It avoided the creation of a new body and a weighty bureaucracy by establishing a series of procedures. The Group proposed the creation of a new *ex ante* political monitoring mechanism involving national parliaments. This included an obligation of the Commission to attach to the proposals a 'subsidiarity sheet' to allow for better case-by-case assessment of the principle by the legislator (the Council of Ministers of the European Union and the European Parliament).

Furthermore, the Group proposed that the Commission should address directly to each national parliament—at the same time as to the Union legislator (Council and European Parliament)—its proposals of a legislative nature and that any national parliament would have six weeks to issue a reasoned opinion regarding compliance with the principle of subsidiarity by the proposal concerned.

The consequences of such opinions for the continuation of the legislative process could be modulated, depending on the number and substance of the reasoned opinions received:

— If, within the six-week deadline, the Community legislator received only a limited number of opinions, he would give further specific reasons for the act with regard to subsidiarity.
— If, within the six-week deadline, the legislator received a significant number of opinions from one-third of national parliaments, the Commission would re-examine its proposal. That re-examination may lead the Commission either to maintain its proposal, amend it or withdraw it.

This 'early warning system' would place all national parliaments on an equal footing. Finally, the Working Group proposed that the Committee of the Regions may appeal to the Court of Justice in the case of texts concerning areas on which it is consulted in the normal context of its duties.

Due to these proposals the 'Protocol on the application of the principles of subsidiarity and proportionality' which formed an integral part of the Constitutional Treaty (Article IV-442) was amended. The Lisbon Treaty accepted in principle the proposals of the Working Group and added detailed rules on the procedure of the ordinary legislative process in Article 7(3) of the Protocol (No 2).[67]

[66] CONV 286/02, 23.9.2002.

[67] See Fischer (n 7) pp 499ff (changes towards the Constitutional Treaty underlined), Article 5(1).

B. The Revised Form of the Principle of Subsidiarity

The principle of subsidiarity was stated in Article I-11 of the Constitutional Treaty under the heading 'Fundamental Principles', with the following wording:

> 1. The limits of Union competences are governed by the principle of conferral. The use of Union competences is governed by the principles of subsidiarity and proportionality.
> 2. Under the principle of conferral, the Union shall act within the limits of the competences conferred upon it by the Member States in the Constitution to attain the objectives set out in the Constitution. Competences not conferred upon the Union in the Constitution remain with the Member States.
> 3. Under the principle of subsidiarity, in areas which do not fall within its exclusive competence, the Union shall act only if and insofar as the objectives of the proposed action cannot be sufficiently achieved by the Member States, either at central level or at regional and local level, but can rather, by reason of the scale or effects of the proposed action, be better achieved at Union level.
>
>   The institutions of the Union shall apply the principle of subsidiarity as laid down in the Protocol on the application of the principles of subsidiarity and proportionality. National Parliaments shall ensure compliance with that principle in accordance with the procedure set out in the Protocol.

The Lisbon Treaty expresses the notion of the principle of subsidiarity in Article 5(1)–(3) TEU using, in principle, the same words.

C. Changes to the Previous Formulation and Application of the Principle of Subsidiarity

Article 5 TEU is close to the former Article 5 EC. The competences of the Union are governed by the principles of conferral, subsidiarity and proportionality. Nevertheless, the Lisbon Treaty—as well as the Constitutional Treaty—contains a number of differences in comparison to the former version in the EC Treaty.

First, the use of all the competences of the Union must be in conformity with the principles of subsidiarity and proportionality (Article 5(1) TEU). Following Article 5(3) TEU '[u]nder the principle of subsidiarity, in areas which do not fall within its exclusive competence, the Union shall act only if and in so far as the objectives of the proposed action cannot be sufficiently achieved by the Member States'. That means that the principle of subsidiarity shall apply only to the areas of shared Union competence.[68] This is a

[68] ter Steeg (n 40) pp 325ff, 329.

clear contradiction to what is stated in Article 5(1) TEU. This contradiction must be resolved by giving priority to the special rule in Article 5(3) TEU. In applying the principles of subsidiarity and proportionality, the EU institutions must act in conformity with the procedural rules laid down in the 'Protocol on subsidiarity and proportionality' (Article 5(3) TEU).

Secondly, emphasis is placed on the close relationship between the principle of subsidiarity and the principle of proportionality. In practice, this was already the case insofar as the wording of ex-Article 5(3) EC, which provided that '[a]ny action by the Community shall not go beyond what is necessary to achieve the objectives of this Treaty' was interpreted as a specific expression of the principle of proportionality. However, the explicit generalisation of this statement to reflect the principle of proportionality was missing. This is now made explicit in Article 5(4) TEU with regard to the content and form of Union measures: 'Under the principle of proportionality, the content and form of Union action shall not exceed what is necessary to achieve the objectives of the Treaties'.

Thirdly, there is a specific reference to the notion of levels and their differentiation into central, regional and local. Subsidiarity operates where the objectives of the proposed action of the Union 'by reason of the scale or effects of the proposed action' cannot be sufficiently achieved by the Member States. In contrast to the former version, the reference to the *level* of the Member States and of 'subordinated' and decentralised political units is no longer a peculiarity of the German language version,[69] but becomes part of all the language versions of the Treaty (in English: 'either at central level or at regional and local level').

[69] Ex-Article 3(b) TEC, ex-Article 5(2) EC) stated: 'In den Bereichen, die nicht in ihre ausschließliche Zuständigkeit fallen, wird die Gemeinschaft nach dem Subsidiaritätsprinzip nur tätig, sofern und soweit die Ziele der in Betracht gezogenen Maßnahmen auf Ebene der Mitgliedstaaten nicht ausreichend verwirklicht werden können und daher wegen ihres Umfangs oder ihrer Wirkungen besser auf Gemeinschaftsebene erreicht werden können'. The French and English wording of Article 5(2) was as follows: 'Dans les domaines qui ne relèvent pas de sa compétence exclusive, la Communauté n'intervient, conformément au principe de subsidiarité, que si et dans la mesure où les objectifs de l'action envisagée ne peuvent pas être réalisés de manière suffisante par les États membres et peuvent donc, en raison des dimensions ou des effets de l'action envisagée, être mieux réalisés au niveau communautaire'. 'In areas which do not fall within its exclusive competence, the Community shall take action, in accordance with the principle of subsidiarity, only if and insofar as the objectives of the proposed action cannot be sufficiently achieved by the Member States and can therefore, by reason of the scale or effects of the proposed action, be better achieved by the Community'. This difference was not a mistake in translation. The German version rather reflected the German understanding of subsidiarity as authorisation for self-administration on a decentralised level, and the specific interest of the German *Länder* in preserving their legislative prerogatives. In this sense, the principle of subsidiarity not only ensured the precedence of national measures over those of the Community, it also recognised and integrated authorities on the federal, regional and municipal levels. See Kempen (n 30) pp 13ff; for a different opinion *cf* Lyon-Caen (n 34) p 386: 'Il s'agit simplement de liberté contractuelle'.

Fourthly, the wording 'by reason of the scale or effects of the proposed action' of Article 5(3) TEU is more precise than the earlier version in ex-Article 5(2) EC. In the earlier German version it was still unclear if the words 'by reason of the scale or effects' referred to the objectives of the proposed action or to the action itself.[70]

Fifthly, the national parliaments are involved for the first time in the history of European construction in the European legislative process in monitoring the application of the principle of subsidiarity. The new role assigned to national parliaments gives them greater information and increases transparency with respect to the Commission's consultation documents and legislative proposals. It allows them to deliver a reasoned opinion if they consider that the principle of subsidiarity has not been complied with. This results from the new provisions laid down in the 'Protocol on the role of national parliaments in the European Union' and the 'Protocol on the application of the principles of subsidiarity and proportionality' which form an integral part of the Treaties (Article 5(3)(2) TEU, Article 51 TEU).

Sixthly, there is furthermore the right of the Member States, national parliaments and, in some cases, also for the Committee of the Regions to bring actions before the CJEU on grounds of infringement of the principle of subsidiarity by a legislative act.

Finally, the 'Protocol on the application of the principles of subsidiarity and proportionality' establishes the conditions for the application of the principles of subsidiarity and proportionality and a system for monitoring the application of those principles by the Union's institutions. Each of them by virtue of Article 1 of the Protocol—as was previously stated in the former Protocol—'shall ensure constant respect for the principles of subsidiarity and proportionality, as laid down in Article 5 [TEU]'. Furthermore, the rights of the national parliaments, as well as the obligations of the Commission and of the European Parliament and Council, are defined in detail. They shall guarantee the observance of the principles in case of legislative activities of the Union.

[70] Paragraph 5 of the 'Protocol on the application of the principles of subsidiarity and proportionality', 2.10.1997, OJ C 340, p 105, attached to the Amsterdam Treaty of 1997 made clear that the scale and effects referred to the proposed action of the Community—see now the explication in Article 5, sentences 4 and 5 of the 'Protocol on the application of the principles of subsidiarity and proportionality' (No 2) 13.12.2007, OJ C 306 of 17.12.2007, p 150: 'The reasons for concluding that a Union objective can be better achieved at Union level shall be substantiated by qualitative and, wherever possible, quantitative indicators. Draft legislative acts shall take account of the need for any burden, whether financial or administrative, falling upon the Union, national governments, regional or local authorities, economic operators and citizens, to be minimised and commensurate with the objective to be achieved'.

V. THE CHANGED CONTENT OF THE PRINCIPLE OF SUBSIDIARITY

A. The Open, Value-based Structure of the Union

The content of the principle of subsidiarity in the Lisbon Treaty can be understood only by looking at the whole structure of the Treaty. According to it, the Union aims to realise the common objectives of the Member States and coordinates the policy of the Member States that concern these objectives (Article 3(1) and (5) TEU). The Member States, on the other hand, transfer competence to the Union so as to enable it to act accordingly (Article 1(1) TEU). The Union has no competence of its own but only transferred competences. It has 'legal personality' (Article 47 TEU) but rather than having a structure such as characterises traditional nation states—as formulated in the Constitutional Treaty—it 'shall be open to all European States which respect its values and are committed to promoting them together' (Article I-1(2) CT, same wording in Article I-58(1) CT). Under the Lisbon Treaty the conditions for the accession of new members to the Union are regulated in Article 49 TEU, which follows the structure of former regulations in ex-Article 49 EU and reads as follows:

> Any European State which respects the values referred to in Article 2 and is committed to promoting them may apply to become a member of the Union. The European Parliament and national Parliaments shall be notified of this application. The applicant State shall address its application to the Council, which shall act unanimously after consulting the Commission and after receiving the consent of the European Parliament, which shall act by a majority of its component members. The conditions of eligibility agreed upon by the European Council shall be taken into account.
>
> The conditions of admission and the adjustments to the Treaties on which the Union is founded, which such admission entails, shall be the subject of an agreement between the Member States and the applicant State. This agreement shall be submitted for ratification by all the contracting States in accordance with their respective constitutional requirements.

First and foremost, the Union is a Community based on *values* of independent and sovereign Member States (Article 2, Article 3(1) and (5), Article 21 TEU). The obligation to 'respect its rich cultural and linguistic diversity' as enshrined in Article 3(3)(4) TEU is also a relevant aspect of subsidiarity. This is also true for the obligation to 'respect the equality of Member States before the constitution, as well as their national identities, inherent in their fundamental structures, political and constitutional, inclusive of regional and local self-government' (Article 4(2) TEU).

B. Regulation of Competences: Conflicting Principles

The enumeration of categories of competence as stated in Article 2 TFEU distinguishes three kinds of competence:[71] the Union's exclusive competence (which means that 'only the Union may legislate and adopt legally binding acts' (paragraph 1, sentence 1)), shared competence (in which the Union has a pre-emptive prerogative to regulate, Article 2(2) TFEU) and the competence for the Union to coordinate, support and complement policies of the Member States (Article 2(3) and (5), Articles 5 and 6 TFEU). This general framework is not very precise; for example, the Member States could legislate and adopt legally binding acts even within the sphere of exclusive competences of the Union if so empowered by the Union (Article 2(1) sentence 2 TFEU).

Nevertheless the Lisbon Conference underlined in Declaration No 18,[72] that competences not conferred on the Union in the Treaties remain with the Member States. The same is valid following Articles 5(2) and 4(1) TEU which provides for a blanket clause in favour of the Member States' competence: 'Competences not conferred upon the Union in the Constitution remain with the Member States'. However, it should be noted that the Treaties just confer primary competence on the Union, for example, in Article 2(1), (2) and (4) TFEU.

The competences are listed in detail in Articles 3–6 TFEU. The catalogues of competences were supplemented by a so-called 'Flexibility Clause' (ex-Article 308 EC, Article I-18 CT). The restriction of this clause in the Lisbon Treaty (Article 352 TFEU) is one of the cornerstones of the difference between the two Treaties: the Constitution enabled the Union to act 'within the framework of the policies defined in Part III to attain one of the objectives set out in the Constitution' even if 'the Constitution has not provided the necessary powers'. This clause goes far beyond the previous provision in ex-Article 308 EC since it is not limited to the objectives 'in the course of the operation of the common market', but rather includes all objectives mentioned in the Constitution. In addition, the enactment of regulations by a unanimous decision of the Council of Ministers was subject to the consent, rather than merely to the consultation of the Parliament (Article I-18(1) CT = Article 352(1) TFEU). According to the new active role of national parliaments within the procedure for monitoring the subsidiarity principle 'the European Commission shall draw national Parliaments' attention to proposals based on this Article' (Article I-18(2) CT = Article 352(2) TFEU).

[71] For a more detailed view see Lörcher (ch 6 in this volume).

[72] ABl C 306 of 17.12.2007, p 249.

These provisions have changed a lot in the Lisbon Treaty. Ex-Article 308 EC was replaced by Article 352 TFEU. Even if the Lisbon Intergovernmental Conference (IGC) tried to give a narrow interpretation to this Article,[73] in the view of the German Federal Constitutional Court this was still not sufficient.

C. From Legislative Supremacy of the Member States towards the Primacy of Decentralised Regulation

The principle of subsidiarity in the Lisbon Treaty is new and different. It no longer prioritises the democratic legitimacy and legislative supremacy of the Member States. Rather, there is a general principle of decentralised regulation on national, regional and local levels. With regard to the above-mentioned differentiation made by John Kincaid between the liberal principle ('rights of persons') and the communitarian principle ('rights of places'), the argument is that, from the Maastricht Treaty to the Lisbon Treaty, there was a clear shift from the predominant liberal interpretation of the principle of subsidiarity (and individual freedom) towards a new communitarian version.

D. The New Communitarian Version of the Principle of Subsidiarity: Towards a Concept of Activating the Individual

However, it would be erroneous to interpret the principle of subsidiarity in the communitarian tradition as formulated in the nineteenth century by the Catholic Church (as it may have been by some German political theorists). Rather, the current interpretation of this principle is inspired by new concepts of government. The idea of the activating state has taken the place of the former concept of a centralised, hierarchical structure of a society governed by the state. The aim of the new concept is to stimulate the power of self-government in all sectors of society: therefore, it is addressed to the individual, and to local and regional spheres. But this version of new communitarianism must be sharply distinguished from the old one. The new concept only seems to reflect radical liberal ideas, such as the predominance

[73] *Cf* Declarations No 41 and 42: Declaration 42 states: 'The Conference underlines that, in accordance with the settled case law of the Court of Justice of the European Union, Article 352 of the Treaty on the Functioning of the European Union, being an integral part of an institutional system based on the principle of conferred powers, cannot serve as a basis for widening the scope of Union powers beyond the general framework created by the provisions of the Treaties as a whole and, in particular, by those that define the tasks and the activities of the Union. In any event, this Article cannot be used as a basis for the adoption of provisions whose effect would, in substance, be to amend the Treaties without following the procedure which they provide for that purpose'.

of structures of a free market, competition and individual responsibility.[74] However, in contrast to classic liberal theory, the state plays not merely a passive role, but rather assumes a general responsibility to create societal structures adapted to improve societal functioning under new (global) challenges. The new task of the state is to 'revive' society, to energise existing structures in order to compel them to adapt to meet inevitable changes.

E. Some Remaining Problems: Conflict between the Principle of Subsidiarity and Fundamental Rights?

The Lisbon Treaty affirms the principle of subsidiarity in the context of fundamental rights. Article 51(1) CFREU defines the field of application of the Charter in light of the subsidiarity principle: 'The provisions of this Charter are addressed to the institutions, bodies, offices and agencies of the Union with due regard for the principle of subsidiarity and to the Member States only when they are implementing Union law'. The Preamble to the Charter also refers to this principle: 'This Charter reaffirms, with due regard for the powers and tasks of the Union and the principle of subsidiarity, the rights as they result, in particular, from the constitutional traditions and international obligations common to the Member States'.

What is the meaning of the evocation of the principle of subsidiarity in the context of fundamental rights? Are the Union's institutions, bodies, offices and agencies generally obliged to respect fundamental rights, or only insofar as they do not contradict the principle of subsidiarity; for example, when they are in conflict with different rights, principles and 'values' at national, regional or local levels? Are the Member States bound by the fundamental rights of the Charter or not? Are the institutions of the EU empowered to supervise the observance by the Member States of these rights?

So far, these are open questions. It must first be acknowledged that the rule of law in the Lisbon Treaty in general, and in the CFREU in particular, is ambivalent. The Lisbon Treaty does not establish the Union as a federal state. In federal states, such as Germany, the possible conflict of different legal provisions between different levels of legislation is governed by the principle '*Bundesrecht bricht Landesrecht*' ('Federal law breaks Member State law'). In Union law, such a principle is not clearly established. In the case of overlapping rights, there is no explicit rule as to which level prevails.[75] In consequence, it will be the task of legal doctrine to develop convincing principles for the solution of this problem.

[74] See Sachße (n 24).

[75] See Declaration No 17 'concerning primacy' with its reference to the 'Opinion of the Council Legal Service' describing, among other things, that it results from CJEU's case-law 'that primacy of EC law is a cornerstone principle of Community law'.

In my view, the Union is strictly bound by fundamental rights and cannot avoid this obligation by reference to the principle of subsidiarity. The same is valid for the Member States, also obliged to respect the fundamental rights set out in the EU Charter. This follows from the pre-eminent status of these rights as fundamental rights on which the values of the Member States—and of the EU in particular—are based (Article 2 TEU). One cannot deny the validity of these rights without destroying their character as universal rights and principles. It follows also from the sentence in the Preamble to the Charter which states that fundamental rights result 'from the constitutional traditions and international obligations common to the Member States'. It follows, finally, from the provision in Article 6(1) TEU, which prescribes that '[t]he Union shall recognise the rights, freedoms and principles set out in the [CFREU] of 7 December 2000, as adapted at Strasbourg, on 12 December 2007, which shall have the same legal value as the Treaties', and indicates in paragraph 3, that '[f]undamental rights, as guaranteed by the [ECHR] and as they result from the constitutional traditions common to the Member States, shall constitute general principles of the Union's law'. These references make clear that there are no differences between the Member States and the Union with respect to the substance of fundamental rights. Fundamental rights, although addressed to the Union, are general principles common to all Member States.

In this sense, the fundamental rights of the Union are to be regarded as a minimum floor of rights common to all Member States. The principle of subsidiarity is only relevant insofar as a Member State stipulates rights with a wider scope than the fundamental rights established in the EU Charter and in this sense Article 53 CFREU could be considered as explicit expression of the principle of subsidiarity.

As to the question of supervision, it seems clear also that the Union has no general competence to supervise the respect by the Member States of fundamental rights which go beyond EU law. This would establish a new power for the Union, which is explicitly excluded by Article 51(2) CFREU. The Union, consequently, has the right to control the respect for fundamental rights in the Member States only when they are implementing Union law.

VI. CONCLUSIONS

The principle of subsidiarity has had an astonishing career in EU law. Since the beginning of the 1990s it has gradually led to a replacement of the French model of European integration and its substitution by the German model. As follows from the German Constitutional Court this led to a new division of competences between the EU and the Member States, even in social matters. In consequence, the Member States have more rights in social questions. Fortunately, Germany is only one of the Member States within the EU. Therefore we see different interpretations of the principle of subsidiarity. Limits on the German interpretation are drawn from the principle of democracy as well as from the universalistic character of human rights. The question arises whether the principle could be helpful to invalidate the measures and acts asked for by the Commission and the ECB (see Bruun, chapter eight in this volume) to counteract the financial crisis of certain Member States. I think it depends on the interpretation given to that principle: in a liberal understanding it seems very clear that the 'better regulation' at EU level ('objectives ... be better achieved at Union level', Article 5(3) TEU) includes respect for fundamental rights and that not only the economic, but the social aims are to be fulfilled (Article 3(3) TEU). In this sense—and although this may be seen differently from a German (old communitarian) point of view—it is also said that the principle of subsidiarity hinders the Member States in diminishing the extent of their social systems.

8

Economic Governance of the EU Crisis and its Social Policy Implications

NIKLAS BRUUN

I. INTRODUCTION

THE EUROPEAN COUNCIL concluded at its meeting of 24–25 March 2011 that it had decided to add the following paragraph to Article 136 of the Treaty (TFEU):

> The Member States whose currency is the euro may establish a stability mechanism to be activated if indispensable to safeguard the stability of the euro area as a whole. The granting of any required financial assistance under the mechanism will be made subject to strict conditionality.

This is the first amendment to be made to the Treaty since the Lisbon Treaty came into force.[1] It has not been much debated nor explained, but it indicates that the economic governors of Europe feel the need for an explicit legal basis for crisis management in the future. It is also a recognition that until May 2010 the EU did not have a mechanism to deal with a debt crisis since stable finances were (and are) not only a Treaty principle for the euro Member States but a condition *sine qua non* of the monetary union.[2]

In this chapter, the author examines the measures that have been taken so far to deal with the euro area debt crisis. What has been the legal basis for these measures? What legal and policy measures form the future economic governance of the European Union in order to prevent a similar crisis in the

[1] In fact, another amendment was agreed upon on 23 June 2010, which amended the transitional provisions concerning the composition of the European Parliament (number of MEPs of certain Member States). See Protocol amending the Protocol on Transitional Provisions annexed to the Treaty on European Union, to the Treaty on the Functioning of the European Union and to the Treaty establishing the European Atomic Energy Community, OJ 2010, C 263/1.

[2] A Antoniadis, 'Debt crisis as a global emergency: the European economic constitution and other Greek fables'. Available at: ssrn.com/abstract=1699082.

future? In this context we especially want to evaluate the implications for European social policy of this emerging new structure of economic governance.

II. WHAT HAS HAPPENED SO FAR?

In the aftermath of the global financial crisis of 2008 the situation in Greece, which has long had a weak public economy with severe structural problems, reached a state of emergency in April 2010. Potential Greece insolvency became a matter of serious concern, especially for the Euro Group in the EU to which Greece belongs, and the situation prompted this group to fulfil the promise they had given at the European Council meeting to take determined and coordinated action, if needed to safeguard the financial stability of the euro.[3]

As a result, negotiations were started between the Greek Government, on the one hand, and a group consisting of the European Commission, the European Central Bank (ECB) and the International Monetary Fund (IMF), on the other. Within a few weeks a complicated contractual and legal structure was built up. A key document in this respect is the detailed Memorandum of Understanding signed by Greece and the European Commission on behalf of the Member States which belong to the Euro Group.[4] Further agreements include the Intercreditor Agreement and a Loan Facility Agreement that settles the availability of credit in the form of pooled bilateral loans for Greece, as well as an agreement between Greece and the IMF in the form of an Exchange of Letters.[5] In the latter, the Greek Government undertook to fully implement the agreed measures, including the Memorandum of Understanding. The European Union was not formally involved in the Agreement except that the Commission coordinated the lending operation on behalf of the Euro Group Member States. The Agreements have also been ratified separately by all the Euro Group Member States.[6]

On 10 May, the Council made a decision on certain measures that Greece had to take before the end of June 2010. Furthermore, the Decision listed measures that had to be taken by the end of September 2010 or by the end of December 2010. The measures listed in the Council decision were the same as those listed in the Memorandum of Understanding.

[3] See European Council 25.3.2010, Conclusions. Available at: www.consilium.europa.eu.

[4] The Memorandum of Understanding comprises a Memorandum of Economic and Financial Policies, a Memorandum of Understanding on Specific Economic Policy Conditionality and a Technical Memorandum of Understanding. Available at: www.imf.org/external/pubs/ft/scr/2010/cr10111.pdf.

[5] See Antoniadis (n 2).

[6] An exception was Slovakia which refused to ratify the agreements.

The Greek bailout package functioned as an alarm-call for the European Commission which during the first half of May 2010 made proposals for measures to be applied in the future in order to preserve financial stability in Europe. These consist of a European Financial Stability Mechanism (EFSM) and a European Financial Stability Facility (EFSF). The EFSM was established by a Council Regulation on 11 May.[7] The EFSF was established by an Intergovernmental Agreement (Framework Agreement) of the Euro Group Member States in the form of a registered limited liability company under Luxembourg law. These Member States own shares in the company in the proportions in which they participate in the arrangement with guarantee commitments. Altogether, the commitments make up a total guarantee of 440 billion euros.

In September 2010, the Government of Ireland revealed that the full cost to the Irish taxpayer of the January 2009 bailout was estimated to be 50 billion euro or about 32 per cent of Ireland's GDP. This sparked a crisis which led to a dialogue between Ireland, on the one hand, and the IMF and the European Union on the other, similar to the one that had taken place concerning Greece.[8] A National Recovery Plan for 2011–14 was drawn up in cooperation with the IMF and the European Union, published on 24 November 2010 after a formal request from the Irish Government for financial assistance from the EU and the IMF on 21 November 2010. The joint Commission, ECB and IMF team negotiated the conditions of the programme and an agreement at the technical level was reached on 28 November 2010 on a comprehensive policy package for the period 2010–13 supported by financing of 85 billion euros. On the same day, the Euro Group issued a statement supporting the policy programme and the loan package associated with it. On 7 December, the ECOFIN Council adopted the formal Decision allowing for financial assistance to Ireland and a Recommendation extending the deadline for compliance under the excessive deficit procedure to 2015. The Irish Parliament approved the programme on 15 December. On 16 December, the IMF board approved the loan arrangement for Ireland. It was agreed that the programme will be financed through contributions from the IMF (one-third) and from Ireland's European partners (two-thirds) through the EFSM and EFSF, but also by bilateral loans from the UK, Sweden and Denmark.[9]

On 11 March 2011, the Portuguese authorities' requested financial assistance. The Euro Group and ECOFIN ministers invited the Commission, the

[7] Council Regulation (EU) No 407/2010 of 11 May 2010; OJ L 118, 12/05/2010.

[8] As late as December 2009 the European Council had concluded that the Irish authorities had taken effective action to correct Ireland's excessive deficit and had postponed the time limit for correcting it to 2014.

[9] See also European Commission, Directorate-General for Economic and Financial Affairs: *The Economic Adjustment Programme for Ireland*. Occasional Papers 76/February 2011.

ECB, the IMF and Portugal to set up a programme and take appropriate action to safeguard financial stability. At the same time, they issued a statement according to which, within the context of a joint EU/IMF programme, the financial assistance package to Portugal should be financed on the European side within the framework provided by the EFSM and the EFSF.[10] It was furthermore stated that the Euro-area and EU financial support will be provided on the basis of a policy programme which will be supported by strict conditionality and negotiated with the Portuguese authorities.[11]

On 3 May 2011, the Memorandum of Understanding on Specific Economic Policy Conditionality was published. It was preceded by a Tripartite Agreement for Competitiveness and Employment already adopted on 22 March 2011. On 17 May, the Council adopted Decision 2011/0122 to make available to Portugal medium-term financial assistance for a period of three years (2011–14) in accordance with Council Regulation (EU) No 407/2010 of 11 May 2010 establishing a European Financial Stabilisation Mechanism. The accompanying Memorandum of Understanding signed on the same day and its successive supplements lay down the economic policy conditions on the basis of which the financial assistance is to be disbursed.

III. THE REFORM PROGRAMME

The European Commission reacted without delay to the Greek crisis, also on the general level of norm setting. Already on 8 May 2010 the Commission announced that it would present to the Council a concrete proposal for a European Stabilisation Mechanism to preserve financial stability in Europe, as indicated above. On 12 May, the European Commission issued a Communication entitled 'Reinforcing economic policy coordination'.[12] Here we already find the main elements of the reform programme that has since been further elaborated.

[10] Statement on 8 April. Memo 11/227.

[11] In accordance with the statement, the programme will be based on three pillars: (i) an ambitious fiscal adjustment to restore fiscal sustainability; (ii) growth and competitiveness enhancing reforms by removing rigidities in the product and labour markets and by encouraging entrepreneurship and innovation, allowing for sustainable and balanced growth and reducing internal and external macroeconomic imbalances, while safeguarding the economic and social position of its citizens—this should include an ambitious privatisation programme; and (iii) measures to maintain the liquidity and solvency of the financial sector.

[12] 'Reinforcing economic policy coordination'. Communication from the Commission to the European Parliament, the European Council, the Council, the European Central Bank, the Economic and Social Committee and the Committee of the Regions. Brussels 12.5.2010. COM(2010) 250 final.

Enhancing economic policy coordination:

- Reinforcing compliance with the Stability and Growth Pact and deeper fiscal policy coordination.
- Towards broader surveillance of intra-euro area macroeconomic and competitiveness developments.
- Integrated economic policy coordination for the EU: a 'European Semester'.
- Towards a robust framework for crisis management for euro area Member States.

On the same day—12 May 2010—the Council also adopted a regulation establishing a European Financial Stabilisation Mechanism.[13] Following a general discussion in the European Council in June, the Commission came out with a new Communication.[14] This document had an annex with a roadmap in which seven concrete legislative proposals were envisaged for the period between September 2010 and January 2011.

The European Commission followed the roadmap quite closely and presented a number of proposals[15] aiming at increased and improved control of economic governance within the European Union. In general terms, the proposals can be divided into three types of instrument. The first try to introduce new procedures for national economic policy and budgetary prudence and also strengthen surveillance. Here too, sanctions can be introduced against a state that does not follow economic policy recommendations from the Council: for example, it might have to pay a fine that can amount to 0.2 per cent of GDP. The second type of instrument is focused on the prevention and correction of so-called macroeconomic imbalances and

[13] Council Regulation (EU) No 407/2010 of 11 May 2010 establishing a European Financial Stabilization Mechanism; OJ L 118, 12/05/2010, pp 1–4.

[14] 'Enhancing economic policy coordination for stability, growth and jobs—Tools for stronger EU economic governance'. Communication from the Commission to the European Parliament, the European Council, the Council, the European Central Bank, the Economic and Social Committee and the Committee of the Regions. Brussels 30.6.2010. COM(2010) 367 (final).

[15] (1) Proposal for a Regulation of the European Parliament and of the Council on the prevention and correction of macroeconomic imbalances, COM(2010)527/final. (2) Proposal for a Regulation of the European Parliament and of the Council amending Regulation (EC) No 1466/97 of 7 July 1997 on the strengthening of the surveillance of budgetary positions and the surveillance and coordination of economic policies, COM(2010)526/final. (3) Proposal for a Regulation of the European Parliament and of the Council on enforcement measures to correct excessive macroeconomic imbalances in the euro area, COM(2010)525 final. (4) Proposal for a Regulation of the European Parliament and of the Council on the effective enforcement of budgetary surveillance in the euro area, COM(2010)524/final. (5) Proposal for a Council Directive on requirements for the budgetary frameworks of the Member States, COM(2010)523/final. (6) Proposal for a Council Regulation (EU) amending Regulation (EC) No 1467/97 of 7 July 1997 on speeding up and clarifying the implementation of the excessive deficit procedure, COM(2010)522/final.

also on the enforcement mechanism to correct them. Here the Commission also proposes that economic sanctions can be introduced of up to 0.1 per cent of GDP.[16] The third kind of instrument is aimed at harmonising and coordinating national budgetary structures and content in order to increase transparency and, among other things, to make accounting systems and statistical reporting comparable.

These proposals are now in the pipeline. At the same time, preparations are under way for the introduction of a permanent European Stability Mechanism (ESM)—in the form of the codification of present practice—and the relevant political decisions were taken at the European Council meeting in March 2011.[17] Here the Council agreed on the need for euro-area Member States to establish a permanent stability mechanism. The ESM will be activated by mutual agreement if indispensable to safeguard the financial stability of the euro area as a whole. The ESM will assume the role of the EFSF and the EFSM in providing external financial assistance to euro-area Member States after June 2013.

Access to ESM financial assistance will be provided on the basis of strict policy conditionality under a macroeconomic adjustment programme and a rigorous analysis of public debt sustainability. This will be conducted by the Commission, together with the IMF and in liaison with the ECB. The beneficiary Member State will be required to put in place an appropriate form of private sector involvement, according to the specific circumstances and in a manner fully consistent with IMF practices. The ESM will have an effective lending capacity of 500 billion euros. The adequacy of the lending capacity will be reviewed on a regular basis, but at least every five years. The ESM will seek to supplement its lending capacity through the participation of the IMF in financial assistance operations, while non-euro-area Member States may also participate on an ad hoc basis.

The ESM will be established by a Treaty among the euro-area Member States as an intergovernmental organisation under public international law and will be located in Luxembourg. The statute of the ESM will be set out in an annex to the Treaty.

The function of the ESM will be to mobilise funding and provide financial assistance, under strict conditionality, for the benefit of euro-area Member States which are experiencing or are threatened by severe financing problems in order to safeguard the financial stability of the euro area as a whole.

The Member States of the euro area will bestow on the ESM the financial sanctions available under the Stability and Growth Pact and the Macroeconomic Imbalance procedures.

[16] See COM(2010) 525 final.

[17] See further European Council 24/25 March 2011, Conclusions.

The ESM will have a board of governors consisting of the Ministers of Finance of the euro-area Member States (as voting members), with the European Commissioner for Economic and Monetary Affairs and the President of the ECB as observers.

IV. THE SOCIAL POLICY IMPLICATIONS

A. Introduction

This is not the place for a detailed study of the mechanisms of the stability instruments in the European Union. Instead, I want to study their impact on social policy in the Member States experiencing economic difficulties and also how these measures fit into the Lisbon Treaty's description (TEU 4) of the European Union as a Social Market Economy and other Articles regarding the European Union and its relationship to the Member States.

B. Some Experiences

In Greece, the report by the Prime Minister and the Governor of the Bank of Greece gives a picture of what took place between spring 2010 and 6 August 2010.[18] The Government reports that the fiscal programme is making good progress, but does not mention anything about the reactions to measures taken—namely the huge nationwide and sectoral collective action that took place during this period, as well as mass demonstrations and street protests. In the report, significant cuts are reported in health care and public administration, which will lead to a significant reduction in employment. From the point of social policy the most contested reforms related to pensions and the labour market. The following reports were made about these sectors:

> *Parliament approved a substantial pension reform ahead of schedule.* It is introducing a new system consisting of a contributory pension to top-up a non-contributory, means-tested, basic pension, aiming to control the increase in pension spending ... These assessments will determine whether further adjustments to the parameters of the pension system would be needed to contain the increase in pension spending to 2.5 percentage points of GDP between 2009 and 2060. Any further adjustments, if needed, will be completed by end of June 2011 in consultation with pension experts, as foreseen in Law 3863.
>
> *Labour market reform is almost completed.* Substantive legislative changes were introduced in July easing employment protection legislation and collective dismissals,

[18] Greece, Memorandum of Economic and Financial Policy, Athens, 6 August 2010. Available at: www.imf.org/external/pubs/ft/scr/2010.

> reforming minimum wages, reducing overtime premia and allowing firm-level agreements to prevail over other levels. Alongside reforms in public employment to reduce labour-market distortions, these will increase the adjustment capacity of firms, ultimately boosting employment. Further measures will be taken to reform collective bargaining, including the elimination of the automatic extension of sectoral agreements to those not represented in the negotiations. Finally, the government will adopt legislation to introduce symmetry into the arbitration system, while strengthening its independence and transparency.

Trade unions in Greece complained to the ILO concerning the policy being implemented in Greece.[19] In its 2011 Annual Report[20] the CEACR (Report of the Committee of Experts on the Application of Conventions and Recommendations) reiterated its established positions on the relationship between economic crisis, public interference in collective bargaining and ILO Convention No 98 on collective bargaining on the occasion of its preliminary comments on Greece within the framework of the mechanism to support the Greek economy with involvement of IMF and EU:

> The CEACR emphasized the importance of holding full and frank consultations with the employers' and workers' organizations on the revision of collective bargaining machinery, in accordance with the principle of the autonomy of the parties to the collective bargaining process and in light of the long-ranging implications of such revision for the standard of living of workers. Furthermore, it must recall that as a general matter, if, as part of its stabilization policy, a government considers that wage rates cannot be settled freely through collective bargaining, such a restriction should be imposed as an exceptional measure and only to the extent that it is necessary, without exceeding a reasonable period, and it should be accompanied by adequate safeguards to protect workers' living standards.[21]

[19] The critical voices from the trade union side described the situation quite dramatically: The General Confederation of Greek Workers (GSEE) concludes that Act Nos 3833/2010, 3845/2010 and 3863/2010 will lead to workers' disempowerment in the face of the combined spillover effect of lay-offs, wage freezes and the abolition of minimum standards with regard to wages, thereby negating the state's fundamental obligation to provide and protect decent work, violating the very essence of individual and social rights and endangering social peace and cohesion. The GSEE emphasises that the measures in question are permanent and irreversible, notwithstanding the specific timeframe and limited duration of the loan mechanism. They are also disproportionate, socially unjust and discriminatory vis-à-vis workers, especially the most vulnerable and have been adopted without examining sufficiently other well-weighed and more appropriate alternatives. Furthermore, they are not quantifiable and their scope has no perceivable causal relationship with the pursued aim of implementing the stability programme. They are not accompanied by adequate and concrete safeguards to protect the living standards of workers and support vulnerable groups in addressing the combined effect of economic austerity measures and the economic crisis, and they have had a serious and direct impact in weakening the position of GSEE during the collective negotiations that began in January 2010 on the conclusion of the new national general collective agreement. See: www.ilo.org/global/standards/WCMS_151490/lang--en/index.htm, Report III (1A) p 84.

[20] See: www.ilo.org/global/standards/WCMS_151490/lang--en/index.htm.

[21] Report, p 83.

The principle of the autonomy of the parties to the collective bargaining process and the right to collective bargaining are enshrined in Convention No 98. In an economic crisis the CFA has further specified the following:

> In cases of government intervention to restrict collective bargaining, the CFA has considered that it is not its role to express a view on the soundness of the economic arguments used by the Government to justify its position or on the measures it has adopted. However, it is for the CFA to express its views on whether, in taking such action, the Government has gone beyond what the CFA has considered to be acceptable restrictions that might be placed temporarily on free collective bargaining.
>
> While the CFA appreciates that the introduction of wage restraint measures must be timed in order to obtain the maximum impact on the economic situation, it nevertheless considers that the interruption of already negotiated contracts is not in conformity with the principles of free collective bargaining because such contracts should be respected.
>
> If, as part of its stabilization policy, a government considers that wage rates cannot be settled freely through collective bargaining, such a restriction should be imposed as an exceptional measure and only to the extent that is necessary, without exceeding a reasonable period, and it should be accompanied by adequate safeguards to protect workers' living standards.
>
> A three-year period of limited collective bargaining on remuneration within the context of a policy of economic stabilization constitutes a substantial restriction.
>
> In any case, any limitation on collective bargaining on the part of the authorities should be preceded by consultations with the workers' and employers' organizations in an effort to obtain their agreement.[22]

The Committee concluded that it should be highlighted that all 27 EU Member States have ratified Convention No 98 on the promotion of collective bargaining and Convention No 87 on freedom of association. These are part of the eight core labour standards Conventions. Over 90 per cent of the 183 ILO Member States have ratified these Conventions. Conventions 87 and 98 have also strongly influenced other regional fundamental rights instruments, such as the European Social Charter, the European Convention on Human Rights (freedom of association is part of this) and the EU Charter on Fundamental Rights.

These strong conclusions by the ILO clearly indicate that the Greece bailout has not been in full conformity with ILO standards. From the government positions above we can also see that there have been strong efforts to

[22] 2006 Digest of decisions and principles of CFA, §§992–1045: www.ilo.org/global/standards/information-resources-and-publications/publications/WCMS_090632/lang--en/index.htm.

change the structural features of the Greek industrial relations system in the context of managing the crisis.

In Ireland, apart from the general increase in unemployment and emigration, the cuts in public services—most importantly in health care—the tax rises, the introduction of new forms of tax that hit the lowest paid, price increases—especially on food—and the serious mortgage debt that families have taken on, the crisis has had a number of negative impacts on the labour market

The Finance Minister has used 'emergency' legislation to do the following:

— Cut public servants' pay and pensions.
— Restrict collective bargaining for certain categories of workers.
— Cut the minimum wage (ignoring the established minimum wage-setting machinery) by 1 euro an hour.
— Reduce social welfare payments, including unemployment benefit, sickness benefit and maternity payments, as well as the duration of payment.
— Remove tax relief for trade union subscriptions.

These strong measures were taken by a government which lost the early spring election in 2011. The new government is now implementing its own programme, but while the situation holds out some prospect of improving, the severe Memorandum of Understanding is still in place. The new majority coalition partner, Fine Gael, is reportedly not very supportive of labour and trade union rights. One of the main things the party has criticised is universally applicable collective agreements. The outcome therefore remains to be seen.

The Portuguese labour market policy package is focused partly on implementing the Tripartite Agreement of March 2011. It encompasses the main areas of labour market policy, including unemployment benefit, employment protection legislation, working time arrangements and reduction of additional pay for overtime as established in the Labour Code. It also addresses wage setting and competitiveness, including some structural issues relating to collective bargaining.

The bailout mechanisms have clearly had a strong impact on social policy and social policy legislation. Formally, the final decision-making power in Greece, Ireland and Portugal is in the hands of their parliaments, but the content of the Memorandums of Understanding were clearly a result of negotiations or even negotiations 'in the shadow of bankruptcy', where the borderline between negotiations and diktat becomes blurred.

The time frame and procedure for reducing spending do not respect nationally or internationally established requirements with regard to altering mutually agreed wage agreements or pension schemes. It is therefore worth investigating how this new economic policy and constitutional practice fit into the framework of the Lisbon Treaty. This is the focus of the next section.

V. THE LISBON TREATY

It is clear that, until May 2010, the European Union did not have a mechanism to deal with a debt crisis. In fact, as Antoniadis has pointed out,[23] such an option was not available to it: since the entire edifice of the Economic and Monetary Union is constructed on the basis of 'no deficit–no debt' he argues that the availability of a mechanism to deal with debt crisis, which was not supposed to happen in the first place, would represent something of a Greek paradox.[24]

For the euro-area Member States, stable finances are a Treaty principle and the rule of economic and monetary policy (Article 119(3) TFEU). In order to ensure that the Member States comply with this obligation, EU economic policy comprises three main areas of coordination: broad economic policy guidelines, multilateral surveillance and the excessive deficit procedure.

In parallel, the Treaty lays down rules to ensure that the stable finances principle may not be circumvented or compromised. For instance, the ECB may not provide an overdraft or other credit facility and may not purchase government bonds (Article 123 TFEU).

Because there is no explicit competence for the European Union to deal with a debt crisis as such one can ask whether Article 3(1)c TFEU, according to which monetary policy is the exclusive competence of the Union, could help in this regard. On the other hand, in economic policy, as in employment policy and social policy, there is only a special competence for EU: it can coordinate national policies, but its competences are usually described as shared in these areas (see Article 4(1) TFEU.

As Antoniadis points out, the arrangements forming the Greek bailout are based on Member State instruments. The euro-area Member States took the decision to react to the debt crisis in Greece by means of an Intercreditor Agreement and a Loan Facility Agreement between Greece, on the one hand, and the other 15 euro-area Member States, on the other. This makes three separate Agreements: the *sui generis* decision of the Member States meeting within the Euro Group formation of the Council to grant the loan, together with the Intercreditor and Loan Facility Agreements between the Member States. Antoniadis argues that this is in principle compatible with EU constitutional law which allows Member States to conclude internal agreements. He points out, however, that they are subject to limitations: it must be ensured that such agreements do not circumvent the procedure for Treaty

[23] Antoniadis (n 2) p 14.
[24] Ibid.

amendment, respect the institutional framework laid down by the Treaties and do not affect existing policies.[25] Antoniadis continues:

> There are major question marks in relation to all three conditions. As outlined above, EU economic policy is constructed on the basis of a no debt–no deficit assumption. The only exceptions the Treaty recognises can be found in Article 122 TFEU and concern supply of energy, a natural disaster or exceptional occurrences beyond a Member State's control. It follows that, if debt crisis falls within the scope of Article 122 TFEU, then any financial assistance must be granted via Union channels; if not, it should not be granted at all. By granting financial assistance in the form of pooled bilateral loans, Member States appear to circumvent an explicit prohibition set out in Article 125 TFEU. Moreover, loans at an interest rate lower than that available to Greece on the financial markets and the acceptance, pursuant to an ECB decision, of Greek debt instruments as collateral, regardless of the rating of the Greek debt, constitute examples of privileged access to financial institutions prohibited by Article 124 TFEU.

Antoniadis also questions the EFSM that is based on Article 122(2) TFEU. It is obviously not self-evident that we can describe the situation in Greece as one in which 'a Member State is in difficulties or is seriously threatened with severe difficulties caused by natural disasters or exceptional occurrences beyond its control'. He also points out that there are numerous legal questions regarding the IMF's role in both procedural and substantive terms.[26] These questions seem to remain unanswered in the proposed new stability mechanism, too. Bruno De Witte has also raised some questions relating to the 'two potential "constitutional" problems' related to the May 2010 package: namely, the intergovernmental non-EU character of the measures and the fulfilment of Article 122(2) criteria regarding what is '*beyond their control*'.[27] He also explains the proposal for a new Treaty provision against the background of complaints that have been lodged before the German Constitutional Court arguing that the Council Regulation of 11 May 2010 was an ultra vires action of the European Union which should be declared contrary to the German Constitution.[28]

The series of Directives[29] that have been proposed seem to be justified on the basis of Article 121(6) TFEU. On the other hand, we find here some interesting proposals aimed at introducing a new decision-making mechanism within the framework of which a decision concerning an obligation to pay

[25] Antoniadis refers to Bruno de Witte, 'Future paths of flexibility: enhanced cooperation, partial agreements and pioneer groups', in JW de Zwaan, JH Jans and FA Nelissen (eds), *The European Union: An Ongoing Process of Integration: Liber Amicorum Alfred E. Kellermann* (The Hague: TMC Asser Press, 2004) 141, 148–51.

[26] Antoniadis (n 2) p 22.

[27] B de Witte, 'The European Treaty amendment for the creation of a financial stability mechanism'. Paper published by SIEPS, Sweden. See: www.sieps.se.

[28] Ibid pp 11–12.

[29] See above (n 14).

a fine 'shall be deemed to be adopted by the Council unless it decides, by qualified majority, to reject the proposal within ten days of the Commission adopting it'.[30]

An in-depth analysis of constitutional EU law is not the main purpose of this chapter. The point here is that the measures taken to deal with the financial crisis have been made on a rather shaky legal basis.[31]

Furthermore, the policy measures undertaken have deep social policy implications. It cannot be a sustainable policy to fully ignore the social partners in contradiction of Article 152 TFEU when intervention in national social policy is taken at EU level, although the final formal decision-making within the framework of economic 'conditionality' is taken at national level. It is also worth recalling that there is an explicit exclusion of wages from EU competences in the Treaty 153(5) TFEU.[32]

The policy is also in sharp contrast with Article 151 TFEU which prescribes that the Union and the Member States shall have as their objectives the promotion of employment and improved living and working conditions, so as to make possible their harmonisation '*while maintain any improvements*' (italics added), proper social protection, dialogue between management and labour, the development of human resources with a view to lasting high employment and the combating of exclusion.

The policy implemented does not pay any attention to existing international labour law—as the opinion of the ILO shows—including the provisions of the European Charter.

VI. THE DEBATE IN THE EUROPEAN PARLIAMENT

The final adoption of the secondary legislation needed in order to create the permanent crisis mechanism for the EU is still under discussion. However, the European Parliament has made numerous proposals for amendments to the new legislation, several of which have the explicit intention of linking the legislation to social policy considerations.

One important debate related to the legal basis for the six proposals on economic governance that was included in the package. For some of these legal measures proposals were made to include also Article 148(3) and (4) in the legal basis in order to emphasise the importance of employment aspects when designing economic governance policy. This was rejected by the Committee

[30] See COM(2010) 524 final p 11, Article 5(1).

[31] See also Oskari Juurikkala, in Finnish newspaper *Helsingin Sanomat* (21.3.2011). Several critics have also pointed out that the ECB interventions go far beyond what Article 123 TFEU allows.

[32] Several MEPs in the European Parliament referred to this fact in a debate in Strasbourg on 10 March 2011.

on Legal Affairs in the Parliament which saw Article 126(6) and/or 126(14) TFEU as the appropriate legal basis for the proposals in two instances in conjunction with Article 136 TFEU.[33]

The Regulation on 'excessive imbalances' now contains a special clause safeguarding the autonomy of collective bargaining. It reads as follows:

> 'It [the regulation] shall not affect the exercise of fundamental rights as recognized in the Member States and by Union law. Nor does it affect the right to strike, to negotiate, conclude and enforce collective agreements and to take industrial action in accordance to national law and practices which respect Union law' (Article 1, subject matter).

An obligation to consult the Social Protection Committee has also been included (proposed new Article 3a).

Furthermore, a broader clause to safeguard wages in general is inserted in the 'preventive action' part: 'The recommendations of the Council and the Commission shall not encroach upon fields such as wage formation which explicitly fall outside the Union's remit' (proposed article 6.2a).

The respect for differences in national industrial relations system is also recognised in a new Recital 16a:

> When the Council and the Commission apply this regulation, they should fully respect the role of national parliaments and social partners and respect differences in national systems, such as the systems for wage formation. In particular, Articles 152 and 153 TFEU and Article 28 of the Charter of Fundamental Rights of the European Union will be taken into account. In accordance with Article 153(5) Article 153 shall not apply to pay, the right to association, the right to strike or the right to impose lock-outs.

The language in the Reports from the Parliament seems to have majority backing so far. But it is still unclear to what extent the European Commission and the Council are willing to accept the amendments. The weakness with the amendments is of course that, from a strictly formal viewpoint, the Commission argues that during the bailout there has been no EU intervention in national wage policy or wage formation.

VII. POLICY CONCLUSIONS

There is a serious debt crisis in Europe. It is not in the interest of any stakeholders to hinder the efforts to stabilise the euro. On the other hand, the current policy is creating severe problems for the whole EU project. The present

[33] See 'Opinion on the legal basis of the proposal for a Regulation of the European Parliament and of the Council on the prevention and correction of macroeconomic imbalances', PE454.699v04-00. Annexed to the Report of the Committee on Economic and Monetary Affairs 6.5.2011 A7-0183/2011.

leadership, represented by Herman van Rompuy and Jose Manuel Barroso, seems to believe that economic policy can be marketed to the public in Germany, France and the Nordic countries as measures of punishment and budgetary discipline, while the same policy is explained as solidarity, help and cooperation to the people of Greece, Ireland and Portugal.[34] As the end result of this duplicity we risk strong populist reactions in many Member States—as was recently illustrated by the Finnish elections.[35]

It seems clear that a Treaty amendment—the first since the Lisbon Treaty came into force in 2009—is needed in order to bring even some legality to the current and future bailouts. In that context, a new social policy conditionality must be built into EU economic policy. A reading of the Treaty which takes the policy goals of the Treaty seriously indicates that EU economic governance must integrate social policy and fundamental rights assessments of proposed policy measures. This is perhaps less a question of legality than of legitimacy. The reactions around Europe have clearly shown that the current bailout policy lacks legitimacy both in Member States that are in economic crisis and in Euro Group Member States that are doing rather better.

Since practice of the bailout policy so far has been based on an interpretation of the present Treaty that makes it possible to conduct an economic and financial policy completely without social policy considerations, a starting point should be that the Treaty needs to be amended in order to clarify that the integration of this dimension is obligatory, both at a European and national level with regard to all policy measures with social policy implications. It is a reasonable requirement that the tabled amendment of Article 136 TFEU of March 2011 should be revised in order to include such a reference.

A technical solution for achieving this is offered by the 'Social Progress' Protocol[36] which was proposed by the European Trade Union Confederation in 2008 in order to solve the problems of balancing economic freedoms and social rights in the European Union in the aftermath of the *Viking* and *Laval* court cases. Such a Treaty revision could be made in the form of enhanced cooperation between the Euro Group Member States. This Protocol should be part of EU primary law to enable it significantly to impact the strengthening of the European social dimension.

[34] An illustrative example of this is the speech given by Herman van Rompuy in Athens on 12 April 2011 (PCE 095/11). Available at: www.consilium.europa.eu.

[35] The vote of the anti-EU party the 'True Finns' rose from 4 per cent to 19 per cent.

[36] See: www.etuc.org/IMG/pdf_social_progress_protocolEN.pdf.

9

Services of General Interest and the Treaty of Lisbon

ANTOINE JACOBS

I. INTRODUCTION

ENERGY AND WATER supply, health care and social services, education, postal services, public transport, waste disposal, social housing, public broadcasting and so on have become cornerstones of the modern state. They were created as far back as the nineteenth century in response to the increased needs and complexities of modern societies. They have become public services (or 'Services of General Interest' or SGI in Brussels jargon) because of the failure of private initiatives to provide them to a sufficient extent and at a sufficient level. They have played and continue to play a massive role in stimulating economic modernisation and improving public health and public order. They meet people's daily needs and are vital to their wellbeing. The quality of citizens' lives depends on these services. As such, they have become an essential building block of the notions of European citizenship[1] and the European Social Model.[2]

However, in recent decades, in which the rules of the market have come to be regarded as a higher criterion for policymakers, public services have come under attack, not the least from EU law.

[1] M Freedland, 'Public and labour law perspectives' in M Freedland and S Sciarra (eds), *Public Services and Citizenship in European Law—Public and Labour Law Perspectives* (Oxford, 1998); W Sauter, 'Universal service obligations and the emergence of citizens' rights in European telecommunications liberalisation' in Freedland and Sciarra (1998); W Sauter, 'Services of general economic interest and universal service in EU law' (2008) 33 *EL Rev* 167; M Krajewski, 'Providing legal clarity and securing policy space for public services through a legal framework for services of general economic interest: squaring the circle?' (2008) 14 *European Public Law* 377.

[2] See Commission Report to the Laeken Council COM (2001) 598, pt 3.

II. A CHANGING VIEW OF SERVICES OF GENERAL INTEREST IN THE 1980S

The economic crisis of the 1970s and 1980s brought a new emphasis on market liberalisation, privatisation and competition. Constant pressure from economists, private business leaders and right-wing politicians diminished the role of these services, challenged the support that governments give them, advocated their privatisation and exposed them to competition from private business. 'Hidebound' public services would be refreshed, 'viscous' bureaucracies would be turned into well-oiled machines and balky officials would be transformed into sympathetic service providers. Prices would drop, while services would improve. The client, finally, would be king.

There was a clear paradigm shift. Until then, the four freedoms of the Common Market and the European Competition Law were directed towards abolishing discrimination against foreign businesses. Since the 1980s, however, these principles have been directed against all sorts of collective and public 'impediments' to the free market. Consequently, the monopolistic character of and state involvement in services of general interest has increasingly been contested. Many have claimed that the existing arrangements gave an unfair advantage to the organisations entrusted by the public authorities with the provision of such services and infringed EU law. They hold that services of general economic interest (SGEI) should normally be subject to EU rules designed to create the single market. This includes monopolies, which may obstruct the smooth functioning of the market.

Although in those years the Court of Justice of the EC (ECJ) continued to protect social services,[3] the Commission's approach to services of general economic interest gradually became more restrictive, as illustrated in the 1996 Communication on Services of General Interest in Europe, which stressed that 'market forces produce better allocation of resources and greater effectiveness in the supply of services, the principal beneficiary being the consumer who gets better quality at a lower price'.[4]

Since those days a number of sectors in which services of general interest are provided have gradually been opened up to competition. The Commission has pursued a policy of market-opening to create competition in, for example, the international rail freight market, the internal gas market, the internal electricity market, telecommunications, postal services and transport. Public authorities increasingly entrust the provision of such services to private undertakings or to public-private partnerships, often by public procurement, and limit themselves to defining public objectives,

[3] *Municipality of Almelo v NV Energiebedrijf IJsselmij (Almelo)* (C-393/92) 1994 ECR I-1477; Corbeau (C-320/91) 1993 ECR I-2533.

[4] COM (1996) 443 final, OJ 1996 C 281/3.

regulating, monitoring and, where necessary, contributing to the financing of such services.

III. TAKING STOCK OF THE EFFECTS OF PRIVATISATION ON SGI: SOME EXAMPLES FROM THE NETHERLANDS

Privatisation, liberalisation and market forces have been given free play. What has been the result for SGI? Let me point to a number of experiences in the Netherlands, as in Western Europe, the Dutch have often led the way in privatisation, liberalisation and the use of market mechanisms.

A. Post, Telephone and Telegraph (PTT): 'Hard Sector' Privatisation

In the 1990s, the state owner divided this company into a number of sectors: the National Giro Service was sold to a commercial bank, while an independent telecommunications company was set up in a growth market and a postal company (TNT) in a shrinking market. The state sold its shares and now 80 per cent of TNT shares are in non-Dutch hands, for example, hedge funds, which have pressed for further division of the company—recently carried out—into a courier service, whose profit and sales prospects are considerable, and a mail service, which is struggling with an annual sales reduction of 10 per cent.

The Dutch State terminated TNT's monopoly position and new commercial mail providers came in. A price war broke out which caused a number of postal delivery rates to decrease, sometimes below cost level. However, the newcomers have also refrained from employing workers on contracts of employment in accordance with the collective agreement for mail services, under which labour costs are 23 euros per hour, instead employing workers on contracts for services at an average remuneration of 8 euros per hour, which is under the Dutch minimum wage. Such competition has driven TNT to embark on all kinds of measures to increase productivity at the expense of working conditions. It established an affiliate company (Network VSP) that operated under the same conditions as the newcomers. In most towns and villages, post offices have been closed and the postal service is hosted by shops. Meanwhile, complaints about poor mail delivery are increasing.

TNT's workforce was reduced by so-called 'natural wastage' from 31,000 full-time jobs to 20,000 in 2009. In 2007, TNT asked its remaining employees to accept a wage cut of 15 per cent in exchange for three years' job security. TNT employees rejected this demand and TNT set out to slash 3500 postmen's jobs by involuntary dismissals and to offer the remaining personnel inferior working conditions.

The government now requires all postal services to have 80 per cent of their staff on permanent contracts of employment by 2012, but the newcomers on the Dutch postal market say they cannot afford that, claiming to be threatened by bankruptcy. They hope that they will be saved by the new Dutch Government or the courts. The new government has called in a mediator.

Proponents of liberalisation say that TNT is still using its strength because of its historical monopoly position to push competitors out of the market and therefore is not letting consumers enjoy the full benefits of competition. However, from a labour law perspective, it is manifestly undesirable that markets are captured by companies undercutting the existing level of employment conditions. Those who cannot live up to current employment conditions should not enter such a market. That is the philosophy behind the legal system of the extension of collective agreements, as it is known in many European countries, including the Netherlands.

In my opinion, a major reason for the catch-22 situation in which TNT and other companies find themselves is the management trend to split up companies into profitable and less profitable parts. The condition of the less profitable part gradually deteriorates, accompanied by substandard conditions of employment and redundancies. When profitable and less profitable parts remain together, however, staff can be shifted relatively smoothly from the less profitable to the profitable part. Such a more harmonious solution may be more time consuming and so likely to encounter shareholder resistance, but under the European Social Model corporate governance should be based on stakeholder value, not merely shareholder value.

B. Privatisation, Liberalisation and Market Forces in the 'Soft Sector'

Formerly, home care for the elderly and disabled was provided by a general social security scheme covering the entire population. In 2007, this task was transferred to the municipalities, but the government provided only modest funding for this purpose. Since then the municipalities have contracted private organisations to provide this service, on the basis of public procurement, the contract being awarded to the lowest bidder. In the public procurement process, hardly any requirements are laid down regarding the quality of the service providers and conditions of employment. The result has often been that institutions with well qualified personnel and good collectively agreed conditions of employment have lost the bidding and have had to lay off hundreds of employees. Some were hired back as self-employed at much lower hourly rates and with no social security in case of illness or retirement. After the government banned such arrangements they could return to work as employees, but with 20 per cent lower wages.

In the past, the government organised school transport and transport for the sick and disabled. Since 2000, however, local authorities have contracted out these services on the basis of public procurement. There is fierce competition and there has been a price war with transport companies forced to make bids well below cost levels. Two-thirds of businesses are now circumventing the collective agreement and more than half of the 38,000 drivers have only a temporary contract. If their company loses a tender drivers are either sacked or transferred to the company that won the tender, where they are employed under worse conditions of employment.

The government used to arrange so-called integration courses for migrants to be implemented by accredited educational institutions with qualified staff in permanent jobs with good conditions of employment. Since 2007, municipalities have offered these courses within the framework of public procurement. As anyone in the Netherlands can run an integration course, there are now many providers whose workers have few qualifications and precarious employment contracts: such providers often win the tender simply because they are cheap. The accredited educational institutions have had to make hundreds of qualified employees redundant.

In the Netherlands analysis has shown that those involved in public procurement have not sufficiently heeded employees' professionalism and the quality of conditions of employment. Work is mostly contracted out via public procurement which does not specify required levels of qualifications or conditions of employment. For years, all parties in the Netherlands have proclaimed loudly from the rooftops that the first (mandatory tendering) is required by 'Brussels', while the second (minimum standards and conditions of employment) are not allowed by 'Brussels'. The reality is much more nuanced (see below, section X.C) and recently the Dutch Government renounced making public procurement in home care compulsory.

Another important factor is that two parallel labour markets have been created in the Netherlands in recent decades: one with traditional employment contracts of indefinite duration, and with good working conditions; the other characterised by 'flexibility', and with inferior conditions of employment. Many SGI employers have exploited this discrepancy for their own advantage.

Clearly, in the so-called 'soft' sector the most important cause of deterioration is the tight budget available for such services: bidders have no other option than to embark on a race to the bottom, tender or no tender.

Of course, such negative developments have not occurred in all sectors. In sectors where a lot of money is at stake, companies must compete on quality and there—as promised by the proponents of privatisation and liberalisation—prices remain unchanged or have fallen, service levels have been maintained or improved, employment has been maintained or even increased and working conditions have not deteriorated or have even improved. It is especially in sectors with poor market prospects, such as mail services, or which are dependent on public spending, such as home care, patient transport and integration courses that consumer services and employment and working conditions have deteriorated.

C. State Aid

In the Netherlands for over a century social housing has been provided on a large scale by housing associations, which are able to borrow money cheaply. The European Commission, however, considered this to be state aid, which is unjustified for people on median or higher incomes. It urged the Dutch Government to cease to provide social housing to tenants with an annual income above 33,000 euros. Eventually, it was agreed that the Netherlands by 1 January 2011 would amend the law so that 90 per cent of rental housing is no longer allocated to tenants with over 33,000 euros' annual income, but 10 per cent can still be assigned to those with an income between 33,000 and 38,000 euros.

This policy, however, has given rise to major problems: first, rental and purchase prices on the open housing market in the Netherlands (the most densely populated country in the EU) are now so high that many people with an annual income slightly above the 33,000 euro mark cannot afford them: researchers estimate their numbers at 650,000 households. Secondly, housing associations have been pushed out of the median market, where they used to earn money to make up for losses in the lower segment of the market. Finally, the new rules may lead to segregation between poor and more expensive neighbourhoods.

The question must surely arise as to whether this is a matter in which Brussels should get involved. Did the authors of the European Treaties have in mind such far-reaching intervention in the domestic social order? Obviously, a single European market will never be realised if each state government continues to support its national businesses: Article 86/87 TEC (now Article 106/107 TFEU) was intended to address this. However, there are sectors of society in which very few foreign competitors are eager to enter and in which it is national private businesses that want to take over parts of the public sector. These sectors include social housing, local sports provision, health care, local media, culture and education. The EU should not get involved in such sectors: delimitating the boundaries between public and private should be left to national politics.

IV. LESSONS TO BE DRAWN FROM DUTCH EXPERIENCES: BE ON THE ALERT!

The foregoing covers only a few examples of the misery that privatisation, liberalisation and the introduction of market forces have brought to services of general interest. Many people in other sectors and outside the Netherlands will be able to add numerous similar negative experiences.[5]

Liberalisation and privatisation are based on the assumption that more competition will lead to better and cheaper services for consumers. However, empirical evidence on the impact of liberalisation on SGI is contradictory. It is often maintained that the results have been positive:[6] from time to time the European Commission makes positive evaluations of liberalisation and privatisation in public services,[7] but others are more critical. For instance, a study commissioned by the European Federation of Public Service Unions (EPSU) suggested that the results of the full-scale privatisation of previously owned companies in electricity, gas, transport, postal services and so on have been disappointing. The network industries experienced 600,000 lay-offs in the period between 1991 and 2001. Productivity growth remained largely unchanged, while price levels increased in the EU15 between 1992 and 2002.[8]

There are also signs of negative impacts of liberalisation on SGI with regard to quality of provision: sharp increases in prices, decreased consumer satisfaction, lower security of supply and lack of efficacy of regulators. Often, liberalisation has had the effect of replacing public monopolies with private quasi-monopolies. Liberalisation and outsourcing have tended to reduce the accessibility and quality of public services and have not always benefited consumers.

Often, the privatisation of services of general interest reduces employment levels and leads to a deterioration of job security and the employment conditions of the workers concerned. It may also have a negative impact on industrial relations in services of general interest. There used to be relatively high trade union membership in these services (higher than in the private sector), which means that in many countries the trade unions had significant industrial muscle in this sector. Therefore, there was often a well-developed system of collective labour relations in this sector,[9] with more favourable

[5] T Brandt, T Schulten, G Sterkel and J Wiedemuth (eds), *Europa im Ausverkauf* (Hamburg, 2008).

[6] See the Report 'Ten years without frontiers' (2003) which claims that the liberalisation of network industries in the EU15 has led to one million new jobs; the European Commission Green Paper on Services of General interest (2003) claims that the income needed for standard electricity consumption fell in most Member States between 1999 and 2002; and the Annual Report of the implementation of the Gas and Electricity Internal Market claims that labour productivity has grown by 5.7 per cent in the EU15 (USA: 0.1 per cent).

[7] See, for instance, the European Commission's evaluation of the performance of network industries providing services of general interest (EPNI) (2005).

[8] See, for instance, the ETUI study by N Noaksson, *Taking stock of the liberalization of public utilities* (Brussels, 2005); see also PSIRO/David Hall, *Evaluating the impact of liberalisation on public services*, EPSU (2005).

[9] At European level the organisation of employers of public enterprises (CEEP) is directly participating in the all-industry European Social Dialogue, the trade unions (EPSU) indirectly via the ETUC; both the CEEP and the EPSU are involved in the sectoral European Social Dialogue.

employment conditions than in the private sector. Consequently, both privatisation and competition have led to anti-trade union pressures. Critics maintain that weakening the trade unions was one of the main objectives of the main protagonist of privatisation, Margaret Thatcher, who accused the unions in this sector of protecting privileges and causing too many strikes.

Although there is as yet insufficient evidence to assess the long-term impact of all these developments, there are concerns that the quality of services of general interest will suffer. Building on these concerns, traditional providers and the public authorities that support them are claiming that the application of EU law jeopardises the structures underlying the provision of such services, which have proved their worth over a long period. Even if many claim that these fears have so far proved unfounded, they are still on the political agenda.

V. SERVICES OF GENERAL INTEREST IN THE TREATY OF ROME, 1957

When the predecessor of the European Union, the European Communities, was established in the 1950s, the organisation of services of general interest was already in full swing. In those years the modern welfare state was under construction in all Western European nations and all political forces in these states were clearly in favour of an important role for such services. In the prevailing political philosophies of those days the services of general interest had an important role to play in the welfare state. In the Eastern European states, indeed, all major economic activities were organised on a public basis. This has changed fundamentally since the end of the Cold War (1989), but also in these countries services of general interest have remained important.

The economic importance of these services has become considerable: even in non-communist Europe public sector companies in their heyday accounted for more than 20 per cent of employment and investments. The sector currently contributes more than 26 per cent of EU27 GDP and employs more than 60 million people in the EU.

Therefore, it was no surprise that the founding fathers of the European Communities made an important exception for these services in the otherwise liberal Treaty of Rome.

The old Article 90(2) of the EEC Treaty (later Article 86(2) TEC, now Article 106(2) TFEU) reads as follows:

> Undertakings entrusted with the operation of services of general economic interest or having the character of a revenue-producing monopoly shall be subject to the rules contained in this Treaty, in particular to the rules of competition, in so far as the application of such rules does not obstruct the performance, in law or in fact, of the particular tasks assigned to them. The development of trade must not be affected to such an extent as would be contrary to the interests of the Community.

This approach meant that the services of general economic interest in principle were subject to the EU rules on competition and the internal market, but that they could claim exceptional treatment. In fact, under this protective aegis services of general interest could retain their specific, often monopolistic position in Western Europe until far into the 1980s.[10]

VI. SERVICES OF GENERAL INTEREST IN THE TREATY OF AMSTERDAM, 1997 AND IN THE EU CHARTER ON FUNDAMENTAL RIGHTS, 2000

As a consequence of the surge of liberalisation, privatisation and market forces in the 1980s and 1990s, it became a serious question whether the constitutional shields protecting services of general interest in the EU were strong enough. Parties fearing liberalisation and privatisation based on EU law campaigned for a stronger basis for public services in the EC Treaty itself. It was argued that high quality public services were not only important to consumers, but formed a significant element of the European Social Model which could at times conflict with the strict application of the logic of the free market and unrestricted competition. Greater emphasis was needed on the specific requirement of services of general economic interest (SGEI) as core values of the EU. Often France was the Member State that acted as standard-bearer for such efforts.[11]

In the Treaty of Amsterdam, 1997, the politicians expressed their sympathy for services of general economic interest in a new Article 16 TEC (now Article 14 TFEU):

> Without prejudice to Articles 73, 86 and 87, and given the place occupied by services of general economic interest in the shared values of the Union as well as their role in promoting social and territorial cohesion, the Community and the Member States, each within their respective powers and within the scope of application of this Treaty, shall take care that such services operate on the basis of principles and conditions which enable them to fulfil their missions.

This Article was accompanied by a Declaration stating that these provisions should be implemented 'with full respect for the jurisprudence of the Court of Justice, inter alia as regards the principles of equality of treatment, quality and continuity of such services'.[12]

[10] G Davies, 'What does Article 86 actually do?' in M Krajewski, U Neergaard and J van de Gronden, *The Changing Legal Framework for Services of General Interest in Europe: Between Competition and Solidarity* (The Hague, 2009) 51.

[11] Sauter (n 1) (2008) p 171.

[12] M Ross, 'Article 16 EC and services of general interest: from derogation to obligation?' (2000) 25 *ELRev* 22; L Girard, 'Les services d'interêt économique général et le Traîté d'Amsterdam' (1999) 2 *Revue des Affaires Européennes* 197–213.

Again in 2000, services of general economic interest were given a place of honour in the Charter of Fundamental Rights of the EU. Article 36 of the Charter provides:

> The Union recognizes and respects access to services of general economic interest as provided for in national law and practices, in accordance with the Treaty establishing the European Community, in order to promote the social and territorial cohesion of the Union.

The official Explanation to this Article is very short. It only says that this Article is fully in line with Article 16 TEC and does not create any new right. It merely sets out the principle of respect by the Union for access to services of general economic interest as provided for by national provisions, when those provisions are compatible with Union law.[13]

It is questionable whether these two texts have brought a substantive change. Sauter, for example, qualified Article 16 TEC as a 'mere consolation prize'.[14]

This more positive approach to services of general interest prompted the European Commission to moderate somewhat its former neoliberal position. The Commission published a Communication on Services of General Interest in 2000[15] and submitted a report on this theme to the Laeken Council on 17 November 2001.[16] It was stated that 'the existence of a network of services of general interest is an essential element of social cohesion … The Community is committed to maintaining the function of these services intact, while improving their efficiency'. The same may be found in the Commission's Green Paper, 2003,[17] in which these services were called 'a pillar of European citizenship, forming some of the rights enjoyed by European citizens and providing an opportunity for dialogue with public authorities within the context of good governance'.

The purpose of the Green Paper was to take stock of the opinions of all affected parties about the place of SGEI under European law. The discussion on the Green Paper revealed old as well as new contradictions in this field. Many voices called for a wholesale restriction of the EU's competition and internal market rules, so that public services would be exempted from liberalisation and privatisation, but in the subsequent White Paper on Services of General Interest,[18] published in spring 2004, the European Commission rejected this. The Commission continued its far-reaching programme on sectoral liberalisation of the public utilities, including the 2002

[13] See OJ EC, C 310/445 of 16 December 2004.

[14] Sauter (n 1) (2008) p 171.

[15] See COM (2000) 580; OJ 2001 C 17/4.

[16] COM (2001) 598 (Report on SGIs to the European Council at Laeken).

[17] COM (2003) 270 final; S Meulman, 'Na het Groenboek' (February 2004) *SEW* 98.

[18] COM (2004) 374.

Regulatory Package on electronic (tele)communications, postal services,[19] railways,[20] the Directives aimed at fuller liberalisation of the electricity[21] and gas industry,[22] and so on. In 2005, the Commission came up with a market-oriented approach to state aid—which was supported by the European Parliament—which described even state aid provided for public hospitals and social housing as a distortion of competition.[23]

VII. SERVICES OF GENERAL INTEREST IN THE DEBATE ON THE EUROPEAN CONSTITUTION

In the same period, the Convention which prepared the draft for a European Constitution debated at length the subject of services of general interest in the Working Group on Social Europe.[24] There was a wide variety of opinions about the meaning of the existing Treaty provisions on services of general economic interest and about the future of these provisions in the new Constitution. In the end, the Group recommended that the relevant Article of the Constitution would include the promotion of efficient and high quality social services and services of general interest. In addition, the Group concluded that the question as to whether Article 16 TEC should be amended to become a legal basis for EU legislation concerning services of general interest should be considered by the Convention.

In the Convention, no fewer than 16 amendments and suggestions for amendments on Article III-6 (equivalent to Article 16 TEC) and seven amendments and suggestions for amendments to Article III-55(2) (the equivalent of 86(2) TEC) were proposed by its Members and observers.[25] One amendment proposed deleting Article III-6 altogether, others wanted to extend Article III-6 and Article III-55(2) to cover all services of general interest, both economic and social. Other amendments proposed defining more precisely the missions of these services and of related European interventions.

In the final version of the draft Constitution adopted by the European Convention, June 2003, Article III-55(2)[26] (compared with Article 86(2) TEC) and Article II-36 (compared with Article 36 of the Charter) emerged

[19] Directive 97/67/EC as amended by Directive 2008/6/EC of 20 February 2008.

[20] Directive 2001/12/EC.

[21] Directive 2003/54/EC.

[22] Directive 2003/55/EC.

[23] In'tVeld Report (February 2005).

[24] Final report of Working Group XI on Social Europe, CONV 516/1/03 REV 1.

[25] See S Rodrigues, 'Vers une loi européenne des services publics' (2003) *Revue du Marché commun et de l'Union européenne* 505–06.

[26] T von Damwitz, 'Die Rolle der Unternehmen der Daseinsvorsorge im Verfassungsentwurf' in J Schwarze (ed), *Der Verfassungsentwurf des Europäischen Konvents* (Baden-Baden, 2004) 251.

almost unchanged. However, Article III-6 (compared with Article 16 TEC) would have brought three substantial changes: (i) 'given the place occupied by services of general economic interest in the shared values of the Union' had been redrafted into 'given the place occupied by services of general economic interest as services to which all in the Union attribute value';[27] (ii) 'that such services operate on the basis of principles and conditions, which enable them' had been redrafted into 'that such services operate on the basis of principles and conditions, in particular economic and financial', which enable them'; and finally, the sentence 'European laws shall define these principles and conditions' was added to the text.

The second amendment highlights more than the Treaty of Amsterdam text the need for answers to the structural problems of financing services of general interest.

The third amendment is certainly the most innovative one. It was a non-debated last minute amendment sponsored by the representative of the French Government.[28] As we shall see (section XI) the French Government had already pushed strongly for a Framework Directive on the services of general interest but was confronted with the reluctance of the European Commission to put forward a proposal on this field. This new specific legislative competence fills a previous gap at EU level, although the apparent limitation to action exclusively by regulations seems curious.[29]

During the Intergovernmental Conference (IGC) 2004,[30] which determined the definitive text of the Constitutional Treaty, not many more amendments were made with regard to the status of services of general economic interest. Apart from some linguistic refinements and a renumbering of the Articles,[31] only the last phrase of the draft Article III-6 (the equivalent of Article 16 TEC) was further extended with the phrase 'without prejudice to the competence of Member States, in compliance with the Constitution, to provide, to commission and to fund such services'.

Also, Article I-5 of the Constitution was inserted under the set of Articles on which draft Article III-6 is not taking prejudice.

[27] This amendment was proposed by the Presidium of the Convention. João Cravinho, observer representing the European Social Partners, remarked that the new wording weakens the status of services of general economic interest within the framework of the future Constitution. Emilio Gabaglio, observer to the European Convention representing the ETUC, unsuccessfully proposed an amendment to this Article, which would have restored the reference to 'the place occupied … in the shared values of the Union'.

[28] R Plassmann, General Secretary of CEEP at a Berlin Symposium, November 2004.

[29] Rodrigues (n 25) pp 503–12.

[30] See CIG 60/04; CIG 81/04 Annex 45.

[31] Article 36 Charter, Article II-36 Draft Constitution had become Article II-96 Constitution; Article 16 TEC, Article III-6 Draft Constitution had become Article III-122 Constitution; Article 86(2) TEC, Article III-55(2) Draft Constitution had become Article III-166(2) Constitution.

Both amendments have presumably been made to give fresh assurances to the Member States that their competences to determine the role of SGEI in their societies will be respected.

VIII. SERVICES OF GENERAL INTEREST IN THE TREATY OF LISBON

However, there was much discontent among the citizens of Europe about this Constitutional Treaty, as appeared from the outcome of the referendums in France and the Netherlands. Concerns about the future of SGEI were undoubtedly one of the sources of this dissatisfaction, notably in France. Apparently, the minor amendments that the Constitutional Treaty offered on the texts of the existing Treaties were not enough to convince the citizens that services of general interest are safe in the hands of European policymakers.

At the IGC of 2007, which decided that the Constitutional Treaty should be converted into an ordinary Treaty amending the existing European Treaties, the first of the three abovementioned amendments to Article 16 TEC was cancelled and the old text restored. Moreover, under pressure from the Netherlands[32] and France a special Protocol was devised.[33]

> Article 1
>
> The shared values of the Union in respect of services of general economic interest within the meaning of Article 14 of the Treaty on the Functioning of the European Union include in particular:
>
> the essential role and the wide discretion of national, regional and local authorities in providing, commissioning and organising services of general economic interest as closely as possible to the needs of the users;
>
> the diversity between various services of general economic interest and the differences in the needs and preferences of users that may result from different geographical, social and cultural situations;
>
> a high level of quality, safety and affordability, equal treatment and the promotion of universal access and of users rights.
>
> Article 2
>
> The provisions of the Treaties do not affect in any way the competence of Member States to provide, commission and organise non-economic services of general interest.

[32] The origin of the Protocol appended to the TEU and the TFEU was a demand expressed by the Dutch Prime Minister at the European Council held in June 2007. This demand was inspired by a formal notice served by the European Commission questioning the organisation of subsidised housing in the Netherlands (see section III of this chapter).

[33] See Protocol No 26, OJ C 115/308 of 9 May 2008.

The Protocol does not have the ambition to change the scope and contents of the existing provisions in the Treaty relating to competition law and the internal market. According to its initial words it contains only 'interpretative provisions'. Even in this limited mission the Protocol is weak as it gives no clarification of key notions. It only specifies somewhat the words of Article 14 TFEU: 'the place occupied by services of general economic interest in the shared values of the Union'. The Protocol therefore seems to add little of substance regarding SGEI. The fact that it was necessary to adopt this Protocol only highlights the deep concerns of the Member States that something essential may slip from their control on this issue.

Although the second paragraph of the Protocol introduces for the first time non-economic services of general interest in a primary text of EU law, this insertion does not bring anything new as it has been undisputed over the years that the European internal market and competition rules do not apply to non-economic activities of the Member States. The problem here is the question what is a non-economic service of general interest, and what is not.[34] The Commission and the ECJ use an extensive interpretation of what is 'economic': most 'social' services of general interest are also considered 'economic' in nature.

In 2005/2006, the Commission issued a Communication in order to clarify the framework within which *social* services of general interest operate and can be modernised. In this Communication a list of Community policies was provided that relate to the provision of social services of general interest. It also describes how these services are organised and how they operate.[35]

The final important innovation brought by the Treaty of Lisbon in this field is the fact that Article 36 of the Charter of Fundamental Rights has more force than in the past, as the Charter has been made binding through the new Article 6(1) TEU.

IX. THE POSITION OF THE ETUC WITH REGARD TO SERVICES OF GENERAL INTEREST

The ETUC has repeatedly reiterated the importance of services of general interest (SGI) for the development of the European Social Model in terms of equal opportunities for citizens, social cohesion and the implementation of the Lisbon Strategy. Emilio Gabaglio, former secretary-general of the ETUC,

[34] U Neergaad, 'The services of general economic interest: the nature of the beast' in Krajewski et al (eds) (n 10) pp 17, 39; see also Krajewski (n 51) pp 7–13.

[35] COM (2005) 33 final, p 11 and COM (2006) 177 of 26.4.2006. In 2007 the Commission updated its view on the role and place of services of general interest as part of a substantial package on 'A single market for the 21st century' (COM (2007) 724 final) in which it devoted particular attention to social services of general interest (COM (2007) 725 final).

has called services of general economic interest 'one of the cornerstones of the European social model'.

In the eyes of the ETUC the provision of services of general interest in the EU in many cases compares very favourably with other areas of the world. Their role is essential for the quality of life of all citizens and for overcoming social exclusion and isolation. Given their weight in the economy and their importance for the production of goods and services, the efficiency and quality of these services are key factors in competitiveness and greater cohesion. It is a condition for the smooth functioning of the single market and for further economic integration in the European Union.

SGI should set an example with regard to 'good governance'. They are often operated by 'emanations of the State'.[36] This means that EC Directives may set minimum labour standards directly applicable to all SGI in the EU. Moreover, it can be expected from SGI that they, more directly than other enterprises, comply with fundamental social rights.

Together with the employers in this field, organised in the European Centre of Enterprises with Public Participation and of Enterprises of General Economic Interest (CEEP), the ETUC adopted a 'Joint Charter on Services of General Interest' as early as 2000.

The ETUC lobbied successfully during the Convention that drafted the EU Charter on Fundamental Rights to have these services included in this Charter. This was realised in Article 36.

During the European Convention, Emilio Gabaglio, observer to the European Convention representing the ETUC, made various proposals to strengthen the texts on services of general interest. However, none of them were accepted by the European Convention and so did not find their way into the text of the Constitution.

Notwithstanding this and other rejections of its proposals, the ETUC supported the adoption of the Constitutional Treaty and in the end the ETUC showed itself equally satisfied with the adoption of the Treaty of Lisbon.

X. SGEI WITH REGARD TO VARIOUS ISSUES ON THE BRUSSELS AGENDA

We have already highlighted how SGEI are affected by the policies pursued by the EU since the 1990s with regard to the liberalisation of markets which were traditionally in the hands of monopolistic state-owned services (see above, sections II–IV). State aid and public procurement were also touched on. These matters, as well as the relationship between SGEI and the Services Directive deserve more discussion, however.

[36] See ECJ Case C-188/89 *Foster v British Gas* [1990] ECR I-3313, para 20.

A. State Aid

Initially, the Commission held the view that aid granted by the Member States to undertakings providing SGEI did not correspond to state aid within the meaning of Article 87(1) TEC (now Article 107(1) TFEU), as long as the public sector only offset any additional costs incurred from the discharge of the imposed public service obligation.[37] This situation changed in the 1990s due to rulings of the European Court which culminated in the *Altmark* decision (2003).[38] In this decision a number of detailed and cumulative criteria were set. Where these criteria were met, the compensation paid for discharging a public service obligation would not be considered state aid and would therefore be compatible with the common market. If not all the criteria were met, the compensation would be regarded as state aid and must be notified to the Commission before being granted. The criteria in *Altmark* relate to the clear definition of public service obligations and to the basis for financing. They also reveal a preference for competitive tendering as the procedure for allocating public service tasks.

In an attempt to expand on the principles laid down by the Court in *Altmark*, the Commission in 2005 issued a Decision,[39] as well as an EU Framework,[40] on the arrangements for financing services of general economic interest. These texts have defined the conditions under which state aid granted with regard to SGEI are compatible with EU rules. In these texts the European Commission also redefined its policy towards state aid in the form of public service compensation. The European Commission wants to require Member States to submit reports to it on such state aid, but it was prepared to exempt public hospitals and social housing from the notification obligation. Unfortunately, on 22 February 2005 a majority could not be obtained in the European Parliament for this exemption. It considered state aid provided for public hospitals and social housing as a 'distortion of competition'. I have already shown (section III) how this problem with regard to social housing has caused difficulties in the Netherlands. The matter is currently before the EU Court of Justice. The European trade union federation in this

[37] CH Bovis, 'The conceptual links between state aid and public procurement in the financing of services of general economic interest' in Krajewski et al (eds) (n 10) p 149.

[38] *Altmark* [2003] ECR I-7747; this ruling was confirmed in the CFI ruling of 12 February 2008, Case T-289/03 *BUPA v Commission*; see M Ross, 'A healthy approach to services of general economic interest? The BUPA judgment of the Court of First Instance' (2009) 34 (1) *ELRev* 127–40; JM Thouvenin, 'The *Altmark* case and its consequences' in Krajewski et al (eds) (n 10) p 103.

[39] Decision relating to the application of Article 86(2) of the EC Treaty to state aid as a form of public service compensation granted to certain undertakings entrusted by an operation of services of general economic interest, COM (2005) 267 of 28 November 2005; OJEU L 312 of 29 November 2005.

[40] Community framework relating to state aid as a form of public service compensation, COM (2005) of 28 November 2005, 2005/C 297/04 OJEU C 297/4.

sector, EPSU, is not only demanding an exemption for public hospitals and social housing, but also wants these exemptions to be extended to all social public services that have no—or no significant—impact on the European internal market.

Although in 2008 the European Commission created an interactive information service to handle questions of the application of Community law to services of general interest, many providers of public services, local authorities and others feel uncertain about the proper content and application of the criteria for state aid, laid down by the ECJ in *Altmark* and by the European Commission in its documents implementing *Altmark*.

B. The Services of General Interest and Services Directive[41]

A further threat to services of general economic interest arose in the form of the proposal for a Framework Directive on services in the internal market which the European Commission tabled in January 2004 (the so-called Draft Services or Bolkestein Directive).[42] This proposed Directive was meant to cover all services that correspond to an economic activity within the meaning of the case law of the Court relating to Article 49 TEC and therefore many services of general interest would be affected. Only the civil service proper, as well as non-economic services of general interest would be exempted.

According to many critics, the relationship of SGI to the proposed Services Directive could give rise to conflicts. More particularly, the ETUC has criticised the regulations in the original proposal with regard to the issue of easier access to health care, especially care provided in another Member State. The Services Directive would amount to the de facto deregulation and privatisation of health services and create even greater legal uncertainty. Consequently, the ETUC has asked the Commission to exempt health care services from this proposal and instead to deal with them in a specific Framework Directive that affirms the principles of solidarity, accessibility, universality and continuity.[43] Similar criticisms of the draft Services Directive were made in a research report by Wouter Gekiere,[44] according to whom the original proposal for the Services Directive did not take into account typical features of health care, welfare care and (non-medical) care services, such as the three-party model, the information asymmetry between

[41] J van de Gronden, 'The Services Directive and services of general (economic) interest' in Krajewski et al (eds) (n 10) pp 233–54.

[42] COM (2004) 2 final 3; see also Document SEC (2007) 1516 final.

[43] See ETUC position paper on the proposal for a Directive on services in the internal market, March 2004.

[44] W Gekiere, Study on the implications of the Services Directive (Institute for European Law, Catholic University Leuven, 24 September 2004).

patient and care provider, the fact that it is partly or mainly financed out of public funding and the fact that it is constricted by social and public health considerations. This study also concluded that these services of general interest should be excluded from the draft Services Directive.

On 16 February 2006 the European Parliament tabled substantial amendments to the proposal for the Services Directive, including the exclusion of health and social services from the scope of the Directive. However, the trade unions in the public service sector, organised in EPSU, were not satisfied. Pointing out that the proposed Services Directive still included water, waste, electricity and gas (metering and billing services and so on), education and culture, it requested a clear exclusion of all public services from the scope of the Directive. EPSU considered it unacceptable that the European Commission may in future block new regulations that a national government introduces to protect the quality and provision of public services, covered by the Services Directive.[45]

The compromise text proposed by the Commission and the Council and finally approved by the European Parliament in November 2006 excluded non-economic services of general interest altogether. It also excluded health care, electronic communications, transport, audiovisual services and specific social services, defined as 'social services relating to social housing, childcare and support of families and persons in need' (Article 2(2)). Finally, Article 17 excludes SGEI which are provided in another Member State, inter alia, in the postal sector, the electricity and gas sector, water distribution, supply and services, waste water services and treatment of waste. However, other services of general economic interest are covered by the Directive and thus subject to the rules of the internal market, but 'only insofar as the application of such rules does not obstruct the performance, in law or in fact, of the particular tasks assigned to them', a phrase which is in line with the wording of Article 86(2) TEC, now Article 106(2) TFEU.

The ETUC was satisfied with the general outcome of the debate, although it would have preferred a non-exhaustive list with examples, as proposed earlier by the European Parliament, to avoid the unintended inclusion of services falling outside the definition.

I submit that the concerns about the negative impact of the Services Directive on services of general economic interest will not disappear since the final text of the Services Directive has not unambiguously excluded all public services from its scope.[46]

[45] See EPSU Newsletter, 24 February 2006.
[46] Services in the internal market (Directive 2006/123/EC of 12 December 2006, OJ L 376 of 27 December 2006).

C. Public Procurement

Equally complex issues have arisen in the context of the relationship between EU procurement law and services of general economic interest. In several Directives, the EU imposes on public entities the obligation of public procurement rules with regard to goods, services or works purchased or commissioned by them. They are applicable mainly to services of general economic interest, but even if such services do not fall within the scope of the EU public procurement law SGEI must nevertheless comply with the relevant rules and principles laid down in the European Treaties.[47] It is often thought that the detailed rules set out in the Directives prohibit authorities from maintaining high social and employment standards when awarding public work contracts. However, in theory this is not correct: the public procurement rules allow the awarding authorities to give the contract not simply to the cheapest, but to 'the most economically advantageous' tender. But this last option requires the public authority to specify in the tender documents the criteria used, with their relative weightings, for the evaluation of the tender. Any failures or inaccuracies in the tender documents could endanger the provision of the services and lead to lengthy court proceedings.[48] It is submitted that many awarding authorities are unable to formulate such standards of quality sufficiently accurately and therefore simply choose the easier option of awarding the contract to the cheapest tender.

As a result, the quality of the relevant SGEI is downgraded (see above, section III).

XI. A EUROPEAN FRAMEWORK DIRECTIVE ON SERVICES OF GENERAL INTEREST

Since the release of the first report on services of general economic interest by the Commission in 1996, a Framework Directive on such services has been considered to be one possible way to put an end to legal uncertainty in this field.[49] Proponents of competition-free management of services, such as the ETUC, have for many years been pleading for a general European Framework Directive that would clearly define and restrict the EU's competition and internal market rules, so that public services would be exempted from liberalisation and privatisation.

[47] See Case C-324/98 *Telaustria*; see COM (2001) 566.

[48] See, for instance, ECJ Case C-314/01 *Siemens AG Osterreich*.

[49] See on this issue also Rodrigues (n 25) pp 509–12; S Rodrigues, 'Towards a general EC Framework Instrument related to services of general economic interest? Political considerations and legal constraints' in M Krajewski, U Neergaard and J van de Gronden, *The Changing Legal Framework for Services of General Interest in Europe: Between Competition and Solidarity* (The Hague, 2009) 255.

Already in December 2000 the ETUC Congress adopted a Resolution on a regulatory framework on SGI. In that year a proposal for a European Charter on SGI was worked out jointly by the CEEP and the ETUC. In February 2002, the ETUC and the CEEP[50] issued a proposal for the structure and principles to be incorporated in a Framework Directive on SGI.

The idea of a general framework for services of general interest[51] initially seemed to garner broad support. The European Parliament in 2001 had called for a Framework Directive on services of general interest[52] and it repeated this request in January 2004.[53] Even the European Council of Barcelona in March 2002 more or less requested that the European Commission draw up a Framework Directive on services of general interest,[54] as the French Government had made its acceptance of further energy liberalisation conditional on the proposal of such a Framework Directive.

At the time of the consultation on the 2003 Green Paper, the majority of the players in the sector (local public authorities, operators, representatives of users and NGOs) emphasised that they felt that there was increasing legal uncertainty with regard to the body of EU legal norms to which they were subject in view of their specific features. They stressed that they were part of a 'grey area' and that this was prejudicial to the accomplishment of the missions entrusted to them.[55]

However, in its White Paper on Services of General Economic Interest (May 2004), the Commission rejected this request. The Commission decided to develop its sectoral approach without issuing a general Directive for the moment. It did so on the grounds that there was no consensus on the need for a legal framework on SGI. However, the Commission promised to revisit the issue once the Constitutional Treaty entered into force.

In 2006, new proposals were made.[56] The Socialist Group in the European Parliament came forward with a proposal for a Framework Directive on services of general economic interest.[57] Some time later a possible EU Framework for services of general interest was published by CELSIG (European Liaison

[50] See: www.CEEP.org.

[51] M Krajewski, *Background paper on a legal framework for services of general (economic) interest*, EPSU, (Brussels, 2006) pp 3–5.

[52] EP Resolution on the Commission Communication 'Services of General Interest in Europe', 13 November 2001, OJ 2002C 140E/153.

[53] EP Resolution on SGI, 14 January 2004, based on report Herzog A 5-484/2003.

[54] Presidential Conclusions, European Council of Barcelona, 15–16 March 2002; request repeated in the conclusions of the European Council in Brussels, 20–21 March 2003, point 26.

[55] Economic and Social Committee, 'Analysis of the implications of the Lisbon Treaty on Services of General Interest and proposals for implementation' (Luxembourg, 2008) p 52.

[56] For a comparison between the different proposals see B Thiry, 'Quel cadre légal pour les services d'interêt économique général? Analyse comparative de cinq projets de "directive-cadre"', Working Paper CIRIEC No 2007/02.

[57] Proposal for a Framework Directive on Services of General Economic Interest, May 2006. Available at: www.socialistgroup.org/.

Committee on Services of General Interest).[58] On 20 September 2006, the ETUC Executive Committee adopted the text of a draft European Framework Directive for services of general economic interest, as a basis on which to work.[59]

The main points of the ETUC proposal for a Framework Directive, 2006, are that general interest should take precedence over market laws; the Charter of Fundamental Rights should be applied; and the principle of subsidiarity and the responsibility of public authorities at all levels should determine how these services will be provided. For the ETUC, it is important that users, trade unions and consumers are consulted and are stakeholders with regard to methods of regulation, and that involvement and consultation of workers and their representatives is affirmed within the context of social dialogue at every level.

However, even if part of the European Parliament on 26 September 2006 still maintained its request to the Commission to table a general Framework Directive on services of general interest, it has become increasingly clear that political division has arisen on this issue. In the text of the EP Resolution of 27 September 2006 it can be seen that the support in the European Parliament for a Framework Directive had dwindled. The European Parliament no longer asked for a general Framework Directive, but called on the Commission only to propose appropriate legal initiatives. It recommended that the sectoral approach be expanded into other sectors and requested that the Commission formulate legal clarifications, guidelines and principles on a number of problematic topics.[60]

Indeed, in those years there was no consensus on the need for a legal framework, neither in the European Parliament (Christian Democrats, liberals and others openly rejected the idea),[61] nor among governments (the Dutch Government, for instance, was opposed to it) nor among the social partners (BusinessEurope[62] did not like the idea).

The ETUC criticised the Commission for having failed to support a Framework Directive on SGI. It pointed to the paradox that, with the new proposal for a Directive on services on the internal market, the Commission appeared to be able to produce a wide-ranging Framework Directive of vast scope on services in general in the internal market that imposes certain basic, harmonised, high-quality requirements at European level. Not surprisingly, the ETUC repeated its call for a specific legal Framework Directive on SGI. In the absence of legislation the ETUC has proposed a moratorium

[58] Draft on a Proposed Law on Services of General Economic Interest, June 2006. Available at: www.celsig.org.

[59] Proposal for a Framework to Guarantee and Develop Services of General Economic Interest, September 2006. Available at: www.etuc.org.

[60] EP Resolution No P6_TA (2006) 0380, points 15, 16 and 31.

[61] See Krajewski (n 51) p 4.

[62] See its letter to the European Parliament of 25 September 2006.

on liberalisation. In support of its demand for a Framework Directive on SGI in November 2006 the ETUC launched a campaign to collect 1 million signatures on a petition demanding 'High quality public services, accessible to all'. Unfortunately, the ETUC did not succeed in gathering the 1 million signatures it needed.

EPSU asserted that the European Commission had been pursuing a cynical strategy of 'stalling and crawling' for the past ten years. A horizontal legal framework for all public services is essential to ensure that the Commission tactic of gradually eroding protected public services on a sector-by-sector basis is stopped. Health and social services, the water sector and even the education sector are all public services under consideration for liberalisation by the Commission. This erosion of public services will continue until a clear EU law ensures that these sectors are not considered only in market terms.[63] EPSU saw a 'framework' text as the bedrock for public service principles. This horizontal approach is particularly appropriate in order to act as a balance with regard to the horizontally applicable Services Directive.[64]

The adoption of the Protocol on Services of General Interest by the European Council in June 2007 seems to have strengthened the European Commission in its refusal to propose a Framework Directive: its position was that sufficient clarification has been provided by this Interpretative Protocol. The Commission stated that it would use the Protocol even before the Treaty came into force as a 'benchmark to check the consistency and proportionality of EU policies and initiatives'.[65]

Given the Commission's monopoly on legislative initiatives this meant that, for the time being, the European Parliament and the Council of Ministers remained blocked.

According to Sauter, the Commission has somewhat cynically embraced this Protocol as finally delivering the clarification that had long been sought during long years of consultation, consequently making a Framework Directive on SGEI superfluous. From the Commission's perspective the entire public debate on SGEI can be seen as a holding exercise intended to diffuse political tension on this topic, which in the final analysis has not had much of an impact on the scope or meaning of SGEI.[66]

Now that the Lisbon Treaty has come into force it make sense to reflect on the options regarding scope and content for implementation of the new responsibility that the Treaty of Lisbon confers on the European legislators in relation to services of general economic interest.

The ETUC has now abandoned its demand for a Framework *Directive*. With regard to the text of Article 14 TFEU, it is now calling for a Framework

[63] Available at: www.epsu.org/a/2314.
[64] Available at: www.epsu.org/a/2314 and 2396.
[65] COM (2007) 725, p 11.
[66] Sauter (n 1) (2008) pp 173–74.

Regulation, as well as detailed sectoral regulations for the various sectors in which SGI are operating.[67]

It is unclear whether Article 14 TFEU leaves the EU legislator with much choice, with regard to either the nature of the act or the procedure for its adoption, as this Article clearly speaks about a regulation and the ordinary legislative procedure. I submit that, in accordance with the legal canon that he who has the power to do the major, also has the power to do the minor, this does not exclude the adoption of other instruments (Directives and Commission Directives/Decisions), for instance for amending the existing Directives on market liberalisation and the Commission Directives/Decisions on state aid in order to bring them into line with the new Protocol on SGI.

Does that mean that there must be one horizontal legal framework for all public services? I submit that it is not necessary that all regulation of SGEI should be in one regulation. The fact that the plural is used in Article 14 TFEU leaves open the possibility of more than one regulation in this field. For example, a combination of a sector-specific and a transversal regulatory approach: sector-based Regulations and Directives under the umbrella of one Framework Regulation laying down definitions and principles common for all sectors.[68]

XII. CONFRONTATION WITH 'LISBON'

One might ask whether the changes introduced by the Lisbon Treaty are to be seen as a major change in the treatment of services of general (economic) interest by the Treaties, both from a formal and a substantive point of view. Can we expect that the Lisbon Treaty will clear the sky above SGI?

To start on the negative side. The existing Articles which define their situation—Article 16 TEC (now 14 TFEU) and Article 86(2) TEC (now 106(2) TFEU—have not been changed substantially.

On the positive side: there is now:

- Protocol No 26 which specifies the values of SGEI and keeps non-economic SGI more explicitly within the competence of the Member States.
- Article 36 of the Charter which now has binding force.
- Greater emphasis on the principle of subsidiarity.

[67] See ETUC Resolution, 'Towards a new impetus for public services', 1–2 June 2010, point 11.

[68] See Rodrigues (2009) (n 49) p 262.

— The affirmation of 'solidarity' and 'equality'—which are both values promoted by SGI[69]—as basic values of the EU (Article 2 TUE).
— The horizontal clause (Article 9 TFEU) mainstreaming the social values of the EU.
— The fact that the idea of an 'internal market where competition is free and undistorted' has been deleted from the basic aims of the EU (Article 3 TUE).
— The last line of Article 14 TFEU, calling for regulations on SGEI.

Therefore it is hoped that in the foreseeable future EU regulations may be adopted to better protect SGEI. The clear insertion of an obligation to issue regulations in this field is a step forward as there were legal doubts under the old Treaty texts with regard to whether there is a legal basis for a general framework.[70] The Commission henceforward can no longer avoid using its monopoly to take legislative initiatives in order to have one or more European regulations on SGI adopted. Should the institutions fail to act, one day there could well be a '*recours en carence*' to the Court of Justice of the EU.[71]

In my view the EU should start as quickly as possible to adopt a regulation on the basis of Article 14 TFEU to provide simple but effective protection of non-economic SGI from the meddling of the Commission.

The ETUC has proposed[72] that the EU should establish a register in which the Member States can enter all their services of non-economic general interest which are excluded from the application of Community rules on the provision of services, on competition and on state aid. This register[73] should not be open to challenge in any legal proceedings except in case of manifest error.[74] The burden of proof should fall on the European Commission or other complainant.

As far as services of general economic interest are concerned the regulation required by Article 14 TFEU should provide that general interest should

[69] M Ross, 'Promoting solidarity: from public services to a European model of competition' (2007) 44 *CMLR* 1057–80; M Ross, 'The value of solidarity in European Public Services Law' in Krajewski et al (eds) (n 10) p 81; European Foundation for the Improvement of Living and Working Conditions, 'Equal Opportunities for women and men in services of general interest' (Dublin, November 2004). Available at: www.eurofound.eu.int.

[70] See the Report on the Commission White Paper on services of general interest, 14 September 2006, A6-0275/2006 (Rapkay Report) p 39. See also Krajewski (n 51) pp 13–19.

[71] Rodrigues (n 25) p 508.

[72] See ETUC Resolution, 'Towards a new impetus for public services', 1–2 June 2010, point 13.

[73] Such a method of creating clarity with a Register also exists in the area of the European coordination of social security systems (Regulation 883/2004).

[74] The 'manifest error' level of scrutiny was already used in CFIEC, 27 February 1997, *FFSA et al v Commission*, Case T-106/95; and in Case T-289/03 *BUPA* CFIEC, 12 February 2008; see Ross (n 38) p 127.

take precedence over market laws and that the principle of subsidiarity and should determine how these services will be provided.

It may be doubted whether there is the political will in the institutions of the EU to issue such a rule, considering the neoliberal winds which still prevail. However, it is important to stress that from now on national parliaments[75] may be more forceful than in the past in opposing effectively the adoption of Directives, Regulations and Decisions that infringe on the freedom of the Member States to organise their SGEI. This is thanks to the new stature of the subsidiarity principle, which can now be enforced by a kind of an early warning system and a right of appeal to the Court of Justice of the EU.

Finally, there is the binding force of Article 36 of the Charter on SGEI, which may lead to greater emphasis on the principle of accessibility as an essential principle of SGEI functioning in the Member States, a principle that the EU legislator should not frustrate in any way by its own rules.

Citizens may invoke this principle against any EU act. Certainly, they can do that in conjunction with other fundamental rights laid down in the Charter, such as the right to social and housing assistance (Article 34(3), health care (Article 35), education (Article 14) and child protection (Article 24(1). For instance, the decisions of the Commission in matters of state aid and so on can all be tested as contrary to the positive attitude of the Charter, Article 14 TFEU and Protocol 26 with respect to SGEI.

XIII. CONCLUSIONS

A few years ago the future of services of general (economic) interest in Europe looked grim. Liberalisation, privatisation, more emphasis on the market and less on state aid seem to have become the general wisdom. However, the financial crisis since 2008 has destroyed this unlimited belief in such 'wisdom'. The financial markets themselves had to call for state intervention, massive state aid and in some instances even the renationalisation of banks.

Our world cannot do without state regulation and state intervention.

Against this background a more promising future for services of general interest is beckoning.

Some say that the Treaty of Lisbon marks an important stage in the adoption of a new architecture for SGI.[76] To date, there has been only a largely ad hoc approach with regard to SGEI in terms of legislation (sector-based Directives) and disputes (depending on complaints or cases brought by

[75] H-J Bieling, C Deckwirth and S Schmalz, *Liberalisierung und Privatisierung in Europa* (Münster, 2008).

[76] See above (n 55) p 49.

the Commission or those which arose in national courts). The new Treaty provisions certainly call for a more transversal regulatory approach with regard to SGEI, so that the current exclusively ad hoc approach ceases to apply.

The Charter of Fundamental Rights together with Article 14 TFEU and the new Protocol 26 on SGI are important cornerstones in the construction of a new SGI architecture. The EU can now skip from a strict derogation approach that has prevailed so far to a more positive stance, based on the shared values embodied by public services across Europe, in other words, solidarity and social and territorial cohesion.[77]

Much will depend on the future elaboration of the last phrase of Article 14 TFEU. Much will also depend on the combativeness of national parliaments in making use of the subsidiarity provisions to defend their SGEI against EU laws that do not contain sufficient protection. And much will depend on the creativity and perseverance of citizens in using the Court of Justice of the EU to prevent the Commission from pursuing its negative approach to SGEI.

Of course, it remains to be seen what the Court of Justice of the EU will do with actions of this kind. It will—as in the famous 'Laval quartet'—again be confronted with the nasty question of how to rank the aims of competition and social demands. However, it may—perhaps more successfully than with regard to the Laval quartet—try to reconcile these aims, 'optimising' them so that such services can no longer be considered 'dysfunctional' exceptions in a competition-oriented Community.[78]

[77] See 'The ETUC, the Lisbon Treaty and public services', Background document for the seminar 'What opportunities for public services?' Barcelona, 28–30 April 2010, point 2; ETUC Resolution, 'Towards a new impetus for public services', 1–2 June 2010, point 10.

[78] S Wernicke, 'Taking stock: the EU institutions and SGEI' in Krajewski et al (eds) (n 10) p 70.

Conclusions concerning the Lisbon Treaty and Social Europe: A Complex Relationship that has only just started to Evolve

I. THE LISBON TREATY: A READING OF THE TEXT

IN THIS BOOK we have tried to show that, from the point of view of its textual content, the Lisbon Treaty marks an advance for Social Europe in a number of ways, compared with the Nice Treaty. We have tried to map these advances carefully in the course of the book. Summing up, a more favourable framework has been achieved in several ways, including reference to the new values and objectives (see chapter by Dorssemont) and also the legally binding Charter of Fundamental Rights of the European Union (Article 6(1) TEU) which in many respects contains fundamental social rights (Kollonay-Lehoczky, Lörcher and Schömann). Furthermore, a social horizontal clause has been introduced (Article 9 TFEU; see chapter by Vielle) and the role of the social partners has been strengthened by the new provision of Article 152 TFEU (see Veneziani's chapter and the Group's Recommendations). Other new elements concern services of general interest (see chapter by Jacobs).

On the other hand, it is clear that the Lisbon Treaty also shows strong continuity in relation to earlier EU law. We might even identify a tendency to neglect some evident, but mainly symbolic implications of the Lisbon Treaty, in the form of a new terminology: for example, the use of 'Community' instead of 'Union' law or the 'European Court of Justice' instead of the 'Court of Justice of the European Union'. Behind this very formal aspect a more general attitude can be perceived: the fact that some new social elements have been added to the Treaty is still not common knowledge and much remains to be done to overcome this neglect. From a social perspective, therefore, the aim of this book is to contribute to a more thorough appreciation of this new framework and its consequences.

II. THE LISBON TREATY IN PRACTICE: THE ECONOMIC AND POLITICAL CONTEXTS

In more theoretical terms, the overall situation in which the Lisbon Treaty is to be applied must be assessed against the background of economic developments, in particular in times of crisis (see the chapters by Deakin and Bruun). Furthermore, it is worth evaluating the role played by social policy in the new political architecture of the EU.

For example, it seems that the economic governance of the EU is in the process of being strengthened. The EU is extending economic coordination and control, especially within the Euro area, but also more generally. In order to make this economic governance constitutionally uncontested, the EU will adopt an explicit amendment to the Lisbon Treaty (see Bruun).

The social implications of this EU (and IMF) economic governance in the Member States that are in serious economic difficulties (Greece, Ireland and Portugal) are severe. The link between economic governance in the EU and so-called national social policy is becoming evident to the broad public. At the same time, the responsibility of the state authorities in the Member States or European institutions (ECB, the European Commission) is becoming evident. There seems to be no return to a strong neoliberal ideology based on the notion that the state (or the regulator) must keep away from European markets. On the contrary, the new debate henceforth will deal more with the issue of what role the state should play, not whether it has a role at all.

In this context we believe that the EU will have to address the linking of economic and social policy in a more systematic way than in the recent past, since institutional reforms are needed to address the adverse social implications of fiscal and economic imbalances, and not only their impact on their financial system (see further Deakin). This is also necessary in order to obtain legitimacy for the European project among the general public (see Bruun).

III. THE COMPLEX RELATIONSHIP BETWEEN EU COMPETENCES AND SOCIAL POLICY

In practice, the Lisbon Treaty will develop in the aftermath of the economic crisis. It is often mentioned that the European Union lacks important competences to regulate social policies. In fact, the competence framework, in principle, remained unchanged when the Lisbon Treaty was introduced (see chapter by Lörcher), but was defined more strictly. Furthermore, the subsidiarity principle, which is seen by many as particularly important in the social policy field, has been strengthened by, among other things, an extended Protocol with new procedural rights (see chapter by Blanke).

At present, however, it seems as if the most important issue regarding social policy is how fundamental social rights are balanced towards economic freedoms and also how social policy considerations and national traditions are taken into account within other policy areas of the European Union.

The debate regarding EU competences in the social field is strongly polarised. Some researchers see strong national competences as the only way of protecting national systems, while others argue that only a strong European Union social policy can end the present process of indirect undermining of national social systems through market regulation (for example, the famous 'Laval quartet' judgments by the CJEU). The contributions in the present publication try to go beyond this debate and to discuss forms in which increased EU competences can be combined with greater diversity and respect for national systems.

IV. THE LISBON TREATY: AN EVALUATION

The general conclusion of the authors of this book is that the Lisbon Treaty cannot be seen as an obstacle—at least compared with the Nice Treaty—facing those who want to advance a more social Europe. On the other hand, it is rather vague and ambiguous and there are many competing actors and views on what its specific content should be. In this context, the role of the European courts (at both national and European level) is becoming increasingly important. The complexity of the system and also the increased fragmentation between different sub-systems make it difficult to foresee and predict outcomes of different cases. The conclusion therefore is that in order to realise the opportunities—or values—inherent in the Lisbon Treaty we need legal activism.

Besides exploring the historical developments and theoretical background of the Lisbon Treaty the contributions in this book also contain practical conclusions which can be used to make the Treaties work more 'socially'. Here we can mention only a few:

- The priority of the EU's values (Article 2 TEU) in relation to its objectives (Article 3 TEU 3) would mean that the CJEU in interpreting EU Directives in the field of social policy should take account of the constitutional values underlying these instruments, instead of interpreting them in light of the conflicting economic objectives of the EU (see Dorssemont).
- The Union is strictly bound by fundamental rights and cannot avoid this obligation by reference to the principle of subsidiarity (see Blanke).
- The Charter of Fundamental Rights, together with Article 14 TFEU and the new Protocol No 26 on services of general interest (SGI) are important cornerstones in the construction of a new SGI architecture (see Jacobs).

- Even though the competence provisions have in principle remained unchanged, the existing possibilities even for secondary legislation offer a wide range of new initiatives, in particular to make the fundamental social rights work effectively (see Lörcher).
- The role of the ETUC as social partner can be strengthened in many procedural respects (see Veneziani and Recommendations on Article 152 TFEU).
- There will be numerous and regular opportunities to invoke the new horizontal social clause (Article 9 TFEU) in the national courts and the Court of Justice in order to reiterate the social aims of the Treaty, including on those occasions when the economic freedoms enshrined in this same Treaty are subject to examination (see Vielle).
- The foreseen (in the Lisbon Treaty) accession of the European Union to the European Convention on Human Rights (ECHR) will also create some opportunities, especially regarding the interpretation of the right to freedom of association (Article 11). Some opportunities might arise even before accession, since the CJEU is inclined to avoid conflicts with ECtHR practice.

In general, we want to underline that the new content of the Lisbon Treaty also opens the way for new interpretations. Such interpretations will be accepted by the European courts only if they are able to assert themselves in practical cases. The legal struggle for social rights in the wide sense of the term will therefore have to be fought at different levels and in different areas. The Lisbon Treaty provides some important arguments in this respect. This publication hopefully contributes to an understanding of these possibilities and makes them visible, as well as to achieving the 'renewal of labour law, both at European transnational level and within the Member States of the EU', as expressed by Brian Bercusson with regard to the EU Charter.[1]

However, legal interpretation alone will not do the job. In order to back legal changes both of interpretation and of legal texts we need to further Social Europe at the level of primary law, namely the Treaty.

Much remains to be done to come closer to or even achieve the general requirement of at least a reasonable balance between economic and social interests within the European Union. More concretely, the most important problems arising from the CJEU's jurisprudence in the cases *Viking*, *Laval* and so on will have to be solved. The most direct approach would be the amendment of primary EU law ('Social Progress Clause/Protocol').[2] It seems that the first opportunity for such legislative action will occur fairly soon, when the amendment of Article 136 TFEU is discussed.

[1] B Bercusson (ed), 'Introduction' in *European Labour Law and the EU Charter of Fundamental Rights* (Baden-Baden, 2006) 13.

[2] ETUC proposal available at: www.etuc.org/a/5175.

Recommendations by the Transnational Trade Union Rights (TTUR) Expert Group to the European Trade Union Confederation (ETUC) on the effective application of Article 152 of the Treaty on the Functioning of the European Union (TFEU)

[B]y virtue of Article 152 TFEU the European Union recognises and promotes the role of the social partners at its level, taking into account the diversity of national systems.

CJEU 15 July 2010 Case C-271/08—Commission/Germany, paragraph 39

Overview

1. The Lisbon Treaty reinforces the role of the social partners at the European Union level. In force since 1 December 2009, the new provision (Article 152 TFEU) must now be properly applied. The Transnational Trade Union Rights (TTUR) Expert Group produced the following paper containing a legal analysis of its procedural aspects,[1] together with recommendations for the ETUC.[2] Background information will be found in the Annex.

Legal Analysis

INTRODUCTION

New Element in Social Policy: Article 152 TFEU

2. In respect of the 'Social policy' Title (Title X of Part Three) of the Treaty on the Functioning of the European Union (TFEU) one major change has taken place: the social partners are addressed by the new Article 152 TFEU. This is an expression of the idea of democratic participation rooted in Part I Title VI of the (never legally binding) Constitutional Treaty (Article I-48). The new provision reads as follows:

> Article 152
>
> The Union recognises and promotes the role of the social partners at its level, taking into account the diversity of national systems. It shall facilitate dialogue between the social partners, respecting their autonomy.
> The Tripartite Social Summit for Growth and Employment shall contribute to social dialogue.

New Legal Framework

3. Important new legally relevant elements must be stressed in order to understand how the Community legal order has changed to become the only existing 'European Union' with its two Treaties (TEU and TFEU) and to describe the legal context for the purpose of interpreting Article 152 TFEU.

[1] The more material issues of Article 152 TFEU to be analysed more in depth would have to include such aspects as its relationship to the economic freedoms, the relevance of the "diversity of national systems" etc.

[2] This paper only addresses the ETUC and its specific role leaving aside the European employers' organisations as counter-parts of the ETUC.

Values

4. The overall architecture of the two Treaties is inspired by and based on *values*, not just principles. They are enumerated in the new Article 2 TEU, which states:

   > The union is founded on the values of respect for human dignity, freedom, democracy, equality, the rule of law and respect of the human rights of persons belonging to minorities. The values are common to the member states in a society in which pluralism, non-discrimination, tolerance, justice, solidarity and equality between women and men prevail.

   References to the values mentioned are also contained in Articles 7(1), 13 and 49 TEU as 'parameters of legitimacy' for the actions of the Union's institutions.

Fundamental Rights

5. The Lisbon Treaty finally achieves the objective of a legally binding framework of fundamental rights, in particular by declaring the Charter of Fundamental Rights of the European Union (hereinafter the 'EU Charter') legally binding:

   — Article 6(1) TEU changes the wording of the previous Article 6 EU: the Union now 'recognises'—no longer merely 'shall respect'—rights, freedoms and principles set out in the EU Charter 2000 as amended in 2007. The Charter 'shall have the same legal value as the treaties'. The EU Charter states rights and principles with the same legal nature and strength as the rights, freedoms and principles recognised by the Union.

   In particular, the role of trade unions is defined by:

   — Article 12(1) on freedom of association (Article 5 (Revised) European Social Charter—(R)ESC);
   — Article 28 on the right to collective bargaining and collective action (Article 6 (R)ESC).

   In respect of both provisions, the explanations to the EU Charter explicitly refer to the European Union level.

   — Article 6(2) TEU: The Union shall accede to the European Convention for the Protection of Human Rights and Fundamental Freedoms (ECHR).
   — Article 6(3) TEU: Fundamental rights, as guaranteed by the ECHR, and as they result from constitutional traditions common to the Member States, 'shall constitute general principles of Union Law'.

6. Furthermore, it should be noted that the 5th recital of the preamble of the TEU, as well as Article 151(1) TFEU refer to the fundamental social rights as defined in the ESC signed at Turin on 18 October 1961 and in the 1989 Community Charter of the Fundamental Social Rights of Workers.

Principle of Representative Democracy

7. The principle of representative democracy at EU level (Article 10 TEU) is clarified explicitly as political representation (para (4)) and civil representation (associations) (Article 11 (1) TEU).
   Civil and political representativeness requires an auxiliary role of the EU institutions in:
   — promoting 'opportunities to make known and publicly exchange their views on all areas of the Union' (Article 11(1) TEU);
   — maintaining 'an open, transparent and regular dialogue with representative associations and civil society' (Article 11(2) TEU), and also
   — that the European Commission 'shall carry out broad consultations with the parties concerned in order to ensure that the Union's actions are coherent and transparent' (Article 11(3) TEU).

8. The new democratic principles prescribe a:
   — broad concept of democracy;
   — political and civil representation;
   — institutional participation; and
   — regular institutional dialogue.

9. In Part One, Title II TEU (Democratic principles) follows Title I (Common provisions) dealing with the fundamental rights and values provided for by the international and Union legal sources which represent the overall legal framework for all its institutions.
   In the words of the new Article 13 TEU, the Union institutional framework:
   — 'shall aim to promote its values, advance its objectives, serve its interests, those of its citizens and those of Member states and
   — ensure the consistency, effectiveness and continuity of its policy and actions' (para (1)).

Further Context

10. It seems consistent that the involvement of the social partners must be read in this renewed context, taking into account:
    - all *'social' objectives* and aims for the EU contained in Article 3 TEU, in particular in para (3):

      It shall work for the sustainable development of Europe based on balanced economic growth and price stability, a highly competitive social market economy, aiming at full employment and social progress ... It shall combat social exclusion and discrimination, and shall promote social justice and protection, equality between women and men ...
    - that the EU shall have *shared competence* with the Member States in matters of social policy and social cohesion (Article 4(2) (b) and (c) TFEU);
    - that the EU shall have a supporting or auxiliary competence in vocational training (Article 6 (e) TFEU);
    - that—according to the new provisions of Part One, Title II ('having general application') of the TFEU—the Union in 'defining and implementing its policy and activities' (Article 9 TFEU) within its competence is obliged by a *social horizontal clause* to respect two principles:
        - the principle of consistency between its policies and activities and objectives (Article 7 TFEU);
        - the principle of 'social responsibility', that is, 'of the promotion of a high level of employment, the guarantee of adequate social protection, the fight against social exclusion and a high level of education, training and protection of human health' (Article 9 TFEU).

General Objective: Reinforcing the Role of the Social Partners at the EU Level

11. The approach used in this Memorandum is based on the '*effet-utile*' method of interpretation developed by the CJEU. By defining the objective, it appears obvious that the role of the social partners should be reinforced. This definition is based on the obligation to promote their role. Furthermore, by introducing the new provision, the legislator wishes to strengthen the role of the social partners in *all* social policy matters.

General Description of the Content of Article 152 TFEU

12. Article 152 TFEU must be seen and analysed in light of this new context. It is a clear expression of the new legal and institutional philosophy

of the Lisbon Treaty process. Reproducing Article I-48 literally, it is now placed in Part Three, Title X of the TFEU on Social Policy and represents, in the areas of labour law, trade union law and welfare, the values of:

— representative democracy (social democracy) and
— participation (social dialogue).

In other words, it also expresses the idea that the 'collective autonomy' of the social partners is a protagonist of a reshaped EU legal system where all collective rights and actions (collective bargaining, freedom of association, participation, strikes) have acquired full legal status.

In fact, collective labour rights are now included in relevant provisions of the legally binding EU Charter (Article 6(1) TEU). The EU Charter must be used as a parameter to scrutinise the legitimacy of all the actions of the European institutions.

13. In this context Article152 TFEU contains rights and obligations:

- a right of the social partners:
  - to be recognised by the Union;
  - to be promoted by the Union;
- an obligation for the Union to facilitate dialogue between the social partners;
- an obligation to respect their autonomy.

14. The role of the Union is described:

- not only as 'passive' ('respecting' a right);
- but also as proactive or promoting ('facilitating') dialogue in general and also 'dialogue leading to contractual relations, including agreements' (Article 155 (1) TFEU).

15. The 'Tripartite Social Summit for Growth and Employment' is institutionalised at the level of primary law and is an expression of *one* of the ways in which the right to recognition and promotion can be make effective.

16. Rights and obligations provided for by Article 152 TFEU must be respected by the Union at 'its level' (para (1)) in line with all provisions stated in the EU Charter dealing with collective social rights. In fact, Articles 12, 27 and 28 of the EU Charter provide for a dense network of collective labour rights protecting not only the *dignity* of workers but also *solidarity* at Union level. Both dignity and solidarity are the substantial roots of the Union as indicated in Article 2 TEU and in the specific Titles of the EU Charter (Title I and Title IV) 'which shall have the same legal value as Treaties' (Article 6(1) TEU).

Scope

Material Scope: At Least All Areas With (Potential) Social Impact Are Covered.

17. Article 152 TFEU does not define exactly the material scope of the role of the social partners. Therefore, an interpretation is needed in order to clarify in what respects the role of he social partners must be recognised and promoted.

18. First, paragraph (2) of this provision makes it clear that it is obviously not only the 'social policy' as defined in Title X of Part Two (and even less the legislative competence areas in Article 153 TFEU) which restricts the role of the social partners. Indeed, the name of the 'Tripartite Social Summit for Growth and Employment' refers in respect of growth to economic questions in the widest sense and in respect of employment at least to the preceding Title IX 'Employment'.

19. Second, this Article must be understood in the context of its general framework (see above), as well as in terms of its relationship to the existing provisions of the Social Policy title. It is placed after the aims of EU social policy (Article 151 TFEU, ex-Article 136 EC), but before the provisions on legislative competences (Article 153 TFEU, ex-Article 137 EC). Therefore, it is not restricted to the areas in which the Union has legislative competences.

20. Third, Article 9 TFEU as a new horizontal ('mainstreaming') social clause (see above) provides for the first time that, in respect of *all* policies and activities ('In defining and implementing its policies and activities, the Union shall take into account') social aims must be taken account of. These aims must also be seen in light of the values and objectives of the Union (Articles 2 and 3 TEU, see above paras 4 and 10). This clause now requires an overall approach. Therefore, any limitation of the material scope of the role of the social partners would not be in harmony with this provision.

21. Therefore all Union policy areas, in particular concerning fundamental rights, economic freedoms and external relations with any sort of social impact are covered.

Personal Scope: Social Partners, in Particular the ETUC

22. On the workers' side, 'Social partners' at Union level include, in particular, the ETUC as the only representative inter-professional trade union organisation at the Union level. Social partners at EU level also include the European Industry Federations, at least as branches of the ETUC.

Role of the ETUC as Social Partner

General Principles

23. The first sentence of Article 152(1) TFEU stipulates that the 'Union recognises and promotes the role of the social partners at its level'. The two dimensions refer, on the one hand, to the recognition of the role of the social partners, and on the other hand, to the promotion of their role.

24. The role of the social partners is defined in different ways and in different provisions of the Treaties. Generally, it should be recalled that the ETUC was present as observer in the Convention on the 'Future of Europe' elaborating the Constitution for the EU. This form of Convention is now foreseen in Article 48(3) TEU in cases of Treaty revision. In particular, Articles 154 and 155 TFEU (ex-Articles 138 and 139 EC) include their role as:

    — partners in consultation, together with the specific form within the 'Tripartite Social Summit';
    — partners in dialogue; and
    — co-legislator.

25. The provision, furthermore, requires that the Union take into account the diversity of national systems. Such an obligation is understandable only if it relates to the larger framework of a European industrial relations system. Therefore, the role of the social partners must be considered in this framework.

26. In respect of EU 'civil society', it should be understood that the ETUC has a double function. On the one hand, it is part of civil society, but on the other hand, it has a specific role which goes beyond the rights attributed to 'civil society' (for example, its role as co-legislator).

Role as 'Partners in Consultation': Consultation With the Union's Institutions

27. Before the Lisbon Treaty, the consulting role of the social partners was limited in several respects (ex-Article 138 EC, now Article 154 TFEU). Major changes have been introduced by Article 152 TFEU:

    — it is no longer only the Commission which is the addressee of consultation, but all the Union's institutions (see below para 43);
    — it is no longer only the 'social policy field' as defined in Article 154(2) TFEU (ex-Article 138(2) EC) but all areas with a social impact (see above paras 17–21);
    — it is now at the highest level that the social partners are partners of the 'Tripartite Social Summit' (see below para 28).

Tripartite Social Summit: A Specific Form of the Role of 'Partners in Consultation'

28. According to Article 152(2) TFEU, the 'Tripartite Social Summit for Growth and Employment' shall contribute to social dialogue. This means that the Tripartite Social Summit—hitherto enshrined only in secondary legislation—is now institutionalised in primary law. It is to be seen as a specific form of consultation with the Union's institutions (see above para 27). The range of topics to be dealt with is vast and it takes in economic and social strategy, from macroeconomic to employment policy, labour law and industrial society. The new body must:

    — 'ensure ... continuous concertation between the Council, Commission and social partners';
    — 'enable the social partners at European level to contribute ... to the various components of the integrated economic and social strategy'.

Role as 'Partners in Dialogue': Dialogue Between the Social Partners

29. The second sentence of 152(1) TFEU specifically mentions the dialogue between the social partners. It thus refers to Article 155(1) TFEU ('Should management and labour so desire, the dialogue between them at Union level may lead to contractual relations, including agreements'). This social dialogue must be facilitated by the Union.

30. Independently of the promotional role of the EU's institutions, there is at European level, a duty to bargain collectively in all cases of multinational labour relations. This is an indispensable legal tool to bring the Social Dialogue to deliver more fruitful results than it has done up to now. Already France, Luxembourg, Sweden and other European nations know in one form or another a duty to bargain. Even American labour law provides for a duty to bargain in its National Labor Relations Law. Of course, this duty as intended by Article 28 EU Charter is different from the duty to conclude agreements and the conditions and modifications of such a European duty to bargain would have to be explored in more detail.

Role as 'Co-legislator': Framework Agreements as Basis of EU Secondary Law

31. In respect of Framework Agreements (Article 155(2) TFEU, ex-Article 139(2) EC) the social partners are to be seen as

'co-legislators' since '(a)greements concluded at Union level shall be implemented ... in matters covered by Article 153, at the joint request of the signatory parties, by a Council decision on a proposal from the Commission'. This role is underlined by the fact that neither the Commission nor the Council have the power to alter the content of the agreement. Their power is limited to 'implementation', whereas the power to 'adopt' (conclude) remains with the social partners.

Content of the Obligations

32. In order to clarify the content of the obligations of the Union's institutions, concrete activities must be defined. In this regard, it appears helpful to refer to the approach developed by the Committee of the International Covenant on Economic, Social and Cultural Rights (ICESCR) in respect of the contents of fundamental social rights (to respect, to protect, to fulfil).

Recognition of the Role: No Regression

33. Defining the notion of recognition, it is in principle related to the protection of the level embodied in the existing situation.

34. At first, recognition refers to the situation prior to the Lisbon Treaty. It does not appear possible that any Union institution will reduce the (procedural and material) impact of the social partners in general and the ETUC in particular. Article 152 TFEU 'recognises' the pre-existing *acquis communautaire* as articulated in Part III, Title X on Social Policy and confirms in the new context the autonomous role of the social partners (Articles 153, 154, 155 TFEU). Therefore, the first obligation (recognition) has a specific content not to reduce the strength of at least the following:

    — promoting consultation of the social partners;
    — adopting measures to facilitate their dialogue;
    — ensuring balanced support for the partners;
    — consulting social partners on the possible direction of Union action;
    — consulting social partners on the content of proposals;
    — accepting their opinion or, where appropriate, recommendation, to be forwarded to the Commission;
    — providing for possible autonomous initiatives by the parties to initiate the bargaining process and autonomous agreement;
    — adopting decisions to implement agreements concluded at European level, at the joint request of the signatory parties.

    Secondly, however, the Lisbon Treaty defines a (reinforced) framework for the social partners.

Promotion of the Role: Action Needed

35. The obligation to promote the role of the social partners is the most important element of the new provision. The word 'promotes' includes continuous (pro-)active measures, which confers a dynamic character on the provision. Different levels must be promoted:

36. The first element is *information*. This fundamental step is the basis of all possible further activities within the Union's framework. (It is surely not limited to the areas of consultation in the current Article 154 TFEU?) Therefore, information must be given at the earliest stage possible and as completely as possible. But this is not the only measure. The provision of information must continue in tandem with the development of documents or procedures.

37. Furthermore, it should be noted that Article 152 TFEU makes it clear that the ETUC as social partner not only has the right, like any EU citizen, to:

    — obtain access to official data sources, such as EUR-LEX or DORIE;
    — apply for access to official documents under regulation; but its own right of access to all documents which are of relevance to any sort of policy with a social impact.

38. The second step concerns *consultation*. The procedure defined in Article 154 TFEU has so far often been seen as a restricted exercise (sometimes even only at the same level as (civil) society) limited to areas which are covered by Article 153 TFEU. This approach is no longer justified, given the new obligation to promote the role of the social partners. Furthermore, consultation must take place in a coherent manner so as to offer the ETUC the possibility to effectively influence any decision-making process.

39. The Commission has stressed the importance of consultation of all 'interested parties' from the 'beginning of the political process' in light of the strategy of transparency, as indicated in the Green Paper of 2007 (COM(2007) 127), stressed in 2008 (COM(2008) 32 final). The initiative is inspired by the logic of 'better support', which includes the improvement of feedback and control of the enforcement of the rules. In going firmly beyond these general consultation principles, Article 152 TFEU provides for the 'promotion' of a distinct consultation status for the social partners.

40. The ETUC also has rights and practices concerning *participation*, which is often related to concertation. Beyond the existing framework of participation, it appears necessary to examine in which bodies

(committees, councils and so on) the ETUC should be included in order to promote its role as social partner effectively.

41. In all its promotional activities, the Union must take into account the diversity of national systems.

Facilitating the Dialogue Between the Social Partners

42. Article 152(1), 2nd sentence TFEU requires that the Union 'facilitate dialogue between the social partners, respecting their autonomy'. This obligation supplements the already existing obligations under Article 154(1) TFEU. This means that there should be a framework which supports the social dialogue in respect of any adequate personal and financial resources.

ADDRESSEE(S) OF THE OBLIGATIONS:
THE 'UNION' AND ITS INSTITUTIONS

43. By definition (Article 13(1) TEU) the term 'Union' means all the institutions of the Union:

— the European Parliament,
— the European Council,
— the Council,
— the European Commission (hereinafter: 'the Commission', including all its agencies),
— the Court of Justice of the European Union,
— the European Central Bank,
— the Court of Auditors.

Therefore, every Union institution must to recognise and promote the role of the social partners.

Practical Consequences

44. On the basis of this interpretation, the TTUR Expert Group considers at least the following measures to be necessary. The following list will have to be supplemented in the process of further discussions.

In Respect of the Commission

Information

45. The Commission in many respects is not prepared to pass on all documents dealing directly or indirectly with social policy to the ETUC.

In order to respect the information obligations (see above para 36) the ETUC should in particular be provided with the following EU documents:

- proposals and initiatives for decisions to open negotiations on amendments to the contractual foundations of the European Union;
- proposals and initiatives for decisions to open negotiations with a view to preparing accessions to the European Union;
- proposals for legislative acts of the European Union;
- negotiating mandates for the European Commission to engage in negotiations on international agreements on behalf of the European Union;
- items for discussion, initiatives, negotiating mandates and negotiation guidelines for the European Commission within the framework of the common commercial policy and world trade rounds;
- communications and opinions of the European Commission;
- reports by the institutions of the European Union;
- action plans of the institutions of the European Union;
- Green Papers of the European Commission;
- White Papers of the European Union;
- political programmes of the institutions of the European Union;
- Recommendations of the European Commission;
- inter-institutional agreements between the institutions of the European Union;
- budgetary and financial planning on the part of the European Union.

46. Furthermore, the regular delivery of the following documents to the ETUC should be ensured:

    - reports of governments, experts and so on, in particular those which serve as a basis for implementation reports, as well as any sort of impact assessments;
    - working documents, non-papers, meeting records;
    - external documents (in particular, research studies by universities, think tanks and so on);
    - internal notes, in particular legal opinions by the Legal Service.

47. Any denial of disclosure of these documents is not consistent with the obligation to recognise and, even less, to promote the role of the social partners contained in Article 152(1) TFEU.

Consultation

48. Since the role of the social partners must be promoted, it can neither be restricted to the consultation foreseen, for example, for civil society

(Article 11 TEU, Article 15(1) TFEU), nor to the consultation provided for in Article 154 TFEU. One key element is the social impact assessment (especially in respect of the new Article 9 TFEU).

49. In order to be effective it appears obvious that any consultation with the ETUC at least would:

- have to take place at a stage at which the relevant decisions have not yet been taken;
- need to be based on complete information (see paras 45 et seq);
- require—on the basis of a 'good faith' approach—an in-depth exchange of views on all aspects relevant for the trade union side; and which
- could not be undermined by any relevant decisions taken during the consultation process.

Participation

50. The participation of the ETUC in EU institutions and bodies should be 'promoted' so as to make less formal the presence of the social partners with regard to topics which affect their responsibility and functions in relation to labour market dynamics. Two examples may suffice:

- It is a paradox that the social partners are consulted only by the Employment Committee as an advisory body (Article 150(2) TFEU). Notwithstanding this limited approach in this provision, it appears necessary to enlarge at least to a maximum this consultation requirement.
- It is not sufficient that unions can play a role within the vast cooperation network provided for by the Council Regulation on the European Union Agency for Fundamental Rights (Article 10 Regulation 168/2007, 15 February 2007), but the ETUC should be directly involved in the structures of the Agency.

(Autonomous) Dialogue Between the Social Partners

51. The obligation to facilitate the dialogue between the social partners (see above para 42) requires a favourable attitude on the part of the Union in general and the Commission in particular. The bipartite social dialogue should be promoted by, among others:

- encouraging the use of all possibilities provided by many directives for issues to be fleshed out through negotiation at all relevant levels;
- stepping up support for bipartite social dialogue and improving its visibility;

— assisting also social partners in following up their agreements, among other things by promoting sharing experiences with regard to good practices;
— reinforcing financial support for joint follow-up actions by the European social partners.

52. More generally, the institutional framework for the social dialogue should include a secretariat with adequate personal and financial resources.

Examination of Legislation and Policies

53. The Commission will have to examine to what extent the existing secondary legislation as well as all other political activities are in line with this provision and propose to amend legislation or to change policies accordingly. The requirements to promote the role of the social partners should also be part of any sort of ex-post evaluation (for example, within the framework of the so-called 'smart' regulation (see COM(2010) 543 final).

In Respect of the Council

54. At least, the inter-institutional agreement will have to be amended in order to conform to the obligation to promote the role of the social partners. This obligation should also lead to a regular consultation by the relevant Council working groups.

In Respect of the European Court of Justice (CJEU)

55. Since the CJEU is one of the Union institutions addressed in Article 13(1) TEU, it derives from Article 152(1) TFEU that also the Court is obliged in the same way as all the other Union institutions to promote the role of the social partners at the European level. Already this legal argument could be sufficient and thus the Court should accept the ETUC as a privileged applicant. In this context it should be recalled that the Court, having initially refused to extend *locus standi* to the European Parliament, reversed this position in *European Parliament v. Council*,[3] allowing the Parliament to challenge the legal basis of Regulations.

56. Even if a direct action of the ETUC would not be accepted, these principles would at least require a direct application in respect of the role as possible third party intervener in direct actions by individuals and in preliminary ruling proceedings.

[3] Judgment of the Court of 4 October 1991 Case C-70/88 ECR 1991 page I-4529.

57. Concerning a third-party intervention by the ETUC in direct action cases (see Article 263(4) TFEU), Article 40(2) Statute of the Court already appears to be open for such a possibility ('any other person which can establish an interest in the result of a case'). Even if there were difficulties, the CJEU would have the obligation of promoting the role of the social partners (Article 152(1) TFEU).

58. As regards preliminary ruling procedures, account should be taken of Article 23(1) Statute of the Court limiting the intervention opportunities 'to the Member States and to the Commission, and to the institution, body, office or agency of the Union which adopted the act the validity or interpretation of which is in dispute'. Nevertheless, this provision appears to be the appropriate legal basis for a third-party intervention by the ETUC in cases dealing with framework agreements concluded between European social partners in which 'the validity or interpretation' of such an agreement (having been implemented by a decision of the Council on the basis of Article 155(2)(1) TFEU[4]) 'is in dispute'. Even if not all conditions were considered as fulfilled, an analogy based on Article 152(1) TFEU would require its application in these cases. Therefore, any granting of leave to an application for a third-party intervention by the CJEU in cases concerning a framework agreement would be an important part of the practical application of Article 152(1) TFEU in judicial proceedings … .

[4] 'Agreements concluded at Union level shall be implemented either in accordance with the procedures and practices specific to management and labour and the Member States or, in matters covered by Article 153, at the joint request of the signatory parties, by a Council decision on a proposal from the Commission …'

Index